LORD BISHOP
The Life of
Samuel Wilberforce

LORD BISHOP
The Life of
Samuel Wilberforce

1805–1873

STANDISH MEACHAM

HARVARD UNIVERSITY PRESS

Cambridge, Massachusetts

1970

Contents

ILLUSTRATIONS

Preface

Samuel Wilberforce is best remembered as Soapy Sam, the bishop who debated Huxley on evolution and lost. He always insisted his nickname derived from the fact that though many times in hot water he emerged in every case with clean hands. Others had a less flattering explanation. They believed he was inordinately ambitious and that he trimmed to a line dictated by that ambition. The reader must judge for himself how near the truth those critics were.

Soapy or not, Samuel Wilberforce is well worth a biography. His former associate and friend, Canon A. R. Ashwell, began one soon after the bishop's death in 1873. It was completed by Wilberforce's son, Reginald, following Ashwell's own death in 1879. It is a good biography notable for the generally full and fair picture it paints, and for the quantity of raw material it presents. This new biography attempts to say something about Wilberforce as a human being and about the Church of England as an institution in nineteenth-century English history. I have published some material which the former biographers decided for various reasons to exclude. And I have arranged the book to give more prominence to those aspects of Wilberforce's life and work that seem to me most interesting and important: his Evangelical upbringing and the subsequent development of his beliefs; his work as a bishop in the diocese of Oxford; his understanding of the part a State Church might play in the life of a nation; and his readiness to undertake the role of defender of orthodoxy against the onrush of Darwinian evolution and higher criticism. Behind the work stands the man, complicated and, for a biographer, always fascinating.

I owe a great debt to David Newsome, who has kindly shared with me his intimate knowledge of the Wilberforce family, and of their letters and diaries which he unearthed to write his fine book on the Wilberforce brothers and Henry Manning, *The Parting of Friends*. I also happily acknowledge the constant advice and encouragement I received from the late David Owen, before his death in 1968; the helpful suggestions of Dudley W. R. Bahlman; the assistance and hospitality of Mr. and Mrs. C. E. Wrangham, Miss Irene Wilberforce, Mrs. Judith Sandwith, and Sir George Clutton; the help of various libraries and librarians—especially Miss Molly Barratt of the Bodleian; and the endless favors received from friends in England, Mr. and Mrs. Michael Teale. Above all I owe my wife thanks for sharing in a project that ended as much hers as mine.

I acknowledge as well, with thanks, the gracious permission of Her Majesty Queen Elizabeth II to publish material from the Royal Archives, and permission from the following persons and institutions to quote from unpublished sources: Sir George Clutton, Mrs. Judith Sandwith, Miss Irene Wilberforce, and Mr. C. E. Wrangham, Wilberforce family papers; The Bodleian Library, Oxford, Wilberforce family papers and Diocesan papers and records; Ronald K. Pugh, unpublished doctoral thesis and copies of Samuel Wilberforce's letter books; Patricia Gill, West Sussex County Archivist, and the executors of the estate of Dr. Octavia Wilberforce, Wilberforce family papers; the Fathers of the Birmingham Oratory, Newman papers; The Archbishop of Canterbury and the Trustees of Lambeth Palace Library, Tait Correspondence; The National Trust, owners of the Hughenden Archives, Disraeli Correspondence; the Governor of Liddon House, Liddon correspondence; the Trustees of the Broadlands Archives, Shaftesbury and Palmerston papers; the Gladstone Trustees, Harwarden, Gladstone Correspondence.

Research for this book was conducted under a grant from the American Council of Learned Societies. Preparation of the manuscript was assisted by grants from The University of Texas at Austin.

S. M.

Austin, Texas
1970

Sources Cited in the Notes

David Newsome included a full catalogue of the Wilberforce family manuscripts in *The Parting of Friends* (London, 1966). Since he wrote, further material has come into the possession of the Bodleian Library and the West Sussex County Library as a result of the death of Dr. Octavia Wilberforce, Reginald's daughter. When used for this book, the papers were disposed as follows:

Bodleian Deposit I (BD, I). A vast, catalogued collection, dealing primarily with Wilberforce's work as Bishop of Oxford, but including as well the correspondence between Wilberforce and Charles Anderson. The Rev. R. K. Pugh has transcribed the almost illegible copies of letters in BD, I. C into Letter Books (BD. d.148, 204, 208–211).

Bodleian Deposit II (BD, II). Mostly family letters, and letters from Newman, Gladstone, Keble, and Sir James Stephen. (These papers are listed as "Wilberforce MSS" in Newsome's catalogue.)

Bodleian Deposit III (BD, III). Further letters, including some from Newman to Wilberforce.*

West Sussex Library (Chichester). Catalogued by Francis W. Steer as "The Wilberforce Archives." Material relating to the Lavington estate, and to the Sargent and Wilberforce families. Includes correspondence between Manning and Wilberforce.

Wrangham Papers. Owned by Mr. C. E. Wrangham. Rosemary House, Catterick, Yorkshire. The correspondence between Robert and Samuel Wilberforce. Also letters from Barbara and William Wilberforce to their children and others.

Sandwith Papers. Owned by Mrs. Judith Sandwith, St. Mark's Vicarage, Harrogate, Yorkshire. Letters and papers of Henry Wilberforce and a few letters of William Wilberforce, Jr.

Irene Wilberforce Papers. Owned by Miss Irene Wilberforce, 2, York House, Church Street, Kensington. Miscellaneous letters from

---

* The Bodleian has recently begun to recatalogue these papers. When completed, all letters and papers from Samuel Wilberforce will be listed together. A second section will contain groups of letters from correspondents who wrote twenty or more, listed alphabetically by correspondent. Other sections will contain family letters, diocesan correspondence, and correspondence about the church overseas. The remaining material will be arranged in chronological series. The entire collection will be shelf-marked 'MSS. Wilberforce.'

Newman, Pusey, Gladstone, Anderson, etc. to members of the Wilberforce family.

Clutton Papers. Owned by Sir George Clutton, K.C.M.G., The British Embassy, Warsaw. The papers of George Dudley Ryder, including his statements concerning Mrs. Mary Sargent's will.

Other relevant material is contained in the following collections:

Gladstone Papers. British Museum. Especially Add Mss. 44343–5.
Peel Papers. British Museum.
Tait Correspondence. Lambeth Palace Library.
Longley Correspondence. Lambeth Palace Library.
Broadlands Mss. (Palmerston papers and Shaftesbury's diaries.) Broadlands.
Newman Papers. Birmingham Oratory.
Hughenden Papers. (Disraeli correspondence.) Hughenden Manor, High Wycombe.
Liddon Papers. Liddon House, London.

There is also useful information among the Oxford diocesan papers (ODP), deposited in the Bodleian, and the Winchester diocesan papers, deposited at the Hampshire County Library, Winchester.

I have quoted from the unpublished sources where they were available. Unfortunately, Wilberforce's diaries for the years 1853–1873 are not among the papers that survive. His son Reginald quoted from them extensively in his biography and was criticized for doing so, the critics charging that they contained a good deal of unsubstantiated and vindictive gossip. He replied (*Times.* Dec. 22, 1882. 6): "Could you see the materials which I have not yet published, you might marvel at my amazing moderation." He may well have destroyed the diaries himself—after finishing the biography.

PART I
Early Years

CHAPTER I

Father and Son

The Evangelicals of Clapham have been called a "sect" ever since Sydney Smith first set the fashion over one hundred and fifty years ago. The designation has helped discourage study of the Claphamites as individuals. Instead, it has encouraged the cliché which sees them gathered together for prayers or pious works: devout, hardworking, and undoubtedly influential reformers, apparently very like each other and very unlike everyone else. In much they were alike, especially in their devotion to God and to the behest of their own consciences. But as soon as one begins to study these men, one encounters the differences in belief, the idiosyncrasies of behavior, which, if historical classification were not as useful as it is inevitable, would tempt one to discard the label, forget the forest, and concentrate on the trees.

If asked to describe that particular forest, most would fill it with oaks. A "tree of righteousness" was how one eulogist described the Evangelical John Thornton when he died in 1790. "Upright," "unyielding," these are the adjectives generally applied not only to Evangelicals of the first generation like John Thornton, but to his son Henry, and to Macaulays and Stephens and Grants who together with other devoted friends nurtured the Clapham "system." Yet William Wilberforce, at the center of that "system," demands some other metaphor. The one that springs readily to mind—quicksilver—won't suit, ignoring as it does the religious faith which lay beneath a supple, fanciful nature. This faith drove him to use the charm God had given him to work His holy will. Faith lent charm its purpose, turning it into relentless persuasiveness. William Wilberforce got his way. He was saintly in London drawing rooms, witty in Clapham libraries, judicious in print, eloquent in Parliament. Wherever he went, men listened to him and, often against their better judgment, allowed themselves to be persuaded by him. He was, even more than his son Samuel, to whom the phrase was so often applied, "all things to all men." As such, he defies simple classification as a man of Clapham. He was an Evangelical with close Clapham friends, but one whose temperament kept him at a distance, while his beliefs bound him to those men who lived and worked beside him, and looked to him as their leader.

William Wilberforce, born into the Yorkshire gentry, was exposed early to the Evangelical teaching that had begun to impress itself upon the

Church of England by mid-century. A Methodistical aunt in Wimbledon, with whom he was sent to live, attempted to work a change in him, only to have his mother—"an Archbishop Tillotson man"—call him back home before overstimulation could result in some sort of irregular "conversion." [1] He went to a grammar school kept by the Evangelical Milner brothers in Hull, but it was not until a trip to the continent with Isaac Milner in 1785 that he experienced the "great change" which was to have such an effect upon his life. By this time he had attended St. John's, Cambridge, was M.P. for Hull, and a close supporter and friend of William Pitt. Both alliance and friendship survived until Pitt's death, but Wilberforce now looked within himself for direction. In 1787 he made his famous declaration, "God Almighty has set before me two great objects: the suppression of the slave trade and the reformation of manners," [2] and from that time these objects absorbed him. He began to desert London for Clapham and to spend his time with the Evangelicals, who helped him organize the moral and religious campaigns which placed his goals before the country.

In these campaigns Wilberforce assumed the leadership. He was from a class above most of his Clapham associates,[3] and his easy manner helped him to win allies where his friends could not. Though occasionally worried lest the stylish seduce him back again, he remained steadily devoted to his new religious principles and to the new concerns they dictated. No doubt to help keep himself conscious of his strong resolves, in 1797, when he was thirty-six, he married Barbara Spooner, the devout daughter of Isaac Spooner, a Birmingham banker. Although there are innumerable letters from Barbara Wilberforce to her family among the Wilberforce papers, she remains a somewhat dim and elusive character. She was many things her husband was not: practical and sharp, yet rather heavy. Wilberforce himself, in a letter to his son Samuel in 1831, referred in a gentle way to her "total incapacity to understand and still less to relish a joke, which was one of the peculiarities of her excellent mother." [4] The Thorntons did not find her attractive or congenial. Henry thought her "a melancholy instance of the evil of long indulged prejudices." [5]

Perhaps her heaviness succeeded in giving to the family a balance it would otherwise have lacked. Barbara was by no means unintelligent.

1. R. I. Wilberforce and Samuel Wilberforce, *Life of William Wilberforce*. 5 vols. 2d ed. (London, 1839), I, 6. Hereafter cited as Wilberforce, *Life*. See also Reginald Coupland, *Wilberforce* (London, 1923), p. 32

2. Wilberforce, *Life*, I, 149.

3. Wilberforce himself once noted the distinction he felt between himself and many of his new allies. "These city people better than at our end of the town." Wilberforce, *Life*, I, 265.

4. March 26, 1831, Chichester, 27.

5. To Hannah More, October 28, 1798, in Standish Meacham, *Henry Thornton of Clapham* (Cambridge, Mass.: Harvard University Press, 1964), p. 40.

"I do not have the faculty of your good mother," wrote Samuel's friend Charles Anderson, "of writing, talking, and listening equally well at the same time." [6] Anderson may not have meant the remark as a compliment, but it acknowledges a talent without which it was hard to survive in the helter-skelter Wilberforce household. It fell to Barbara to supervise the moves—to friends, to Bath, to the seashore, for her peripatetic husband refused to light for long in one place. In a house almost never without a stream of visitors, she labored to keep expenses down. Above all, she tried to order her husband's life, though she was not noticeably successful; for, as Thornton once remarked, "Wilberforce is a man who, were he in Norway or Siberia, would find himself infested by company, since he would produce a population for the sake of his society, in the regions of the earth where it is least." [7]

His friends despaired at the dissipation of such extraordinary talents and constantly urged him to undertake less, to see fewer people, to live more quietly within his family. His life often seemed no more than a series of interruptions. Some were the result of his multifarious activities and responsibilities. Abolition of the slave trade and then of slavery itself were only the most famous of his concerns, and his reputation as both a Christian and a reformer made him into a sort of touchstone without whose presence in the chair no charitable society could conduct its annual meeting, without whose name on the letterhead no cause could call itself worthy. Many more of the interruptions were the result of his own nature. Never at rest, he thrived upon change and abhorred a settled existence.

If his life was kaleidoscopic, religion brought the pieces into pattern. Like his Evangelical friends, he worshipped a God whose nearness was at once comforting and terrifying. He could carry his problems to God and God would help him bear them. Through Christ's death on the cross, he could feel sure of his own ultimate salvation.[8] The price God extracted in return for this glorious promise was high. Man labored to attune his conscience to God's will and, having done so, to obey the stern demands that conscience laid upon him. Only by constantly probing into one's own soul, only by repeated questioning of one's motives, could one be at all certain that the spark of faith struck in the soul at the time of conversion was burning with brightness enough to insure ultimate salvation. Hence the private nature of an Evangelical's religion. Churchgoing, though an important and satisfying duty, could not take the place of daily prayer, when, by agonizing conversations with God, one found comfort by coming to understand his will. For a man as publicly occupied as

6. April 8, 1831, BD, I. C189.
7. To Hannah More, October 20, 1799, in Meacham, *Henry Thornton,* p. 39.
8. Unlike some of his Evangelical friends, Wilberforce was not a Calvinist predestinarian.

Wilberforce, such quiet communion must have been most difficult. That he achieved it, his diaries and letters attest. They show him able to turn away from the world and into himself to find the support which faith provided him in the conduct of his busy life.

Faith—the Evangelical's "real" religion—had not come to William Wilberforce until he was twenty-six. He took pains to see that his children would never experience such deprivation. He lavished attention upon them naturally, for his was a loving and in many ways a childlike nature. But Clapham recognized a duty to ensure that its sons and daughters heard the great religious truths as soon as they could understand them. The family into which Samuel Wilberforce was born on September 7, 1805, was one in which even the very young were constantly made to feel the presence of God in their lives.

Unfortunately, there is no domestic memoir to draw upon for a picture of life in the Wilberforce household. Samuel was the third son and fifth child,[9] born when his father was forty-six and at the busiest point in his career. Amidst the constant comings and goings, the children's upbringing may have been in some respects haphazard.[10] In view of the extraordinary public life he was leading, the care William Wilberforce took with the training of his children is an indication of the importance he attached to it. Driven to use education as a means of leading his children to God, his concern for their proper upbringing stemmed from more than this very private motive. Anxious to reform the manners of their fellow countrymen, leading Evangelicals felt themselves compelled to set forth their educational precepts as examples for others.

These precepts centered upon the concept of duty. Intellect was not tutored for its own sake. Nor was it stretched without simultaneous attention to the exercise of conscience. Intelligence was a tool, a gift from God like everything else, and one to be put to use for his sake. As such it must be ready to do the duty conscience prescribed. Hence the constant appearance of words like "self-denial," "application," "motive," in the Evangelicals' educational lexicon. Samuel once recorded a conversation with his father that suggests both the method and purpose of this sort of training.

He spoke of forming early habits of self-denial in childhood. He said it was a deficiency which could never be thoroughly supplied. That no effort of mind could form a habit. It must be formed from the repetition of little instances. That therefore accustoming children whilst very young to call for what they like at table has the very worst effect upon the mind, namely of fostering a habit of self indulgence.[11]

9. William, Junior, born 1798; Robert Isaac, born 1802; Barbara, born 1799; Elizabeth, born 1801. A fourth son, Henry William, was born in 1807.
10. Thomas Mozley suggests Samuel was too often allowed his own way. *Reminiscences, Chiefly of Oriel College and the Oxford Movement*, 2 vols. (Boston, 1882), I, 28.
11. Notebook containing conversations with his father, 1823, BD, II. W.

The teacher's major task was neither to sharpen the intellect nor to instill a love of learning. It was, by constant precept and careful example culled from books, and by "the repetition of little instances" derived from the experience of daily life, to impart to the student what Henry Venn had, a century before, called the complete duty of man. The lesson, to stay learned, had to be taught early. Though complete duty meant partial self-denial, and such self-denial might lead occasionally to sternness, it never, in the case of the Wilberforces, led to cruelty. Children were too precious, families too close, to permit it. "I do not like to write merely on the *outside* of this cover," William wrote to Samuel at school. "Yet as when you were a little boy I used to delight in taking a passing kiss of you, so now, it is quite gratifying to exchange a salutation with you on paper, tho' but for a minute or two." [12] With such a father in close charge, sternness was not likely to harden into severity nor self-denial into repression. William lamented once that the son of a friend was neither benevolent nor kindly. "S[another friend] thinks that he was over-dosed with religion, and that of an offensive kind, while young. It is an awful instance, and well-deserves the study of all parents. They should labour to render religion as congenial as possible." [13]

This congeniality had come to Wilberforce only after he had made his own flawed nature accord as closely as possible with God's. He had worked hard, as all Evangelicals had to, to achieve this nearness, until at last what he had once struggled to attain came easily. With his own experience in mind, he began, gently but persistently, to urge upon his children the cultivation of "the *Root of all Holiness,* by endeavouring to obtain a closer union with Jesus Christ." [14] Intellect and spirit were to be trained together and gradually grow together during a period of learning which, if difficult and sometimes painful, yet promised spiritual happiness.

This was, at any rate, the ideal. Its realization demanded concentration—indeed, consecration—from parents, teachers, and pupils. William and Barbara Wilberforce undertook the task with the zeal characteristic of all Evangelical enterprise. Their children appear to have striven readily enough. The problem was to find the right sort of teachers. All the boys were educated by private tutors; none went to a public school, where at that time, life and learning were the antithesis of that which an anxious Evangelical would want for his children. Only in the household of a clergyman, and one certain to profess "real" religious sentiments, could a parent know that such a conflict would not arise.

The Wilberforces were in no hurry to send their sons away from home. Samuel did not go off until March 1817, when he was placed with a Reverend S. Langston at Hastings. By the end of the year his father had

12. 1819, BD, II. P.   13. Wilberforce, *Life,* IV, 152.
14. October 5, 1819, A. R. Ashwell and R. G. Wilberforce, *Life of Samuel Wilberforce,* 3 vols. (London, 1880–83), I, 10–11. Hereafter cited as Ashwell and Wilberforce, *Life.*

moved him to Nuneham, near Oxford, to the household of the Reverend
E. G. Marsh. There he remained for just a year, when he was removed
once more, this time into the care of the Reverend George Hodson, later
canon of Lichfield and Archdeacon of Stafford, but at that time chaplain
to a friend of the Wilberforces, Lewis Way of Stanstead Park near Ems-
worth. Hodson's clientele was small: six sons of the upper middle class,
among them Henry Hoare and Way's son Albert. Hodson, a nephew-in-
law of Wilberforce's Clapham ally James Stephen, apparently gave
satisfaction. Samuel remained with him when Hodson removed from
Stanstead to accept a curacy at Maisemore, near Gloucester, in 1820.
Not until 1822 did Samuel change tutors again, this time moving to Bid-
borough, near Tunbridge, for intensive study with the Reverend F.
Spragge prior to matriculation at Oxford.

Thomas Mozley, an Oxford contemporary, criticized the education
that the Wilberforce brothers received at the hands of these divines.
Some of them, he wrote, "whatever their other qualifications, were not
scholars, or men of common sense, or even quite gentlemen, or even
honest in the sense necessary for the fulfillment of a positive and very
important contract. [This last, perhaps, may suggest why Samuel was
moved about so much.] "Of the best of them," he continues, "the Wilberforces said that, after spending the whole day in his parish, and returning
to a late dinner, he would take them just from nine to ten, when both he
and they were good for nothing but bed. A scrambling lesson at any odd
hour was the common rule." [15] Mozley also suggests that had they gone
to public school, the boys would have better learned how to distinguish
between true and false appearances, "how to give and take, when all
must offend more or less, and how to accept differences and even dis-
agreeables with comparative indifference." [16] Yet he credits their education with endowing them with a lifelong regard for truth, and, he concludes somewhat surprisingly, "Upon the whole, though perhaps an
Etonian would say that he detected more than a want of high scholarship
in the Wilberforces, it is difficult to deny that they stand to the account
in favour of private education." [17]

Mozley, who was a High Churchman, was understandably unenthusiastic about Low Church divines. Samuel himself had little good to say
for Hodson, with whom he resided longest. Although he wrote early in
his stay that he liked both tutor and wife,[18] he complained in later letters
to a fellow student, Patrick Boyle, that "it certainly is a striking proof of
the iniquity of Hod's plan that I never knew of anyone who after he had
left him spoke a good word for it. Even the favorite H. H. [Henry Hoare]

15. Mozley, *Reminiscences,* I, 102–103.   16. *Ibid.,* p. 115.   17. *Ibid.,* p. 103.
18. See excerpt of letter from William Wilberforce to Samuel Wilberforce, February 13,
1819. Ashwell and Wilberforce, *Life,* I, 5.

is as strong as anyone." [19] Hod's plan, it seems, was a "mode of boyishing us to an extreme degree and treating us with uncommon strictness. . . . Hodson's was certainly a most excellent place for making progress in classics," Samuel concludes, "but his method of treating us was, I think extremely injudicious." [20] Despite the care that had gone into his selection, Hodson appears to have been little more than a crammer. But Samuel, it should be added, was not a scholar, nor an overly zealous student. What he once described as "the sufferance and wretchedness" [21] he underwent at Hodson's may have been the result of his own unwillingness to work at Hodson's pace. Soon after his transfer there in March 1819, his father had written:

I fear you do not apply to your business with energy. This, remember, was your fault at Mr. Marsh's, and you alleged, not without plausibility, that this arose in a great degree from your wanting in spirits, in consequence of your having no playfellows for your hours of recreation, no schoolmates for your season of business. A horse never goes so cheerfully alone as when animated by the presence of a companion, and a boy profits from the same quickening principle. But my dearest Samuel has not now this danger to plead at Mr. Hodson's, and I hope he will now bear in mind that his indisposition to work strenuously is one of his besetting sins.[22]

Samuel did need then, as he was to need all his life, the company of others to make him go cheerfully. He studied diligently enough and performed in the end as well as he was expected to, but, unlike his truly scholarly brother Robert, he was not happy long when by himself. His first report to Boyle from Mr. Spragge's, where he had been sent to prepare for Oxford, reflects his taste for society. After listing his studies—algebra, Sophocles, Demosthenes, Tacitus, and Hume—he describes his hopes for "a day or two's shooting over Lord Abergavenny's vast manor," and reports his pleasure at the proximity of Tunbridge Wells, "where there is a succession of company." [23]

Although he enjoyed company and preferred conversation to books, Samuel was in no sense anything but a generally sober and circumspect young man. Nor did he chafe at the instruction poured out to him in letter after letter from his father and mother during the years he was away from home at school and college. This correspondence, of which over six hundred letters from his father and nearly as many from his mother have been preserved, shows how remarkably close the parents remained to their child, and how desperately anxious they were about each accomplishment and misdemeanor. William dashed off letters to Samuel in his

19. 1827, BD, I. C205.   20. To Patrick Boyle, *ibid.*, April 25, 1823.
21. To Patrick Boyle, *ibid.*, March 6, 1828.
22. A. M. Wilberforce, ed., *The Private Papers of William Wilberforce* (London, 1897), pp. 181–182. Hereafter cited as *Private Papers*.
23. November 16, 1822, BD, I. C205.

large and rather elaborate hand at any place, at any time, much as Samuel was himself one day to conduct his correspondence. "Though some company who are to dine with me are already in the drawing room," he begins characteristically, "I must leave them for two minutes to write. . ." [24] One of the first letters from father to son, written just after Samuel, aged eleven, had gone to live with his tutor Mr. Langston, reflects Wilberforce's concern, both for his son's soul and for his position and reputation as a member of the country's leading family of Evangelicals. "Though the grand motives on which I wish you to act are those of Christianity, yet I may fairly superadd another—that of your not discrediting your family and friends." [25]

Wilberforce constantly urged Samuel to remember the special duties that were incumbent upon him because of the blessings he enjoyed as a Christian. "You have enjoyed and still enjoy many advantages for which you are responsible. Use them honestly." "Remember, my dearest boy, that you have enjoyed advantages which probably R [a student with whom Samuel was quarreling] has not, and therefore more than kindness and patience may be expected from you than from him." [26] Samuel was not to press an argument or refuse to come more than halfway. "Nine times out of ten, if one of two parties be really intent on healing the breach and preventing the renewal of it, the thing may be done." [27] He was never to forget that he was acting not to please himself, his father, or his friends, but to please God. When Samuel expressed disappointment at having fallen below a rival in school: "You should do your business and try to excel in it, to please your Saviour, as a small return for all He has done for you . . . The Heavenly Shepherd . . . may have designed this very incident to discover to you that you were too much under the influence of emulation, and to impress you with a sense of duty of rooting it out." [28] Emulation led to the worship of false, worldly standards, and Wilberforce, always quick to draw a general moral from some particular misstep, did so when Samuel failed to report a student wrongdoer to his master.

This is one of the numerous (they are almost innumerable) class of cases in which worldly honour teaches one lesson and Christian morality another. For the point of honour governs boys in schools with as arbitrary a sway as men in life: and the very same principle which, I suppose, led you not to mention to Mr. H. the misconduct of your schoolfellow, would prompt you, when a man, to obey the laws of honour in fighting duels, or in all the other instances in which the World goes one way and the servants of Christ another. [29]

24. November 1817, BD, II. B.   25. July 5, 1817, Chichester, 27.
26. June 30, 1821, Chichester, 27. November 15, 1821, BD, II. P.   27. *Ibid.*
28. November 18, 1820, *Private Papers,* pp. 188–189.
29. November 30, 1821, BD, II. P.

As Samuel grew older, his father's letters to him dwelt less upon the lessons to be drawn from schoolboy scrapes, more upon the great truths of Christian religion. In answer to a question from Samuel about repentance and predestination, he wrote that "the grand mark" of true repentance was very simply "its providing a dread of sin and a watchfulness against it." [30] In this same letter, Wilberforce expressed the hope that Samuel would never feel what he knew other sons had felt, that "strange shrinking back from opening their minds to the parent they cordially loved, and of whose love to them they were fully satisfied. I hope you will continue, my dear Samuel," he adds, "to speak to me without constraint or concealment." Nothing in the few schoolboy letters to his family which remain suggests that Samuel was anything but readily confiding. Despite occasional indulgences and infrequent mishaps, the method worked. School, Samuel's mother once wrote him when he was homesick, was not an affliction but a trial.[31] Samuel passed through the trial without apparent emotional torment or even discomfort. Although his tutors may not have suited him, he suffered them willingly enough. He accepted the exhortations and admonitions from his parents with filial obedience. And, although occasionally bothered by doubts, he gladly received the religion which they had been at such pains to pass on to him. In a long letter to his sister Elizabeth, written while on vacation when he was almost fifteen, he displayed the fruits of the earnest apprenticeship through which he had been so carefully led.

In answer to your letter I write a short one. I think that you really may comfort yourself about Barbara, as she is so very *very much* better than when she came here and is I think *very very much better* than when I came home [Barbara Wilberforce, Samuel's oldest sister, was to die in 1821.] . . . You say that we must not *depend* on the earnestness of our prayers but yet I think that when we do feel that great earnestness in prayer we may safely augur that our hopes are founded on Jesus Christ the only true foundation and that the holy spirit has in some measure at least touched our hearts. So that the praying earnestly is the fruit of faith.

We are very comfortable here. We go on the water very much, bathe a good deal, ride and shoot. Mamma is going to buy you a very nice pony which I found and hope you will like. I am to ride it for a few days before it comes up to you.

I hope that you will now be more comfortable. Only, dear Lizzy, how much more trying is prosperity than adversity. I find it much more difficult to keep my temper good etc. in the holidays than at school, but prayer is the great thing, prayer is the shield that wards off the temptation thrown out by our great enemy the Devil. Prayer it is that obtains for us the sword of the spirit and all the other parts of the Christian armour. Prayer is the guide to God. Pray earnestly, placing confidence entirely in God and God alone, and our bark can never be tossed about by the sea of trouble and of temptation.

30. February 20, 1822, Chichester, 27.   31. No date, BD, II. M.

Oh, how should we ever reach the haven of peace and happiness without the star of Nazareth. Oh my dear Lizzy, I fear that in the day, in the bustle and pleasure of the day, I forget my God but I am sure that when I reflect I prefer God, Christ, and The World to Come to all the bubbles of the present world, and that we may finally meet in the world of bliss and glory is the earnest desire of my dear Lizzy's affectionate brother, Samuel Wilberforce.[32]

Such pious virtuosity is hard to credit. The fruits of William Wilberforce's lessons are in that letter, but displayed so facily as to raise doubts as to their genuineness. They should not be dismissed as insincere. Young Samuel Wilberforce was a devout, believing Christian. His belief had come upon him slowly. Unlike his father, he was not engulfed by the powerful emotions of a religious rebirth after a youthful period of comparative indifference. Indifference was impossible in a household where the immediacy of the Christian message was constantly preached. William Wilberforce could not expect his sons to undergo the same sort of "change" that had come to him. Samuel believed, but he believed what his father had always told him Christians should believe. He accepted the tenets of "real" religion without a struggle, and therefore without any sudden illumination. He talked and wrote the language of Evangelical piety because everyone he knew talked and wrote it to him. And because writing and talking came easily to him, he unhesitatingly poured out the thoughts he had been urged to think in the language he was accustomed to hear.

Samuel and his brothers, though always encouraged to "think through" their religion, were in fact never allowed to consider an alternative to it. They left their tutors for Oxford intellectually naive, and without the ability to defend what they had been taught from serious challenge. Robert Wilberforce, who had a brilliant mind, soon taught himself to think with independence, and once self-taught, thought himself away from Evangelicalism. Henry, younger than Samuel by two years, and by nature a disciple, found himself unable to hold to what he had believed, once confronted by the persuasiveness and charm of his friend and mentor, John Henry Newman. Only Samuel, no intellectual, yet certainly not one to follow others willy-nilly, remained untroubled and ready to subscribe to the beliefs his father had taught him, to the simple truths expressed in a letter Samuel had received when he was only thirteen: "You have a Heavenly Father. . . who loves you dearly, and who has promised He will never leave you nor forsake you if you will but devote yourself to His service in His appointed way." [33]

Though many of Clapham's young men were entrusted to Cambridge Evangelicals, William Wilberforce chose to send his three younger sons to Oxford. David Newsome has sought and found convincing reasons

32. July 27, 1820, BD, II. W.   33. May 25, 1819, *Private Papers*, p. 183.

for the apparent contradiction.[34] Wilberforce did not think as highly of Cambridge as did some of his Evangelical friends. He believed that he had wasted his time at St. John's shamefully, and could not help but know for certain that his eldest son William had done so, after he was sent down from Trinity in 1819, following a series of public indiscretions. In a letter to Samuel in 1823, his father refers to "the more relaxed discipline of Cambridge," [35] suggesting that he felt it a generally demoralizing place for young men to live. Nor, as Newsome points out, was Cambridge without religious indiscipline as well. Evangelical enthusiasms there had a tendency to disintegrate into unseemly effusion. Meanwhile, Oxford— and particularly Oriel—was gaining a reputation for both learning and piety. William knew Edward Hawkins, the Oriel tutor; Edward Copleston, provost since 1814, had Evangelical friends and supporters. Charles Simeon, doyen of Cambridge Evangelicals, visited with Hawkins in 1822, "and held most profitable conversation. He accords more with my views of scripture," Simeon noted, "than almost any other person I am acquainted with." [36] Such recommendation, and the reputation Copleston was at that time making as an educational reformer, would have been enough to persuade Wilberforce to settle his sons at Oriel.

Under Copleston and his predecessor John Eveleigh, Oriel had become an outstanding college. Both provosts were determined to counter a legacy of eighteenth-century lethargy and nepotism with a tighter intellectual regime among the undergraduates and a fellowship of able and original thinkers. By the time Samuel Wilberforce matriculated in October 1823, the Senior Common Room contained an extraordinary galaxy: Thomas Arnold, John Henry Newman, E. B. Pusey, and Richard Whateley. John Keble had only just resigned his Fellowship for a curacy in Gloucestershire. Hawkins, a future provost, was still a tutor. Hawkins, Copleston, and Whateley, later to be joined by the theologically eccentric Blanco White, an honorary member of the Oriel Common Room, were the most important of the so-called Noetics, an ill-defined and almost undefinable group of liberal theologians and scholars who contributed most to Oriel's reputation in the 1820's. The Noetics [37] welcomed reform; they championed biblical criticism; they subscribed heartily to the principles of the Protestant Reformation. In the early 1820's, their

34. Tom Macaulay and Henry Sykes Thornton were sent to Trinity; Charles and Robert Grant to Magdalene; James Stephen to Trinity Hall. Ford K. Brown, in *Fathers of the Victorians* (Cambridge University Press [Eng.], 1961), insists that Wilberforce's choice proves he was not really an Evangelical. Newsome replies to this argument in the *Historical Journal,* 6: 295–310 (1963), and in *The Parting of Friends* (London, 1966), pp. 57–62.

35. October 14, 1823, Chichester, 27.

36. Charles Simeon, *Memoirs,* ed. W. Carus (London, 1847), p. 396.

37. Noetic is a Greek word meaning intellectual. No one appears to know who first applied it to the Oriel men.

abilities as individual scholars and polemicists had only begun to achieve for them distinction as a group. Had they then the reputation they were soon to earn, William Wilberforce might not have been as ready to let them educate his sons. Oriel was not yet, however, the center of fierce theological storm and counter-storm that it was to become by 1830. Rather it was perhaps the only Oxford college already distinguished for those three cardinal attributes of Victorian education Newsome has defined: intellectual toughness, moral earnestness, and deep spiritual conviction.[38]

The latter two were, of course, the important ones for Wilberforce. In a letter to Samuel in the summer of 1824, his father wrote urging him to join his friends Henry Ryder and Sir George Prevost who were reading classics with Keble at Southrop. "Much as I value classical scholarship I prize still more highly the superior benefit to be derived from associating with such good young men as I trust the two gentlemen are whose names I have mentioned, and I have the satisfaction of knowing that you have the privilege of calling them your friends." [39] Robert Wilberforce, in company with two other good young men, Isaac Williams and Richard Hurrell Froude, had spent the long vacation of 1822 studying under Keble's direction. He professed a pronouncedly High Church position, but his transparent piety recommended him as a proper tutor and counselor to earnest young men. William Wilberforce remained willing to judge a man not by his label, but simply by his reputation as a religious individual. Was he in earnest? Did he truly believe the Gospel message of sin and redemption? If so, his opinions about Church and sacraments mattered as little, ultimately, as did his scholarship. Enough that he could be proved a man of real spiritual worth. The Wilberforce brothers thus found themselves in the company of many at Oriel who, although unquestionably devout, relied for their devotion upon a system of beliefs far more complex and intellectually challenging than the one their father had passed on to them.[40] Robert's scholarly mind could not for long ignore this implicit challenge to his faith. Samuel, on the other hand, whose interests lay in individuals and not in ideas, could, as his father did, respect "good young men" without allowing their beliefs to disturb the tranquillity of his own.

Never had William Wilberforce counseled Samuel more carefully than in the choosing of his Oxford friends. For the first time, Samuel lay exposed to the world. Might its temptations prove too much for him?

38. David Newsome, *Godliness and Good Learning* (London, 1961), p. 25.
39. August 6, 1824, Chichester, 27.
40. Isaac Williams records an interesting illustration of Robert's initial surprise and confusion when confronted by Keble's High Church reserve. "He observed one day, 'what a strange person Keble is; there is "[William] Law's Serious Call," instead of leaving it

I am sure you will not deny that you ought not to make a part of any society in which you will be hearing what is indecent or profane. . . As to the wine parties, if I have a correct idea of them they are the young men going after dinner to each other's rooms to drink their wine, eat their fruit, etc; and with the qualification above specified, I see no reason for your absenting yourself from them, if your so doing would fairly subject you to the charge of moroseness or any other evil imputation. I understand there is no excess, and that you separate after a short time. . . But in all these questions the *practical* question often is, how the expenditure of any amount of time and money (for the former I estimate full as highly as the latter) can be made productive of the best effort.[41]

"Its being more *agreeable* to you to stay away," Wilberforce notes in the same letter, "I should not deem a legitimate motive if alone," suggesting that attendance might serve an other than purely social purpose. Earlier the same year, Wilberforce had written of the advantages of bringing together like-minded men "who may at some time or other combine and concert for the public good." [42] So Clapham and its work might have been defined. Wilberforce hoped no better than that his sons would find themselves among such a like-minded group at Oxford.

Samuel did much as his father hoped he would. "I like Oxford very well," he wrote Patrick Boyle soon after his arrival. "I know a tolerable number of Oriel men and could know many more but that I do not wish to do so. I think I know most if not all the best: i.e. the quiet, gentlemanly, clever men." [43] His closest friends were men like Sir George Prevost, Charles Anderson, and Henry Ryder, all of them sober, none of them over-serious or morose. Samuel avoided friendships within the Evangelical enclaves of Wadham and St. Edmund Hall. He had a fear of being thought "peculiar," and, in any case, reported to his father that he found the young men who advertised themselves as religious a dull and vulgar lot.[44]

Although William did not want him "peculiar" in the accepted sense of that word, he found it difficult to set the limits of Christian behavior for his son. Two and a half years later he was still worrying about the problem. "Singularity in indifferent manners" was wrong.

The very contrary is our duty. But from that very circumstance of its being right that we should be like the rest of the world in exterior, manners, etc., etc., results an augmentation of the danger of our not maintaining that diversity, nay, that contrast, which the Eye of God ought to see in us to the worldly way of thinking and feeling on all the various occasions of life, and in relation to its various interests.[45]

about to do people good, I see he reads it and puts it out of the way, hiding it in a drawer.'"
Isaac Williams, *Autobiography*, 2d ed. (London, 1892), p. 28.
41. October 14, 1823, Chichester, 27.   42. *Ibid.,* June 14, 1823.
43. October 31, 1823, BD, I. C205.   44. June 21, 1823, BD, II. M.
45. January 22, 1826, *Private Papers*, pp. 228–229.

By the time Samuel received this advice—1826—he had set his course. At the beginning of his career he had apparently determined to establish a name for himself academically. In the spring before coming up, he submitted a poem about Stonehenge, intended for the Newdigate Prize competition, to William Shirley for criticism. Shirley's replies are interesting, for they suggest Samuel was both ambitious and impatient of success, as indeed he was. "Though there are some very good lines and several poetical ideas," Shirley wrote in February, "yet as a whole it will not do." Replying to a new draft: "I can perceive that you have not yet arrived at by any means an adequate idea of the minute and elaborate polish which must be applied to a Newdigate Prize Poem"; and again: "A freshman who has not yet come into residence has no business to think of success." [46]

Success meant a great deal to Samuel, and when he discovered that he would not achieve real distinction as a scholar, he turned to the newly founded Union, where he soon established a reputation for himself as a forceful speaker and an outspoken liberal. The liberalism comes as a surprise, in view of Wilberforce's later conservatism. Mozley suggested that it stemmed from loyalty to his father, who was at that time a particular target for Tory abuse.[47] *John Bull,* for example, in an account of a debate on the dethronement of Charles I, reported that

the most active and virulent of the disputants in favour of the deposition of Charles I were the two sons [Robert and Samuel] of Mr. Wilberforce!!! And one of them [Samuel]—more indiscreet, perhaps, than the other, or untutored in a higher quarter—let out one of the secrets of the prisonhouse at Clapham and Kensington, by making a direct attack upon the Established Church.[48]

Whether or not it was in response to such attacks that Samuel continued to espouse liberalism, he clearly enjoyed his role and reputation. He attacked the Crown, slavery, censorship, and the Irish Union; defended Hampden, the English barons, and Roman Catholic Emancipation, and once organized a demonstration to protest the vice-chancellor's regulation forbidding the Union to meet publicly. During an awarding of honorary degrees, the undergraduates, under Wilberforce's direction, set up a loud and continuous groaning "to the great discomfort of some of the

46. February 18 and April 1, 1823, BD, I. C195.
47. In a letter to a friend, William Gray, written in December 1830, William Wilberforce declared that "from myself and the general tenour of our family and social circle, it might have been supposed that my children, though averse to party, would be inclined to adopt Liberal, or so far as would be consistent with part, Whig principles." He notes that contrary to expectations, all had become "strong friends to High Church and King doctrines," which by that time they had (*Private Papers,* p. 157).
48. "The Oxford Union," *Macmillan's Magazine,* 28:567–568 (1873). At this time the Union still met in the rooms of its members, and debates were not normally reported. The informant was reputed to have been Walter Farquhar Hook, then an undergraduate, whose uncle, Theodore Hook, was at that time editor of *John Bull.* See Mozley, *Reminiscences,* I, 118–119.

recipients," writes Patrick Boyle in a reminiscence, "although we tried hard to show that they were not the objects at which our groans were directed." [49]

William Wilberforce worried that all this notoriety might turn Samuel's head, but although there was more than a touch of flamboyance in his Union career, and although he was unquestionably anxious to make a name for himself, Samuel did nothing to give his father real cause for alarm. He hunted, and was developing a taste for natural history that lasted him his life. He enjoyed his circle of friends, dubbed the Bethel Union because of its generally serious demeanor. And he studied diligently enough to take a first in Mathematics and a second in Classics at the end of Michaelmas term, 1826.

Samuel was barely twenty-one. His father hoped he would eventually take Orders, but he was not yet old enough, nor certain himself that he was suited for the clergy. If not the Church, he would soon have to choose something else, for William Wilberforce could not afford to support his sons indefinitely. Wilberforce, although he had retired from Parliament in 1825 and although he remarked himself that he felt like "a bee which has lost its sting," [50] yet remained extraordinarily busy. He had purchased a small estate at Highwood Hill, outside London. Here he entertained visitors constantly, when he was not himself traveling about. "Except last Sunday, Monday, and Tuesday, being Christmas Day," wrote an apparently exhausted Mrs. Wilberforce to Samuel in 1827, "our house has been constantly full (and will be so till Saturday morning). Those three days I felt most glad to get a little quiet time." [51] That a purpose lay behind the comings and goings Wilberforce was at pains to make clear. "My chief object in these visits," he wrote to Samuel following a journey through Derbyshire in 1822,

was to provide future intimacies and I hope friendships for you and your brothers. And how thankful ought we to be, to be enabled thus to select for our associates the best families in so many different counties; best, I mean, in the true sense of the word—men of real worth, who, I am sure, will always receive you with kindness for my sake.[52]

Less than a month before, he had written Samuel of his concern lest, with such a peripatetic mother and father, the children might feel deprived

49. To R. G. Wilberforce (Samuel's son), August 16, 1873, BD, I. C206.
50. Wilberforce, *Life,* V, 263.
51. December 27, 1827, BD, II. B. In the same vein, a note from Robert to Samuel, December 22, 1830. "The dear father has just returned with a man who came down just by the coach to ask him some things, not a little to mother's dissatisfaction" (BD, II. C).
52. November 22, 1822, Chichester, 27. Samuel, who complained in 1825 at the constant comings and goings, was instructed by his father that a life of that sort might be a blessing. "We are less likely to lose the consciousness of our true condition in this life; less likely to forget that while sailing in the ocean of life we are always exposed to the buffeting of the billows, nay, more, to the rock and quicksand" (*Private Papers,* pp. 206–207).

of "the notion of a home." Perhaps, he remarked, he should have bought a country residence and tried to raise them all together there. "I say a *country* residence, for as extremes meet, London, from the multitude of the *individuals* it contains, destroys all *individuality.*" [53]

The Wilberforce household must at times have seemed designed to destroy peace of mind. Henry Thornton's eldest daughter Marianne, writing of a visit paid in 1820, describes the domestic confusion that apparently followed in the wake of William's gentle good nature.

Things go on in the old way the house thronged with servants who are all lame or impotent or blind, or kept from charity; an ex-secretary kept because he is grateful, and his wife because she missed poor Barbara, and an old butler who they wish would not stay but then he is so attached, and his wife who was a cook but now she is so infirm. All this is rather as it should be however for one likes to see him so completely in character and would willingly sit in despair of getting one's plate changed at dinner and hear a chorus of Bells all day which nobody answers for the sake of seeing Mr. Wilberforce in his element.[54]

The confusion abounded still at Highwood, and Wilberforce appeared to thrive amidst the disorder. But such a life cost a great deal of money. He owned property, but he had been forced to reduce his rents by a quarter in 1821 and, as he remarked to his son Robert, such a diminution of income, a fourth, was not at all convenient, especially for one who had never, throughout his life, saved anything. He could not stint himself. In a letter to Samuel at Oriel, warning him to be neither lavish nor stingy, he explained his own philosophy of spending. He had kept no country house, he explained, and therefore felt himself justified in entertaining at London dinners which "as they could not be imputed to a disposition to offer up a splendid sideboard etc. and suited people's convenience etc., made me extremely popular and excluded all ideas that in the more important particulars in which I saved money I was influenced by any narrowmindedness." [55] Spending money, like everything else an Evangelical did, was done with a purpose; in the Wilberforce household it was freely done. William hoped to leave his sons "what, with the ordinary emoluments of a profession, may afford a comfortable competence," [56] but while their father lived, they could not look to him for much financial help.

Help of another kind he could of course give them. Mozley argued in his *Reminiscences* that by 1825, William Wilberforce "was a man of

53. October 26, 1822, BD, II. P. During 1822 Wilberforce was organizing the campaign to emancipate British-owned slaves. Perhaps the time thus spent made him feel he was neglecting his family.
54. Marianne Thornton, Recollections, in E. M. Forster, *Marianne Thornton* (London, 1956), p. 143.
55. October 12, 1823, BD, II. P.
56. To Samuel Wilberforce, October 14, 1823, Chichester, 27.

broken health and strength, diminished means, almost out of the political world, a noble wreck and no more." [57] He had retired from Parliament; he was sixty-six and troubled by his eyesight; of those who waited upon him many could hardly be classed as anything better than second-rate. Yet he remained one of the most famous Englishmen alive, and one to whom the country as a whole felt itself indebted. A son of William Wilberforce would have little trouble establishing himself. He would, however, bear the burdens of a famous name, as well as enjoy its privileges. "You, as *my* son, will be tried by a different standard from that which is commonly referred to," William wrote Samuel, "for it would be folly rather than merely false delicacy to say that from various causes, my character is more generally known than that of most men of my own rank in life. . . You have *my* credit in your keeping as well as your own." [58] Nothing suggests that his sons found these charges upon them too heavy to bear. But by the time they came to choose their professions they must have learned that although their name would accord them instant recognition, such recognition could as easily result in an unpleasant notoriety as in a rapid advancement.

William Wilberforce had never disguised his hope that all four of his sons would enter the Church. He wrote a friend that his only wish was to see all his sons "real Christians, rather than great scholars, or eminent in any other way." [59] He appears to have had little ambition for them, success meaning nothing more to him than the discovery and practice of the religion by which he lived. In 1821, when Samuel was only sixteen, his father wrote that nothing would give him greater pleasure than seeing him a minister of God. If he was to be a good one he must be zealous.

There are so many clergymen who are no better than tradesmen, whether you regard the motives from which they enter the Church or discharge its offices, that their sacred function sinks in the scale below that of a lawyer for instance. But let a TRUE minister of Christ meditate fairly on the subject, and fix in his mind a just sense of the real importance of the ministerial office, and all others fall below it. . .[60]

Samuel did not make up his mind to be a clergyman until the spring of 1827. His brother Robert had already settled into a Fellowship at Oriel, and for a short time Samuel thought to do the same at Balliol. He stood as candidate in November 1826 but did not win out. He had apparently abandoned the idea by the following March, for it was then that he resolved to take Orders and become a parson. His brother's friend Richard Hurrell Froude wrote, first to urge him on, then to congratulate him upon his decision.[61] Little in the letters that survive helps to explain why

57. Mozley, *Reminiscences,* I, 103ff.   58. October 12, 1823, BD, II. P.
59. To ?. 1813, Wilberforce, *Life*, IV, 138.   60. October 12, 1821, Chichester, 27.
61. March 19 and March 28, 1827, BD, I. C193.

Samuel decided as he did. His success in the Union had for a short time
suggested the law as a possible alternative. William, naturally relieved
that he had chosen otherwise, wrote during the following summer that
he rejoiced in the prospect of his becoming a clergyman.

> . . . it is due to you, my dear Samuel, to say that it is a very striking proof of
> your having been enabled by, I humbly trust, the highest of all influences, to
> form this decision, when from your talents and qualifications it appeared by no
> means improbable that in the legal line you might not improbably rise into the
> enjoyment of rank and affluence.[62]

That "highest of all influences" was a call from God. Years later, Samuel,
as bishop of Oxford, delivered an ordination address in which he argued
that no one should enter the ministry without such a call. Other reasons—
family hopes, for example, might help one to a decision. But without
God's blessing, some tangible stirring of the soul achieved by watchfulness and prayer, a man would do wrong to offer his services as a minister.[63] Samuel probably felt the call himself. In view of his respect for
his father and willing acquiescence in his wishes heretofore, it would
have been most surprising had he disappointed him by turning from the
course so lovingly and painstakingly set for him.

In that same letter William had remarked that Samuel's determination
"may have been in part produced by that connection to which you look
forward." The connection—marriage to Emily Sargent—was one to
which Samuel had been looking forward for at least six years. Emily was
the daughter of John Sargent of Lavington, rector of Lavington and
Graffham in Sussex, an Evangelical "squarson," whose wife was a cousin
of William Wilberforce. Evangelical families, because they tended to
fight shy of the world and because the world was not ready to live according to their sober model, saw a great deal of each other. The children
visited back and forth and, encouraged perhaps by the pious intimacies
their religious frankness enjoined upon them, when they grew up they
often fell in love.[64] The Wilberforce and Sargent children had known
each other since youth. Samuel first met Emily Sargent while a student
at Hodson's. Stanstead Park lay close to Lavington, and John Sargent
was a good friend of Lewis Way, Hodson's patron. The two children
formed an "attachment" before Samuel left Stanstead, and from that
time they determined to marry. Both were remarkably handsome, if the
typically soft lines of Richmond's portraits are to be believed. Their love
for each other was deep and binding. "As I cannot be certain my own

62. August 25, 1827, Chichester, 27.
63. Samuel Wilberforce, *Addresses to the Candidates for Ordination* (Oxford and London, 1867; 1st ed. 1859), pp. 7–8.
64. The Wilberforces were also connected to the Stephens, the Thorntons, and the
Birds—all prominent Evangelical families.

dearest Emily of seeing you this morning," Samuel once wrote Emily on her birthday,

I cannot help telling you in this way how sincerely I feel for you this day. With no commonplace congratulations my most fondly beloved creature would I wish you many very many happy returns of this day. My prayers indeed my sweetest love are earnestly offered for you to Him who can grant it, that *many* successive years may still find and leave you happy upon this day... And my own dear Emily may He grant in His infinite mercy that I may still be with you to share your sorrows and your joys and may every year find us more united, more knit together to each other and to Him. I cannot tell you my darling what I feel for you... Once more from my heart I pray that God may bless you my sweet dear. Goodbye my own most fondly, most tenderly, most exclusively beloved Emily. Your own most inexpressibly affectionate Samuel Wilberforce.[65]

Such ardor does not bespeak a long engagement, and Samuel and Emily wanted to marry as soon as they could. From the parents' point of view the match was an eminently suitable one. William Wilberforce could not help but enjoy the prospect of his son's marriage to a Sargent. John, Emily's father, had intended at first to study law; but his tutelage under Simeon at King's had left its mark upon his conscience. In 1805, following marriage to Mary Abel Smith, he was ordained deacon, and settled in Sussex as curate of the livings of Lavington and Graffham, both in the presentation of his father.[66] A friend and later the biographer of two Evangelical missionaries, Henry Martyn and Thomas Thomason, he was, in every way, a worthy. Sargent, in his turn, could have found nothing to object to in Samuel as a prospective son-in-law. Yet he was not as ready as the children wished to give his permission for their early marriage. Samuel and Emily had an ally in William, who wrote Sargent, urging that the wedding take place before Samuel's ordination. It was, he contended, a matter of expediency, "I ought rather to say . . . absolute duty." Chastity was, for the Evangelical, a cardinal virtue, but there was no need to thwart passion if it could be legitimately assuaged. "I own," he wrote Samuel at the end of 1827, "your marriage is likely, d.v., to take place at an earlier period in life than I commonly think advisable, but . . . dear Emily and you appear to have been intended by Heaven for each other, and I am almost ready to adopt already the language of Scripture and to say whom God has joined together let no man put asunder." [67]

65. No date, Chichester, 29. This letter is a copy in Emily's hand. She has dated it "c. 1817," but it is obviously of a much later date. In a letter to his brother Robert after Emily's death, Samuel speaks of his "great dream of life of 1821," suggesting that it was then—when Samuel was sixteen and Emily fourteen—that they fell in love (Wrangham papers, January 30, 1846).

66. The property had come into the possession of John Sargent, Senior, through his wife, Charlotte, the daughter of Richard Bettsworth of nearby Petworth.

67. December 27, 1827, Chichester, 27. Mrs. Wilberforce was ready to see them wait. "Do not be in a hurry," she wrote Samuel more than a year before his marriage. "You are

Financially the union was more blessed by future prospects than by immediate provision. When deciding upon his profession during the early spring of 1827, Samuel had written his father asking what he might expect from him, in view of the requirements of primogeniture. William had replied that the subject had cost him "many an anxious reflection," but remarked only that he felt Samuel was far too despondent about his chances of preferment within the Church.[68] At the same time he had written John Sargent, explaining that he disapproved of primogeniture, and reassuring him that he had "resolved to do more for my younger children than men of my fortune usually do." [69] Meanwhile, he was prepared to lend him what support he could.[70] John Sargent, on his part, agreed to an annuity of £100 a year, with £5000 to come to Emily at the time of Mrs. Sargent's death, assuming that she would outlive her husband. "Viewed in a worldly light, the connection cannot be deemed favorable to either of you," [71] William wrote Samuel in the summer before his marriage. He would not have had it otherwise. "I can truly say I had rather you should possess your dear Emily with her future fortune or even without it than most females with whom you could have united yourself with 20 or 30,000 in their pockets." [72] Nor would Samuel have had it otherwise. Yet, because throughout his life he was to worry about money, and because the Wilberforce family was soon to be plunged into financial disorder, it is well to understand that although Samuel and Emily could live comfortably, they were not by any means rich, and that they were dependent upon both Wilberforces and Sargents for the comforts they did enjoy.

They were married by Charles Simeon on June 11, 1828, in the Lavington Church. Without question they were an extraordinarily happy couple. Several months before their marriage they had written a pledge in Samuel's engagement book: "We do faithfully promise to tell one another everything (ie *little things, very, very* little things such as the thoughts seamen on board ship exchanged) because without it they [*sic*] cannot be *quite, quite* happy. Sam/Emily." [73] This freshness and simple confidence never went out of their marriage, and Samuel continued Emily's suitor long after he had become her husband. "Never, my own darling, *never* before did I get such precious letters from you as this

both far too young and three or four years will do no one any harm" (February 2, 1827, BD, II. A).

68. February 19, 1827, Chichester, 27.   69. March 12, 1827, Chichester, 24.

70. See letter from William Wilberforce to Samuel Wilberforce, July 6, 1830, in which William agrees to help support Samuel in his new position as rector of Brighstone, "so long as I am able, if your income does not suffice" (Chichester, 27).

71. August 25, 1827, Chichester, 27.   72. November 12, 1829, BD, II. E.

73. Engagement Book. Entry for March 13, 1828, BD, I. C186.

time," he wrote three years later. "How very much more than ever of old I dote upon and love you now far more than ever you are all to me." [74]

The young Wilberforces traveled on the continent during the summer of 1828. When they returned to England in the fall, they lived for a time at Lavington and at Highwood, while Samuel prepared for his ordination and for his first ministry, the curacy of the tiny parish of Checkendon in Oxfordshire.

74. July 19, 1831, Chichester, 29.

CHAPTER II

Rector

The matter of Samuel Wilberforce's first appointment had been a subject of discussion and arrangement within his family for almost nine months before he assumed the duties of his curacy in January 1829. William Wilberforce had hoped that his cousin Charles Sumner, the bishop of Winchester, might find a place for Samuel within his diocese. Sumner, a gentlemanly Evangelical whom the Sargents knew as well, offered Samuel the curacy of Chiddingfold in Surrey in the spring of 1828, very soon after Samuel's decision to take Orders. John Sargent, a good friend of the rector of Chiddingfold, Dean Pearson of Salisbury, pressed Samuel to accept. The Wilberforces considered the duties too heavy, and Samuel declined. In June, Sumner wrote William to say that he could offer nothing else, and that, although he would in future be pleased to have Samuel serve under him, he could only for the time recommend his acceptance of the curacy at Checkendon.[1]

Checkendon, near Henley and only eighteen miles from Oxford, had much to recommend it to a young curate. Both church and parish were small, affording time for study and for careful attention to the spiritual needs of the few parishioners—about three hundred. Samuel had apparently balked at the small stipend. He might have had Adderbury, a better-paying curacy within the Oxford diocese, but its size—a population of two thousand—made him hesitant. The presence of friends at Oxford, and especially of his brother Robert, now a Fellow and tutor of Oriel, naturally helped attract Samuel to nearby Checkendon. He was offered nothing else that combined the advantages of a rural Oxfordshire parish—it was small enough to allow him to begin his ministry modestly, yet near enough Oxford to afford him a chance to keep in touch with the world he would have been loath to live without. It seemed a pleasant prospect. He welcomed it and accepted the appointment.

His parishioners engrossed him. "The good Mrs. Whitfield is as happy, as contented, and as lame and suffering as ever. . . The old man father of the ostler still 'wags' much as of old." [2] He met for the first time the problems of agricultural poverty and depression. "At present," he wrote his father, soon after he began his duties,

1. June 13, 1828, BD, I. C195.
2. To Charles Anderson, February 7, 1830, BD, I. C191.

I am thankful to say that though we have much poverty we have very little urgent distress. Still as I suppose in all cases of agricultural labourers, the one borders very closely upon the other. For nine shillings a week to support a family of five or six children is the best case, and in old age, sickness, and bad weather they suffer very much.[3]

Much as he enjoyed the chance to understand and to help the little village full of people, he believed that his primary duty was to save their souls. Returned from a visit to three deathbeds, he wrote his father: "It is a very awful feeling to think that one of those committed to your care is gone to his account . . . it should be made I think always a season of self-examination and prayer." [4] The realization that he, as the spiritual head of his parish, had not simply a responsibility for their welfare but an awful commission to prepare them for eternity impressed him deeply. "Never allow yourselves," he later told a group of young ordinands, "to think of them as 'the people'; remember they are SOULS; each one has a soul; that wonderful, that enduring gift which you are to shape for eternity." [5] Wilberforce fought to shape the souls committed to him according to Church principles. He could find only three Dissenters in the parish, but two nearby meetings threatened an invasion. What he saw of their activity strengthened his belief that Dissenters worked nothing but confusion. "They catch those whose minds are in some measure awakened and lead them off from sobriety of mind, to feelings and fancies and I fear spiritual pride." [6]

Before he was more than two months at Checkendon, Wilberforce was offered the chance to battle against more pernicious doctrine. John Bird Sumner, brother of the bishop of Winchester and himself recently consecrated bishop of Chester, proposed that Wilberforce accept the vicarage of Ribchester, an isolated but heavily populated parish near Preston and nearer Stoneyhurst, a center of northern Roman Catholicism. The offer was flattering and a great challenge to a curate of only twenty-three. Samuel consulted with his father who advised strongly against the move, pointing out that Ribchester lacked all the advantages which had made Checkendon so attractive and so appropriate a place to begin his ministry. He was certain that Samuel possessed neither knowledge nor experience enough for the job. He was not well enough grounded in divinity, nor did he possess a broad enough acquaintance with human nature to tackle the problems of the place.[7] Two weeks later he wrote to warn Samuel again of the dangers of putting himself "in circumstances in which he would almost necessarily be almost incessantly arguing for Protestant

---

3. February 16, 1829, BD, I. C196.   4. *Ibid.,* March 30, 1829.
    5. *The Ministry of Reconciliation* (London, 1840), pp. 23–24. The sermon was preached at one of Bishop Sumner's ordinations at Farnham Castle on December 13, 1839.
    6. To William Wilberforce, March 30, 1829, BD, I. C196.
    7. March 3, 1829, *Private Papers,* p. 245.

principles—in short, would be occupied in the religion of the head rather than of the heart." [8] Samuel did as his father advised and remained at Checkendon. He was not one to back away from a challenge, but he must have recognized that he was still very much an apprentice and that he needed the quiet that Checkendon afforded him in order to take stock of his resources. William understood rightly that Samuel was best suited to preach a "religion of the heart." "Religion of the head" presumably meant a religion of doctrinal attack and defense. For this, Samuel was by nature ill-equipped. He enjoyed debate, but more often because he relished the occasion than because he appreciated the intellectual niceties of the argument at hand. His reputation as a speaker rested not so much upon his powers of reasoning as upon his manner and style. As a polemicist he was never a great success. His strength lay, rather, in his ability to reach people. He listened well, sympathized readily, and had the rare ability to convince those who came to him that he understood their problems and, further, that he could help solve them. In this respect he was much like his father. When William instructed Samuel to avoid debate and instead acquaint himself with human nature, when he encouraged him to be in earnest and to set that earnestness to work among his parishioners, he was giving good advice and showing sound knowledge of his son's strengths and weaknesses.

In the spring of 1830 the bishop of Winchester again offered Wilberforce a position in his diocese, this time the living of Brighstone, an agricultural parish on the Isle of Wight. It was worth about £500 a year and contained a substantial population of yeomen farmers. There seems to have been no question about its suitability, Brighstone's proximity to Lavington making the offer especially attractive to the Sargents. Wilberforce accepted readily and moved his family—Emily and their three-months' old daughter, Emily Charlotte—to the new rectory in August.

Wilberforce would later remark that his ten years as rector of Brighstone were the happiest of his life. Much did run smoothly for him. He took pleasure in his increasingly large family.[9] He enjoyed his work within the parish and was a success at it. His patron, the bishop, became a good friend, and encouraged his career by appointing him first a rural dean and then an archdeacon. He traveled to London and about the country with increasing frequency, much in demand because of his growing reputation as a fund raiser and organizer, often remarked upon as a very bright and coming young clergyman. The single heavy blot upon the otherwise happy period was a domestic one, occurring at the beginning of the year

8. *Ibid.*, March 17, 1829, p. 247.
9. Herbert William, born 1833; Agnes Everilda, born 1837 and lived only one day; Reginald Garton, born 1838; Ernest Roland, born 1840. Albert Basil Orme, the Wilberforce's youngest child, was born in 1841, after his father had been appointed rector of Alverstoke.

1831. Samuel's eldest brother William, a pathetic and eminently unsuccessful man, lost a great deal of money on an ill-advised farming venture into which he had sunk not only his entire fortune but a sizeable part of his father's as well.

William Wilberforce, Junior, has left few traces behind him. The three younger brothers seem to have had little to do with him; their references to him in letters to each other are almost invariably accompanied by distressful remarks about deplorable shortcomings or recent misadventures. Undoubtedly their father took as great pains with William as he did with his other children; more, perhaps, since he was the eldest son. For some reason he amounted to nothing and was one of those men who could with no trouble find someone else to blame for his own conspicuous lack of fortune and ability. Following his inauspicious departure from Cambridge, the younger William had intended to practice law; he was prevented by delicate health, or so Robert and Samuel maintain in the biography of their father.[10] Instead, with a large initial outlay from his father, he invested in a dairy-farming business—at the behest of its religiously minded secretary, if Mozley is to be believed.[11] By 1827 the farm had already begun to lose money. William, Senior, mentions the "real inconvenience" to which he had been put by further large advances in a March letter to John Sargent. "Mischievous competition" is blamed for the difficulties, and Wilberforce remained sanguine about future prospects.[12] The first severe jolt came in March 1830 when it appeared that the agent who had been managing the farm, a Major Close, was incompetent and perhaps worse. Wilberforce discovered that his entire investment had disappeared and began a program of domestic retrenchment. Not until a year later did the full extent of the loss become apparent. Wilberforce found himself saddled with debts of £50,000 and forced to leave his estate at Highwood.

Friends and admirers hurried to offer assistance, none of which Wilberforce would accept for himself.[13] He was not unwilling to refuse help on behalf of his sons, and when Lord Brougham offered Robert, as a favor to his father, the living of East Farleigh in Kent—worth about £800 a year—Robert took it. William not unexpectedly accepted the loss with gentle resignation. John Sargent, who spoke with him shortly after the decision to leave Highwood, recorded the conversation in a letter to his wife. "'I regret my books,' he said, 'and not having a house for

10. Wilberforce, *Life,* V, 314.   11. Thomas Mozley, *Reminiscences,* I, 123.
12. March 12, 1827, Chichester, 24.
13. There is a letter from Barbara Wilberforce to Samuel, undated, which suggests that the children for some reason did not tell William of all these offers. "Your father lately said to me speaking of Mr. Gladstone's offer which you remember, how strange it is that none of my own friends have ever offered any help under my circumstances. I felt myself bound to say nothing but is it right he should not hear something from Robert of what you hinted to me" (BD, I. C191).

my friends, but I cannot call this an affliction—it will draw me nearer my dear children.'" "And surely," Sargent adds, "he might have said 'to my Saviour' which it has done." [14] For Barbara Wilberforce the wrench was painful and one she could not accept with grace. "She lies awake for hours in the morning," William wrote Samuel, "and cannot banish from her mind the carking cares that haunt and worry her." [15] In fact, she came near to complete breakdown. Her husband, who had resigned himself to the calamity, assigned to her the task of reorganizing their life. For a time there was talk of their moving permanently to Brighstone, but Barbara disliked the idea of "imprisonment" on an island and that plan was abandoned. William longed to find a small house near Kensington Gardens, but this would mean sharing a house with the young William Wilberforces, and that, "your mother thinks and I own I believe justly," would be of all plans the most undesirable.[16] "All this," Wilberforce adds in the same letter, "is sad trifling." But to Barbara it was a constant and apparently overwhelming problem. She wished to accept the money that had been offered them to pay their debts. She wrote to Samuel:

How much I wish instead of offering a house which we do not wish for they would have made up a sum to pay our heavy debts and leave us what your father hoped and fully expected he should have—about 1500 per annum.

Through the confusion the visitors still streamed in and out of her house. "He has been quite overcome with all these people pestering him about slaves and colonies, and I know not what." She ends with a plea for help to "fence him from all those who trouble him as much as if he was quite young and strong." [17]

Within a few weeks, affairs had begun to straighten out. A new partner agreed to manage what remained of the business with the understanding—"established as a principle"—that the incapable William was to have nothing to do with it.[18] He, meanwhile, removed himself and his family for a time to Switzerland with the intention of returning to England to practice law. Samuel did not put much faith in his new resolves. "He has that unbounded sanguineness of temper," he confided to Charles Anderson, "that he finds out some good reason why he should not gather experience from every past failure." [19] The senior Wilberforces decided

14. March 22, 1831, Chichester, 25.   15. February 8, 1831, BD, II. E.
16. February 2, 1831, Chichester, 27.   17. No date, BD, I. C191.
18. William Wilberforce to Samuel Wilberforce, February 25, 1831, Chichester, 27.
19. April 19, 1831, BD, I. C191. Samuel was not far wrong. In 1838 William stood as a Tory for Kingston-upon-Hull, but was unseated on a petition charging bribery. Samuel helped him prepare a pamphlet in his own defense (*The Law and Practice of Election Committees in a Letter to the Electors of Hull* [London, 1839]), in which he charged that the committee itself was corrupt. Samuel appears to have agreed, for he noted in his diary on March 16, 1838: "William's committee said to be the worst that has been struck" (BD, I. C186).

to spend a part of each year with both Samuel and Robert and to divide the rest of their time between visits with other friends and prolonged sojourns at Bath.

The Wilberforces did not fit easily into the Brighstone rectory when they came to stay. Their visits were long ones—a month or two was not uncommon—and Barbara Wilberforce was difficult to satisfy. To William, happy domesticity was a state of mind divorced from the tribulations of managing an overfull household. He tried occasionally to settle quarrels and ease the strains that inevitably developed. "Considering your Mother's being Mother," he wrote regarding an early disagreement between Barbara and Emily, "considering her age, her anxieties and misfortunes and privations, all which, I am sorry to say she feels very painfully, I strongly advise . . . that all such points should be left entirely to be regulated according to her own pleasure." [20] To the credit of all, and especially, one suspects, of Emily, these initial discomforts and disputes appear to have resolved themselves. Not only the Wilberforces, but the Sargents as well, came with regularity to Brighstone and remained for weeks at a time. In the summer of 1832, soon after the birth of Emily's second child, Mrs. Sargent, Mrs. Sargent's mother-in-law, Emily's three sisters, and Henry Wilberforce were in residence. A week after their departure in September, William and Barbara Wilberforce, Robert, and his new wife Agnes arrived. They were succeeded by another round of Sargents during the winter.

Nothing in letters from either Samuel or Emily suggests that they felt themselves unduly put upon. Even had they wished to see less of the Wilberforces they would have found it difficult to refuse them their hospitality, since they continued throughout the period of William's greatest difficulties to receive an allowance from him. "My father does not of course intend that the fortunes of his younger children should be injured," Samuel wrote Anderson soon after the crash. "We give up some of our present allowance to increase my father's income." [21] Samuel's

---

In 1841 William contested Taunton, again lost, and again was charged with bribery, this time, apparently, with good cause. "I see in my own mind that he lost that entirely through bribery," Samuel wrote Robert at the time. "He now, he says, sees that is wrong and will never do it again. But!! All his present correspondence turns on this and I feel little doubt that had his hands been clean some case would have been found out on the other side" (Wrangham papers, November 30, 1841).

Almost the only other mention of William occurs in a letter from Samuel to Robert in 1846, in which a plan is mooted for putting William into the consular service. Samuel is to speak to Sir James Graham and wonders if Robert would be willing to approach Gladstone (Wrangham papers, February 16, 1846). In 1863 William turned Roman Catholic. He outlived his three brothers and died in 1879.

20. March 18, 1831, Chichester, 27. The disagreement was over the salary and duties of a maid Barbara proposed to bring with her to Brighstone.

21. April 9, 1831, BD, I. C191.

allowance was reduced by £100 to £300 per year; while the Wilber-forces lodged at Brighstone, they paid him an additional £75 a month.[22] All the children continued to rely on their parents for partial support, and even after William's death in 1833, Barbara lent Samuel large sums of money, although her income was not sufficient to allow her a home of her own.[23] Tempting as it is to read acceptance of whatever came his way as selfishness on Samuel's part, the fact remains his parents did not think it so, nor did his brothers or his sister act otherwise. All apparently considered the money from their father as their due.

Samuel found it difficult to manage his affairs prudently, and although his mother did not begrudge him the money, she could not refrain upon occasion from upbraiding him for his extravagance. In a letter of 1837 she complains

... you and Emily have such talents for spending, and would both grace a very handsome income, but while you have only what you have, tho' you have no occasion to save, you should live within your means and some self-denial is needed.

She urged them to make do with only two horses and adds: "*I should be content with a good ass, fed with corn now and then, to draw me about, if I had the courage to drive it.*" [24] Samuel would not have felt himself able to advance in the profession his father had so strongly urged upon him had he been forced to ride about his parish behind an ass. If he could not stay within his income, it was because it cost money to live a life of ex-ample as one of God's ministers to the Established Church of England. Ministry was "doing" as much as "being." "Doing" meant spending, and he justified the loans and the allowances on those grounds.

His advance, if rapid, was based upon the zeal he exercised as rector of Brighstone. The more work he undertook outside his parish, the more he claimed to realize the importance of his ministry there. "I never come home to my parish without a saddened spirit, saddened with myself and with the state of things around me," he wrote to the family's friend Louisa Noel. "The *prospect* of work and of exertion promises more than the reality performs, and the new forms of sin and of suffering which have accumulated in a few weeks absence come with a force which the *daily* load possesses at no one time." [25] Convinced that his first duty was to

22. William Wilberforce to Samuel Wilberforce, February 2, 1831, and March 18, 1831, Chichester, 27; Barbara Wilberforce to Samuel Wilberforce, July 11, 1833, BD, II. P.
23. There are records of a £200 loan in 1837 and one for £80 a year later. By the time Samuel moved to the parish of Alverstoke in 1840, he owed his mother a total of £472 (see Barbara Wilberforce to Samuel Wilberforce, March 14, 1837, BD, II. C; December 13, 1838, BD, II. B; and an undated letter (circa October 1840), BD, II. P.
24. March 14, 1837, BD, II. B.
25. November 5, 1834. BD, II. F. Louisa Noel was the daughter of the Hon. and Rev. Gerald Noel, Vicar of Romsey, Hants., and brother of the Earl of Gainsborough. A close friend of both Samuel and Emily, she corresponded with Samuel both before and after

save souls, he worked to perfect his preaching and soon added a second sermon on Sunday, a weekday evening service, evening services with sermons on saints' days, and a daily service during Holy Week. He read his Church Fathers diligently, but his sermons reflect not so much the erudition of Hooker or Latimer as the simple Evangelical faith his father had taught him. Sin and its consequences, redemption and its fruits, were his most frequent themes.

He remained, as he had been at Checkendon, a conscientious visitor. Typical, as reflecting the sort of work he was doing, is this diary entry in 1830:

Thought of sermon for Sunday. About the benches in church and dearest E's door. Saw Betty Shotton about not going to church. She seemed really penitent I hope and I permitted her coming to the Sacrament. Also the Newlands who promised to come and Tailer Shotton to whom in particular I spoke very strongly etc.[26]

The weeks were made up of such fragments: more often than not simply encouraging a man to understand the sort of life he should lead, then goading him to lead it. Occasionally he compromised. Parents, for example, found it hard to hunt up sponsors for their baptized children. "I fear if I were *at present* to enforce the sponsors having received the Lord's Supper it would lead to half the children in the parish being unbaptized." [27] Deathbeds depressed him; they showed him how frequently both the dying sinner and he as well had left undone the things they ought to have done. Last-minute confessions might hold a promise of eventual salvation, but "it is a matter of painful doubt," Wilberforce lamented to Anderson, "to endeavour to catch the signs of penitence and faith on the death bed of one who we fear has forgotten God while in health and the habits of whose mind and conduct have all been formed without reference to him." [28]

Dissent plagued him at Brighstone as it had at Checkendon. At the start he had taken what his father thought a far too pronounced and public a stand against Methodism. At Brighstone he made an effort to tread more cautiously. He worried, for example, about a Baptist prayer meeting which he felt certain did nothing more than encourage self-righteousness; yet, he warned himself, "I dread to do anything which may quench

---

Emily's death. Almost no further information exists about her. Presumably she lived with her father at Romsey until his death in 1851. Her sister Emma married the clergyman C. E. Kenneway, a friend and confidante of Wilberforce. On her father's side she was a first cousin of Henry Hoare, Wilberforce's schoolboy friend, with whom he later worked for the revival of Convocation. Although Wilberforce's letters to her in the Bodleian extend only to 1849, she did not die until 1863. Whether the correspondence ceased in 1849, and if so, why, remains a mystery. I am indebted to Dr. J. F. A. Mason, Christ Church, Oxford, for this information.

26. December 23, 1830, BD, I. C186.   27. *Ibid.*, January 4, 1831.
28. May 10, 1831, BD, I. C191.

the spark of heavenly grace." [29] By 1838, he reported to his colleague Walter Farquhar Hook, the Methodists had left his parish and he could claim "outward conformity" to the Church of England. Now he was invaded by ranters—thirty to thirty-five regulars—with large attendance as well from the curious.[30]

To combat disloyalty to Establishment principles, Wilberforce worked to remodel Brighstone into a Church of England community. His task was made easier by the fact that he had no strong-minded squire to combat and by his own extraordinary energy. He edited and printed a hymn-book, he organized a Sunday School, and soon raised the money for a school building. He encouraged his fellow clergymen on the island to form a clerical society, meeting frequently to pray and to discuss mutual difficulties. Before he left he had raised money for the restoration of his church. Like every incumbent he was sensitive to interference, especially from the government. He wrote a pamphlet in defense of tithes in 1831, when there was talk of their abolition,[31] and he opposed any tampering with Church rates.

Sentiments of this sort drew Wilberforce into local politics. He had, by the time he came to Brighstone, forsaken the extreme liberal attitudes of his Union days for a moderate conservatism more appropriate to his position in the parish. He could not enthuse about the Reform Bill of 1832 and joined the majority of his class and profession in bemoaning the country's future. He enjoyed a political role and in 1835 could not resist an opportunity to speak publicly for the Tory candidate, a Mr. Ward. He had been asked to second him, or at least to speak from the hustings, but this, on the advice of his bishop, he had refused to do. He furnished Robert with an account of his speech:

> . . . this afternoon, after the nominations, when Mr. Ward's friends mustered in the Bugle Inn, about 100 strong, after drinking 'The Church,' there was a call for me, and I got up thinking it was a good opportunity, as the room was full of substantial yeomen, both of explaining why all the clergy were with Ward, and of striking while the iron of political excitement was hot, and leaving an impression of Churchmanship hereafter. I spoke to this effect for some ten minutes in the midst of amazing cheers, and then they drank 'The Church and Mr. Wilberforce,' etc. I do not expect to carry Ward's election this time, but I think Simeon [the Liberal] will never sit again.[32]

He added that the election confusions impressed upon him "the vanity of earthly things," but the letter clearly shows him prey to that vanity. He felt himself a force—"I do not expect to carry Ward's election this time"—not just in Church affairs, but in general community matters as

29. Diary, November 3, 1830, BD, I. C186.   30. August 29, 1838, BD, I. C194.
31. The pamphlet was entitled *A Conversation on the Hardship and Injustice of Tithes.* I have not been able to discover any existing copies.
32. To Robert I. Wilberforce, January 12, 1835, in Ashwell and Wilberforce, *Life,* I, 79.

well. The letter shows him thoroughly enjoying his role. He believed it a clergyman's duty to associate himself with the gentry, and without doubt his beliefs corresponded to his predilections. He thought seriously of buying land for himself on the island, in order that he might claim a proper gentryman's title, and was dissuaded, according to Canon Ashwell, only because he realized that he would probably not remain at Brighstone for the rest of his life. His purpose was not simply to make a name for himself. As rector and leader of a rural community, he had a responsibility to learn as much as he could about the problems of land and of farming. He could not begin to help the people of his parish without sharing in some way the occupation of almost all their waking hours.[33] His interest was genuine and undoubtedly appreciated. With the farmers of his parish he denounced the ruinous effects of the old Poor Law, and with them shared the simple pleasures of ancient rural customs. Although anxious to live amidst the gentry, he refused to toady to them and made a point to treat them as severely as he would a laborer when the occasion demanded. Once he even dared upbraid a gentleman for swearing, while at the same time dunning him for money he had promised for a schoolhouse stove:

How should I acquit myself as sincere in the sight of God if I allow myself to be the witness of such sin without remonstrance? or how can I better return the kindness which upon many occasions I have experienced from you, than by pointing out to you the existence of so fatal a habit? [34]

As so often happens in the case of Wilberforce, one is brought up short by the unworldliness of this very worldly man: the Wilberforce of the hustings, so obviously excited by his success; the Wilberforce of this letter, so straight and sharp with a man who has done him favors. The contrast is as pronounced as it is persistent. The explanation lies in his protean character. Like his father, he was in the world because of the sacred task he felt he must perform there. But he was of the world as well and loved it in a way his father never did. His success at Brighstone sprang from his ability to keep his complicated nature in balance; of that success there can be no doubt. "I wish we might see you," Robert Wilberforce wrote Newman in 1836,

if it was but for two days, that you might get more of a domestic knowledge of my brother. It is curious to me to see the ascendency he has got in this little island; it must be worthwhile to live Gyari clausus scopulis, if one is thus to have all of it to oneself.[35]

33. On this point see Diana McClatchey, *Oxfordshire Clergy, 1777–1869* (Oxford: Clarendon Press, 1960), p. 98.
    34. To ?, June 9, 1832, BD, I. C196. One wonders if he got the money for the stove.
    35. July 26, 1836. Copied in Newman's notebook. Newman papers, Birmingham Oratory, A7 36.117.

By that time his success had brought him one important offer of advancement and would soon bring two more. The first came in May 1834 when Charles Simeon, in whose hands rested a sizable share of Evangelical preferment, offered him the city living of St. Dunstan's.[36] The chance to work and make a name in London tempted Wilberforce, but the disadvantages of such a change were great. The recently passed Act, requiring residence by an incumbent within the limits of his parish, would have imposed a burden upon Emily and the children by forcing them into the none-too-healthy region of Temple Bar. London living was expensive, and although the rector of St. Dunstan's received an income substantially higher than the rector of Brighstone, the difference would undoubtedly have been devoured by city prices. Even from a worldly point of view, Wilberforce could see no compelling reasons for the move. "I should say," he wrote Robert, "it was a lottery in which I staked certain comfort against the chance of rising to an uncomfortable eminence. But," he quickly added, "I earnestly desire and pray *constantly* to be able to put these thoughts altogether aside." [37] Being the man he was, he would not altogether dismiss such thoughts. He did take care to reach a right decision, doing so for the first time in his life without the support of his father's advice. He turned for counsel to Bishop Sumner, who reassured him that his usefulness at Brighstone was as great as it would be in London and, with a hint that he understood the temptations to eminence, comfortable or uncomfortable, to which his young friend was prey, warned that "to you, personally, I think the collision with London character would be unfavorable." [38] Wilberforce took the advice and declined the offer, even after Simeon had promised him a house in Lincoln's Inn Fields. He did not regret this decision, once made. In September he wrote Anderson of his delight in the life he was still leading "in quiet" at Brighstone.[39]

Three years later another offer came. Sir Robert Inglis, the respectable and preeminently Tory Member for Oxford, and a trustee of Simeon's Church livings since the latter's death, asked Wilberforce if he would be willing to undertake the heavy duties of the vicarage of Leeds. This was a challenge far greater than St. Dunstan's. Leeds, with new factories and raw hands to work in them, posed problems complex enough to try even the most hard-working and zealous clergyman. "I see the importance of the post," Sumner wrote when once more his advice was asked, "and I

36. He had previously been offered the chaplainship of the Old Chapel at Tunbridge Wells. For a time he considered taking it, on the understanding that he would reside for only six months, but Bishop Sumner advised strongly against it and he declined. See Sumner's letter to Wilberforce in Ashwell and Wilberforce, *Life,* I, 70: "You will scarcely choose to descend from the parish priest to the pulpit preacher; and in my judgment the two situations are not tenable simultaneously."
37. May 23, 1834, Wrangham papers.   38. May 23, 1834, BD, I. C195.
39. September 14, 1834, BD, I. C191.

do not hide from myself that by God's blessing you might exercise in it an immense influence for good. In this respect the proposal differs in my judgment immeasurably from the former London offer." [40] Wilberforce agreed and was ready to accept. He worried, however, and his friends and family along with him, whether his health would stand the strain. He had never been particularly strong, and in the winter of 1835 had suffered a severe inflammation of the lungs. He consulted the family physician who "was disposed to think it very doubtful, but that with care I might manage it." A specialist whom he consulted the same day reported "he had no doubt that I was unequal to it." [41] This second opinion appears to have been welcomed; at any rate it settled the matter, and Wilberforce again remained in the south. He attempted to persuade his brother Robert to take the post, but there is no evidence that Robert wanted it, or, indeed, that the trustees were particularly interested in him as a candidate. They offered it, instead, to Walter Farquhar Hook, who accepted and, in the twenty-two years he remained at Leeds, made himself the foremost metropolitan vicar in England. A year later Hook himself offered Wilberforce the chance to exchange Brighstone for Leamington. In this case Samuel declined on the ground that he could not force his bishop's hand, compelling him to accept in exchange someone he might not have himself chosen to fill a vacancy at Brighstone.

Offers of this sort no longer came to Wilberforce because he bore a venerated name, or because of Oxford friendships and connections. Inglis wanted him, Hook wanted him, Sumner wanted him, because he was an extremely hard-working and effective clergyman, and because he had managed to establish his reputation as one. Even during his early years at Brighstone, before he was thirty, he spent a good deal of time in London in the frequent company of those who mattered. His diary entry for March 23, 1833, for example: "Went to Clapham to dinner at the Bishop of Chester's—with Bishops Winton, Bristol, Lichfield, Chester, Knowles, two Henry Thorntons, Mrs. and Emily Ryder. Pleasant evening." [42] When in London he would often preach a sermon or attend the meetings of charitable and religious societies. He made use of Bishop Sumner's house and of Lord Calthorpe's,[43] where Emily was confined during the birth of their daughter Agnes. Frequently, on a Sunday he would travel round the town, listening to as many preachers as he could:

Morning to James Street to breakfast. [This in March 1838.] Then in fly to Boone's (St. John's, Paddington) very pretty church. Sermon much too essay,

40. February 5, 1837, BD, I. C195.
41. To Robert I. Wilberforce, February 8, 1837, in Ashwell and Wilberforce, *Life,* I, 105.
42. BD, I. C186.
43. Calthorpe was a cousin of Barbara Wilberforce, through the Spooner family.

some thought and one good hit—'chamber of licentiousness the antechamber of hell.' Back, read a little of Froude's 'Journals.' To Westminster Abbey, heard Lord J. Thynne. Met C. Anderson and Ey Anderson [his wife] in the Abbey. Evening to Melvill's, quite inferior to former times. 'Hear, O ye mountains,' etc. Yet some fine passages, especially near the end. The sinner testified against by Creation at the bar of Judgment. Home at 11.[44]

These excursions had their purpose. Wilberforce was working to develop his own considerable talents as a preacher, carefully noting the strengths and weaknesses of others in order to improve himself. He quickly succeeded, and his ability and reputation brought him continual requests to preach outside his parish. His sermon before the University during Lent 1835 was well received and the first of many. He took special care with these, generally working on them for at least a week, often sending them or reading them aloud to the bishop. His concern betrayed the natural anxiety he felt when summoned from his parish to address an audience of bright, argumentative scholars, ready to listen to a sermon only to catch at a phrase on which to hang an argument of their own. Wilberforce, who usually retained both parochial text and manner when preaching at Oxford, was never at home in the University pulpit in the way that Newman, Pusey, and his brother Robert were.[45]

When called upon to speak at large meetings to plead for missions or Bibles for the heathen, however, Wilberforce was extraordinarily effective. He began to travel for both the Church Missionary Society and the Society for the Propagation of the Gospel during the early 1830's and established such a name for himself that in the fall of 1838 Dr. Vowler Short, rector of Bloomsbury and a member of the standing committee of S.P.G., asked him to undertake a lengthy tour for the Society the following year. Wilberforce agreed, and Short arranged for him to travel into Devon and Cornwall with Henry Phillpotts, the bishop of Exeter, during his triennial visitation of his diocese in the autumn of 1839. A cantankerous and litigious man, Phillpotts made a formidable traveling companion. He is reputed to have screamed when told he would have to listen to the same man preaching the same cause for a month and a half.

Wilberforce spoke at least once a day from August 8 until September 20, and traveled 1467 miles, carefully logging each day's journey in his diary. He was remarkably successful, even winning Phillpotts' unstinting admiration. "Mr. S. Wilberforce, R. of Brighstone Isle of Wight, is going with me on my visitation, advocating the cause of the S.P.G. in Foreign Parts," he wrote to a friend. "The effect is astonishing. He is,

44. Diary, March 18, 1838, BD, I. C186.
45. James Mozley in a letter to his sister Anne, February 11, 1839, reported a sermon of Wilberforce's he had just heard at St. Mary's, "better than ever I had heard from him, with high ideas in it. He is sadly pompous though, both in style and delivery" (J. B. Mozley, Letters, ed, Anne Mozley [London, 1885], p. 88).

I think, the most interesting and captivating speaker I ever heard. Pray try, at some future season, to induce him to make a similar tour in the north." [46] So impressive was his performance that the bishop of London, in the name of the Society and the Archbishop, requested Wilberforce to address a public meeting in April 1840, convened with the hope of persuading leading city bankers and merchants to contribute to a scheme for colonial bishoprics—a most flattering invitation and a most important occasion, both for the Society and for himself, since he had never before spoken at a public meeting in London. "The two Archbishops and all London are to be there," he wrote Robert. "It is most absurd having me. . . However, I have clearly no choice, as it has come unsought, so I have assented." [47] He was at great pains to make his speech a good one, and it was, as he reported to Robert:

Our meeting went off very well. It appears I gave satisfaction to all but myself. I spoke not nearly so well as in the West, and infinitely below my own perceptions of excellence. Yet I trust it answered its purpose in stirring up the meeting. The Bp. of London spoke most kindly to me about my speech yesterday and today, only saying, 'I do not quite like hearing you, for you make me cry.'

Then, lest Robert think success had turned his head, he added,

Dearest R., I do not tell you this with a feeling of vanity. I am sure I do not, but because I know you, from affection, will wish to know *just all*. I greatly fell below my own standard, and the opinion of others somehow does not alter that.[48]

Nor, as he knew, could his own opinion alter the fact that he had made his mark in London, before the archbishops and the bishops, the bankers and the businessmen, and that for a clergyman not yet thirty-five this was a remarkable achievement.

The speech was only one of a series of achievements which Wilberforce had to his credit by 1840. Long before his father's death it was understood that he and Robert would together undertake the authorship of his biography. Samuel had begun a journal of his father's thoughts and opinions in 1823; his letters and diaries were at hand. Shortly after William's death in 1833, his sons began laboring on the five volumes which they eventually published in 1838. Their father's fame guaranteed the book a brisk sale—between six and seven thousand copies in five weeks—and assured it, as well, a widespread critical reception. Reactions varied. James Stephen accorded it favorable notice in the *Edinburgh Review*. John Wilson Croker, however, accused the authors of mistreating their father's memory by quoting too freely from his diaries.[49] In Evangelical papers they were taken to task for turning their father from an Evangelical

46. To the Reverend T. Baker, August 28, 1839 (Spencer Mss. in G. C. B. Davies, *Henry Phillpotts* [London, 1954], p. 163).
47. March 24, 1840, Wrangham papers.   48. *Ibid.*, April 9, 1840.
49. *Quarterly Review*, 62: 214ff (1838).

into a High Churchman. The most hostile attacks came from old Thomas
Clarkson and his friends, who charged, with some foundation, that the
Wilberforces had deliberately underrated Clarkson's role in the abolition
movement in order to reflect more glory on their father.[50] Whatever the
critical reaction, Samuel, who had already written and edited several
shorter books, found himself with something of a reputation as an
author.[51]

His work away from the diocese had not led him to neglect his duties
there. In 1836 Sumner appointed him rural dean of the northeast division
of the Isle of Wight. The new position accorded recognition to the fact
that he had been for some time the leading clergyman on the island. He
helped organize a Diocesan Building Society and a Board of Education,
taking readily any commission his bishop sent him. In November 1839,
soon after his return from the western tour, he received Sumner's offer
of the archidiaconate of Surrey, and surprised no one by accepting with
alacrity. The pace Wilberforce set for himself during these years was
phenomenal. He had hired a curate to help him at Brighstone, though he
managed still to spend almost two thirds of his year there. When he
traveled it was seldom solely for pleasure: there were always meetings
to attend, a sermon to preach, an ecclesiastical fence to mend. In 1835, for
example, on a trip with Emily, he went first to the Sumners' at Farnham
Castle, thence to Oxford, to Eccleshall with Bishop Ryder of Lichfield—

50. Clarkson attacked the biography with a pamphlet, *Strictures on the Life of William
Wilberforce* (London, 1838). Samuel and Robert retorted in the introduction to their edition of William Wilberforce's correspondence. James Stephen thought their reply warranted; "yet," he wrote Samuel, "it gave me great heartache to think of the pain which the
old man would have to endure" (August 21, 1838, BD, II.H). The sons eventually admitted
that they had been wrong to make an issue of Clarkson's role in the antislavery movement.
In a generous, if belated, apology, they wrote to him in 1844: "We were in the wrong in the
manner in which we treated you in the Memoirs of our father. We desired certainly to speak
the strict truth in every mention of you (nor indeed are we now aware of having anywhere
transgressed it), but we are conscious that too jealous a regard for what we thought our
father's fame, led us to entertain an ungrounded prejudice against you, and this led us into
a tone of writing which we now acknowledge was practically unjust. It has pleased God to
spare your life to a period far exceeding the ordinary lot of man, and amidst many other
grounds for rejoicing in it, we trust that you will allow us to add the satisfaction which it is
to our own minds to have made compensation for the fault with which we may be charged,
so far as it can be done by its free acknowledgment to the injured party" (November 15,
1844, BD, II.M).
51. By 1840 Wilberforce had published *The Notebook of a Country Clergyman* (1833),
a series of moral tales designed for a simple, rural audience; *The Journals of Henry Martyn*
(1837), which included a memoir of his father-in-law, John Sargent, who had died in 1833;
Eucharistica (1839), sacramental prayers which Wilberforce revised for publication;
his *University Sermons* (1839); and *Agathos, and other Sunday Stories* (1839), another
set of moral tales, this one for children. So successful was *Agathos* that he published a
sequel, *The Rocky Island,* in 1840. His *History of the American Church* was published in
1844, and his edition of John Evelyn's *Life of Mrs. Godolphin* in 1845. With Robert he
edited two volumes of his father's correspondence (1840). Throughout the period he contributed occasionally to various reviews and religious periodicals.

Emily's sister Sophia having recently married the bishop's son—to Hanbury with the young Ryders, to Birmingham for a church meeting, to Leamington, to Oxford again, and finally, for a rest, to the Sargents' at Lavington. Samuel's journeyings remind one of his father's; his attendance at innumerable committee meetings and boards recalls William's ceaseless good works. What William accomplished with the haphazard wizardry of his charm, Samuel, though charming, achieved through a meticulous attention to hours spent and miles traveled. He planned his life with a concern for detail which his father might well have admired, but which he would have found himself constitutionally incapable of emulating.

An archdeacon's duties depended upon his bishop's zeal and his own willingness to work. Bishop Blomfield of London, when pressed, once remarked that they were "to be going up and down the diocese discharging Archidiaconal functions." [52] Although Sumner had more precise notions of the task he wished his archdeacons to perform, Wilberforce was nevertheless left to steer a course that was basically his own. In his first attempt to define the course, made in his Charge of 1840, he allowed himself a latitude that suggests he may not yet have known just what he intended to do. The use of the office, he wrote,

is to carry out into the detail of cases the bishop's office and care;—not regarding merely the fabric of the church; or its external possessions and endowments alone,—but taking cognizance of persons as well as things; and hearing on all points, which are not of necessity limited to the episcopate, its portion of the bishop's spiritual charge.[53]

Whatever the definition, the duties were manifold and heavy. The archidiaconate included the South London parishes, and for the first time Wilberforce saw the problems the Church faced in the cities. He was hampered by the fact that he continued to live in the south, and by the requirement, necessitated by his concurrent appointment to a cathedral stall, that he reside for forty days a year at Winchester.[54] He determined to bring the clergy into more frequent contact with each other. To this end he organized quarterly meetings in each rural deanery and attended these meetings himself as often as possible. His annual Charges, substantial essays in which he discussed matters of far more than local ecclesiastical interest, again carried him from one part of the county to another, since he was required to "charge" his clergy by addressing them

52. Ashwell and Wilberforce, *Life*, I, 282.
53. Samuel Wilberforce, *A Charge Delivered to the Clergy of the Archdeaconry of Surrey* (London, 1840), p. 5. Hereafter all Wilberforce's official reports, or Charges, both as archdeacon and bishop, will be given the short title *Charge*.
54. At the bishop's request Wilberforce had surrendered the endowments of the archidiaconate, which were then transferred to the parish of Farnham. To compensate for this loss, the first vacant stall was annexed to the archdeaconry.

in person. Both clergy and laymen were occasionally startled by his readiness to prosecute his duties. In one such instance, illustrative as well of the teapot-tempest world into which Wilberforce had often to descend, he wrote to a parish priest:

You are perfectly right in your view of the matter. The Ordinary whether Bishop or Archdeacon is invested by law with the power of visiting Churches that he may judge what ought to be done to them, in the way of restoring or repairing etc. etc. He makes *an order* to this effect; and that order he can if necessary *enforce,* by monition, citation, and other processes of his court. . . I need not add that desirable as their removal is, I would not have forced the removal of the hatpegs on a reluctant parish: but this is not the point. Mr. Cox [a vestryman] is not aware that the Archdeacon's office is clothed by law with this authority and he therefore not unnaturally resisted it. But when he learns that by law the Archdeacon can not only (like the Rural Dean) *inspect,* but also *order,* it will alter his view I doubt not of the whole matter.[55]

Wilberforce was not trying to assert authority he did not have. Rather Mr. Cox lost his hatpegs because his archdeacon chose to exercise his power in a way it had not been exercised before in Surrey. Occasionally, Wilberforce found himself at a loss to know how far to go, how firmly to pronounce. William Gladstone, to whom Wilberforce had sent his Charge of 1843, wrote to warn that he might be taking too much upon himself. Wilberforce acknowledged the danger but added, "It is most difficult to know what at the present time to do in the sort of pseudo-episcopate into which so many causes have changed the Archidiaconate. For so much is some expression of opinion looked for by the clergy, that its suppression would appear like a shifty evasion of difficulties." [56]

With one of his most ambitious plans for the Archidiaconate Wilberforce went out of his way to court difficulty. He attempted to organize a Church Fund into which the money raised by all the various Church societies within the Archidiaconate would be pooled and subsequently spent under the direction of the clergy and the supervision of the archdeacon. The current practice of including only a few select societies within one Church Union led to constant bicker. The Union's directors only served, Wilberforce argued, "to break up the Church into cabals, instead of knitting it into one band." [57] The number of societies, and their antagonisms toward each other, made the sort of rational solution proposed by Wilberforce impossible, despite the advantages apparent to the nonpartisan outsider. He forced the societies to accept his plan in 1841, but a year later in his Charge, he admitted defeat. "Practical difficulties in the way of its accomplishment convinced me that we are not yet ripe for the full blessing of such visibly united action." [58]

55. To the Reverend W. W. Walpole, March 28, 1843. Letter Book, BD, d. 208.
56. December 18, 1843, Add Mss. 44343.   57. *Charge* (London, 1841), p. 21.
58. *Charge* (London, 1842), p. 33.

More apparently encouraging was the work going forward to subdivide some of the most overcrowded of the South London parishes. As a result of the Ecclesiastical Commissioners Bill of 1843, two new districts were formed from the parish of St. James Bermondsey, and similar reorganization was proposed for Horsleydown and Southwark. Progress was slow and the task formidable. The parish of St. George the Martyr in Lambeth, with a population of 50,000 in 1844, had sittings for only 2500, and of those, 1300 had been provided within the past two years.[59] Wilberforce, who went where he could and talked with everyone he knew to find money for these new parishes, must have occasionally turned with relief from city problems to act as Solomon to the rural squabbles that still took a great share of his time. "Perhaps," he wrote to an angry parishioner who had been called upon to maintain a churchyard hedge adjacent to his property, "perhaps the Churchwardens might compromise the matter with you—by undertaking a share of the expense of erecting and maintaining, instead of a hedge, a sufficient rail. This would be a great improvement both to the Churchyard and to your garden." [60]

Travel now took even more of his time. In November 1843 he reported proudly that he had visited one hundred and thirty-four parishes in Surrey —almost the lot. His letters often read like a timetable: "I am here [London] today from Camberwell, going tonight to the Geological Society. Tomorrow, to the new Camberwell Church consecration. Then to Addington till Saturday. To be at Battersea rectory on Sunday and all next week charging." [61] Not that Wilberforce looked upon such activity as a chore. More often it was a tonic, for these visits were occasions upon which he could indulge a favorite pastime—meeting new people and studying the effect of the Church on their lives. When at rest once at Lavington, he could not resist a drive to Goodwood, though not within his province,

where the Duke [Richmond] was holding a great festival as the anniversary of the agricultural association for rewarding meritorious labourers. The Bishop attended to give a Bible and prayer book to the three first prize men. The Dean and thirty clergy were present. All the gentry of the neighborhood, all the yeomen and the prize labourers, about 260 in all. We dined in the tennis court and the Duke did it admirably. Such things when so managed and the Church put forward tend greatly to bind up the wounds of society amongst us, and are a great blessing.[62]

Opportunities to enjoy such edifying rural occasions were rare. Less than six months after his outing to Goodwood, Wilberforce received still another commission from Sumner, the rectory of the sprawling parish

59. *Charge* (London, 1844), pp. 16–17.
60. To Richard Horley, February 11, 1843. Letter Book, BD, d. 208.
61. To Louisa Noel, November 20, 1844, BD, II. F.
62. To Charles Anderson, June 15, 1840, BD, I. C191.

of Alverstoke, outside Portsmouth. Wilberforce, whose close ties with
Sumner had helped persuade him to reject the offers he had received to
go north, was now prepared to do his bishop's bidding, seeing in Alverstoke a challenge worth the sacrifice of his beloved Brighstone. Alverstoke was a parish of extremes. Originally a farming district, it now
included the fortified town of Gosport and the recently fashionable resort
of Anglesey-ville. Although, in a letter to Robert, Wilberforce reported
that he would be addressing himself to "a much more educated class,"
he was to find that Gosport, adjacent to military and naval barracks,
spawned a vicious low life. The parish, with a population of 12,637, contained only three churches: one at Alverstoke, one in the Gosport suburb
of Forton, and one, a large chapel without a legal district, in Gosport
itself.[63] He had the assistance of a group of devoted curates, among them
one who became a good friend, Richard Chevenix Trench. A pair of
Evangelical clergymen, at Gosport and nearby Portsea, had worked
to promote a revival of sorts, but not to an extent that would satisfy Wilberforce. As he had at Brighstone, he increased the number of services
and communions and reorganized the system of district visiting. He
devoted a major share of his time to a campaign to build new churches
within the parish. In a plea for funds issued in 1842, he presented statistics to prove the inadequacy of present accommodations. With a population exceeding 13,000, the three central churches contained sittings
for only 4,294. Wilberforce proposed a chapel of ease at Gosport and a
church at Elson, a community of about 900 people, "chiefly in the middle
and lower ranks of life." To build them a church large enough for their
needs—with sittings for 400—would cost £1400. Additional funds were
solicited for endowment, for, as the circular boldly pronounced, the intention was to build the church "without pews and that EVERY SEAT
IN IT SHOULD BE FREE." [64] Work of this sort was in a different
class from any Wilberforce had undertaken at Brighstone. As he had
done there and at Checkendon, he managed his days so that he could
spend time watching over the people committed to his charge to see
whether his busy ministrations were having an effect. "My great parish
in a confirmation has been an immense interest to me," he wrote Louisa
Noel in the fall of 1841.

We have had 130 catechisms from our own district alone: and I trust that many
of them are setting in earnest their seal to the promises of their baptismal covenant
with a firm trust in the promised help of God's holy spirit. A very large proportion

63. A fourth, begun at the direction of his predecessor, was soon finished at Anglesey.
The population figure appears in the letter from Bishop Sumner to Wilberforce offering the
living (October 24, 1840, BD, I. C195). Ashwell gives the population in 1841 as 13,510
(*Life*, I, 169).
64. Printed circular dated April 6, 1842 (BD, I. C204). Wilberforce himself is listed as
having contributed £100. He saw both churches completed before leaving Alverstoke.

of them will I trust be for the first time at the Holy Communion on Sunday morning at half past seven.[65]

Piling the heavy offices of Alverstoke upon those he already bore as archdeacon often left even the indefatigable Wilberforce exhausted. Exhaustion now helped to bring him relief from a burden far heavier than that imposed by his duties. On March 10, 1841, a month after giving birth to her sixth child, Emily Wilberforce died. Samuel never freed himself from the pain of that blow. Work brought him some relief, and so he worked to wear himself into insensitivity and make himself too tired to think. "All day long," his mother-in-law Mary Sargent wrote

he is most busily occupied as if he were afraid of giving himself time to think and his whole life seems altered. . . Dearest Sam spends the great part of every afternoon and evening with his poor or sick parishioners and comes in about nine or later (half dead with fatigue) for some tea and unable to do more than look at a book when he is eating his toast.[66]

He traveled as never before to London, to Winchester, to Lavington, back to Alverstoke; seldom any more to Oxford, although had it not been for Emily's death, he would have delivered the Bampton lectures there in 1841.

Often he was summoned now to preach at Claremont or at Windsor, for the Prince, impressed by a speech he had heard Wilberforce deliver in London, had made him a royal chaplain. Albert and Victoria found both his sermons and his company edifying, and when Thomas Turton was translated from the deanery of Westminster to the bishopric of Ely in the spring of 1845, Peel did not hesitate to suggest his name for the vacancy. "I shall be inclined to offer the Deanery of Westminster to Archdeacon Wilberforce," he wrote Bishop Blomfield, "in whose behalf the Queen and Prince take rather a warm interest." [67] In reply to a similar notification, the Archbishop signified his approval and remarked that "a man of Archdeacon Wilberforce's traits and activity cannot but be useful in London." [68] Wilberforce appears to have been genuinely uncertain if he should accept. It meant surrendering the archdeaconry and perhaps Alverstoke as well. With typical dispatch, he set about to seek advice.

March 28, 1845.—Whilst at dinner with Trench etc., a messenger came from Sir R. Peel with offer of Deanery of Westminster. Much perplexed by it. Greatly disposed to refuse it. Resolved to consult Anson [Prince Albert's secretary]. Off at midnight. Got to Windsor at half past 7. Found it was the Queen's wish. . . Resolved; and off with A. to Farnborough and on to Farnham. Bishop [Sumner]

65. October 14, 1841, BD, II. F.
66. To Emily (Mrs. Charles) Anderson, June 16, 1841, BD, II. W.
67. March 26, 1845, Add Mss. 40563.254.
68. William Howley to Robert Peel, March 29, 1845, Add Mss. 40563.260.

Samuel Wilberforce as Dean of Westminster. From a drawing by George Richmond, R.A.

at Godalming. Thither after him. Affecting conversation, and away to rail. Down to Winton. Wrote and accepted.[69]

Sumner urged him to keep Alverstoke, and he acquiesced, although he realized that he would lay himself open to the charge of pluralism. He defended the decision on the ground that he was in the midst of his church building campaign, that his plans for the reorganization of the parish necessitated the passage of certain Acts of Parliament, and that he was the one best able to manage this difficult work.[70] His rationalization did nothing to forestall an attack, which came in the fall in the *Morning Post* and which prompted him to make an accounting to himself in his diary.

Upon reckoning up, I think I have hardly *drawn* above £400 per annum [from a total of £1287] for myself, the rest having gone in charities, repairs, churches, schools, etc.; and I have been able to obtain [*i.e.* from others] or contribute to permanent Church objects in the five years . . . £9980. I am most thankful that God has suffered me to *see* the labour of my hands.[71]

Wilberforce anticipated that his duties in London would still allow him four full months "and many several Sundays and Mondays" in Alverstoke, and apparently intended to retain the living only until the complicated reorganization he had undertaken had been successfully accomplished.[72] In fact, he kept both deanery and rectory for only six months, surrendering them together in October to become a bishop.

As dean of Westminster he became administrator-in-chief of an institution part school, part church, part shrine. His business was with his Chapter, stall holders jealous to exercise every jot and tittle of their inherited privilege, with the Ecclesiastical Commission, even with the Prime Minister, who was anxious to see reforms attempted in both the school and the Abbey. Wilberforce plunged into the work with characteristic concern. He preached for the first time in the Abbey on June 10. "I looked on it with dread; but the sight of the large congregation, the mass of heads, the number of *men* moved me greatly." [73] He wrote in August to Louisa Noel of difficulties he was encountering. The school was in disrepair, and he wanted to see to its restoration. "If you treat boys as savages, they will be savages." The choristers and lay vicars were as well "a grief of heart" to him.[74] He recognized that the Abbey

69. Diary, March 28, 1845, BD, I. C186.

70. See A. P. Stanley's report of his conversation with one of Wilberforce's curates—probably Trench—in a letter to his sister Mary, October 31, 1845 in *Letters and Verses of A. P. Stanley,* R. E. Prothero, ed. (London, 1895), p. 95.

71. October 12, 1845, BD, I. C186. The deanery of Westminster was worth £2000 per year (William Howley to Robert Peel, October 4, 1845, Add Mss. 40575.101).

72. To R. C. Trench, March 29, 1845, in Ashwell and Wilberforce, *Life,* I, 264; and A. P. Stanley to Mary Stanley, October 31, 1845, in *Letters and Verses of A. P. Stanley,* p. 95.

73. Diary, June 10, 1845, BD, I. C186.

74. August 7, 1845, BD, II. F. In a letter to Peel just after his appointment to Oxford, Wilberforce urged him to concern himself with the school, which he felt needed new

was as much a national monument as a church and managed to open it to public sightseers, an innovation opposed vigorously by certain Chapter members, whose objections the dean stilled to some degree by an admission charge of sixpence a head.[75]

Wilberforce did not remain dean long enough to accomplish much. The announcement of his appointment, in the fall of 1845, to the bishopric of Oxford surprised almost no one; his reputation had prepared those who followed ecclesiastical politics for the news. Some had expected it sooner. Wilberforce himself had, in 1841, recorded James Stephen's "assurance that Sir R. Peel would *quam citissime* call me *episcopari*"; Lady Lyttelton, after hearing him preach at Windsor in 1842, wrote that "everybody says he will be a bishop." [76] He was, of course, still very young, but in a letter in 1843 to an ecclesiastical friend, Thomas Fosbery, he observed soberly that "a Bishop may *look* as old as he pleases and not be respected if his *actions* are young, and he may look as young as you like and be respected if his acts are grave." [77] Youth did not apparently worry Peel, for in January 1842, when Wilberforce was only thirty-six, he had proposed him to Archbishop Howley as the most suitable candidate for the vacant bishopric of Chichester. He added that he had asked the Bishop of London to inquire of Sumner "what is the real state of Mr. Wilberforce's opinions in matters connected with the theological differences at Oxford." [78] Wilberforce stood a middle ground during those disputes [79]—many, not unexpectedly, saw his caution dictated by a desire for place. Sumner, although responsible for his archdeacon's rapid advancement, apparently allowed his Evangelical scruples to convince him that Wilberforce was too sympathetic to the Tractarians to warrant promotion to the Bench and returned a letter effectively removing him from the running.[80] The next year, when Peel

---

buildings and was suffering from a "general vulgarity of tone." Peel replied that he agreed, and considered "the present state of so noble an endowment is a great scandal." He recommended the retirement of the headmaster, Dr. Williamson, a capable scholar but a poor administrator. Following charges about the conduct of the school addressed by a parent to Peel in 1846, the latter invoked the powers of the Crown as Visitor. After an inquiry the captain of the school was dismissed, and Williamson retired to the living of Pershore, in the gift of the dean and chapter (J. D. Carleton, *Westminster School* [London, 1965] pp. 52, 54). Samuel Wilberforce to Robert Peel, October 24, 1845, Add Mss. 40576.338; Robert Peel to Samuel Wilberforce, October 28, 1845, Add Mss. 40576.334.

75. To Robert Peel, August 1, 1845, Add Mss. 40571.363; and to George Anson, August 6, 1845, BD, I. C193.

76. Diary, November 12, 1841, BD, I. C186; Lady Lyttelton to her daughter, 1842, in Ashwell and Wilberforce, *Life*, I, 220.

77. January 22, 1843, BD, I. C193.   78. January 14, 1842, Add Mss. 40500.88.

79. See below, Chapter III.

80. Peel wrote a second letter to Howley on January 14: "I received the accompanying letter from the Bishop of London this morning. I am sorry for the impediment to the selection of Archdeacon Wilberforce—but I feel the force of the Bishop of Winchester's observations" (Add Mss. 40500.90). Sumner's letter to Peel has not been preserved.

considered moving Bishop Bagot of Oxford to Lichfield, he again consulted Blomfield as to candidates, but this time himself wrote Wilberforce off. "I may have Wilberforce's name mentioned to me"—a reference
presumably to the Queen. "I do not think his appointment to Oxford
would be advisable." Blomfield concurred, adding that Wilberforce was
young enough to wait.[81]

Bagot in any case refused to remove himself to Lichfield, remaining
at Oxford for another two years. In September 1845 he accepted Peel's
offer of Bath and Wells, and Peel, now without the qualms he had felt
two years before, offered the See to Wilberforce. Unfortunately, his
correspondence on this occasion gives little indication of the reasons
behind his change of mind. Undoubtedly, the Prince and the Queen
pressed for the appointment, as they had for the deanship. Nor was the
competition particularly stiff. "I do not think the supply of distinguished
divines for the Bench is a very abundant one," Peel wrote the Archbishop
while as yet undecided. He mentioned as another possibility Edward
Cardwell, principal of Low Church St. Alban's Hall. "But," he added,
"my desire is to place on the Bench the divine best entitled by professional character and merit to preferment." [82] On those straightforward
grounds his ultimate choice was eminently justifiable. Cardwell, although
a respectable enough candidate, lacked Wilberforce's experience and
ability. Bagot, although by no means an unsuccessful bishop of Oxford,
possessed neither taste nor talent for administration. The diocese was
in need of the sort of energetic attention which Wilberforce had clearly
shown he could give it. Tractarian controversy still raged, and Blomfield
favored the appointment of the safer Cardwell. Peel, though aware that
he had undertaken a "hazardous measure," now presumably believed
Sumner's reservations overcautious.[83] He wrote Wilberforce on October 13, offering him the See of Oxford and was accepted the following
day. "I have just received your letter," Wilberforce wrote,

conveying to me in terms expressive of the greatest personal kindness and with
an assurance most deeply gratifying to me, of the cordial approbation of Her
Majesty and the Prince the offer of the See of Oxford.

I assure you that I feel most unfeignedly my own lack of qualification for such
a post: yet I cannot, when so selected, for a moment doubt as to the duty of
accepting it. I can but express in doing so at once my heartfelt gratitude for the
good opinion which has suggested and approved the choice, and my earnest
desire that I may be enabled to discharge the high and important duties which
will devolve upon me, as not to disappoint entirely the too favorable estimate
which your letter expresses of me.[84]

81. Robert Peel to C. J. Blomfield, October 13, 1843 (Add Mss. 40533.403); C. J.
Blomfield to Robert Peel, October 15, 1843 (Add Mss. 40534.168).
82. September 26, 1845, Add Mss. 40574.261.
83. P. J. Welch, "Blomfield and Peel: A Study in Cooperation between Church and
State, 1841–46," *Journal of Ecclesiastical History,* 12:75 (1961).
84. October 14, 1845, Add Mss. 40575.376.

The stiff language of self-deprecation masks the excitement and gratification Wilberforce unquestionably felt. As soon as he had written to accept, he put his very human reactions into a letter to his friend Louisa Noel.

My dearest Sister—you must hear this day from me, that a messenger has arrived from Sir Robert Peel, with a *very* cordial letter, in which he states that he has just heard from the Bishop of Oxford that he will accept Bath and Wells in lieu of his present preferment; that, when at Windsor Castle, he had suggested to Her Majesty that in case of that acceptance, I was the fittest person for the See of Oxford; that her Majesty had most cordially acquiesced on the suggestion, 'with very kind expressions towards yourself on her part and on that of the Prince'; and that he therefore, offered me the See of Oxford.

Ah! dearest sister, when you and I have talked of such matters, how different has it looked from what it does now! I thought I knew my unworthiness of such a post; but now I see that I never felt it at all. My soul is penetrated with a thrilling sense of it. Yet you will understand how, without real inconsistency, I yet feel I could not decline the offer so made. I have written to accept it. Pray for me, dearest sister, that neither may Christ's Church suffer damage, or I ruin my own soul in these new responsibilities being committed to me.[85]

That night Wilberforce wrote a line in his diary that said it all. "I had wished for this, and now it comes it seems *awful*." [86]

Without question he had worked to be a bishop. He had served his Church with skill and energy enough to earn advancement. Bishops were no longer called to the Bench without having displayed genuine distinction as clergymen, and Peel was sincere in expressing himself anxious to appoint men of merit and ability. Wilberforce possessed those qualifications. Yet if he had worked for the Church, he had done it so as to insure that those who could advance him knew what he was doing. When at Brighstone his friendship with Sumner kept him from what might otherwise have been premature burial in a small island parish. From the start, Wilberforce cultivated Sumner's confidence and attention. He and Emily visited at Farnham Castle when they returned from their wedding trip. As soon as Wilberforce began to travel up to London frequently, the Sumners pressed him to stay with them there. Wilberforce accepted with pleasure and came as often as he was bid. He, in turn, entertained Sumner whenever he traveled to the Isle of Wight for a meeting or a confirmation tour. Sumner, who quickly recognized Wilberforce for the able young man he was, undertook to counsel him as his protégé. He foresaw that his clergyman friend would not remain for long a parish priest. He fretted at the pace Wilberforce set himself, urging him to focus his energies toward a more "permanent usefulness." Sumner's friendly attentions to Wilberforce sprang originally from the close ties that already existed

85. October 14, 1845, BD, II. F.
86. October 14, 1845, BD, I. C186.

between their two families.[87] His later readiness to support Wilberforce's advancement came with a profound admiration for his undoubted accomplishments. With one exception—when he advised against the appointment to Chichester in 1842—he promoted Wilberforce's steady ascendancy. It would be unfair to accuse Wilberforce of battening on his superior with a view to preferment. Sumner offered friendship which Wilberforce accepted willingly and assiduously cultivated. But the rapid rise from Brighstone to Oxford was due far more to Sumner's fortuitous respect for Wilberforce than to any sort of active campaign by Wilberforce to win his bishop's favor and support.

The same cannot be said for his relationship with Peel. In this case, Wilberforce did call attention to himself and, one suspects, did so with his eye on an eventual episcopate. For a time in the late 1820's he had had little good to say for Peel. Although he had supported a mild reform ministry in 1827, he found Peel's attitude on Catholic Emancipation unendurable and turned on him with the sort of invective he had in his Union days saved for place hunters, slavers, and borough mongers. The reality of reform and the hostility of reformers to the Church establishments dispelled the remainder of his racy undergraduate liberalism, leaving him for a time one of the mass of sour, frightened Tory clergymen. He tried, nevertheless, to teach himself the lesson he had preached as long ago as 1827, when, in a letter to Boyle, he remarked that he was hoping to moderate his political feelings, "which only become a clergyman, I think, when mildly held." [88] Soon he was back to the middle of the road, claiming that although he thought modern liberalism a devil's creed, his politics had "always been what Tories would call liberal." [89] As he admitted to Anderson, Church politics—that is, the government's policy toward the Church—were all he really cared about.[90] With attitudes of this sort, Wilberforce found himself absolving Peel of his earlier mistakes and welcoming him as an astute and thoughtful politician. In May 1837, with Peel out of office and Wilberforce two years away from his archdeaconry, he wrote him suggesting a plan to counter the anti-Church rate proposals of the Ministry.[91] Peel must have been impressed, for only a year later Robert Wilberforce reported a conversation Peel had had with

87. Interestingly enough, however, Bishop Sumner did not realize that he and Wilberforce were cousins until 1837. See the letter from Sumner to Wilberforce in Ashwell and Wilberforce, *Life*, I, 82.

88. October 25, 1827, BD, I. C205.

89. To Charles Anderson, August 21, 1837, BD, I. C191.

90. April 13, 1837, BD, I. C191.

91. May 9, 1837, Add Mss. 40423.201. The plan involved an entailing of the episcopal estates and subsequent leasing of the lands, "providing at the same time that all additional income so created should be paid over to the Ecclesiastical Commissioners."

Sir Robert Inglis, in which he announced himself ready to make Samuel "at least a dean." [92] Wilberforce continued to remind Peel of his existence. He wrote to congratulate him and to bless him upon his assumption of office, and throughout the early 1840's at every opportunity sent him his sermons and his Charges. Nor did he neglect to cultivate his Alverstoke neighbor John Wilson Croker, a privy councillor to whom Peel turned for ecclesiastical advice, yet a man whom Wilberforce had not hesitated to call a "clever dung-feeder" when it appeared that he was blocking Samuel's admission to the Athenaeum in 1838.[93] Again, as in the case of his relationship with Sumner, it would be wrong to accuse Wilberforce of simple toadying for office. He had come to believe in Peel's sort of conservatism, which he found consistent with his own attitudes toward Church reform; Peel had become his natural political leader. Yet there is no question that Peel's respect for him, his intention *"quam citissime* to call me *episcopari"* spurred Wilberforce to keep himself in Peel's good graces, as it encouraged him to lay his sermons before Peel's eyes.

Wilberforce did not court political favor indiscriminately. While ingratiating himself with Peel, he had managed to win himself an enemy in Palmerston. He had first crossed him at a meeting in Winchester in support of a diocesan church building society in 1837. The presiding bishop had summoned a London galaxy to grace the platform. Wellington took the chair, and Palmerston spoke, directing his remarks in a way that convinced Wilberforce he was less interested in building churches for the Establishment than in wooing his Dissenting constituents. Wilberforce made a sharp reply, drawing from Wellington, according to tradition, the retort that he would himself have sooner faced a battery.[94] Wilberforce was willing to judge politicians by one simple standard: the loyalty they showed the Church of England. Palmerston, "willing to court the Dissenters in order to maintain political consistency," had been weighed,

92. April 30, 1838, Wrangham papers.
93. To Robert I. Wilberforce, July 6, 1838, Wrangham papers. With this compare his character of Croker to Robert two years later: "I really think that I have never heard him make an unkind remark on any one. He is very attentive at Church" (*Ibid.,* November 1840).
94. Palmerston was at this time M.P. for Tiverton. He had been returned by South Hampshire in 1833 but rejected by the voters there the following year. There is no account of the speeches of either Palmerston or Wilberforce. The *Times* of April 3, 1837 (p. 5) mentions only that the meeting took place and that contributions of from £7 to £8000 were announced. Wilberforce noted in his diary that it had been a "very good meeting," and that "I spoke answering Lord Palmerston well" (BD, I. C186).
To Charles Anderson, on April 13, he wrote: "I quite agree with you in what you say about the misery of having to court the Dissenters in order to maintain political consistency. I saw it very curiously at the Winchester Church meeting, where Lord Palmerston was *really* speaking throughout to his *Dissenting* constituents" (BD, I. C191). The alleged remark by Wellington is in Ashwell and Wilberforce, *Life,* I, 107–108.

found wanting, and was consequently attacked. Wilberforce continued to have no use for him, and Palmerston, in turn, developed an antipathy for Wilberforce that lasted well into the years when both men had power enough to try to hurt each other.

Meanwhile, Wilberforce cultivated friendship with a young politician of whose solid churchmanship there could be no doubt. Robert had written his brother of William Gladstone in 1835, recommending that Samuel make his acquaintance the next time he went to London.[95] This Wilberforce had lost no time in doing. By 1838 he was writing him at length, though more as a self-appointed and ardently admiring counsellor than as a friend, urging upon him the future leadership of a party that would make the support of Church Establishment a cardinal principle. "There is no height to which you may not fairly rise in this country," he urged. But to do so, he explained, a politician must keep himself from compromise. "I would have you view yourself as one who may become the head of all the better feelings of this country, the maintainer of its Church and of its liberties, and who must now be fitting himself for this high vocation." [96] The solemn notes of this prognostication struck a responsive chord in Gladstone. "I have not to charge myself inwardly with having been used to look forward along the avenues of life rarely or neglectfully," he replied,

but rather with that weakness of faith, and that shrinking of the flesh, of which at every moment I am mournfully conscious, but most so when I attempt to estimate or conjecture our probable public destinies during the term to which our natural lives may extend—a prospect which I confess fills me with alarm.

He foresaw a coming period of decline, although not for the Church, for which he expected "new developments of religious power which have been forgotten in the day of insidious prosperity." Rather it was the principles of civil government that were in decay, and "if we look around for the masses of principle, I mean of enlightened principle, blended with courage and devotion, which are the human means of resistance, *these* I feel have yet to be organised, almost to be created." [97] The two men continued to talk this mild sort of gloom when they met in the London clubs to which they belonged. Both were earnest, both ambitious, and both enjoyed sober discussions of a future in which they assigned each other major roles.

Perhaps it was his sense of impending national disaster that led Wilberforce to defer in such exaggerated fashion to Royalty, once he had

95. January 31, 1835, Wrangham papers. Samuel's first letter to Gladstone was written May 1, 1834, requesting his signature on a petition protesting Russell's marriage bills. "You will not, I hope, think that I am making too free an use of the slight acquaintance which I can personally claim with you in sending you these few lines" (Add Mss. 44343).
96. *Ibid.,* April 20, 1838.   97. *Ibid.,* April 25, 1838.

been admitted to the hothouse *gemutlichkeit* world of Windsor and
Osborne. More probably it was that dizziness that affected many upper
middle-class Victorians when they discovered themselves seated at
dinner across from Royal Personages. The throat goes dry, the knees
wobble, while the critical faculties sink into slumber, anesthetized by the
august feeling of occasion that accompanies even the raising of an oyster
fork. Afterward the evening was "so pleasant," the company "so engaging," the Personages themselves "so kind." Wilberforce's account to
Louisa Noel of his first meeting with the Prince following his appointment
as chaplain set the tone for all his accounts of royal visits thereafter. "The
Prince received me most pleasantly. His manner was kind and so easily
self-possessed that he set me quite at my ease at once. He spoke very
kindly and talked for five or six minutes in a very sensible way." [98] And
from Windsor, where he was summoned for a visit:

> All has gone most pleasantly and smoothly here. I felt no nervousness about
> the service [he preached on the Widow of Nain] because there I was on high
> ground: but about the first dinner, etc., I did. However, things fell rapidly into
> their proper places; and after dinner when the Queen came to speak to me, she
> spoke so pleasantly and kindly that I was composed by it.[99]

Wilberforce found himself ill at ease only upon the rare occasions
when, surprisingly, he felt that the conventions of the Victorian court
might better have attuned themselves to Christian propriety. Once he
had made the mistake of accepting the Prince's invitation to play chess on
Sunday. Albert, who had already expressed his distaste for English
Sabbatarianism to Wilberforce, and whose conscience was as Lutheran
as his upbringing, could see no reason to deny himself a game in the evening. Wilberforce sat through only one. "I have never been asked again
to play at chess," he later reported to Louisa Noel, "since the time I
told you of, when (the only time I played) I explained afterwards that I
wished not to play: deeming it though not wrong in *act* yet very inexpe-
dient and especially so for me. This last time I sat with the Queen talking
all the time." [100]

During another visit, at Eastertime, he was embarrassed to find himself unable to fast. "At home one can do it easily; but here I hardly know
what is right. To be at all singular would be wrong certainly, yet I fear
our not fasting must scandalize good Roman Catholics like the Queen of
the Belgians [who was visiting at the time]." [101] The routine seldom
varied when he came to preach. Dinner Saturday night, a sermon the
next morning, and often in the afternoon as well, a quiet Sunday evening,
and away the next day. Gifts were exchanged, a volume of sermons for

98. June 7, 1841, BD, II. F.
99. To Louisa Noel, September 26, 1841, BD, II. F.
100. *Ibid.,* September 7, 1846.   101. To Louisa Noel, April 4, 1844, BD, II. F.

the Queen, a lithograph for Wilberforce. Frequently a new prince or princess was carried up to be admired—the Prince of Wales: "a singularly engaging child. Quite lovable"; Princess Alice Maud Mary: "are they not quite grand names. So new and yet so old. And so English. The Princess Alice of England sounds charming I think." [102] Occasionally Albert would take him off for a talk, and once confided to him in a refreshingly frank way his despair of English phlegm.

He urged English want of amusements for common people of an innocent class— no *gardens* . . . 'I never have heard a real *shout* in England. All my German servants marry because they say it is so dull here: nothing to interest—good living, good wine, but there is nothing to do but turn rogue or marry,' etc.

"He very intelligent, right-minded and remarkably pleasing," Wilberforce is quick to add in his record of the conversation, as if to suggest that after such an openhearted confession, the Prince's *bona fides* as a sound and proper Consort needed reestablishing. [103]

Wilberforce recognized that he was a ready prey to temptations court life laid in his path. "I hope, dearest brother," he once wrote Robert, "that you pray for me on these occasions that I may *do good* and not *get harm*. . . There may certainly, I think, be something wholesome in one's knowing that quantities of ill-natured things are said of one just because one is, as people think, thus put into a post of honor." [104] He bore the ill-will believing he served a useful and a holy purpose by preaching to the Queen and her court. He was plainly delighted that God had set his lines for a time in such a pleasant place. The chance to live among royalty thrilled him. More than that, the opportunity to press indirectly for a royal favor by dropping hints encouraged him to cultivate his court connections for the good they might do his friends and himself. He wrote a revealing letter to Louisa Noel in 1843:

The Prince hearing quite incidentally that I should like to secure E. Farleigh (where poor Mr. Lutwidge is said to be just dying) for Henry, has written himself to the Lord Chancellor to say that it will be a great satisfaction to the Queen and himself if he will give it to Henry [Robert having left East Farleigh to become rector of Burton Agnes in Yorkshire in 1840]. . . The Prince said in his note that his and the Queen's great reason was a wish to gratify Archdeacon S. W., who was, they knew, anxious to secure such a post for his brother. [105]

The text for his sermon on the occasion of that visit was "Every man shall bear his own burden."

Before leaping to condemn, we must remember that place-hunting

102. Diary, January 30, 1843. BD, I. C186. To Louisa Noel, May 28, 1843, BD, II. F.
103. Diary, March 6, 1843, BD, I. C186.
104. January 9, 1843, Wrangham papers.
105. January 15, 1843, Ashwell and Wilberforce, *Life,* I, 222. The Queen had appointed Wilberforce her sub-almoner—that is adviser on charitable contributions—in October 1844.

was often a necessary and certainly not a disreputable clerical pursuit. Even the saintly William saw nothing amiss when Brougham favored him by giving Robert preferment. Henry was a capable young cleric, less scholarly than Robert, but as well qualified as the next to take East Farleigh. Why should he not have it? Perhaps the Prince *had* heard only incidentally of Wilberforce's hopes for Henry. Perhaps, but probably not. The place-hunting does not grate; the self-deception does: complaining of that "quantity of ill-natured things" spread about concerning his activities at Court while at the same time airing desires, priding himself on his ability to win favors from his distinguished friends.

But an honest picture of Wilberforce must reflect as faithfully as possible the many planes and shadings from which his complex nature took its shape. Charm softened the harsh edge of his ambitions, and self-knowledge lay alongside self-deception. Most people, even those predisposed to dislike him, rated him a delightful and sympathetic companion. Charles Greville, encountering him for the first time in 1845, thought him "a very quick, lively, agreeable man." [106] F. D. Maurice, the Christian Socialist, whose tastes were certainly far from Greville's, found him as congenial. "Far less finished [than Manning]," he reported, "but therefore more suitable to me, of the greatest geniality and cordiality, open to receive any truths, and with singular capacities for imparting all he has received." [107] His ability to enjoy the society of all kinds of people and to give them pleasure was the result of his delight in the variety of human nature. He was forever observing, jotting down a quick impression, noting a glance or a phrase that might give a clue to character. From his diary, March 17, 1838, while in London:

Struck exceedingly by *faces*,—history or prophecy in:—a poor woman especially in the street today—poor, sickly, and most distressed-looking,—suddenly lighted up with a face of *perfect pleasure*. I saw *she was carrying a baby which smiled.* Then she relapsed.[108]

In a letter to Louisa Noel of May 27, 1845, he described a woman he had encountered in a London drawing room:

The type of a class, deeply worldly, beginning to age, fighting against it to desperation, and playing off two daughters of very great beauty, dressed admirably in a sort of exquisite green, with light flowers; and their hair like a mist floating around them, and only girdled by a wreath of lovely flowers, but seeming decked out like victims, played daily, hourly, minutely in this their sweet girlish youth, by a very clever, reaching mother, for coronets and a settlement.[109]

106. Charles C. F. Greville, *Memoirs*, ed. Lytton Strachey and Roger Fulford, 8 vols. (London, 1938), V, 197.
107. To Edward Strachey, September 15, 1843. Frederick Maurice, *The Life of Frederick Denison Maurice*, 2 vols. (New York, 1884), I, 35.
108. Diary, March 17, 1838, BD, I. C186.
109. May 27, 1845, BD, II. F.

Like his father, he was an excellent mimic.[110] One can picture him delighting Emily with an imitation of the curate of Newport, here caricatured in a letter to Anderson:

He is a famous hand at his knife and fork. He sent to me with a most engaging smile for some pigeon pie—'and plenty of the crust and gravy,' a charge first delivered to the waiter and afterwards repeated to me. I had afterwards to help him to some crab and the eagerness with which he answered my query of what part—'The inside, the inside'—was quite astonishing.[111]

Observation of this sort was not infrequently accompanied by judgment. Clapham had trained its sons to attend not only to their own shortcomings but, as a favor and a duty, to those of others as well. Barbara Wilberforce had been particularly predisposed to help her friends understand the nature and extent of their failings; perhaps she passed the predisposition to her sons. Some, in any case, found the habit trying. A mutual friend wrote Manning once that "both he [Samuel] and others of his family are, I think, in the habit of talking over and exercising acts of judgment on their friends' characters in a way which both produces evil externally and injures their own minds." [112] It is true that Wilberforce's diary is peppered with disparaging opinion, yet probably no more so than were the journals of his friends. If he judged his acquaintances severely, so did some of them judge him—especially those who, like Newman and the Mozleys, disliked the way Wilberforce steered shy of Tractarian commitment.

His delight in good society, his own genial nature, and his frequent trips to London led to election to a variety of clubs and societies: the Sterling, that collection of disparate yet alarmingly clever men; "The Club," more political, longer established; and, in 1840, the Athenaeum, without membership in which no would-be bishop could think his aspirations worth a chance.[113] Wilberforce enjoyed London life; he could as easily enjoy the countryside. Lavington never ceased to delight him; he was an ardent naturalist and loved to ride the countryside and walk the shore. To Anderson he had once written that he liked nothing better than his accounts of a day's shooting. "That poetry of shooting is what I would

110. Daniel Wilson, the bishop of Calcutta, in a memoir included in the *Life of William Wilberforce,* recollected that "observations minute, accurate, graphical, and often with a tinge of humour, dropped from him [William] in conversation, and when quiet in his family he would imitate the voice and manner of the person he was describing (generally some public man) in a way to provoke profuse merriment. Then he would check himself and throw in some kind remark" (Wilberforce, *Life,* V, 295).
111. September 20, 1830, BD, I. C191.
112. S. F. Wood to Henry E. Manning, November 15, 1837, in E. S. Purcell, *Life of Cardinal Manning,* 2 vols. (New York, 1896), I, 192, n. 2. Wood, a lawyer and a friend and disciple of Newman's, had been at Oriel with the Wilberforces.
113. He had hoped to receive election two years previously, but had been blackballed, apparently by Croker. See letter to Robert I. Wilberforce, July 6, 1838, Wrangham papers.

of all things enjoy. The solitary, meditative observation of nature is de-
licious." [114] He was by no means all dash and go, and when at rest remembered to let his conscience upbraid him for his shortcomings. His
diary shows him awake to the dangers of worldliness, self-deception—
all the sins which could be entered against the name of an ambitious
young clergyman:

September 8, 1832 [the day after his twenty-seventh birthday]. Resolved to
pray more constantly against sensuality, irritability, vanity: for singleness of
heart toward God. Love to God and therefore to his word, prayer, and work.
The Lord grant that this new year may be more devoted to Thee: in *heart*, in
work.
January 21, 1838. I shrink from the severe countenance of perfect devotion to
God despicably. Lord have pity on my miserable weakness; and yet while I so
pray I am scarce sincere, for I fear being *scourged into devotedness.* Lord, give
me a will for Thee. I wish earnestly that I more wished to be a flame of fire in
Thy service, passionless for earth, impassioned for Thee.[115]

He understood what Hook had meant when, writing to congratulate him
on his appointment as archdeacon, Hook had remarked that "the great
danger to men like you and me, actively employed, is, lest we should be
found thinking of self, instead of looking only to the glory of God." [116]
Wilberforce thanked God for what he called "cooling days": "If it is so
hard to make ahead against sin," he remonstrated to himself in his diary,
"what would it have been if I had been a successful lawyer." [117] On one
such "cooling day" he wrote Robert of his belief that God would never
grant him success without sending misfortune with it to balance him,
giving him reason to regret the ambition that pushed him forward.

How strange is life. The last few months to an outside observer would seem to
have been likely to slate me with many successes. In truth I never remember a
time when I had been oftener more deeply depressed; when anxieties and disap-
pointments and troubles and humiliations and burdens had pressed on me more
heavily. 'Lord THOU knowest my groaning.' [118]

He sought success yet feared its consequences, when God who gave
could so easily take away. His conviction led him to anticipate Emily's
death, although it did little to ease the almost unbearable pain he suffered
after she was dead.

Emily had much of her husband's brightness and gaiety. Like him, she
enjoyed observing and caricaturing the slightly absurd. Sir George
Prevost's mother, who had come to visit, "is something quite horrible,"
she wrote Mrs. Sargent.

114. December 22, 1829, BD, I. C191.   115. BD, I. C186.
116. Letter of December 5, 1839, in W. R. W. Stephens, *The Life and Letters of Walter
Farquhar Hook,* 2 vols. (London, 1879), II, 44.
117. BD, I. C186.   118. December 13, 1840, Wrangham papers.

She is huge and black with a long, long grey beard and she was dressed in a short blue common coloured gown *just* like the maids and would sit the whole evening behind the blind looking at the black night. In short she was so odd, so hideous, so huge, so like an ogress that I expected every moment to be devoured.[119]

She and Samuel kept as close to each other as husband and wife can. When he went on tour for the S.P.G. he missed her dreadfully. His diary records his constant loneliness. "At night exceedingly depressed. Rarely felt greater loneliness of spirit. Thought if ill how lonely etc. Prayer against it and strove." [120] Sickness and death close at hand bound them together. One by one Emily's family was struck down in the 1830's by heart disease. John Garton Sargent, Emily's brother and heir to the Lavington estate, died in 1829; their grandfather in 1831; their father in 1833; and Henry Martyn Sargent, the sole surviving son, in 1836. Caroline, a younger sister, who had married Henry Manning in 1833, died in 1837. Within eight years Mrs. Sargent had buried her husband, her two sons, a daughter, and her father-in-law, leaving her with three daughters: Emily; Mary, married in 1834 to Henry Wilberforce; and Sophia, who in the same year married the Reverend George Ryder. Wilberforce had lost his father, his sister Elizabeth, and his sister-in-law, Robert's wife Agnes, who died in childbirth in 1834. Samuel and Emily buried two children, one born prematurely in 1835, another, a day old, in 1837. Even in that age, this was a heavy toll. If in much of the family correspondence there is an apparent preoccupation with death, such preoccupation is understandable, more especially since Evangelicals believed that the supreme task of life was preparation for a life beyond the grave. After attending the funeral of Agnes Wilberforce, Samuel wrote to Emily that they must resolve

that if we are spared to each other we may help each other to glory, and if we part it may be with a comfortable hope of a blessed meeting. I cannot help recalling to mind a conversation we had on this very day three years ago—a Sunday evening when you opened your whole heart to me and when you set yourself to love God earnestly.

He saw in Agnes Wilberforce's death a lesson both of them must learn. God was warning them not to set too great a store by their own happiness in each other. "I well know that I have wanted such a chastening and that I need to learn its lessons quite as much or more than you do, and I press them on myself in pressing them on you." [121]

Although he tried to prepare himself to bear a loss that other family deaths and his own foreboding warned him might soon come, he found it no easier to do so once Emily was gone. She suffered her family's weak heart and had undoubtedly borne too many children. When pregnant in

119. July 30, 1829, Chichester, 25.   120. August 10, 1839, BD, I. C186.
121. November 19, 1834, BD, II. A.

October 1840 she caught the fever that proved fatal. Day after day Wilberforce recorded its deadly progress. Some days she was better, other days "still poorly and suffering greatly." On February 14 she gave birth to a son, and the doctor hoped she might now regain strength enough to live. But on March 5: "Dearest E. *very* ill . . . very low about herself. 'I have seen my face: shocked: it is the stamp of death. It is *the* look all the rest had.'" [122] She read the mirror right. Five days later at Winchester, where they had gone to keep Samuel's required residence, Emily died.

The love Samuel had felt for her since he was sixteen now poured out as grief in the letters he wrote his friends. He had received an incurable wound that lasted his lifetime. He wrote Louisa Noel the day Emily died:

Oh Louisa I cannot write: I cannot speak: I cannot even feel about it. It is all unreal to me. Some dreadful tale of a blighted life of which I am a mere spectator: it is not my Emily with her joyous spirit her sparkling unwearied unpalling love who has been taken from me and my poor boys and sweet girl. I do not believe it. I only know if I know anything that I do most earnestly desire to bow to the will of God; to receive His loving correction meekly . . . but I am so utterly crushed that I cannot tell what else I feel or what is real around me. I can hardly pray: I seem only in a muffling, horrible dream. . . She is gone, and Checkendon, and Lavington, and Brighstone and every place and every friend and every joy are so entirely fragrant with the remembrance of her dear love that I know not how to bear them.[123]

Places meant much to Wilberforce. He was the sort of person who noticed furniture, rooms, flowers, fields, and views, and associated them in his mind with the people who had enjoyed them with him. A return to Winchester, to Brighstone, to Lavington, of which he was now heir, was never again to be an altogether happy experience for him. He went back to Brighstone for the first time in 1846, following a visit to Osborne. "All was as fresh as if it were yesterday," he wrote Louisa Noel,

and I could hardly believe that I should not be called by that voice at every turn. I am very glad I have been, though my heart feels utterly crushed within me. Most happily for me the family were not there, so I walked about alone, and stayed a good while in her room; and went down to the sea where we all used to go. Really every crack in every cottage wall, every stone in the roadside bank, seemed to be clear and bright in my memory as if I had seen it yesterday.[124]

These associations remained with him always. Preaching at Brighstone in 1871, thirty years after Emily's death, he found his reaction "as abrupt as if my own great sorrow was not a week old: and as I looked down from the pulpit there for the first time since 1840 I caught myself looking to *her* corner in the Church." [125]

Wilberforce believed that God had brought about Emily's death as a

122. Diary, BD, I. C186.   123. March 10, 1841, BD, II. F.
124. July 13, 1846, BD, II. F.
125. To Ernest R. Wilberforce, March 30, 1871, BD, I. C205.

punishment to him for his sins. God meant to teach him a lesson and, believing this, he struggled to make himself understand it. As his conscience instructed him, he wrote out in his diary the things he was learning about himself. At first, he could do nothing but grieve.

March 10, 1841.—A day of unknown agony to me. Every feeling stunned. Paroxysms of convulsive anguish and no power of looking up through the darkness which had settled on my soul. . .
March 11.—In some degree, yet but little, able to look to God, as the smiter of my soul, for healing. . .

Then, a week later in a remarkable entry, he set down the conclusions he had been able to draw from the chastening he had suffered.

March 19, 1841, Winchester.—As I firmly believe that upon my use of this bitter anguish depends under God the very cast of my future life, I put down such thoughts, recollections, and resolutions as may hereafter be useful to me. . .
It is a call to a different mode of life. This is my settled conviction. I have had the best of this world's blessings, the fullest enjoyment of the most faithful and strong affections. Now what [else] *can* the sudden removal of all this mean than that I am to serve Him in a different way: in a more severe, separate, self-mortifying course? I am called as Abraham was to 'come out,' to care no more for the things of this world.
This view is greatly strengthened by what I know of my temptations, which may have caused this blow—self-indulgence, covetousness, vanity.
If this be so, I should make up my mind *for my life;* yet not as *vowing,* or making resolutions, which were presumptuous, but yet make up my mind not to shrink back from this burden of *desolate* service which God binds on me.

He believed God had not meant him to enjoy domestic happiness— "or why taken away?" He apparently determined not to marry again— "to think no more of weaving other webs"—but to lead instead a life of self-mortification. He would work hard, and pray constantly and in that way "still, settle, and strengthen" his heart. The next day, he again wrote at length, this time determined to battle the worldliness which he recognized was still very much a part of him.

I shall be greatly in danger, by degrees, of ambitious desires, now that I have lost the holding back of domestic affections. *She* always checked them in me. Therefore I must pray more for a simple mind, watch the risings of ambition, seek after the fit of lowliness and look to Christ as *the* object. . .
I must specially guard against self-contemplation and vanity. I am conscious of danger here, even in my very sorrow. God help me. Oh, if all this should pass away and leave me no nearer to God, *ie, more worldly!* [126]

Canon Ashwell, when writing of the effect Emily's death had upon Samuel, called it a turning point. Henceforth, he wrote, "it is scarcely too much to say that all the mere personal aims of ordinary ambition were burnt up by the fiery fierceness of that one great sorrow which fell upon him at the exact moment when he was passing into a sphere where such

126. BD, I. C186.

aims would naturally have their fullest influence." If he was later ambitious, it was for his Church, not for himself. By arguing for Wilberforce as he did, Ashwell admitted he was hoping to silence those who "regarded him as keenly alive to the accidental advantages of his position, and as being ambitious of social distinction and of professional advancement." [127] His is the charitable interpretation of an admirer too honest to evade an issue altogether, yet too faithful to a recently dead friend to face it squarely. In fact, Wilberforce remained very much in the world, ambitious for his family and for himself.

It would be wrong to dismiss Ashwell's contentions completely and say that Emily's death resulted in no lasting changes whatsoever. Wilberforce continued to believe that Emily had died because he was not good enough to deserve her. "If I did not *always* feel how my unworthiness of such a blessing had led to its being taken," he once wrote Louisa Noel, "I should really hardly suffer, compared with what I now sometimes do." [128] And on the twentieth anniversary of Emily's death: "Oh, if my sins had not forced the enduring chastisement of this day, my life had been too bright for earth." [129] Bearing that thought constantly with him, he could never again enjoy unalloyed the pleasure his achievements would otherwise have provided him. He soon recognized that he would not succeed in giving up the life he had been used to leading. "I am far too fond of this old world," he wrote Anderson, "even embittered as it has been to me." [130] But with each compliment, with every advancement, there came the sharp reminder that clever, talented, wise as others thought him, God had not thought him good enough for Emily. And when later he lost favor at Court, when he failed to succeed to the archbishopric his ambition had led him to expect, he was able to console himself with the thought that painful though his humiliation was, it was nothing to the pain he could still feel from the great loss which his own inadequacies had forced God to bring upon him. Emily's death, if it did not change his life, gave it a point of reference. It brought him self-knowledge and taught him resignation. From the almost feminine intensity of his grief, he was able to derive strength he had not possessed before. Without a belief in God's power to enter the lives of men, to "scourge them into devotedness"—without the conviction that Emily had died by God's command—he would have never felt the harsh blessings of the lesson he was certain God had meant to teach him. It is a mark of his father's lasting influence upon him and of the simplicity of his own faith that through so many years he clung so steadfastly to that Evangelical truth.

127. Ashwell and Wilberforce, *Life,* I, 178.   128. October 3, 1847, BD, II. F.
129. Diary, March 10, 1861, in Ashwell and Wilberforce, *Life,* I, 187.
130. March 10, 1845, BD, I. C191.

CHAPTER III

Churchman

The Evangelicalism that William Wilberforce worked to instill in his sons was less a theological system than a way to live one's life: a "practical" religion.[1] By the time Samuel Wilberforce had taken Orders, Evangelicalism had become an even more amorphous creed. Dependent upon individual devotedness and based upon the assurance that man could best discover God by himself, it began to lose whatever center it had once possessed when professed by increasingly large congregations. A flock of popular preachers and a host of worthy societies won innumerable converts, many of them with little notion of the painful process of personal commitment which had endowed the Evangelicalism of an earlier generation with its real substance. Without that commitment, the substance began to disappear. Evangelicalism within the Church of England became a sect determined to defend itself against equally strident attacks from equally determined adversaries.

Central to their scanty theology was the Evangelicals' conviction that only an invisible Church—a communion of saints with nothing but their saintliness to bind them to each other and to God—could serve to shelter their precious faith. For the Church visible and its earthly manifestations —the apostolic succession, the sacraments, and the prayer book—they began to have less and less respect.[2] Unable to appreciate or to make use of these sacred institutions as aids to their own faith, they fought shy of a corporate Church, instructed instead by their ministers to seek salvation with nothing more than a Bible and a willing heart. The union others discovered through the mystical sharing of the Eucharist, they achieved in zealous work on behalf of their thriving network of missionary and philanthropic societies. Evangelical leadership rested not with clergymen,

---

1. See Y. Brilioth, *The Anglican Revival* (London, 1933), "One can speak of an Evangelical party [ca. 1800–1820] but it had no sharp limits. Rather was it that all who strove for a warmer religious feeling, all who were really spiritually minded, to put it differently, came to be counted that way even if they had little sympathy with the theoretical principles which marked Evangelicalism in the narrower sense" (p. 36).

2. Evangelicals of an earlier generation, on the other hand, had by no means dismissed them as readily. Simeon, for example, called liturgy lawful, expedient, and acceptable to God, and declared that if he were to ground his sentiments on human authority "it would not be on the dogmas of Calvin or Arminius, but on the Articles and Homilies of *The Church of England*." See Robert S. Dell, "Simeon and the Bible," in A. Pollard and M. Hennell, *Charles Simeon* (London, 1959).

but with the lay presidents of such organizations as the Church Missionary Society and the African Institution. Emphasis was on doing, upon the
"practical," with the result that Evangelicals found themselves drawn
further than ever from any sort of useful theological discussion or debate.
So intent were they to organize crusades among the heathens that they
had neither time nor inclination to think steadily or creatively about the
challenges thrown up to them by the Noetics or by the young men who
were coming to be called Tractarians. Nor was this the sole disadvantage
of lay leadership. The prominence and success of Evangelical enterprise
led others to accuse its enterpreneurs of a worldliness that ill-accorded
with their professed abomination of the things of this world. Their claims
to sanctity often rested upon a self-advertised withdrawal from precisely
the kinds of feuding and controversy into which their multifold activities
were constantly entrapping them.

Other heirs of the Evangelical tradition were strong enough and sensitive enough to preserve only the good in the system that had been passed
to them, or to reshape it into a faith that could withstand the challenge not
just of conscience but of a demanding intellect as well. Such was Wilberforce's contemporary Sir James Stephen who, in the final chapter of his
Essays in Ecclesiastical Biography, set out his own reworking of the
Evangelicalism he had inherited from Clapham. For every Stephen,
however, there were now hundreds prepared to take their Evangelicalism
ready-made, as expounded from fashionable London pulpits, in the pages
of the monthly *Christian Observer,* or in the more vociferous columns
of the recently founded *Record.*

Wilberforce, by reason of his own religious inheritance, naturally felt
the effect of changes brought about by the proliferation of Evangelical
teaching and activity. By the time he had settled at Brighstone, he had
heard enough from members of the Oriel Common Room to allow him
if he wished to modify the system his father had bequeathed him. Newman, Hurrell Froude, and his own brother Robert were taking the first
of those steps which were to lead them in logical progression to Rome.
Samuel refused to follow them. He quickly identified himself at Brighstone with the Evangelicals' Church Missionary Society. "My favorite
society," he wrote Anderson, adding rather surprisingly: "so thoroughly Church of England, so eminently active and spiritual." [3] The
Church Missionary Society was, in the opinion of many, far from thoroughly Church of England. One of the first manifestations of Newman's
dissatisfaction with the Evangelicals was his attack on the C.M.S. in
1829, recommending in a pamphlet that clergy join in numbers sufficient
to give it a Church character he felt it lacked. Wilberforce, who continued
to support the Society throughout the 1830's, soon altered his own opin-

3. September 12, 1833, BD, I. C191.

ions as to its nature. In 1837, wholly satisfied with neither the men nor the doctrines the C.M.S. exported, he urged its directors "to send out *The Church,* and not merely *instructions about religion.*" [4]

These sentiments led many Evangelicals to suspect Samuel of decamping to join his brother Robert among the Tractarians. Their suspicions received further confirmation with the appearance of their father's biography in 1838. William Wilberforce had by that time been accorded sainthood by a generation of Evangelicals who had barely known him. Their determination to penetrate the privacy of his beliefs so that they might venerate him led to their discovery that while Wilberforce was an undoubted Evangelical, his infinite good nature had endowed his religion with a generosity that scarcely accorded with their own narrow creed. Doctrine meant almost nothing to him—always excepting the two all-important foundation stones of free grace and justification by faith. If an inspiring preacher happened to be a Nonconformist, he nevertheless went to hear him. If a suitably qualified tutor happened to be a Roman Catholic, he persevered in hiring him to teach his grandson.[5] William Wilberforce maintained that the sole requirement for a holy life and a happy death was a conscience constantly attuned to God's will. All else mattered little. Although Robert had found this a hopelessly inadequate basis for belief, and although Samuel too had moved beyond it, both sons, by quoting extensively from their father's letters and diaries, allowed him to speak for himself in the biography. Evangelicals, therefore, who read the book expecting to discover a Wilberforce in their own image sensed a sort of fraud. Distressed to find a man they could not recognize, they seized upon the several remarks that did reflect Tractarian inclinations to suggest that the entire work was a distortion wrought by two traitors to their father's faith.[6]

Such attacks made it difficult for Samuel to remain on good terms with the Evangelicals who were now beginning to demand allegiance as if to a party standard. Although he continued to accept much that Evangelicals professed to believe, although he could eulogize the purity of his father's and his father-in-law's Evangelical rule of life,[7] he could not identify

4. August 31, 1838, BD, I. C191.
5. William Wilberforce to Samuel Wilberforce, July 12, 1832, *Private Papers,* p. 281.
6. The *Christian Observer,* for example, severely criticized the Wilberforces for their defense of the doctrine of baptismal regeneration. Noting the remark that William's religious upbringing had "fostered that baptismal seed which though dormant was destined to produce at last a golden harvest," they commented: "The question involved in the hypothesis is, whether, if Mr. Wilberforce had lived and also died a profligate, and had been lost forever, there would be any scriptural warrant for saying that because he was baptized, and sacramentally dedicated to God, he had really been once in possession of a renewed, a transformed, a 'heavenly' nature, though so it was that it perished without ever giving any visible token of its existence" (*Christian Observer,* no. 1, n.s., September 1838. p. 570).
7. See the introduction to his edition of *The Journals and Letters of Henry Martyn* (London, 1837), p. 3: "He walked in the low valley where the pastures of God's presence

himself with the sect. He referred to its spokesmen, in a letter to his
mother in 1835, as "self-contented religionists of small attainments." [8]
Interested as he was in human beings as individuals, he felt constrained
by the Evangelicals' determination to judge by no standard other than
party label. Along with many, he was offended by the unpleasant odor of
self-satisfaction which seemed to linger in the air whenever an Evangelical delivered himself of an opinion. To one such, Baptist Noel, who
had written to announce that he had recently found Wilberforce not nearly
so offensively Tractarian as he had originally supposed him to be, Wilberforce returned a sharp reply. He had, he confessed, been pained to
learn that Noel had judged him "needlessly and uncharitably." And now,
to write "almost to congratulate me on having been replaced in your good
opinion," suggests nothing more than "a most fearful want of humility."
And he continued:

Let me tell you also, in all kindness, that in the affectionate exhortations which
end your letter, and which the pen of an aged Bishop might have written for a
young Deacon [Noel was seven years older than Wilberforce], I trace, even
amidst all their affection, the self same spirit. Such a spirit is ever the snare of
men who, like you, are possessed of shining talents, are fond of action, are thrown
into busy life and take a prominent part in their own province of society. It leads
them to love singularity, to trample on rules, to have little respect for those
above them, to assume a tone of superior age, wisdom, and spirituality in their
intercourse with others; it injures above all things the holiness and true peace of
their own spirits. From such evils, my dear brother, may God in his great mercy
keep us forever free.[9]

Wilberforce had no desire to disaffiliate himself completely from the
Evangelicals. He continued to preach during the 1840's on behalf of the
Church Missionary Society, hoping to encourage its members, as he had
hoped previously, to adopt principles more consonant with their claim
to be a Church society. His distaste for religious warfare and his unwillingness to subscribe to many of the Evangelicals' principles of battle
compelled him to keep his distance. He best expressed his attitude toward
them in an article he contributed years later to the *Quarterly Review*.
"Of that party, in its merits and its defects," he wrote,

the life of Bishop Daniel Wilson, of Calcutta, is in many respects a sufficient
exposition. Warm-hearted, zealous, earnestly pious, but withal shallow and
eminently technical in his views of religion, with an amount of self-importance
which often invested even the most sacred subjects with a hue so simply personal,
that it made him at once unawares exquisitely comic and most unintentionally

are often greenest, where the dews of his spirit fall in richest and most proliferating abun-
dance, and where, if anywhere upon earth, the notes of purer beings might still be heard to
float upon the air, and blend with the praises of the children of men."
  8. April 28, 1835, Wrangham papers.
  9. September 25, 1843, Letter Book, BD, d.208.

irreverent; possessed so strongly by party spirit, that even his kind heart could not always save him from harshness and injustice, he manifested, we think, in his administration of the great diocese of Calcutta what his scheme of theological life could, and even more signally what it could not accomplish.[10]

Not only did Wilberforce exasperate the Evangelicals by refusing to enlist with them; he provoked the Tractarians who might as naturally have expected him to join their ranks. For a short time in the early 1830's a clash between the two camps seemed unlikely. Many of the leading Tractarians had been raised in Evangelical households, and all cherished the habits of private prayer and self-communion; Keble had, after all, impressed William Wilberforce with his piety and with *The Christian Year*. Moreover, Evangelicals were pleased with the anti-Erastian temper of the *Tracts for the Times*. It soon became apparent, however, that the Tractarians were not interested simply in enshrining an inheritance or in protecting it from the encroachments of the State. While it is true that the Oxford Movement occurred as a natural progression from the Evangelical revival and not simply as a reaction to it, it is equally true that the Tractarians did far more than enrich a tradition that had been passed to them. With a respect for the mind as well as a concern for the soul, they looked into the past with fresh interest and understanding. They rediscovered and then devotedly resurrected the High Church doctrine of apostolic succession and, with increased respect, received the sacramental evidences of Christ's presence in the Church. Renewed reverence for ecclesiastical institutions fused in the minds of the young Tractarians with the already strong traditions of Evangelical piety and Noetic scholarship to produce an unshakeable belief in the power of a visible Church to remake the lives of men. Some eventually found it impossible to resist what seemed to them the logical consequences of this belief. By 1840, when Newman published *Tract XC,* he was only the most prominent of those who felt an increasing strain in trying to reconcile faith in a Church Indivisible with continued membership in the apparently schismatic Anglican communion. No one foresaw that strain nor the alarm that would ensue once Newman and his friends gave it expression when the Tracts first made their appearance. Instead, the Tracts impressed most as the worthy production of a zealous yet eminently respectable and learned society endowed with a will to labor for the good of the Church of England.

Wilberforce agreed with much of the Tractarians' early thinking and was in sympathy with their enthusiasm. In 1833, upon the occasion of Bishop Sumner's visitation, he preached a strong sermon in support of the doctrine of apostolic succession. Two years later, he answered his mother's accusations that he had forsaken his Evangelical heritage by

10. "The Church of England and Her Bishops," *Quarterly Review,* 114:545 (1863).

declaring that although there were many points at which he differed with the Tractarians, "I do agree as far as I can with all these great lights whom God has from time to time given to his Church; with Hooker and Bramhall and Taylor, with Beveridge and Stillingfleet, and with the primitive Church of the first three centuries." [11] He reviewed for the High Church *British Magazine* and, for a time, for Newman's *British Critic.* For the latter he wrote a review in 1837 of *Lyra Apostolica,* so generally favorable to its authors and so hostile not only to Evangelical poetry but to Evangelicalism itself as to suggest that Wilberforce was ready to cast his lot permanently with the Tractarians. To expect true poetry from what he called the Puritan school "would be not a whit less absurd than to look for the graceful folds of Grecian elegance in the drab straight-cut of a Leadenhall Street 'friend.'" The Evangelical William Cowper's poetry, he wrote, compels readers "to substitute a set of internal feelings, unconnected with practice, for actual holiness; and then it encourages frames and feelings which are directly morbid and unhealthy." The *Lyra,* on the other hand, are free from morbid subjectivism. Drawing their inspiration from "those purer and holier fountains wherewith the Church Catholic abounds," they contain "nothing of that sickly sentiment which so often infests devotional poetry." Although some of the verses struck him as constrained and inharmonious, and though he found others obscure, Wilberforce gave them the highest marks for their objective truths, their exaltation of the sacraments, and their elevation of those "ennobling associations which are the heritage of the true Catholic Church." [12]

He singled out "the exquisite lines" of Newman's "Lead Kindly Light" for special praise, and not surprisingly, for he was most impressed at this time by Newman's talents and achievements. A conversation with him in 1836 "was really most sublime as an exhibition of human intellect," Newman pouring forth "a sort of magisterial announcement in which Scripture, Christian antiquity deeply studied and thoroughly imbibed, humility, veneration, love of truth, and the highest glow of poetical feelings, all impressed their own pictures upon his conversation." [13] Although Wilberforce sat very seldom in this fashion at their feet, he saw a good deal of all his former Oriel acquaintances whenever he went

11. April 28, 1835, Wrangham papers.
12. *British Critic,* 21:170 (1837). Strangely enough, Newman was apparently offended by the few strictures Wilberforce did level against his poetry. Wilberforce had included him among a list of occasionally "inharmonious" writers, but his praise of "Lead Kindly Light" was generous in the extreme. Isaac Williams, however, maintains that Newman was much annoyed, and suggests that this explains his long refusal to write further poetry (*Autobiography,* p. 68).
13. To Louisa Noel, April 1, 1836, Ashwell and Wilberforce, *Life,* I, 95.

to Oxford, and his occasional letters to them convey an impression of allegiance to their cause.[14]

In fact, he drew back from any sort of full commitment. In his letter of 1835 to his mother he had boasted that he belonged to no school, and his attitude toward the Tractarians in times of crisis showed him no more securely bound to them than to the Evangelicals. He sided fervently with Oxford against the government's appointment of the Latitudinarian R. D. Hampden as Regius Professor of Divinity in 1836, canvassing the Isle of Wight to arouse opposition and traveling to Oxford to vote against him. That vote, he wrote Anderson, pitted "loose Churchmen against sound Churchmen"; [15] though Tractarians opposed Hampden, so did many Evangelicals. The next year, however, following an attack by Wilberforce on the Tractarians' doctrine of sin after baptism,[16] Newman refused to accept further reviews from him for the *Critic*. Wilberforce was hurt and disposed to see Newman's move as nothing more than a pettish display of party spirit. "He knows well that I am a strong and dutiful Church man," he wrote Anderson, "and to refuse cooperation from such because the *colour* of their opinions is not exactly the same as his, is to prefer *party* to truth; and to seek rather to attach himself to a body-guard of men than to disseminate through the existing Church a higher measure of Church sentiments." [17] He was in no mood to stand with the Tractarians in opposition to the Martyr's Memorial, erected as much as anything as a monument to "the errors of the Church of Rome" and in reaction to the over-fervent outpourings of Hurrell Froude's Romish *Remains* which had been published in 1838. Wilberforce, who had found the publication of the *Remains* distasteful, and who was certain that their appearance would simply incite party feelings on both sides, hoped that the Tractarians would contribute to the Memorial "as an opportunity of shewing in some measure a different state of feeling from that which Froude's *Remains* exhibit—but in vain." [18]

His next opportunity to publicly declare himself found Wilberforce again opposing the Tractarians, and again with the hope of restoring religious harmony. In 1841 Isaac Williams announced his candidacy for the Oxford Poetry Professorship, from which Keble was retiring at the close of his second term. Pusey circulated a letter requesting support for

14. Writing to ask if Newman could recommend anyone to fill the headmastership of the Islington Proprietary Grammar School, Wilberforce inquired: "Can you suggest anyone who will creep into the midst of the bee's hive and poison the Islingtonians [*i.e.* Evangelicals]? He must of course be a man who will not *shock* the Peculiars—and to be useful, equally, of course, must be a Churchman. . . Will there be a fresh supply of Tracts on July 1? I wish to know that I may order." (June 25, 1836, Newman papers, Birmingham Oratory, Miscellaneous No. 99).

15. May 31, 1836, BD, I. C191.   16. See below, page 87.

17. August 31, 1838, BD, I. C191.

18. To W. F. Hook, December 26, 1836, BD, I. C194.

Williams on the basis of his religious views, and the Evangelicals, who had not unnaturally taken particular offense at Williams' tract on "Reserve in Communicating Religious Knowledge," soon persuaded one of their number, Edward Garbett of Brasenose, to stand. Wilberforce, although pressed by Robert and by his good friend Sir George Prevost to vote for Williams, found he could not. "I have promised to vote for Garbett," he wrote Robert.

It seems to me that, at present, the Tract men are threatening us with two great dangers: (1) Romanizing our best men of one tone; (2) driving into utter Low Church our best men of the other. I think it necessary to give them the strongest check we can, and especially needful, if we *do* hold really Church views, strongly to testify against their modification of them, in order to prove to young men that they have another choice between *them* and the Low Church.[19]

Robert replied that though he granted Williams had his faults, and though in fact he wished both candidates would withdraw, he considered Garbett "a piece of worsted velvet-plush—so pulpy and unctuous that Poetry is a manufacture out of the question with him." [20] But, as Robert and Samuel both realized, professional ability was no longer an issue. Gladstone tried at one point to bring forward a compromise candidate, but Wilberforce rejected this plan as well; he refused to consider Garbett as nothing more than the captive candidate of the Evangelicals.[21] He reported to Gladstone that he had consulted with Bishop Sumner and that Sumner was "so very strong" against his taking a part in raising a third candidate "that in the relation I stand to him, and being in some uncertainty myself, I feel hardly at liberty in a matter not of direct duty to go counter to [his advice]." [22] Though never unwilling to listen to Sumner's counsel, Wilberforce was in no sense knuckling under to his bishop. He had already decided that he would work to make Garbett appear more than the tool of the Low Church interests, hoping in that way to draw together enough of a "Church party" to counteract the extreme Tractarians. "It does seem to me," he explained to Robert, when writing of his sorrow at their disagreement, "that our only hope of maintaining Church principles is by showing strongly our power of separating them from the extravagancies and party feelings of that school." [23] Williams eventually withdrew after a comparison of votes indicated that he had little hope of winning the election, and Garbett took the chair by default.

Meanwhile, Wilberforce had found himself forced to disagree with Robert on yet another issue. The King of Prussia had expressed his desire to cooperate with the Church of England in establishing a bishopric

19. December 16, 1841, Wrangham papers.
20. *Ibid.*, January 2, 1842.   21. December 19, 1841, Add Mss. 44343.
22. *Ibid.*, December 20, 1841.   23. January 2, 1842, Wrangham papers.

at Jerusalem. Through his emissary, the Chevalier Bunsen, he had proposed the plan to the English Establishment, where in most quarters it
met with a cautious though not unfavorable reception. Bunsen befriended
Wilberforce, who took up the scheme enthusiastically, delighted to find
himself *confidant* to the *confidant* of yet another Royal Personage. "I
have of late got *very* intimate with Bunsen," he wrote Louisa Noel.

Once I went with him to Lambeth. He showed me numbers of the King's private
letters and detailed to me his conversations. The King's intention is most pure.
He quite wishes to gain over his people to true Episcopacy; he longs to give up
the keys to the Church, but says, 'No thank you,' to the Lutherans, who wish to
take them from him, 'because,' he says, 'God gave them me no doubt to keep till
I could give them up to His Bishops, and then I will.' The King seems to me to
have acted in the best way.[24]

To the Tractarians, it seemed that whatever the motives of the King
of Prussia, the Church of England was acting in the worst way possible.
They listened with horror as leading Evangelicals pronounced the plan
the first step toward a union with Protestantism. "The Church," Newman
complained when he wrote the *Apologia,* "was not only forbidding any
sympathy or concurrence with the Church of Rome, but it actually was
courting an intercommunion with Protestant Prussia and the heresy of
the Orientals." [25] Robert Wilberforce shared this indignation, though
Samuel tried to temper his brother's opposition and, more important,
to convince him that his fear for the Church was groundless. "I confess,"
he wrote rather testily, "I feel furious at the craving of men for union
with idolatrous, material, sensual, domineering Rome, and their squea-
mish anathematizing hatred of Protestant Reformed men." [26]

This disgust with what he considered an alarmingly extreme position
led Wilberforce to continue to throw his weight in the balance against
the Tractarians. In the fall of 1844 he traveled to Oxford to vote in convocation for the Evangelical, Dr. Benjamin Symons, for vice-chancellor.
Symons, in company with five other doctors of divinity, had the previous
year suspended Pusey from preaching within the University for deliver-
ing what they judged to be a heretical sermon on the Holy Eucharist.
Again, Samuel and Robert were in opposite camps. At first, apparently,
both agreed to abstain from voting for the vice-chancellor. Samuel subsequently changed his mind, rather to Robert's surprise and discompo-
sure, and cast for Symons. The election was little more than a preliminary
skirmish in the battle fought the following winter over the teachings and
writings of W. G. Ward, the most forward, and, to those who disagreed
with him, the most personally obnoxious of the Tractarians. Ward's

24. October 20, 1841, BD, II. F.
25. J. H. Newman, *Apologia Pro Vita Sua* (London, 1890), p. 143.
26. February 2, 1842, Wrangham papers.

Ideal of a Christian Church Considered, published in 1844, had shocked
a great many by its frankly sympathetic discussions of Roman Catholic
doctrines and practices. The Hebdomadal Board was pressured to
censure not only Ward's book, but Ward himself, by declaring that *The
Ideal* contradicted the Articles of Faith to which he had subscribed when
admitted to his B.A. and M.A. degrees. The Board agreed to put these
propositions to a vote of Convocation, at the same time proposing a more
stringent subscription to the Articles than that in force, with the hope of
preventing doctrinally tainted candidates from taking their degrees in
the future. This third proposal met with widespread condemnation; its
terms were vague in the extreme, demanding conformity to some sort of
University-dictated affirmation that remained unspecified. Wilberforce
opposed this particular proposition as formulated by the Board, but he
was by no means adverse to the idea of some sort of test. He argued
with Robert that rather than a new and unnecessary barrier, affirmation
within more strictly defined limits would simply represent "a protest
against a new mode of evading the *old* test." [27]

Many moderate High Churchmen considered the proceedings against
Ward vindictive, but Wilberforce remained convinced that both the book
and the man must be condemned. Gladstone had written him to protest
that if Ward was to be censured for supposedly heretical leanings toward
Rome, others—among them Whately—should then likewise be condemned for tending too far in other directions.[28] Wilberforce could not
agree. No other man, he wrote, stood in Ward's position.

He avows a 'non-natural sense' as that in which he signs our Articles; declares
his affection distinctly to the dogmatic teaching and practice of Rome in all
points where Rome and England differ; and then challenges the University and
the Church to punish him for so doing and holding. I think that, if his punishment
be not certain and condign, it is better to give up all subscription to Articles.[29]

Wilberforce ultimately became convinced that the Board's third proposition—the controversial affirmation—was unworkable and therefore
unwise, and drew up the address to the vice-chancellor that resulted in
its withdrawal.[30] He voted in favor of the degradation of both Ward's
book and Ward himself, however, thus separating himself not only from
Robert and Henry, but from his more moderate friends, Gladstone and
Hook.

At a time, then, when it was becoming increasingly difficult to avoid
commitment to either the Evangelical or the Tractarian party, Wilber-

27. December 31, 1844, Wrangham papers.   28. December 29, 1844, BD, II. K.
29. January 14, 1845, Ashwell and Wilberforce, *Life,* I, 256.
      30. *Ibid.,* to W. E. Gladstone, January 7, 1845. Wilberforce also unintentionally en-
couraged F. D. Maurice to write his pamphlet, *Two Letters to a Non-Resident Member of
Convocation,* in which he protested the University's arbitrariness in its proceedings against
Ward (*Maurice,* I, 395ff).

force had tried his best to escape a label of any sort. That he had by no means succeeded, he himself suggested in a plaintive aside to Robert in 1842. With regard to the Tractarians, he says, "dearest H[enry] says that for three years I have indulged in the most unChristian bitterness against them." On the other hand, "The *Record* says I countenance them." [31] Some had a ready explanation for Wilberforce's unwillingness to stand with a side. "This see-saw state must be a most difficult and agitating one to keep up," J. B. Mozley wrote to his sister after Isaac Williams' defeat. "He will require a bishopric for the benefit of his health before long, if for no other reason." [32] Oxford acquaintances were at first puzzled and then angered by Wilberforce's apparent readiness to call himself their ally when with them, while at the same time preaching and talking against their doctrines elsewhere. Following a series of University sermons in which Wilberforce attacked Pusey's views on sin after baptism, Mozley reported again to his sister: "This is uncommonly silly in S. W.; he professes himself of our party and talks of *us,* and *we* and so on, and yet splits from us in public." [33] Isaac Williams had much the same reaction to Wilberforce's behavior at the time of the contested election. "The most trying case to me," Williams later wrote in his autobiography,

was that of Bishop Wilberforce (not then the Bishop of Oxford). He had always been in familiar intercourse with me—asking me for my new books, getting me to introduce Newman to him in every way. On receiving the college circular he wrote to our President, expressing his great interest in the election, as I was his old and intimate friend; but some one observed at the time, 'Don't you notice how cautiously throughout he abstains from giving his promise?' And in the end, though an old friend, he took part against me, and voted for my opponent.[34]

The Tractarians grew to believe that the caution Wilberforce displayed was dictated by his hopes for advancement and by his knowledge that both the Queen and her prime minister disparaged the Oxford reformers. They found no other way to reconcile his acceptance of their friendship with his repeated willingness to desert them when they needed his vote or his voice. Yet Wilberforce had cultivated them not so much as friends —his friends, Anderson, Boyle, Louisa Noel, were a far different sort— but rather as interesting and important personages whom it would pay to know and to talk to. The Tractarians were themselves much talked about. To be able to meet with them, to report their conversations, was to be in the midst of the most advanced, the most discussed ecclesiastical world of the moment. Newman, Williams, the Mozleys, fascinated Wilberforce as people; he wanted their company, and to obtain it for a time he courted them. In turn, to court them he was ready on occasion to speak

31. February 2, 1842, Wrangham papers.
32. May 22, 1842, J. B. Mozley, *Letters,* p. 131.
33. *Ibid.,* March 4, 1838, p. 74.   34. *Autobiography,* p. 142.

in their particular party accent, as he did in his review of *Lyra Apostolica*. Yet he had beliefs of his own, which varied at many points from those of the Tractarians. When his conscience—and it should be added as well, his desire for advancement—began to compel him to articulate those beliefs as publicly as possible, his relations with the Oxford luminaries deteriorated, much to his surprise. Because Wilberforce took such delight in the company of every sort of human being, he seldom felt the need to sacrifice an interesting acquaintance for conviction's sake. He saw no reason why he could not continue to meet on friendly terms with Tractarians in University common rooms while at the same time challenging their doctrines from the University pulpit. When he preached against Pusey's theory of sin, he insisted that his sermons should in no way be construed as an attack upon his friend, only upon his misguided doctrinal notions.[35] But the Tractarians, unlike Wilberforce and like all reformers, could not for long tolerate the company of a man who did not share their convictions. Once Wilberforce had shown himself less than committed to their way of thinking, they pronounced judgment against him as a hypocrite, and explained his apparent cautiousness as a symptom of his desire for place.

One or two fragments of evidence might suggest that these insinuations had some basis in fact. Without question Wilberforce did his best to give no offense to his bishop, though to say that he tailored his convictions to match Sumner's would be doing him a grave injustice. Once after he had sent Sumner a sermon for his comments he recorded his perplexed feeling about their relationship:

I am in a false position with him. I do not hold what he truly dislikes in Pusey and Newman, etc., and I hardly know how to disavow this without seeming to disavow what I do hold, being more High Church in *feeling* than he is. Lord keep me humble and free from the fear of man *which bringeth a snare*.[36]

Sumner reassured Wilberforce, after he had made him an archdeacon and moved him to Alverstoke, that he "never thought of preferring Evangelical men as such." Instead, he insisted, he tried simply to pick the fittest man for the post. "This of course implies being satisfied of his soundness: but I never that I know of thought whether a man belonged to the Evangelical school or not." [37] Though the claim rings with a disingenuous note, the implication for Wilberforce was that he need not bridle his own beliefs to please his master. The following year Sumner did warn Peel against appointing Wilberforce to Chichester, but there is no evidence that Wilberforce knew of Sumner's advice, or that, if he did, he in any way tried as a result to bolster his reputation as an anti-Trac-

---

35. ? to J. B. Mozley, April 7, 1838, J. B. Mozley, *Letters*, p. 74.
36. Diary, November 24, 1837, BD, I. C186.   37. *Ibid.*, November 19, 1841.

tarian. His position throughout the crises of the early 1840's—both before and after the vacancy at Chichester—was a notably consistent one, the only discrepancy occurring in his willingness to remain friends with many of the people whose opinions he renounced.

Only in one letter during the period is there a suggestion that he was afraid to speak what he believed for fear of the damage it might do his reputation. To a Mrs. Agnew, who wrote him in 1844 requesting his help in establishing a sisterhood, he replied that in view of the current mistrust of any plan bearing even the slightest taint of Rome, he would advise extreme caution. "And on this account I must say that I do not think we are yet at all ready to announce the plan to friends: certainly not with my name at present in connexion with it." [38] He justified his reticence on the reasonable ground that, in such cases, the wisest plan was to "begin with small and unobserved steps; to let all we do *grow* as much as possible out of what we have in the Church round us." But, he cautioned, "we must not disguise from ourselves the difficulty of establishing clearly this difference between ourselves and 'solitaires' or 'Nuns' and we must, therefore, walk with the utmost circumspection." Wilberforce offered to take the matter up with Sumner, but insisted that his application to the bishop be kept private, "that he may feel himself at full liberty to express his unbiased judgment on the whole proposal, both as to its own merits and as to this being the proper time, way, and place of attempting it." No doubt had it become public knowledge that Wilberforce was in league with the foundress of some sort of ecclesiastical sodality, the Evangelical papers which already considered him a Tractarian sympathizer would have embarrassed him with a distorted report of the facts. Yet his arguments for a policy of *festina lente* were perfectly sound, and his offer to take the matter up with Sumner suggests a willingness to do what he could to make a success of the enterprise.

The evidence that Wilberforce kept himself free from party in order to win himself a bishopric is flimsy. It is worth examining because of the reputation he acquired among those highflying Tractarians whom he had been led to cultivate by his insatiable appetite for acquaintances. These men of mind and character far different from his own had ascribed his apparent hypocrisy to the motive they felt most nearly suited the Wilberforce they knew, and had troubled to look no further for an explanation of his behavior toward them.

Had they pursued the question, they might have recognized that this very difference in their temperaments helped hold Wilberforce at a distance from them. The subtleties of Newman's personality and the paradoxes of his thinking fascinated Wilberforce. Humility struggling against

38. February 5, 1844, Letter Book, BD, d.208.

self-centeredness, emotional subjectivity reaching for an external authority: the tensions struck exciting sparks; their brilliance kept Wilberforce away. He had neither the strength of mind nor the willingness to blind himself that he would have needed to stand for more than a short time in the circle that surrounded Newman. Pusey, not nearly as complicated or as exciting a person, attracted Wilberforce far less. He was both scholarly and ascetic, two things Wilberforce was most certainly not. The ruthlessness with which he disciplined himself—his debates, for example, as to the propriety of a smile—struck little response in Wilberforce's congenial heart. This almost morbid sensitivity disturbed him when it appeared spread through the pages of Hurrell Froude's *Remains*. He thought the decision to publish the *Remains* irresponsible and, indeed, "quite shocking," and termed Froude's religion "Henry Martyn unchristianized": as emotional and overly-personal as Evangelicalism, without its saving sense of God's simple and direct message to man.[39]

Of the leading Tractarians, only Keble possessed a mind and temper which Wilberforce could understand and admire. The sense of pastoral responsibility that had led him to remove himself from Oxford to the quiet parishes of Fairford and Hursley, his preference for traditional rather than theoretical authority, which had kept his thinking, as well, one remove from the center of the movement, the generally old-fashioned and gentle tenor of his existence—all of this appealed to Wilberforce. A good part of the appeal was the sort felt by any active man when he encounters a life lived to a beat far different from his own. He is at first charmed by the uninterrupted pace and the chance for contemplation. Soon enough, however, he recognizes that he could never endure what to his active nature would amount to semi-idleness; and then his admiration assumes a touch of envy, and—in self-defense—of condescension. So Wilberforce described an encounter with Keble at the seaside in 1837: "He has the simplest and most childlike mind conceivable. Playing with his nephew and a son of Davison's on the shore as if he had never had a higher thought in his head than how he should make two boys happiest." [40] Attractive though such a life might be, Wilberforce knew it could not be his, so far was it from the world to which he felt himself bound.

There was an exclusiveness, a "specialness," about the Tractarian movement that derived from the very inward-looking character of its foremost adherents. Their distress at the public and, as they felt, vulgar nature of much Evangelical soul-searching, led them to reserve their

39. Diary, March 28, 1838, BD, I. C186.
40. To Charles Anderson, August 9, 1836, BD, I. C191. John Davison was an Oriel contemporary of Keble's.

most precious thoughts to themselves and to a tight communion of their closest friends. Since these friends had known each other well from the days when they had first met at Oriel, the movement began to bear the appearance of a religious club. Despite their pronouncements to the world, its members were concerned primarily with themselves and with each other. They were astonished at public reaction to Froude's *Remains* and Newman's *Tract XC,* which, though when read within the group might have seemed far from sensational, to outsiders came as a great shock.

Robert and Henry Wilberforce, by virtue of their continued attachment to Oriel and to its Tractarian coterie, belonged from the beginning to this club in a way that Samuel did not. Robert's Fellowship had kept him within the small world of an Oxford common room, than which there are very few smaller. He took pleasure in the sort of colloquies and campaigns such society fosters. He joined with Froude, Newman, and Blanco White in a letter-writing association for the purpose of airing a variety of theological and philosophical problems; in 1828, upon the removal of Provost Copleston to the bishopric of Llandaff, Robert allowed Newman and Pusey to persuade him to vote for Hawkins rather than for his friend and former tutor Keble. Newman was convinced, with reason, that Hawkins was the better administrator; yet within a year, he, Wilberforce, and Froude, all college tutors, were battling their new provost to sanction a major revolution in the tutorial system. Hawkins, who saw the plan as a threat to his own authority within the College, refused them everything they asked, and when they persisted, neglected to assign them any further pupils. Robert's departure to East Farleigh, dictated by the circumstances of his father's financial plight, was thus hastened by the loss of his Oriel tutorship. The battle with Hawkins doubtless drew him closer to Newman, and so strengthened his ties with Oxford. He continued to enjoy the society of the College. The fellowship whose members Samuel found "pettish, priggish, and ungentlemanly" [41] rather pleased his older brother. Robert, in turn, shared none of Samuel's pleasure in general society; Marianne Thornton found him dull, and presumed it was because he had inherited a large share of his mother's Birmingham blood.[42] Though the two brothers differed and grew to have less and less in common, they remained devoted to each other—Samuel forever anxious to win his older brother's approbation and upset when forced into disagreement with him; Robert steering a course further from the public eye, though pleased at the success that meant so much to Samuel. "I can never think of you," he wrote once,

41. To Robert I. Wilberforce, November 10, 1835, Wrangham papers.
42. E. M. Forster, *Marianne Thornton* (London, 1956), p. 147.

oppressed as you are with public cares, but as a different being from what you were, when I used to visit you in the days of your early happiness at Checkendon and Brighstone . . . and amidst all the trials and difficulties of life, it is a great comfort that we have been able to keep up such unity of feeling, and even of opinion (and the first more than the last even) so that we can tell what effect the same event or statement will produce on one another.[43]

Robert and Samuel were not as close to their younger brother Henry as they were to each other. Henry had inherited his father's airy charm, but not, apparently, the discipline that by some paradoxical magic had complemented it. "There was a thorough natural force and brilliancy in his wit," J. B. Mozley wrote years later, "which I never heard equalled; but I suppose he lacked the power of work—a defect which comes out in subsequent life. Copleston, however, when Provost of Oriel, put him above both his brothers." [44] Henry chose to stay on at Oriel following his graduation with the hope of gaining a Fellowship. Robert, fussing over his progress, reported to Samuel that Henry was wasting his time. "It is a very trying thing when you are anxious about an object of this kind, and see it lost by the dawdling of another person." Henry could not work with either the sober industry of Robert or the perpetual zeal of Samuel; he began with reluctance, only to finish in a burst of eleventh-hour exuberance—laboring, in one instance, twenty-seven and a half hours out of a total of thirty-three and a half, in order to hand a paper to Newman on time.[45] If the exertion was for Newman's sake, the chances were it would be performed not only with alacrity but with devotion as well. "I cannot bear seeming in any way to influence others," Newman once wrote Robert; [46] he unquestionably worked a spell upon Henry, who, even after his marriage to Mary Sargent, Emily's sister, and removal to the perpetual curacy of Bransgore in the diocese of Winchester, continued a close and diligent disciple.

Samuel was fond of Henry, and, as a handsome favor, saw him settled by royal request at East Farleigh. Yet both he and Robert tended to continue treating him as a charming, slightly incorrigible boy. "I wish you would write to Henry and try if you could *quiet* him," Samuel wrote Robert at the time of the Ward controversy. "He has just seen a furious attack (I believe) against Wynter in the 'Christian Remembrancer,' and this is sure to stir him up to some great extravaganza." [47] The two brothers—Samuel and Henry—were not unlike each other. Both possessed their father's charm, both had had enough of the world in them to think seriously of the law as a career. In Henry there was an immaturity—

43. March 1842(?), Wrangham papers.
44. J. B. Mozley to Mrs. Wilkinson, August 30, 1873, J. B. Mozley, *Letters,* p. 334.
45. April 28, 1831, Wrangham papers; May 3, 1832, Sandwith papers.
46. July 29, 1828, Irene Wilberforce papers.
47. December 31, 1844, Wrangham papers.

fostered in part by his perpetually youthful appearance and reflected, perhaps, in his willingness to live at Newman's side—that worried Samuel and kept him from confiding in his younger brother as he did in Robert.

The differences that make it possible to distinguish between the characters of the three brothers make it easier to understand why two were attracted to the Oxford Movement while the third was not. During the 1830's, Samuel seemed to bear a far closer resemblance in both temper and ambition to his brother-in-law Henry Manning then to either Robert or Henry. Manning, rector of Lavington and, from 1841, an archdeacon of Chichester, found himself fighting the same sort of daily battles Wilberforce fought. Church rates, church building, the time-taking matters of parish and diocese, were the usual subject of letters between them. Manning, too, had discriminated in his attachment to the Tractarians.[48] He had been careful to dissociate himself, in his first archidiaconal Charge, from the doctrines of *Tract XC,* although he had until then cultivated Newman assiduously. He had voted for neither Garbett nor Williams, but, at a late stage, did decide to oppose the degradation of Ward. These inconsistencies exposed him to the same sort of accusations that had been leveled against Wilberforce. Manning's by no means reliable biographer, Purcell, implies that he allowed his desire for a bishopric to dictate his beliefs. Newsome makes it clear that Manning was carving out a genuine and impressive Anglo-Catholic theology during these years. Like Wilberforce, he was without doubt prey to personal ambition and to the pleasures of the world.[49] It was as unlikely for him as it was for Wilberforce to attach himself wholeheartedly to an essentially Oxford-bound movement whose leaders led their lives and cast their thoughts in a manner quite different from his own.

When Wilberforce sought friends rather than acquaintances, he looked among men very much like himself. Hence his closeness to Gladstone and Hook, devout Christians and staunch Churchmen, yet both of them— layman and cleric—possessed of breadth and steadiness that carried them into the world in a way that the leading Tractarians were not. Though Charles Anderson, his oldest and best friend, lived a more retired life, he too had interests, common sense, and balance that now make him seem almost the epitome of Victorian probity and charm. Anderson, who was six months older than Wilberforce, came from a distinguished Lincolnshire family. His father, the Reverend Sir Charles Anderson, was rector of Lea and a prebend of Lincoln. He himself served as vice-chairman and then chairman of the Lincolnshire quarter sessions for fifty

48. David Newsome, *The Parting of Friends,* pp. 195ff.

49. See his debate with himself about the propriety and wisdom of accepting the sub-almonership, offered to him upon Wilberforce's elevation to the See of Oxford, in E. S. Purcell, *Life of Cardinal Manning,* I, 278-279.

years, and as a lay member of the Lincolnshire Diocesan Conference. Politically he journeyed, as Wilberforce had, from the far right to the center, all the while calling himself a Whig. "I feel that I am a Whig because my father is," he told Wilberforce, "so that is settled." [50]

Anderson's religious views were remarkably akin to Wilberforce's. He looked to Wilberforce as a spiritual adviser, especially when he was a young man. "It moves me to envy," Wilberforce wrote once when his father seemed on the point of death

to see such as he is stand upon the brink of eternity, their work done, waiting the summons to enter into the joy of the Lord and secure in their everlasting reward. May we both, my dear Charles, be found at last so doing. The present is a very important point in your life. [Anderson was about to marry.] Be diligent to seek spirituality of mind in it. . . There is a peril of your sinking into a sort of indolent self-gratification to the eminent peril of your spiritual state.[51]

A quietly devout High Churchman, Anderson at first saw in the *Tracts for the Times* a means of stirring up renewed interest in the Church. "I am thinking of trying to establish a depot for the Oxford Tracts at Lincoln," he reported in 1836. "I have only seen one but I like it extremely. I doubt whether any of our clergy will read them. The Residentiaries of the Minster are of that stamp of High Church which ought to be called Low, for their affection to it only extends to it in a temporal point of view." [52] Like his friend, he eventually grew alarmed at Oxford's excesses and took to restoring the life of the Church in less controversial ways, rebuilding Lincolnshire churches and helping to "awaken the laity to the necessity of opening their purses." [53]

Despite his self-imposed isolation, Anderson continued to be a man of wide interests and many talents. He painted pleasant watercolors, drew funny caricatures, and was perhaps even cleverer than Wilberforce at sketching in words. Describing Professor Sedgewick, the professor of geology: "His Phiz a most extraordinary one. His nose like a large range of mountains rugged and long with two large fishy tho' penetrating eyes like two lakes far asunder in the valleys below. A mouth with a long underlip made to enjoy a glass of champagne." [54] His letters, as well as his paintings, reflect his own maxim that the most effective pictures are those which "represent a scene as correctly as possible with small trouble and without stiffness." [55] Throughout all he wrote and did, there runs side by side with his worthy purposefulness, a robust perversity that

50. February 9, 1828, BD, I. C189.   51. August 31, 1832, BD, I. C191.
52. October 28, 1836, BD, I. C190.   53. *Ibid.,* (?) 1840.
54. June 22, 1830, BD, I. C189. For one of his best caricatures see his letter to Wilberforce, *ibid.,* February 17, 1830, in which he has sketched a monstrously fat Duchess of St. Albans calling out "Duke, Duke, where's my potatoe pie?"
55. *Ibid.,* April 1, 1830.

makes him seem very English indeed. "This abominable railway pro-
jected through Lincolnshire," he growled in 1836, "intends to go straight
through my father's kitchen garden, within a stone's throw of the house,
cutting off two farm houses from the land attached to them, through a
village, a *fox cover,* and will not benefit us one sixpence." [56] The Wilberforces and the Andersons saw a great deal of each other, and were god-
parents to each other's children; in 1863 Samuel's son Ernest married
Charles's daughter Frances. Until Wilberforce died in 1873, he continued
to visit and to write his great friend with a regularity that showed how
much he enjoyed the sharing of their mutual interests and affections.

The more one considers Wilberforce's friendships, the closer one
studies his own habits of mind and watches him pursue his interests and
ambitions, the easier it is to understand why the Tractarians had so little
appeal for him. His was certainly the motto which Brooke Foss Westcott
attributed to the Cambridge of his own generation: "I act, therefore I
am." [57] His energy, his compulsion to be always up and doing—so foreign
to the Tractarians' scholarly and occasionally studied reserve—was a
symptom of the busy early Victorian age in which he lived. To such a
man, with such a temperament, distinctions that were to the Tractarians
a matter of agonizing concern would appear unimportant and a hindrance
to his one supreme task of drawing men to Christ. "It is of the utmost
moment for the right understanding of any subject," Wilberforce preached
in 1839,

that we seize distinctly upon its leading idea. Minute acquaintance with a multiplicity of details; strong perceptions on peculiar points; these are apt to trouble
and confuse the mind which has not first singled out and mastered the principal
and governing features of any subject.[58]

Wilberforce believed that clergymen preached and wrote tracts for
the sublimely simple purpose of bringing men into the Church and thus
into communion with their Savior. This was the "leading idea" to seize
upon; anything that hindered its expression was beside the point. In
the same sermon he expressed his impatience with Tractarian reserve.
"For even when reserving much Himself, our blessed Master taught us
that 'what He had spoken in the ear, we were to proclaim on the house-
top.'" [59] Wilberforce worried when anything distracted the Church from
this mission. Accomplishment depended equally upon inspiration and
organization, but inspiration, to be genuine, had to serve a purpose and
not distract from that all-important proclamation. Doing, because of
what had to be done, thus took precedence—not over thinking—but over

56. February 21, 1836, BD, I. C190.
57. David Newsome, *Godliness and Good Learning,* p. 20.
58. *The Ministry of Reconciliation,* p. 5.
59. *Ibid.,* p. 16.

the contemplative theorizing that was the Oxford Movement at its best, and over the sectarian squabbling that was Church politics at its worst. "Yours is the very opposite of the cold, effete and repressive temper in which at Oxford and elsewhere Oxford excesses are commonly opposed," Gladstone wrote Wilberforce at the height of Tractarian controversy. "You do not allow that opposition, though you are very warm in it, to draw off the energy which should be spent upon the work of real development and improvement in the Church." [60] True enough. But the energy that drove Wilberforce to do the work of the Church so single-mindedly made him distrust "details" and "strong perceptions." It left him without much inclination to appreciate to their depth the intellectual satisfactions and spiritual comforts the Tractarians' more sensitively tuned mentalities had tutored them to find.

Many an energetic nineteenth-century clergyman engaged in round after round of activity in order to avoid confronting his own doubts. Walter Houghton has described the manner in which they concealed "the misgivings from their own eyes by the passion with which they flung themselves into their work." Activity might serve as a "rational method of attacking anxieties or an irrational method of escaping them." [61] True though this was of many, it was not true of Wilberforce. He never appears to have questioned the basis of the belief he had inherited. Inclination and experience did lead him to enrich it, the better to serve himself and those to whom he ministered. Although resting within the Evangelical creed his father had passed to him, and agreeing at many points with the teachings of the Tractarians, his faith bore his own stamp, and he felt secure in its strength. Borrowed from widely differing sources of inspiration, and by nature designed to steer a true *via media,* it served, as much as temperamental disinclination, to keep Wilberforce from affiliation with some particular Church party.

So many Tractarian attitudes and beliefs had their roots in Evangelicalism that it has now become common practice to see both movements as consecutive steps in a general revival of English pietism.[62] The emphasis upon conscience and nearness to God, the renewed attempt to reach men through preaching, the stress upon personal holiness—all these the Tractarians carried with them when they drew apart from the tradition they

60. December 29, 1844, Add Mss. 44343.
61. Walter Houghton, *The Victorian Frame of Mind* (New Haven, Conn., 1957), p. 262.
62. Y. Brilioth, *The Anglican Revival,* p. 42; Dieter Voll, *Catholic Evangelicalism* (London, 1963), pp. 37–38.

considered otherwise narrow and sterile. Wilberforce, who had been taught to cherish these same elements by his father, incorporated them into his own faith. He rejoiced in the simplicity of the Evangelicals' close communion with God. Describing John Sargent's death, he wrote that "when, just before the last struggle, one said to him, 'the everlasting arms are under you,' he answered with eager joy, 'I know they are—I feel them—that is enough.'" [63] To receive the blessings of that divine reassurance—the one support an Evangelical craved—he had first to pledge obedience to a Holy Will laid upon his conscience by God's continuing nearness. In a dream Wilberforce once recounted in his diary, "my whole soul seemed to float away, to see the earth at a distance—God near. . . Earnest desire to bow to HIM in all." [64] He could not believe that God would in anger drive him into submission. "Oh Lord," he prefaced a sonnet, "correct me, but with judgement."

> Not all at once! Nor in thy wrath O Lord!
> Break Thou these stubborn hearts of ours, we pray:
> Not all at once! For we are weak, and they
> Draw trembling back from that thy fiery sword.
> But as a tender mother day by day,
> Weans the weak babe she loves, lest it should pine;
> So wean us Lord! So make us wholly Thine. . .[65]

If man was to have God's help in battling sin, he had to learn first how to approach him. In one of his University sermons, Wilberforce spoke, as an Evangelical would speak, of "the temper of mind in which to receive the Christian mysteries"—not with the sharpness of observing scrutiny, but with simple reverence and adoration. "To receive [revelation] rightly, the will must assent to it no less than the understanding." [66] To know for certain that he was to receive it at all, man had to work ceaselessly to understand God's message and to press forward toward his own salvation. The importance of "this very moment," the resolution that "today you begin to fight the good fight," this theme, again Evangelical in its personal urgency, appears throughout Wilberforce's sermons. "Always, indeed, the NOW is important, because always it is ALL we have. It is the only opportunity of which we can be sure for working out our salvation." [67]

63. *The Journal and Letters of the Reverend Henry Martyn,* p. 23. Newman insisted that even after his conversion he remained unwilling to allow anything to come between himself and God. "It is face to face, *'solus cum solo,'* in all matters between man and his God" (*Apologia Pro Vita Sua,* p. 195).
64. April 9, 1842, BD, I. C186.
65. December 30, 1838, Notebook, BD, I. C203.
66. "The Temper of the Mind in Which to Receive the Christian Mysteries," in *Sermons Preached before the University of Oxford* (London and Oxford, 1839), pp. 67–69.
67. *An Address Delivered at a Confirmation* (London, n.d.n.p. [an Eton confirmation of 1847]).

This "practical" religion—the sort that taught man how best to lead a life pleasing in the sight of the Lord—was what Wilberforce taught in his parish and in the little books of homilies and moral tales he published. Over and over he preached the lessons of vigilance and preparedness. The stories in his *Notebook of a Country Clergyman* are almost all written to impress the reader with a sense of the transitoriness of earthly life and of God's power to end it at his will in his own way. Young Harry St. Aubyn, a character in one of the tales, fails to profit as he should from the lesson of his mother's death. "Harry was just what he had been before, as high-spirited, as hopeful, as fearless of evil, and also as ill-prepared to meet it." [68] His own horrible death occurs soon after, when, in a violent fever, he hurls himself out of his chamber window. His brother Arthur is by this singular means brought finally to a clearer understanding of God's purposes. In conversation with the country clergyman he was

weaned from earthly things, and when . . . in prayer, with what an eagerness of aspiration did he ask for spiritual grace! How earnestly did he pray for pardon for the many times wherein he had resisted the gracious purposes of God; and turned his merciful dealing into occasions of iniquity. 'Oh!' said he, 'that I could pray for the dead too. I would live centuries even in this misery of mind, could I but spend them in prayer for him who is taken away, but it must not be.' [69]

In his books of parables for the young, Wilberforce sounded the same theme, and often none too gently. Two children are placed by their father in a garden. He warns them of the lion that lurks there and instructs them to call him should they see it. "Day after day passed away, and the children became more and more watchful, and even in their sport and play, they were mindful of the lion; and when he was stealing near to them, they called always on their father, and he ever stood beside them and saved them from his fangs." The moral: "Be sober and be vigilant, because your adversary the devil goeth about as a roaring lion, seeking whom he may devour." [70] Ministers of Christ could not by themselves shield their parishioners from the devil's teeth. That was God's task. Their duty was to make those parishioners understand how ready God was to help them, once they had showed themselves prepared to follow him. In a passage in his ordination sermon of 1839, remarkable for its Evangelical emphasis upon the doctrine of atonement, Wilberforce urged the young clergyman to address the conscience of a parishoner without fear.

Lift up before him the cross: let all your ministry be the bringing him as a sinner to a Saviour's blood: let this be the very font of your address; let it fill your own

68. *The Notebook of a Country Clergyman* (New York, 1833), p. 184.
69. *Ibid.,* p. 197.
70. "The Children and the Lion," *Agathos and other Sunday Stories,* 2d ed. (London, 1840), p. 37.

soul, when you deal with his; and as the 'rivers of the south,' the hardened hearts shall, of God's mercy, 'turn again.' . . . Keep ever in view, as you look out upon your flock, the true cause of man's wretchedness and its only cure—separation from God, to be done away through the blood of Christ.[71]

This was the pure milk of Evangelical doctrine, and probably pleased Bishop Sumner, before whom it was preached. Yet on this very point Wilberforce began to part company with the Evangelicals. Man was not to suppose that the atonement, although it released him from the burden of his sins, released him as well from the responsibilities of membership in the Church Christ had established while on earth. Too often men who had heard of Christ's sacrifice for them assumed that because his infinite love had brought him down to them, they might as easily ascend to him. This "self-idolizing tendency," [72] as Wilberforce termed it, this readiness to see oneself specially ordained to traffic with the Almighty, was in his opinion Evangelicalism's chief danger. Instructed to seek God by themselves, Evangelicals believed they had been granted a special grace to find him. When Charles Simeon, lamenting in his old age the coldness he found in much of the religion around him, punned: "there's a *do* everywhere, but a shower nowhere," Wilberforce queried: "(1) The truth of the statement? (2) If true, *does it not arise from a mistaken expectation of some effusion of the Holy Spirit different* from that vouchsafed by God in His ordinances to all who seek for it." [73] These men who disdained the aids to faith willed them by Christ while looking within themselves for the "effusion" that was to be the talisman of their salvation, merely deluded themselves and damaged that one vessel—the Church—which by God's will contained his truth. Even the best of men needed more than their own conscience to lead them to God.

They needed the Church, its history and its sacraments—those ancient elements which the Tractarians, and Wilberforce with them, grew to venerate and to insist must no longer remain half-forgotten. Wilberforce attached great importance to the doctrine of the apostolic succession. The blessing, passed down the centuries through that chain, gave Christians a strength they could never have gathered by their own exertion. This conviction led Wilberforce to insist that the Church Missionary Society send bishops—that is, the Church Apostolic—into the world to

71. *The Ministry of Reconciliation,* p. 18.
72. To Charles Anderson, January 23, 1838, BD, I. C191.
73. Diary, September 29, 1831, BD, I. C186. A year earlier he had recorded an experience with a family of this "self-idolizing" sort: during a visit he was asked to pray with them, "and before I could begin [the husband] began. Then his wife prayed. A good deal too much of 'God I thank Thee' and of phraseology. As soon as I got upon my feet I told them very plainly my entire disapprobation of things of the sort. Why I disliked it. That I could never allow of another leading when the minister of God was present etc. She apologized and he took the rebuke humbly and I trust will be profited by it" (Diary, October 25, 1830, BD, I. C186).

convert the heathen. "If episcopacy, a native clergy, visible communion, the due administration of the Sacraments, Confirmation, etc., etc.—if these things be really important, then how can we expect full success till we send out missionary bishops, *i.e.,* bishops and a missionary clergy as a visible Church?" [74]

No more could a Christian do without the blessings of the sacraments. Those who refused to partake of the Eucharist on the grounds that its liturgy led to a repressive formalism were in fact "pulling down the scaffolding *because* its work is not yet accomplished." The sacraments, far from disturbing the growth of a truly pious spirit, were indispensable to its very life. To think otherwise, as some Evangelicals professed to do, was to pervert the teachings of the Church. "This is the fruit of the low and degenerate mysticism which is everywhere abroad," Wilberforce wrote in the preface to the collection of meditations on the Eucharist which he edited and published in 1839; "setting out by seeking to promote the essence and inner life of piety, it ends by destroying its very existence." [75] The Eucharist, he insisted, is a specially appointed means of grace. "It were no true *sacrament,* if there were not in it greater blessings than in any of the ordinary means and opportunities of grace which men may at their will appoint, or at their discretion intermit." Because Romanists had perverted the Eucharist, Christian men ought not therefore fall into an opposite error "and lower down into a mere commemoration rite that which Christ hath given them for a higher purpose." [76] Wilberforce quoted Hooker in his support; [77] none of the doctrines which he espoused and which led him to sympathize with Tractarian teaching was in any way inconsistent with those of the English Church fathers. Further than that he refused to go; and two colloquies—one with Newman, the other with Pusey—showed the very limited extent of his willingness to make Oxford doctrine his own.

In November 1834 Wilberforce wrote to Newman to acknowledge the gift of the first volume of Newman's *Parochial and Plain Sermons.* He remarked that he had seldom read "anything of the sort which has provided a like present effect upon my own mind." He regretted "a few casual expressions and the tone of address upon one subject because I think these likely to make them much less generally useful than they are in other respects likely to be. I have no claim to intrude my remarks upon you," he added, "but would gladly refer to the pages if you thought it

74. To Charles Anderson, August 31, 1838, BD, I. C191.
75. *Eucharistica: Meditations and Prayers with Select Passages on the Most Holy Eucharist from old English Divines* (London, n.d. [1839]), pp. x–xi.
76. *Ibid.,* p. xvi.
77. "It is not ordinarily God's will to bestow the grace of sacraments on any but by the sacraments" (*Ecclesiastical Polity,* vol. V, para. 57. Quoted in *Eucharistica,* p. xvii).

worth your while to receive such references." [78] Newman wrote that he would welcome a critique, and Wilberforce replied with a long letter in January 1835. Newman had apparently expected Wilberforce to criticize him for launching too intemperate an attack upon the religious trends and sentiments of the day. Yet Wilberforce insisted that "it is not that you testify too boldly or harshly against the open or secret schismatical spirit of the day." Rather, he wrote, "the *single* point which has most continually met and surprised me [is] an apparently studied effort to suppress the doctrine of spiritual influences." [79] He argued that God's spirit can act instantaneously and as a free agent. To insist, as Newman did, that salvation required a certain length of time was to "undervalue the clearness of the working of God's grace in all established believers."

Wilberforce criticized a further passage in which he thought Newman had overstressed the difficulties of receiving God's grace, a gift attained only after "fear and much trembling."

Surely this passage limits the power of God's spirit in a most unscriptural way. Have there not been very many who in a far shorter time have attained to very high measures of Christian grace—and can we be permitted to speak thus of His operations to whom time is not, and who 'measures life by love'—as our Christian Year has it. Of course I know your object and highly value it—but surely Scripture provides in a *different* way for rousing man out of the sluggishness of a low standard of Christianity.

In order to support his arguments, Wilberforce appended a further comment on Newman that he had received "uncalled for and unexpected" from James Stephen:

What a pity that a man of so vigorous an understanding, of so much independence of thought and with such lofty conceptions of what is wise and holy, should contrive to invest Christianity with an aspect so harsh and repulsive. . . However to render justice to Mr. Newman, he raises a standard both of thought and sentiment which elevates him immeasurably above the poor Evangelicals whom he despises—in every quality, excepting only that of touching other men's hearts and influencing their conduct. In these respects Charles Simeon is worth a legion of Newmans.

Both Wilberforce and Stephen found fault with Newman for denying God the power to work within the souls of men at his own pace and by his own will. They were disturbed by what they considered a harsh and demanding tenor in Newman's preaching, one which seemed to them designed to repulse rather than to inspire potential Christians. They understood Newman's disgust with much of the easy, rhetorical assump-

78. November 5, 1834, Newman papers, Birmingham Oratory, Miscellaneous No. 62. The correspondence which ensued has been treated in full in David Newsome, "Justification and Sanctification: Newman and the Evangelicals," *The Journal of Theological Studies,* n.s. vol. XV, pt. 1 (1964), pp. 32ff.

79. January 23, 1835, Newman papers, Birmingham Oratory, Miscellaneous No. 66.

tion and assurance of Evangelical preaching; they could not acquiesce in his sharp and, to them, unscriptural corrective.

Newman replied to Wilberforce in two letters, the first dealing with his views on justification. In the second he explained at greater length why he felt it necessary to lay such emphasis upon sanctification—salvation by works—rather than justification—salvation through a faith in the indwelling spirit of God.

My reason . . . was my conviction *that we required the law* not the Gospel in this age. We want rousing—we want the chains of duty and the details of obedience set before us strongly. And this is what has led us to enlarge upon our part of the work not on the Spirit's. . . In truth men *do* think that a saving state is one, where the mind merely looks to Christ—a virtual antinomianism.[80]

Wilberforce found this answer unsatisfactory. The message of the New Testament was not Newman's message. Christians

are never urged to repent etc. because it necessarily takes a long time [and a life of sanctification] to become Christian, but because the influence of the Holy Spirit may be withheld from them—and will be withdrawn if they continue in their present careless state. . .

Surely the scriptural account would lead us to believe that there was a beginning of holiness formed in the mind of man as soon as ever he sincerely looked for deliverance from sin to Jesus Christ—a seminal principle of holiness, which should expand in glory; and then, without denying this, that Christians should be urged to trust to the hope that this would be wrought in them at the last when they may be abandoned utterly by that Blessed Spirit without whose influence they can do nothing, and whom they have so long refused to listen to; and then to urge upon them growth in grace by a desire to glorify their Saviour, to make their calling and election sure.[81]

A further exchange of letters followed, but to no avail. On April 21 Newman wrote: "As I see that I cannot by letter sufficiently explain to you my view. . . I write this to save both of us the trouble of writing more. . . I do not feel that you allow your mind swing enough to put yourself into my views." [82]

So ended the correspondence, though not the rather distant friendship. Wilberforce continued to attend to what Newman said and wrote. Yet when his *Lectures on Justification* appeared in 1838, Samuel wrote Robert to state once more his complete disagreement with Newman's doctrine of sanctification, which, by this time, was becoming Robert's as well. Faith was "the formal instrument of our justification," and that faith remained independent of good works. Time would eventually bring forth good works from a life of faith, but by "a necessary accident." "It is not, I mean, the future production of good works which makes the

80. February 4, 1835, BD, III.
81. February 23, 1835, Newman papers, Birmingham Oratory, Miscellaneous No. 67.
82. April 21, 1835, BD, III.

difference between the one and the other, but the *present difference of the Will.* The man may die before he has had time to produce one good work, yet his living faith is not made to have been dead by Christ." Such faith, originating with God, discouraged self-pride. It served, as well, to prevent despair. "'When shall I have worked enough to convince me I am justified?' What a question!!'" Newman's harsh insistence upon sanctification was "like a man trying to build under a shower of bullets piercing his hands." [83]

Throughout the debate, Wilberforce had been objecting to Newman's doctrines upon practical as well as theological grounds. A theory which emphasized, as Newman's did, "the chains of duty" and "the details of obedience," ran the risk of driving men with "timid conscientious minds" out of the Church altogether. Evangelicalism was a stern religion; but it tempered its rigorous demands with a promise of salvation to all who sought God with humble and contrite heart. Newman appeared unwilling to offer his hearers that one glorious consolation. The implications of his doctrine of sanctification—"election" following a lifetime of self-mortifying good works—restricted salvation to a small and, one suspects, intellectually as well as spiritually superior band. To the Tractarians, this prospect was not particularly upsetting. To Wilberforce, who had set himself the task of saving souls, it offered far too confined a vision of the Gospel message. "They hold up a glorious standard of Holiness," he wrote Anderson, "and for us, my dear Charles, who know well the riches of the Gospel and can supply all they leave deficient it is the very thing needful—but there are ignorant and bowed-down souls who need I think a more welcoming treatment than their view of penitence will allow." [84]

This desire to offer sinners a more "welcoming treatment" led Wilberforce that same year to attack Pusey's doctrine of sin after baptism. In *Tract LXVII* Pusey had defended the sacrament of baptism from Protestant heresies, proclaiming it "a living seal stamped upon our souls by the Spirit of life, and bearing with it the impress of Divine Nature," renewing continually "the image of Him who created us, our Father, our Redeemer, our Sanctifier." [85] Yet he devoted the major portion of the Tract to a discussion and defense of the doctrine that sin after baptism "is not only a step towards final impenitence, but weakens Baptismal grace, and tends to deprive the individual of the ordinary means of restoration." Once having sinned, Pusey argued, man could never be completely restored to favor in God's eyes. "In Baptism we are washed, once for all, in His blood . . . if we again sin, there remaineth no more such complete ablution in this life." Like Newman, he argued that sinful Christians had grown too confident of an eventual return to grace: "Until we

83. May 24, 1838, Wrangham papers.   84. January 23, 1838, BD, I. C191.
85. E. B. Pusey, *Scriptural Views of Holy Baptism* (London, 1836), pp. 38–39.

lay deeper the foundations of repentence the very preaching of the Cross of Christ becomes but a means of carnal security." [86]

These strictures drew from Wilberforce a public answer that pro-claimed his disaffection with Tractarian insistence upon the oppressive nature and presence of sin. Two of the six sermons he preached before the University in 1838 dealt directly with the doctrines set forth in Pusey's Tract and in a previous and much discussed sermon at Christ Church.[87] In the first, on "The Moral Consequences of Sin," he was careful not to underestimate the damage that sin wrought upon the soul. "Even if the sinner could at once be forgiven by God, by an act of sovereign and partial favour, still he would not be in the same condition that he was before; because there would remain in his very nature the accursed consequences of past pollution." The moral consequences of sin were therefore dread-ful. But for the truly penitent there was hope. By encouraging the action of the Holy Spirit upon the mind, one could effect the necessary cure. If Christ was not resisted, "His holy work will at last, and in His good time, be perfected within us. . . And in our training, too, we answer to our discipline; for our own souls become more pure—there is more good brought into their nature, and their remaining evil is continually subdued." The promise was sure; the process remained long and painful.

We cannot promise [sinners] a speedy deliverance from that bitter fruit of their own ways with which they are not filled; we must rather bid them bear their burdens patiently, nor fret against God's way of healing them, but take up the bitter cross of present suffering, meekly acknowledging that it is indeed a fearful thing to have polluted a soul which God created holy.[88]

Having treated his subject from the point of view of sinful man, Wil-berforce, in his next sermon, "The Penal Consequences of Sin," tried to describe mortal sin as it appeared to the eyes of God. Directly chal-lenging the Tractarians' theory of sanctification, he asked whether a baptized sinner, "upon his turning unto the Lord," might be assured of "a full and free and ready pardon, even as before his baptism." "Is there, *from* his baptism, that assurance of a Father's waiting favour?" Wilber-force was certain there was, and he took as a text to prove his conviction the story of the prodigal son. Just as the father saw his returning son from a great distance and rejoiced, so

the eye of the heavenly Father rests upon the wanderer; a great way off He sees him; whilst his own heart, clouded over by his own sin, and weaned from God by willful transgression, though it begins to turn to Him with longing, yet dares not look up with confidence . . . even then His thoughts and ways, whose thoughts

86. *Ibid.*, pp. 49, 62, 63.   87. Thomas Mozley, *Reminiscences*, II, 148.
88. "The Moral Consequences of Sin," *Sermons Preached before the University of Oxford*, pp. 6–7, 13, 24.

and ways are not as ours, are 'thoughts of peace,' to 'give' to the returning wanderer 'an expected end.' (Jeremiah XXIX. II)

Sinful man, Wilberforce argued, cannot be baptized afresh. Even if he were seeking that sacrament for the first time, he would, to make its seal sure for *him,* have to come in sincerity and faith. "And now, if he comes in sincerity and faith, the seal is still sure, and is for him; his baptism is on him, fresh as when its waters glistened upon his infant brow."

Finally Wilberforce turned his attention directly to the Tractarians. He attacked those whose tendency was "to reprove with harshness those sensible marks of joy and favor with which the threshold is crowned for the penitent; of a Novation readiness to diet the returning sinner long on doubts and fears, rather than to fling wide the doors, and kill the fatted calf." He despaired at the Tractarian inclination to readmit sinners only conditionally, to "bid them to doubt the goodness of the Lord of Mercy." This, said Wilberforce, is "to drive our sinful but repentant brother to despair." "They who would blot out, or only cloud over, the fair face of mercy to the guilty, surely thereby bring on equally the might of desperation—that deadliest and most hopeless state of sin." Forgiveness, he urged, need not lessen the bitterness of repentance: "it is the very glory of Christ's gospel, that it can combine a thankful assurance of pardon with the deepest sense of undeserving." [89]

While they continued to preach their harsh and overly demanding religion, therefore, the Tractarians would remain a none-too-healthy influence within the Church. Although Wilberforce readily admitted that they had done much to stimulate religious revival—to encourage, as he wrote Anderson, a "high tone of intellect and morality" [90]—he continued to find their exclusiveness unattractive and, with an increasingly large number of critics, to deplore the doctrines which seemed to be drawing their disciples much too close to Rome. In 1840, in response to accusations that his second book of parables for children, *The Rocky Island,* reflected Tractarian dogmas, he wrote a lengthy defense and exposition of his own beliefs to a fellow clergyman, Thomas Fosbery. He acknowledged the personal piety of the Tractarians, but, he insisted, his opinions had been formed "in a far different school."

They are those of my beloved father, as I could prove, were it needful, from many written records of his judgment as to the tenor of my ministry, of which, during his late years, he was a most kind, but a close observer. But why do I say all this, which you well know. You know my dread of the 'Tract' doctrine of Reserve, of its coldness, and suppression, and earthly wisdom; you know my love and gratitude towards the memory of our great Reformers; you know my fear of robbing religion of its true spiritual character in the heart of faithful man; you know my

89. "The Penal Consequences of Sin," *ibid.,* pp. 31, 39, 40, 44–45, 52, 55, 57.
90. May 31, 1836, BD, I. C191.

abhorrence of Rome, and of the result of Popish doctrine, that *caput mortuum* of piety, whether reached through the Papacy or any other system.[91]

Wilberforce ended the letter with a declaration of allegiance to the Church of England. "I am indeed, on the conclusions of my reason and the convictions of my conscience, a decided and uncompromising Churchman." But, he added, "it is because I believe the Church system is God's appointment for maintaining the life of God in the souls of men; and I cannot, therefore, substitute a veneration for the instrument for that result for the sake of which the instrument is valuable."

This unwanted veneration of the Church, Wilberforce believed, was leading Tractarians to Rome. "Their craving after a visible centre of unity," he explained to Robert, their belief "that the Church is to us instead of an absent Christ" [92]—these notions would almost surely carry them away not just from Anglicanism but indeed from God's presence. Robert, who seemed to his brother in danger of slipping into this very error, received a similar warning the following year:

> ... I do not agree with you as to the—in fact—impossibility of substituting the Church for Christ. Indeed, as I speak of it, I believe it to be *the* prominent danger, amongst the many, of the Tract system. The Church, I say, *separated from the head* is substituted for Him! I refer to such passages as, *e.g.* that in one of Newman's sermons, where he is dealing with the case of one in dejection under the sense of sin, where he says: 'It is true you can have no assurance; there is no second Laver in which you can wash; but still you need not despair. You are still in the Church and that is something. Go on using her ordinances in the hope that perhaps, after all, you will find you have life in you,' etc.[93]

The longing for authority, for a sure and steady source of comfort and assurance, is one that drives many men to religion. It drove the Evangelicals to throw themselves upon God's mercy. It drove the Tractarians, whose doctrine of sanctification plunged them into a limbo of doubt, to worship the authority of the Church. Individualism, so much a part of the Evangelical faith, was central to Tractarianism as well. Both traditions demanded personal commitment, which in the case of Evangelicalism, led to a close and continual relationship with God. Tractarianism, straining, as it seemed to Wilberforce, to doubt the promise of the atonement, and insisting upon an incredibly high standard of personal holiness for salvation, separated man from God and led him to welcome the certain reassurances of Rome. "Newman's book [*Essay on the Development of Christian Doctrine*] is wonderfully clever and full of Ecclesiastical history, but the most deeply sceptical book I ever read," Wilberforce wrote Louisa Noel in 1845. "It is in fact an assertion from beginning to end that all religion is so uncertain except the *fact* of there being the Church that

91. March 30, 1840, BD, I. C193.   92. February 2, 1842, Wrangham papers.
93. *Ibid.*, December 18, 1843.

we can only go to its living authority to convince us there is a God at all." [94]

His dismay at what he considered a blind allegiance to Church authority did not lead him to disparage the true Catholic Church as a holy institution. It was a part of the foundation upon which he attempted to build his own faith. His conception was of a Church of England as part of the Church Universal, a conception far different from that upon which the advanced Tractarians relied for support. He believed firmly in the principle of a State Church. In a letter to Gladstone, following the publication of the latter's *The State in Its Relation to the Church*, Wilberforce wrote to approve the notion that all governments had a duty to support and defend what they believed to be religious truth.[95] Yet he was no more pleased than most clergymen when the government of the day stepped in to interfere with the management of the Church. He consulted with both Pusey and Newman in 1836 concerning ways to put an end to the laws of *praemunire* as they affected the election and consecration of bishops. He was upset by the government's grant of money to Roman Catholic Maynooth College in 1845, but his desire to maintain the State-Church connection, his assumption, which he seems to have taken *a priori,* that such a connection was vital to the nation's well-being, led him to swallow the indignity of support for an alien and indeed heretical faith. In a rather dispirited letter to Anderson, he reported

... I am quite for the Maynooth Grant; not as a thing that I like in itself, but as a necessary step in our position when Church and State are rather at the fag end of an old alliance than identifiable terms ... we do not want deep Laputan principles of legislation, to change everything on an abstract idea, but just the practical modifications of existing systems which the change of all things makes unavoidable.[96]

The Tractarians were wedded to just such abstract ideas and principles. Although naturally not averse to a government grant in support of the Catholics of Maynooth, they had by that time been sufficiently dismayed by governmental willingness to let politics dictate Church policy and to traffic with as offensively Protestant a notion as the Jerusalem bishopric, to declare themselves no longer able to support Erastian compromises. They pledged their support, instead, to the Church Catholic and championed the divine right of that mystical hierarchy of Church, Saints, and Fathers through whom they traced their lineage. Their lines of allegiances were vertical rather than horizontal. Whereas the Tractarian thought of his Church as part of a universal Catholicism that flowed from past to present, transcending time and history, Wilberforce, although by no means slighting the apostolic tradition, placed it inside the web of human

94. December 20, 1845, BD, II. F.   95. May 15, 1839, Add Mss. 44343.
96. April 26, 1845, BD, I. C191.

activity and thus saw the Church as a force that might, through prayer and hard work, be made to play a part in the lives of men and nations. His "horizontal" allegiances were to the all-too-imperfect institutions man had created, and to the idea that the Church might hold a mission to improve and sanctify them. He remained ready to "hoist the Church flag" [97] upon any occasion—secular or ecclesiastical—where there was strife to be settled, or division to be healed. Although he saw the Church as the repository of the true faith, he did not assume, as did many of the Tractarians, that her sole task was the guardianship of that faith. Her role, according to Wilberforce, was the more dynamic and creative one of changing man and, through him, the world he lived in.

To accomplish its appointed task the Church required authority to lend it necessary strength. General toleration, Wilberforce insisted, led only to a denial of truth; lack of clerical discipline resulted in doctrinal contradiction and confusion. "The Kirk establishment of Scotland, the Methodist conference, etc., proceed upon generally admitted and maintained principles," he wrote Hook in 1840. "But the great bulk of our clergy are still so ignorant of Church principles that we have no sufficient bond of union to resist the necessary division of opinion which must always spring from shades of individual opinion." [98] The traditional patterns and formularies of the Church were in themselves a form of authority. In the Episcopal Church in America, Wilberforce saw them as the one bulwark against religious excess. The Church possessed the further authority vouchsafed by the apostolic succession. Although, in the face of Roman claims to Catholicity, some high Tractarians felt uncertain of their own ecclesiastical descent, apostolicity remained for Wilberforce a sure support.[99] Yet the ultimate sanction and authority was neither tradition nor the laying on of hands. It was for Wilberforce, as it had been for his father, the Bible. The truth lay as nowhere else within the Testaments.

The Bible being to *each one* of us *the* rule of faith; and being, as I believe, the very living word of God, it *will* speak straight to the heart of each one who uses faithfully whatever aids God has given him to understand it; these aids are, for the first, the teaching of the Holy Spirit to be obtained by earnest prayer; then the singleness of eye which belongs to Sincerity in God's sight; and then, beyond these, all the external aids God gives each man, *ie* pious parents and pious friends to the child; and, to all, the guides and directors whom His providence has furnished.

97. To Robert I. Wilberforce, December 16, 1841, Wrangham papers. His remark was in regard to the contested poetry professorship.

98. April 12, 1840, BD, I. C194.

99. Y. Brilioth, *The Anglican Revival,* pp. 146–147: "The Anglican imputation against Rome was, that Rome lacked the mark of apostolicity and abandoned the ground of the early Church. But could not Rome reply by denying the name of Catholic to the Church of England? Was not this Church a sect cut off from other branches of the Church? Thus Catholicity was opposed to Apostolicity."

Men who refuse to use these aids are refusing to use the Bible itself as God intends. The aids are "glasses for weak eyes," which they will make use of if they are sincere, and which God will bless. "Of all the aids to faith, however, none is so great as the uniform and consenting judgment of all God's Saints upon the meaning of God's word." Individuals are not free to interpret at will, as some Evangelicals seemed to think. They must remember that there is but one meaning to Scripture, that attached to it by "God's Saints from the beginning. . . This, I think, is what our article means by calling the Church the keeper and witness of holy Scripture." [100]

The letter bespeaks Wilberforce's own *via media* clearly and succinctly. Its Evangelicalism is striking: the aids to faith—prayer and conscience; the reliance upon biblical authority. Its admission at the same time that the weakened eyes of man's faith must rely upon the judgment of "God's Saints" shows Wilberforce transcending Evangelicalism, preaching not just Christ crucified but Christ within his Church. He recognized that many found his religion a shabby compromise. He defended it, nevertheless, as the true faith of *ecclesia Anglicana,* "not a faint and ill-defined middle . . . [but], in the truest sense, a positive position. We maintain," he wrote in his Charge of 1843, "on the one hand, the ever-renewed mystery of the individual spiritual life in every faithful child of God. . . And yet, with this, on the other hand, we maintain the existence of a true spiritual kingdom in the Church of Christ." [101]

He believed this middle position afforded the Church an unparalleled opportunity to bring God into the lives of men, if only she would first put her own house in order. And to Wilberforce, order meant unity. "In union must be our strength," he wrote in his first Charge.

And between men engaged in action there cannot long be union without concert. Perhaps one of the main causes of want of strength within the Church of England, at this time, is the want of concert, combination, and therefore of strict union between her clergy. We act separately in our parishes—we grow to act as units on society; the man, therefore, and not the systems, is brought to bear upon the various hindrances we meet with.

100. To Miss M. S. Elliott, May 18, 1842, Ashwell and Wilberforce, *Life,* I, 214–215. Miss Elliott had written Wilberforce a criticism of Manning's book, *The Rule of Faith,* charging that Manning relied too much upon authority, too little on the Bible. Wilberforce admitted that "I could not have written as he has done; but when I have talked with him, I have found it difficult to fix him to any meaning beyond what all Churchmen hold." Wilberforce did not believe in a doctrine of development. Truth came to man from God through Scripture and through the apostles. Nothing written later was more than a comment upon that truth. See his letter to Gladstone, December 6, 1845 (Add Mss. 44343), expressing his belief that "the first Divine afflatus conveyed to the Church in the persons of the Apostles all truth concerning God which man could know and that the inspired Word of God is the written transcript of that entire knowledge which it was but given to the Church afterwards to draw out and define with logical accuracy as heresy created that necessity."
101. *Charge,* 1843, pp. 36–37.

Separateness breeds selfishness and suspicion, and so the "compact phalanx of the Church, which in her union would be terrible as an army with banners," is rendered ineffective against the assault of her enemies.[102] Here lies the reason for his reluctance to take sides. Controversy weakened the Church and hence doomed the human beings whom the Church had been called into existence to serve. Dedicated to that service himself, Wilberforce found it hard to sympathize with others who defined the Church's role more personally, searching meanwhile for truth among distinctions which were to them far more than "different modes of speech." To Wilberforce, these men were living apart from history, and communing with a Church apart from time. "It is of no use to rail against the spirit of the times in which God has cast our lot," Wilberforce declared in the same Charge. "Our business is to mould and sanctify it; and this we may do, if we bring the influence of the Church to bear upon it." [103] This was the true Churchman's task; and it was the task Wilberforce set himself to perform as bishop of Oxford.

102. *Charge*, 1840, p. 5.   103. *Ibid.*, p. 32.

PART II
Oxford

CHAPTER IV

Clergy and People

Wilberforce entered upon his duties resolved to think of nothing but the service he might perform for God and the Church and aware of the dangers that his new position held for a person as active and as worldly as he was.

Nov 2, 1845. *Alverstoke, Sunday.* . . The first great *necessity* seems to me to be to maintain a devotional temper. The first great *peril*—SECULARITY. To guard against this by self-examination, and above all by living in prayer. . .

Among other practical hints specially needful and necessary, I put down,—

1. *Beware of exaggerating,* either in praise or blame; guard my conversation more. υι διάβολος [let me not slander].

2. Be a 'father in God' to men of *all* opinions amongst my clergy.

3. Take *time* to answer letters. Give no opinion on hearing one side. Beware of *confiding*—of speaking on feeling. . .

Nov 27. . . Never to hurry men who come to consult you. Mere venting themselves is a relief. The receiving of this a duty of sympathy.

Residence and Labour. God numbers the Bishop's absent or idle days. Satan *always* busy. Evil sowing; the good fainting; time passing; men dying; Christ coming. . .

Nov 28. . . My object: I. To serve God.
II. In His way.

All else indifferent. All around the *media* for this. For this thou wast created and redeemed. This is Heaven. To serve anything else, especially thyself, this is Hell. Lord, teach me to love thy service.[1]

These reflections, which say a good deal about Wilberforce's ability to assess his own failings, say as much about the sort of task he saw before him. "Satan *always* busy. Evil sowing; the good fainting; time passing; men dying; Christ coming." Wilberforce was to work in his diocese as if those words rang constantly within his head. They insured that he would try as hard as he could to save the souls of as many as he could reach. He was to be a "doing" bishop.

In this he was not unlike others on the Bench at the time of his appointment. Wilberforce has often been described as the first of a new diocesan breed, but such a description ignores the tradition which had already been established by Blomfield of London, Otter of Chichester, Ryder of Lich-

1. Diary, BD, I. C186.

field and Coventry, and the Sumners. This is not to say that the Bench no longer numbered gentle relics of eighteenth-century episcopal ineffectiveness. Bishop Gilbert, who succeeded the reforming Otter at Chichester in 1842, "followed the Georgian rather than the Victorian tradition." [2] But after the reforms of the 1830's and the noisy criticisms tossed at the Bench's refusal to countenance them, bishops took pains to be about their business and to look for ways to justify that business to the country. Moreover, once Peel determined to interest himself in Church extension and reform, he began to make use of those among his natural allies, the bishops, who appeared ready to cooperate with him. In most cases the cooperation proved only tenuous or half-hearted. Conflict over the exact nature of Church property—whether it was public or private—and natural reluctance to countenance the disarrangment if not the actual dismantling of cathedral administration kept the bishops wary. This, too, at a time when the campaign to curtail pluralities and nonresidence was placing more and more livings and hence more and more power in the bishops' hands. Both Church and State might wish for reform; inevitably both undertook it by different means and with differing ends in view.[3] The mutual confidence that bred cooperation between Blomfield and Peel was rare.[4]

Richard Bagot, Wilberforce's predecessor as bishop of Oxford, had himself run afoul of the State. He had acceded to the bishopric in 1829, while dean of Canterbury, and had continued to hold that post, as well as the rectorship of Blithfield, in Staffordshire, *in commendam*. Much of the revenue of the See of Oxfordshire had been granted in lease for fines by previous incumbents; as a result the bishop's income had been substantially diminished, and on this ground Bagot, with some justice, defended his plurality. In 1836 the Ecclesiastical Commissioners, through an Order in Council, annexed the counties of Berkshire and Buckinghamshire to the diocese, in the course of a general redrawing of southern ecclesiastical boundaries. Bagot, though he accepted the addition of Berkshire, bridled at the thought of Buckinghamshire as well, "there being many points besides that of annual income to be settled previous to my acceding to the formation of so large a diocese as Oxford would be with the addition of both counties."[5] Income certainly had something to do with his unenthusiastic response. He fought hard to have the income for the even partially enlarged diocese brought to £5000 per annum, and to this the Commissioners eventually agreed, settling at the

2. J. B. Atlay, *Ernest Wilberforce* (London, 1912), p. 222.
3. See G. F. A. Best, *Temporal Pillars* (Cambridge University Press [Eng.], 1964), chap. VI.
4. P. J. Welch, "Blomfield and Peel: Study in the Cooperation Between Church and State," *Journal of Ecclesiastical History*, 12:71–84 (1961).
5. *Report of the Ecclesiastical Commissioners*, XLII (1851), 268.

same time that Buckinghamshire would not come into the diocese until the accession of Bagot's successor.

Bagot's reluctance to undertake the heavy reorganization implicit in the Commissioners' proposals does not mean that he was an inactive diocesan. On the contrary, he instituted a number of reforms, among them a diocesan Board of Education and a small training college for schoolmasters. Perhaps the most noteworthy was his restoration of the office of rural dean, an innovation that proved of great service to Wilberforce during the early years of his episcopate, when he relied on those agents to supply him quickly with the quantities of information he craved.

Wilberforce succeeded to a diocese that was generally rural in nature. Reading and Oxford were the only large towns.[6] Oxfordshire and Berkshire divided generally into middle-sized estates. In the former, 40 per cent of the total area was occupied by estates of from 1000 to 10,000 acres; in the latter, 37 per cent.[7] Buckinghamshire, with a heavy sprinkling of larger estates, and closer to London, presented a somewhat different picture and a different set of problems. The diocese as a whole was distinguished by several idiosyncrasies which set it apart and added to its bishop's difficulties. It maintained no cathedral of its own, Henry VIII having united the cathedral bodies of both the See and Christ Church College in 1546. The bishop had even less than a bishop's normally tenuous hold over his dean and chapter. Appointment to some of the stalls came automatically with appointment to positions within the University. Pusey and Hampden, for example, both held canonries by virtue of their professorships of Hebrew and Divinity. Nor was this the sole area in which the University and its affairs intruded upon those of the diocese. Oxford colleges possessed a number of livings, most of them in Oxfordshire, and most of them not generously endowed. These the colleges treated as material investments, using them to reward Fellows whose talents might be scholarly rather than pastoral—or might be neither. They expended on their maintenance and expansion only those sums that could be spared from the management of the colleges.[8]

Wilberforce could do little but make the best of University intrusion into diocesan affairs. If it brought disarrangement it often added distinction. A far less complicated but more immediately exasperating problem was the lack of an episcopal palace. Bagot, who had been virtually nonresident, had hoped to have a suitable residence built at Shotover. The country house with which he had been obliged to make do was at nearby Cuddesdon, six miles from Oxford and, as he reported to the Commis-

6. With populations, respectively, of 18,937, and 24,258 in 1841.
7. F. M. L. Thompson, *English Landed Society in the Nineteenth Century* (London, 1963), pp. 30–32; 113–117.
8. V. H. H. Green, *Oxford Common Room* (London, 1957), pp. 30, 229ff.

sioners, inconvenient and inaccessible.[9] Wilberforce thought Cuddesdon would suit, if enlarged. He was taken with the charm of the place and with the chance it offered him to keep his hand directly in matters pastoral. "The palace is not a bit of a palace," he wrote Louisa Noel on first seeing it.

It is an old H-shaped house, a rambling sort of country gentleman's house, very small grounds, but a pretty garden, very unmagnificent. There is a nice lawn, with fine old elms, and a very pretty Church close by. I *am* Rector, and like very much keeping up with that pastoral character our Bishops are so apt to lose. There is a curate, who of course must be the effective parish priest during a great part of the year. But it will be my flock. It is 500 *quite* agricultural people. This I greatly like, and think it will be very useful for my dear children. It is, so far, more true country than Alverstoke. . . The gardens, etc., seem small, and productive, and 2 men do them; a little land, but no Manors or anything great— all of which I think quite good for me and less expensive I hope than if otherwise.[10]

If the house was to serve as a proper palace, Wilberforce was convinced that it would have to be reconstructed on a more generous scale. He pressed the Archbishop and the Commissioners, and by the middle of February 1848 had received a grant of £3500 toward the reconstruction of the palace and one for £1300 to improve the desmesne.[11] At least one Oxfordshire incumbent, Thomas Fosbery, complained to his new bishop about what he considered an unwarranted extravagance. Wilberforce replied that the Commission had pledged itself to build a "See House"— a more modest phrase than "Palace"—and that there was "nothing of finery or decoration" about the alterations. "They are the addition of rooms in which the bishop can and does receive the candidates for orders, etc.," and for that reason were not only excusable but absolutely indispensable.[12] Wilberforce insisted upon the renovation so that he might bring together the clergy to learn what they had to tell him and to tell them how they might best assist him.

His clergy—what sort of men they were, what sort of job they were doing—remained Wilberforce's central concern throughout his years as a bishop. His strength was his ability to impress himself upon the men he worked with. His interest was in these men as men and as servants of the Church. He was not alone in recognizing the importance of parochial clergy to the community and to the Church, especially in country parishes, where the priest might often be schoolmaster, magistrate, and even squire. The movement from the 1820's onward to make livings equal

9. Best, *Temporal Pillars,* p. 364.
10. November 9, 1845, Ashwell and Wilberforce, *Life,* I, 309–310.
11. Best, *Temporal Pillars,* p. 366. In all, £6819 was spent on the reconditioning of Cuddesdon (Best, p. 362, and Table I).
12. December 26, 1846, BD, I. C193.

and to ameliorate the lot of the parish priest may have stemmed in part from simple humanitarian impulse; it stemmed also, as one historian has noted, from "the realization of the manifold uses of the resident incumbent in a rural area, outside his church as well as inside." [13] This realization spurred the drive to reduce instances of pluralism and nonresidence. In a survey of 1827, 6,120 incumbents out of 10,533 who troubled to reply were not residing upon their benefices.[14] Many clergymen held two or more livings, and were nonresident simply because they could not be in more than one place at one time. Pluralism in the diocese of Oxford was common enough at the beginning of the nineteenth century. With legislation introduced in 1838, however, no clergyman was allowed to hold more than two livings, a maximun of ten miles was to lie between the two, and in no case was their joint value to exceed £1000. Further legislation in 1850 all but abolished pluralism. The allowable distance was reduced to three miles, and possession of a second living was permitted only when the value of the first was less than £100. Nonresidence also all but disappeared as a result of these two acts; ill health and lack of accommodation were stipulated the sole grounds for absence, and legitimate absenteeism required an episcopal license.[15]

Legislation of this sort helped guarantee the presence of a clergyman in every parish. It could not insure clergymen enough money to live on. McClatchey estimates that in 1786 forty-five per cent of the Oxfordshire livings were poor and inadequate.[16] Though the situation improved in the following century, Wilberforce reported in his Charge of 1860 that more than one third of the benefices possessed incomes of less than £200, and that seventy-two were worth less than £100 per year,[17] hardly enough to allow a clergyman to maintain the position which tradition and, in this case, his bishop required of him. Curates naturally felt the pinch especially hard. After years of work in a parish with little thanks and less remuneration, they would doubtless have been tempted to add amen to the conclusions expressed by Fitzjames Stephen in the *Cornhill Magazine* in 1864: "Considered as a profession, the Church is a very good profession for a rich man, and not a very bad one for the sort of man who is extremely anxious to be considered a gentleman, and who,

13. Diana McClatchey, *Oxfordshire Clergy*, pp. 17–18.
14. Owen Chadwick, *Victorian Miniature* (London, 1960), p. 10.
15. 1 and 2 Vict., c. 106; 13 and 14 Vict., c. 98. For a detailed discussion of the effect of these acts upon the clergy of Oxfordshire, see McClatchey, *Oxfordshire Clergy,* chaps. IV and V. To further decrease the incidence of nonresidence, Wilberforce himself introduced a bill which became law in 1871, allowing clergymen to resign their livings because of ill health or old age. See *Hansard,* 3rd ser., CCII, June 14, 1870, 3; CCIV, February 20, 1871, 477–482.
16. McClatchey, *Oxfordshire Clergy,* p. 13.
17. *Charge,* 1860, p. 43. The richest living in the city of Oxford was worth only £164; the average for the city parishes was £113.

if he had been employed by a bustling shopkeeper, would never have had any chance of being taken into partnership. For an ambitious, able, intellectual man, who is also poor, no profession can well be worse." [18]

Stephen added that no man should hesitate to sacrifice a comfortable income if convinced that he had a calling to deliver God's message for his Church. But the critic's tone suggested that those who entered the profession too often did so for lack of a better alternative. Given the size and amorphous nature of the clergy, and the haphazard and patchwork way in which appointments to it could be made, he might have found many examples to prove his implication. Though there were fewer drunkards, foxhunters, and farmer-parsons within the Church in 1845 than there had been in 1800, though fewer entered out of indifference and more with a calling, enough lackluster clergymen remained to blot the Church's reputation and hamper its effectiveness. All a man had to do in many instances to present himself for Orders was to produce evidence of an Oxford or Cambridge degree, express willingness to subscribe to the Thirty-nine Articles, and find a patron to present him with a cure of souls.

Wilberforce, who was as awake as anyone to the role a parish clergyman might play in effecting the Church's mission, appreciated the fact that many had neither the talent nor the inclination to play it with determination. He knew the sort of men he wanted to attract and train as clergymen, and the extraordinary amount of time he devoted to that difficult and often exasperating work reflected his conviction that they were the life's blood of his diocese. The ideal clergyman was one who lived to set his parishioners an example. "The Church without the Parsonage," Wilberforce argued,

was altogether inadequate and incomplete. . . for not only should the clergyman be able to reach the people, but the people reach the clergyman: he should be accessible at all hours whenever he might be wanted: he should be capable of illustrating by his life the doctrines he taught, and affording his parishioners the example of the amenities of family life, especially valuable where there were few resident gentry. And this was at once evident when they remembered that the livings in which there were no parsonage houses, were, firstly, poor livings, and, secondly, poor livings in poor districts, where in all probability, there was no gentleman's house, no clergyman to consult, no family bestowing a blessing on the whole neighborhood, dispensing its charity, and by example enforcing improved habits of life among their poor neighbours.[19]

In saying this he was preaching what he had himself practiced at Brighstone and Alverstoke, where duty and inclination led him to assume a position among the leading gentlemen of the community. But by gentleman he meant more than landowner and local arbiter. "What we mean

18. "The Church as a Profession," *Cornhill Magazine*, 9:760 (1864).
19. *Rules, Proceedings . . . of the Diocesan Association for the Increase of Church Accommodation, etc.* (1849), p. 5; McClatchey, *Oxfordshire Clergy*, p. 24.

by 'gentleman,'" he remarked upon another occasion, "is just this—it is that habit of putting self down and of exalting to an equality with himself those to whom he is ministering." [20] This equality was equality before God and not necessarily among men or within the parish. Clergymen had a duty to stand a bit apart from their fellows, to display in their conduct "the separated character of Christ's ambassador," and to prove that although men of this world they were nevertheless "but more decent men of this world." [21] What he did and what he was seen doing would in large part determine the nature of the community a clergyman led. *"Esse quam videri,"* Wilberforce once remarked to Ashwell, "is a maxim which has its application; but, for a clergyman, the *videri* is essential to his having even the chance of realizing the *esse* in his actual work. How are people to be encouraged to come to you for what you are ready to *be* and *do,* if you do not take care that what you are and what you do be seen and known." [22]

With this object before his clergymen, little wonder that Wilberforce frowned upon their hunting, dancing, and drinking. He clipped and kept newspaper lists of subscribers to county balls and applicants for game certificates, duly checking the names of clergymen and dispatching appropriate reprimands.[23] He insisted that his clergy do far more than restrain inclinations to indulge in pastimes frivolous or perhaps worse. They should strive, of course, to keep their minds limber. Clerical life, as Stephen noted in the *Cornhill,* afforded little scope for strenuous intellectual exercise. "There is hardly any profession—certainly no liberal profession—which makes such small demands on the mere intellect, the power of thinking and weighing arguments. A man with quick sympathies, businesslike habits, and some power of expression, has pretty nearly all the intellectual gifts an average clergyman requires." [24] Wilberforce recognized that unless the parish priest could argue intelligently with the intelligent parish agnostic, the faith would be in mortal danger; thus the call for University-educated gentlemen. At one point in his career—significantly, perhaps, the year following the publication of *The Origin of Species*—he seemed to despair of attracting bright young men into the ministry. "The number of men endowed with the highest gifts of intellect who give themselves to the Christian ministry," he reported in his Charge of 1860, "appears to me to be smaller than it was fifteen years ago." [25] By 1866 he reassured the diocese that he was encouraged by the intellectual caliber of recent candidates for orders, "a complete practical

20. Speech at the Oxford Diocesan Society for Augmentation of Small Livings, November 25, 1864, in Ashwell and Wilberforce, *Life,* III, 156.
21. *Charge,* 1848, p. 66.   22. Ashwell and Wilberforce, *Life,* I, 345.
23. ODP, d. 550. 90. 156.
24. "The Church as a Profession," *Cornhill Magazine,* 9:752–753 (1864).
25. *Charge,* 1860, p. 8. The total number of ordinations for the three years 1857–1860 had shown a slight decline over previous triennial periods. See *Charge,* 1860, p. 5.

answer to the taint we have sometimes heard of late [in the *Cornhill,* perhaps?] that the ministry was now sought only by those who were hopeless of distinction in secular professions." [26]

An educated clergyman would serve his parish badly were he, though educated, unholy. "An ignorant clergy are a reproach to any Church," Wilberforce wrote at the time of his appointment to Oxford, "and must injure its efficiency; but an ungodly clergy threaten the removal of its candlestick, and the extinction of its life." [27] The "momentous question" was not "Is your mind ready to accept Christ's message?," but rather "Is your spirit able to accept Christ's calling?" The anser to this question came not from books but from prayer. And not until it had been answered could a man undertake the real work of ministry, the all-important task Wilberforce believed the Church had before it: "Your one work is to win souls to Christ: not to produce a certain general decency and amendment in the face of society round you, but as God's instrument and through the power of Christ's name, to work in living souls the mighty marvel of their true conversion." [28] Wilberforce insisted that those under his charge accept this challenge that he had accepted for himself. He was ready to coach them by precept and example. He warned them against "mere professional decency." He cautioned them against discouragement. Above all, and perhaps because he himself knew something of the dangers of haste, he counseled patience. One could not win souls by the lightning stroke of a powerful sermon. "It must be by conversation with them"; he told his ordinands,

by putting the truth before them with the briefness of statement, the reiteration, the plainness, and the meetness for their peculiar errors, which are only possible in conversation; it must be by catechizing child after child, and talking privately with adult after adult, that we can make them understand our statements.[29]

If a clergyman refused to undertake this painstaking work, he was shirking his duty and turning back from the goal his vows had pledged him to pursue. "Your ministry has failed as to every soul entrusted to you, who is not under it converted to the Lord, or built up in His holy faith." [30] Wilberforce believed that with this solemn responsibility upon him, a clergyman was compelled to lead a life distinct from that of other men. Ministers of God, he had written in his archidiaconal Charge of 1843, are "men of another stamp from those of this world; [with] more self-government, greater habits of devotion, purer aims than other men... We must rebuke the chilling, cramping, debasing trade-spirit of the present day by the visible nobleness of a willing self-sacrifice. We must be felt to be true men, really serving God and our neighbours." [31]

26. *Charge,* 1866, p. 10.   27. *Charge,* 1845, p. 6.
28. *Ibid.,* p. 16.   29. *Addresses to the Candidates for Ordination,* p. 103.
30. "The Inward Call," in *ibid.,* p. 13.   31. *Charge,* 1843, p. 38.

That Wilberforce, as he constantly confessed, fell far below these lofty standards need not qualify his sincerity in setting them both for himself and for the clergy of his diocese. His sincerity received expression in his painstaking devotion to the preparation and examination of candidates for ordination, the first general reform he initiated and the one that probably mattered most to the clergy themselves. Ordination was in some dioceses at this time formal, in others informal, but in most insipid and uninspiring. Bagot had allowed an archdeacon to examine for him and had contented himself with preaching a charge to the candidates and conducting the ordination service in the Cathedral. Candidates were lodged at hotels in Oxford, and the experience was often as much a pleasant University reunion as a serious final preparation for the work of a parish priest. Even before he was enthroned as bishop, Wilberforce determined upon a series of radical changes. "My wish," he wrote Louisa Noel from Cuddesdon, "has been to bring all the candidates as much as possible under my own eye, and to secure all opportunities of social, friendly, and spiritual intercourse." He would hold the examinations at Cuddesdon, and require candidates to assemble for three days of questions and prayers. The ordination would take place in Christ Church Cathedral on Sunday. "I shall lodge as many as I can in the house, the others in the village round. Oh I earnestly trust that God may enable me to make this season a blessed sowing-time." [32]

With the exception of the fact that he soon performed the ordination services in parishes throughout the diocese, "so as to show the Church in action as widely as possible," [33] he followed the pattern outlined in this letter throughout his years as bishop of Oxford. Candidates were summoned a month in advance and requested to submit credentials for examination a week before their arrival. These included testimonial letters from beneficed clergymen, certification of baptism, of attendance at required University lectures, and of appointment to some clerical post. On at least one occasion, candidates were also required to submit a sample sermon.[34] Accompanying each summons was a list of the subjects for examination.[35] Wilberforce had a reputation as a tough examiner, and took great pains to read the papers with care.

Not every candidate who presented himself on Thursday remained to

32. December 12, 1845, Ashwell and Wilberforce, *Life,* I, 323.
33. October, 1848, BD, I. C194.   34. ODP, c. 239.
35. Typical subjects: Old Testament, New Testament, doctrine and liturgy, parochial duties. Typical of the questions asked in the latter exam: "How do you deal with the landlord of the public house in your parish." For candidates for priests' orders: "State what you experience to have been the greatest impediment to your ministry during the last year, either from within or from without." Francis Pigou, who recalled these questions in his autobiography, recalled as well the answer of one candidate to the second question: "My rector" (Francis Pigou, *Phases of My Life* [London, 1898], pp. 124–125).

receive the sacrament of ordination the following Sunday. Some withdrew their intention before arriving at Cuddesdon. Others came, often after a previously unsuccessful session, to try once again to satisfy both themselves and their bishop as to their readiness. "I had a moving interview with Mr. Dakes," Wilberforce reported to Louisa Noel during the December 1846 ordination. "He still does not come. He hopes that the time will come when he may: but at present he is not in his own judgment fit. There seems to be nothing morbid in his resolution." [36] Throughout the three days the candidates saw Wilberforce constantly, and in the surviving accounts of the experience all agree that it was his presence that gave coherence to the convocation. He determined to make not simply the examinations but the experience as a whole the focus of the retreat. He took pains over the addresses he delivered twice a day to the candidates, and in more informal meetings with them would whenever possible rehearse some of the particular difficulties they might expect to encounter in the parish to which they had been called.[37] Perhaps the most evocative of the several existing accounts of these weeks at Cuddesdon is that by J. W. Burgon, written the week after his ordination in 1848 to his brother-in-law Henry John Rose.

It was impossible not to admire the Bishop's tact. On Thursday after dinner (which followed Chapel immediately) and on Friday after the less substantial repast at which we all (about fifty in number) were assembled, as soon as the servants had withdrawn, the Bishop raised his voice and his head, and in the cleverest manner possible made the conversation general. He addressed a remark to one of his chaplains, and speedily, in reply to the question of some one present, made some remarks on ruri-decanal associations, education of the poor, prayers for the lower orders, and all those topics which were sure to be most interesting to those present. This was excellently well done, for all were entertained, all *edified,* and it was optional to anyone present to ask whatever questions he chose. . .

I must tell you that about forty had beds provided in the palace, his plan being to have all candidates for his guests. . . He also contrived to see everyone twice—some even three times—and not only remarked on the papers (which it was clear he had *read)* but discoursed leisurely and kindly on one's prospects, hopes, wishes, etc., etc. It really was most admirable. . . On the Saturday morning we all partook of the Eucharist; and in the evening he gave a very powerful and eloquent charge, one of a series which when collected will form a commentary on the Ordination Service.

Burgon was a Tractarian; Wilberforce, who was not, did not hesitate to air with him his longstanding disagreement with the Puseyite doctrine of sin after baptism.

I supposed (and still believe) that Grace is given in Baptism. He says, 'No, but the dead bud is grafted into the living stock,—man's fallen nature into the Body

36. December 26, 1846, BD, II. F.   37. Pigou, *Phases of My Life,* p. 127.

of Christ.' All absolution is moreover simply declaratory 'thy sins are forgiven thee'—spoken by Christ himself—revealed a fact, not made it. (Here I think there is a fallacy.) I am to read Jacobson—Hooker's Sermon—Luther on Galatians.

Disagreement with his bishop's theology did not temper Burgon's enthusiasm for his mannner, nor his respect for the dignity of his position. "The history of Sunday"—again to Rose—"you can fancy very well.

All was most solemn and reverently managed. Not like the Archbishop of York [Musgrave] who, I am shocked to hear, walks round the Communion rails putting a single hand on the heads of the kneeling candidates for Orders—*our* Bishop sits in the best throne the Dean of Christ Church will provide, and conveys the gift of clasping each head in his hands. Nothing *could* be better done. . . I really must say the Bishop of Oxford's entire deportment is truly Apostolical, and I shall henceforth be his defender, as in duty bound.[38]

Burgon's commentary is all the more valuable in that he was not predisposed to admire Wilberforce unduly. Other accounts, such as that by a Reverend C. H. Grundy who was ordained in the fall of 1869, gush unstinted praise and are therefore of less value. Grundy's detailed report does confirm the fact that Wilberforce took as much pains with ordinations at the end of his Oxford regime as he had at the beginning.[39]

Without doubt the system met with success. Yet Wilberforce believed that it took more than a few days of solemn concourse to prepare men for Orders. From the first he determined to found a theological college within the diocese.[40] He did not consider undergraduate life as led at Oxford and Cambridge particularly conducive to the study and contemplation he felt the ministry should require of its prospective members. Not that he wished candidates to eschew the pleasures of that life. They should be allowed to enjoy them unalloyed, then placed under the stricter regimen of seminary life. What he objected to was any attempt to combine the two steps; on these grounds he opposed an honors program in theology at Oxford. Sacred and profane could not successfully be mixed.

Although the new college was to foster the study of God's word and God's truth, that study was to be only a means to the end of producing "an able minister of God's word." What Wilberforce wanted was the opportunity to bring together a group of young men for a prolonged and

38. January 5, 1849, E. M. Goulbourn, *Life of John William Burgon*, 2 vols. (London, 1892), I, 158–161. Henry Rose was a younger brother of the High Church theologian Hugh James Rose.

39. C. H. Grundy, "Wilberforce in Ember Week," *The Church of England Pulpit and Ecclesiastical Review,* May 29, 1880, pp. 259ff. ("The Bishop examined us in the Hall, made us laugh in the dining-room, made us cry in the Chapel, yet somehow there seemed no incongruity between the three.") See also the recollections of J. R. Woodford, one of Wilberforce's examining chaplains in Ashwell and Wilberforce, *Life,* I, 330.

40. Two had already been established, at Chichester and Wells.

intensive period of preparation of mind and soul for the role of parish priest. His intention and his goal were practical, plainly stated in a series of suggestions to students which he composed upon the occasion of the opening of Cuddesdon College in 1854.

I. Threefold object of residence here—1. Devotion. 2. Parochial Work. 3. Theological Reading.
II. Aids to be given—to Daily Prayer. Opportunities of private seclusion. Constant access at all times to the Bishop and the Principal.
III. Aids in learning Parochial Work—Schools. Visiting. Sermons. Missionary meetings.
IV. Dangers as well as advantages of Collegiate Life—The habits of lounging. Waste of time. How such habits will bear upon future ministry. Habits of self-denial to be learned here.
V. Shortness of the residence of some makes the amount of reading necessarily small. Sketch of studies—Scripture. Pearson and Hooker. Apostolic Fathers. Such lectures as may be obtained from occasional Lecturers.
VI. Great importance of *conduct* in the eyes of others. The *Village* and *University* Men.[41]

Wilberforce hoped above all else that his college would temper the mind of university men to suit the manner of village work. In a letter to Charles Anderson in 1858, he complained that the students devoted too little attention to parochial duties. "They are fond of speculating on what the *early* Church did (which is a very vague term) and then they lose sight of what the English Church orders to be done and does by her rubrics when interpreted in a common sense way." [42] When he worried the following year that his choice for vice-principal, Edward King, might not have the scholarly credentials for the post, J. W. Burgon wrote to reassure him.

King is the right man. You do not want Hebrew, my dear Lord. You want to make men *read their Bibles,* and *understand their Prayer Books; know how to prepare children for confirmation,* and *imbibe the pastoral spirit.* You want to make *exemplary parish priests*—good *preachers*—good *teachers*—good *visitors of the poor.*[43]

That was precisely what Wilberforce wanted. The story of the founding of Cuddesdon College has been told fully and well by Owen Chadwick. Its importance in this history of its founder lies in his intention that it serve a particular end, one which reflected his determination to preach direct, soul-saving religion to the people of his diocese.[44]

Difficulties did not end with the training of clergymen. They had to be

41. Ashwell and Wilberforce, *Life,* II, 245–246.
42. November 28, 1858, BD, I. C190.
43. February 11, 1859. Quoted in Owen Chadwick, *The Founding of Cuddesdon* (Oxford, 1954), p. 98.
44. See below, page 197, for the account of Wilberforce's early difficulties in achieving that goal.

placed. Bishops were believed to have vast powers of patronage. Most wished they had, for it would have made the task of filling their parishes with worthy incumbents far simpler than it was. When Wilberforce went to Oxford in 1845, the bishop had the patronage of only fourteen benefices out of three hundred fifty-six; only three were in towns of any size: Oxford, Banbury, and Aylesbury. By the time of his translation to Winchester he had secured a total of one hundred and three from the much larger total of six hundred and thirty.[45] Even this improvement left him in direct control of but one in seven livings. For the rest, he was compelled to cajole the patrons—colleges, gentry, corporations, Crown, clergymen—to appoint men who might be expected to serve the needs of the parish and satisfy the particular requirements of their benefactors.[46] The case of the vacancy in the vicarage of Astwood in 1856 exemplifies as well as any the way in which Wilberforce scurried to get his man home. In April the Duke of Bedford presented the incumbent of Astwood to the living of Woburn. Astwood's patron, "the Lord Chancellor (on Lord Spencer's, who on Lady Lyttelton's, request) offers it to Thomas Burrow's brother-in-law. [This from one of Wilberforce's diocesan notebooks.] He finds that it is only worth £128 net and is obliged to decline. Cumberlege [the original incumbent] applies for his nephew late of our college: I apply to the Chancellor who says he gave [the chance to nominate to] the D. of Bedford after Lord Spencer. So I to D. of Bedford who May 12, 1856 comes to me at Harts, and assents to Cumberlege's appointment." A second entry on the same page, dated March 16, 1859, records the successful sequel. "Charles Cumberlege doing well. . . Brings some well prepared [confirmation] candidates to Crawley." A further note suggests, however, that Astwood vicarage may have required further episcopal solicitude: "Marries 1860 Miss Williams who will have £2000 a year. He very anxious to restore the church but Mrs. Williams a sad opponent." [47]

45. Ashwell and Wilberforce, *Life,* I, 351, 381. Of those Wilberforce secured, four were in Reading, two in Oxford, and twelve in other towns of some importance in the diocese. Most of the new parishes came into his hands as a result of subdivision, or the exchange with diocesan patrons of livings in his possession outside the diocese.

46. Wilberforce did not altogether oppose the practice of simony. He regretted the existence of advowsons separate from the possession of land. But, he once wrote a clergyman, "I do not venture to pronounce it to be wrong; and where therefore I find it existing I should have no scruple in acting on it and trying to extract good from it." To the Reverend Stobard, December 15, 1862, BD, I. C197.

47. Diocesan Note Book, ODP, d.178. 32. A letter to Lord Aberdeen in 1853 shows Wilberforce attempting to consolidate his patronage. "May I ask whether you would be disposed to enter into any arrangement under the Act of the last session for the exchange of any Crown livings *in* the Diocese of Oxford for any of the Patronage of the Bishop *out* of his Diocese?" Aberdeen replied that he had not known of the Act, and that no other bishops had written with similar requests, but that he would bear it in mind (Add Mss. 43251.81; 43251.98).

The notebooks in which remarks of this sort were recorded helped keep Wilberforce in touch with his clergy. Whenever he visited a parish, or whenever special circumstances required him to attend to its well-being, he would note the particulars on an allotted page. In this way, during his twenty-four years as bishop, he compiled hundreds of minute histories of his year-by-year dealings with the diocese. The notebooks and the copies of his official correspondence which survive [48] suggest the limited extent to which he was able to implement the ideal of a whole-heartedly devout, hard-working clergy, and the energy it took to attain even the success which was his. Many times he would have to persuade men too old to keep up their work that the time had come to lay it in another's hands. To one such he wrote that "the infirmities of age come through God's merciful appointment so very gradually upon a robust man that he is generally the last to perceive their increasing effect, and it is therefore highly probable that you may hardly be aware to what a degree the slow march of age has lessened your power of service." [49] Of another old and more pathetic man, the vicar of West Hendred, he noted: "Out of sight for debt. A most grievous case. Curate charged [he] used to leap ditches to escape sheriff's officers." [50] A few instances recall the gaunt miseries of the Crawleys of Barsetshire. "Confirmed here [Brill] again to please old J. B. [Baron, the perpetual curate.] A small confirmation. Snow on the ground. Poor Baron in a peck of trouble about harmonium, school matters etc. Had followed six children and their mother to the grave." [51] Wilberforce handled most clerical difficulties with forthrightness. He was anxious to persuade the Reverend George Pretyman, a notorious pluralist, to resign the living of Aylesbury, where he had accomplished little for the Church, and take instead the country parish of Barley. But, he warned him bluntly: "Unless you can trust yourself to bear the wearing and irritating treatment which you are sure to meet with from its rough tithe-paying dissenters, without losing your hearty interest in their spiritual welfare, I do not think it would contribue to your happiness to take it." [52]

Despite corrective legislation, pluralism and nonresidence remained a thorn. As one instance, the following letter, written in reply to the Reverend G. W. St. John, rector of Bladon, illustrates the legal snarls these

48. These letters have been transcribed from almost illegible copies by the Reverend R. K. Pugh. I have used his copies and record his permission to allow me to do so with thanks.
49. To the Reverend J. Penson, December 25, 1853, Letter Book, BD, d.148. 44.
50. Diocesan Note Book, ODP, d.550. 102.
51. Diocesan Note Book, ODP, d.178. 89.
52. January 6, 1853, Letter Book, BD, d.204. 339. Of Pretyman, Wilberforce wrote once in exasperation: "Oh the lifelong mischief this miserable pluralism has done as it has fattened Pretyman for the day of slaughter!" (Diocesan Note Book, ODP, d.178. 115).

problems engendered. St. John claimed he had no legal call to provide for duty in Woodstock chapel, which was within his benefice. Wilberforce stated his readiness to countenance a temporary curtailment of services, but added:

I consent to this as a provisional arrangement mainly from your stating to me what is quite new to me, that the Woodstock House was given by Bishop Fell [of Oxford (1625–1686)] for the use of the Rector of Bladon and not the minister of Woodstock. Upon this point I must beg you to give me as full information as you are able. I shall be glad if you can send me Ist the exact words of Bishop Fell's gift. II. the grounds of your opinion that Woodstock Chapel is not an ordinary consecrated Chapel of Ease to Bladon III. a statement of any payment which is made for the service of Woodstock Chapel: its amount; the persons by whom it is paid; and the date of its commencement. IV. A Statement of the Exact Sum for which the tithes of Bladon are commuted; and whether any part of those tithes are paid in respect of Woodstock.[53]

Such a paragraph is a reminder that Wilberforce had to deal with clergymen not only as minister but, with the aid of the diocesan chancellor, as lawyer.[54] Tithes and title deeds were as much a part of his daily life as charges and exhortations. He must not simply implore a man to hold services; he must first make certain of his legal grounds, and then implore. Even so, he could not always expect to be obeyed without a tedious fight. He tried to make whatever accommodation he believed he properly could. To a clergyman unwilling to undertake two services each Sunday: "I could not allow the double duty to be discontinued; still less that you seek another parish from which to serve Wexham. But if you think, upon full consideration, that it would aid you if you obtained for a time a license of non-residence, to seek another duty, and leave me to appoint a curate to Wexham, I will allow you to make a trial of that plan." [55]

On matters of morals and public conduct Wilberforce took a far more rigid stand. In the case of one clergyman—"in the highest degree unclerical; devoted to Hunting, Shooting, Fishing, and Races"—he applied for advice to the Archbishop and finally turned the case over to him for his private judgment, though aware that the man's position as a Fellow of St. Johns, Oxford, would make his action most unpopular.[56] Even in in-

53. August 19, 1848, Letter Book, BD, d.209. 36–38.

54. Wilberforce was capably served by his two chancellors, Dr. Joseph Phillimore, who was also chancellor of Worcester and Bristol, and his son, Sir Robert Joseph Phillimore, also chancellor of Salisbury and subsequently dean of the Court of Arches.

55. To the Reverend A. A. Kempe, September 2, 1848, Letter Book, BD, d.209. 73. This compromise, if adopted, may well have worked to Wilberforce's advantage, since it gave him the opportunity of placing a curate of his choice in a parish where the rector was unwilling to exert himself.

56. Letter Books, BD, d.204. 220, 222ff; d.209. 130, 154. The sportsman, the Reverend F. Burgess, was known as "the lying parson." He shocked Wilberforce by remarking to a mutual acquaintance that he considered *the* one day of the year to be that of the Goodwood races.

stances of this sort a bishop's hands were tied by more than opinion. So exasperated was Wilberforce by the so-called Brogden case, in which the rector of Deddington, a debtor and drunkard, refused to countenance the appointment of a curate in his place, that he agitated successfully in Parliament for a law clarifying a bishop's power to intervene.[57] In dealing with the adulterous rector of Woughton on the Green, the Reverend Francis Rose, Wilberforce found himself forced to appeal to the Queen's Bench for the right to remain unsatisfied with Rose's meager certificate of good behavior, following a three-year suspension, and was less than overjoyed when Rose returned to the diocese as rector of Balking with Woolstone, Berkshire, soon after.[58]

Probably the most exasperating and surely the most prolonged of Wilberforce's parochial battles was fought with the Reverend H. Paddon of Wycombe. Paddon made enemies wherever he set his foot. One of the first of Wilberforce's letters to him attempted to settle a squabble between the rector, who wanted to rid himself of an organist he suspected of ritualism, and the parishioners, who retaliated, once the organist had been driven off, by locking up the organ. The following year, 1849, began his never-ending trouble with curates. Paddon sent Wilberforce a sermon preached by his curate, which Paddon declared contained "fundamental [*i.e.* Tractarian] errors." Wilberforce replied that it did not, and advised the curate to leave. In 1853 Paddon requested a three-year leave for reasons of ill health, one of the two grounds upon which such leave could be granted. This Wilberforce agreed to, if Paddon would agree, in turn, to a suitable curate, and to abstain from the business of the parish while on leave. The parish, meanwhile, objected that Paddon was not in ill health, but that his request stemmed from the fact that he had hired a house for three years at Rugby to educate his sons and did not want to sacrifice the rent. Wilberforce pressed him to undergo a medical examination. Paddon, who had returned to Wycombe to superintend the hay-making on his property and appeared in good health, refused to do more than submit the certificate of a Rugby doctor which Wilberforce considered insufficient. All this time Paddon had continued to harass the

57. 34 and 35 Vict., c.45. See debates in *Hansard,* 3rd ser., CCI (May 17, 1870), 791–795; CCII (July 4, 1870), 1344–1346. From Wilberforce's diocesan notes on the parish of Deddington: "Rev. J. Brogden. '56. March. His difficulties increasing. He says he must speedily send his wife into union etc., that I resolved to starve him out of his miserable vicarage etc. March 10, '58. Confirm here. At first a miserable confirmation from children in aisles etc. After they gone all mended. John H. Burgess curate [the living was at the time sequestered.] A good deal of opposition, but from bad people... Jan. 19, 1859. Sequestration withdrawn. Oct. 11, 1861. Yesterday poor Brogden taken up drunk by policemen on the road. Had got £5 from a grace spent it in Brandy and drink... Ash Wed. '64. Poor Brogden after service ordered by me and makes himself drunk at Public inn and in afternoon is struck down senseless with apoplexy and never recovers!" (ODP, d.178. 178).

58. Letter Book, BD, d.209. 134; also ODP, b.71. 52.

curates whom Wilberforce had introduced in his place. "No man worth having will take such a post," Wilberforce wrote him in December 1853, "to be continually interfered with; and therefore I say, again, for three years, give up the matter to him." All to no avail. By November 1854 Wilberforce moved to sequester the living on the grounds of unjustifiable nonresidence. "I now entirely abandon the hope of doing anything more than I can enforce by law and solemnly cast upon you the responsibility of all the loss of souls which will be entailed on it by your having defeated my efforts."

Wilberforce appointed two curates and was pleased with their progress when he came to confirm in Wycombe in March 1856. "All different since Rice and Turton [the curates]," he noted. "Some 120 confirmation candidates instead of 30. D. G. But what when poor Paddon returns." Paddon was ready to return by June 1856, although a group of parishioners had offered him £100 a year if would agree to stay away. The rest of Wilberforce's notes on the parish spin out the dreary tale.

1856–7. He quarrels with the Committee of the National School and goes to British School instead. I license curate and enjoin him on attendance.

November 7, 1857. I try again in God's sight to win the poor man over, but all in vain. . . He wrote me a bitter denunciatory letter. . . I tried to make peace.

1858. At last I heal the quarrel between the school committee.

December, 1858. He quarrels with his new curate Johnson.

October 11, 1861. Hear that Paddon gone out for three months leaving all in charge of a deacon!

Confirm here March 24, 1862. Paddon giving my health at luncheon. Begging for more frequent confirmations. Lamenting dissent. No chance of amendment until the Church restored.[59]

Without Paddon's side of the story, we cannot be sure that the fault was all with him. He was a Low Churchman and believed that Wilberforce hounded him for that reason. He had his faction in Wycombe, though apparently a small one. The long history is worth the telling for the light it sheds on the limited extent of a bishop's power to rid himself and his diocese of a trial such as Paddon, and for the impression it conveys of the perpetual care that a bishop had to devote to the nurture of his clerical charges.

Fortunately, many Oxfordshire clergymen did their work in a useful and generally competent manner. The notebooks contain, along with accounts of squabbles small and very small, many entries similar to the following: "warmhearted, kind, useful man"; "very much in earnest";

59. Correspondence and notes on the Paddon controversy are in BD, I. C197; Letter Books, BD, d.148. 34–35, 48–50, 161–162; d.209. 83ff, 135–136; Diocesan Note Book, ODP, d.178, 591ff.

"moderate low churchman. Very anxious about his parish"; "active little man"; "a very excellent man." Some of these were younger men, very much of the breed of Wilberforce himself: a new school, and so described by the *Bristol Times* in December, 1847:

The new clergyman is of the new school—zealous, anxious, ever in his work. He is evidently one of the race of clergymen who have in late years sprung up to replace the old high and dry denomination, and compete in energy and zeal with the Evangelical order. If some of them have lacked discretion [a reference presumably to ritualistic experiment], none of them have been deficient in devotedness, and many have awakened a new spirit in the parishes over which they were placed, filling churches that before, morning and evening, boasted but a cheerless few, and crowding schools that before were neglected and in decay.[60]

Among this new breed were men such as W. J. Butler, who received the living of Wantage, in the gift of the dean and chapter of Windsor, in June 1846. He had gone to visit the parish the month before and found the church in decay and the services dreary. "I only wonder so many people can sit through such discourses," he wrote his wife. "I was as fidgety as possible, and were I likely to undergo such things continually I must join one of the sects with which Wantage is rife."[61] Butler soon took hold and stirred the parish to life and to action, leading a campaign for drains and gas while increasing church services and enlarging the schools. Wilberforce, though for a time worried that Butler might leave the Church for Rome, delighted in the work he had carried forward in Wantage. "More by far is doing than in any other parish in my diocese. I rejoice and I tremble," he wrote Louisa Noel, "I wanted to strengthen his hands: being sure that *shewing* the Church in action is a great part of our duty."[62]

Wantage, whatever its liabilities as a clerical post, was, at least, a town of three thousand, in which Butler presumably could find companions to share his interests and concerns. Other clergymen, with parishes buried in rural wilderness, faced the same problems Butler faced, and more beside. Francis Pigou, when he went as curate to Stoke Talmadge in 1855, found himself fifteen miles from the railway. His stipend was £100 per year, and £25 went the first year to pay a college debt. He had hoped to marry but could not now afford to do so. "The Church," he wrote in his memoirs, "was in a woeful condition. Cocks and hens roosted on weekdays in the pulpit." The Methodist preacher, a butcher, "as a token of 'Godly concord' and the 'Union of Christendom'" lent Pigou the lamps from his chapel so that he could conduct an afternoon service in the wintertime.[63] Despite what must have been an achingly lonely situation, Pigou stayed on and did what he could to improve the life of the Church and the parish.

60. A. J. Butler, *Life and Letters of William John Butler* (London, 1897), pp. 55–56.
61. *Ibid.,* pp. 36–37.   62. March 30, 1848, BD, II. F.
63. Pigou, *Phases of My Life,* p. 133.

Although Wilberforce by no means founded singlehandedly the "new school," he can be counted among its earliest and most successful products. He remained an ardent exponent of its social doctrine, enthusiast in the cause of the Church and champion of its place in society. By the attention he paid to the clergy who worked for him he won the respect and support of a great many; through them he broadcast his enthusiasm for the Church across the diocese, and in this manner did much to alter the life of many a parish.

Wilberforce entered directly, as well as vicariously, into parish life. The New Parishes Bill of 1843 had provided for the division of parishes into smaller, more manageable units. Wilberforce was quick to take advantage of the opportunity, and it was largely by means of a succession of Orders in Council sanctioning such divisions that he increased the livings in his diocese from three hundred and fifty-six to six hundred and thirty. The consequences were not always entirely beneficial. Hook at Leeds found that subdivision brought problems of its own. Benefactors were no longer willing to subscribe to a general fund for the city as a whole. Each wished to support only his own parish. Parochialism thus complicated the work of any citywide charitable or religious organization and "parochial" began to be used as a term of derogation, describing a narrow and confining approach to difficulties many felt should receive broader treatment and solution.[64] Wilberforce, whose problems were as much rural as urban, fared better than Hook, though it was often difficult enough to parcel out country souls, especially when no church existed to accommodate the newly separated parishioners. The perpetual curacy of Longcot cum Fernham, for example, was separated from the vicarage of Shrevenham in the late forties. The curate, the Reverend John Hughes, wrote Wilberforce, complaining of the unfairness of requiring Fernham to pay a £300 annual rent charge, "where there is [at Fernham] no church and no room which could be made available for Church services, the cottages being all of the lowest description and sort." [65] Wilberforce was in this case able to resolve Hughes' problem. Pasted alongside his letter in the diocesan record book is a photograph of Fernham Church with the note that it was consecrated by the bishop on June 22, 1860.

64. W. R. W. Stephens, *The Life and Letters of Walter Farquhar Hook,* II, 254. Wilberforce remained a strong supporter of multiplicity. In a speech in the Lords on a Church Building Bill in 1854, he warned of the dangers in tearing down older, smaller churches in the cities in order to build large, central ones. The shock would be great to those who had worshipped for years in the same building *(Hansard,* 3rd ser. CXXXIII [May 12, 1854], 218–222; 229–230.)

65. ODP, b. 71. 338.

Church-building, in consequence of subdivisions and of the need in many undivided parishes to accommodate increasing populations, became one of Wilberforce's main concerns. Churches were often built in the nineteenth century by proprietors or developers in the hope of attracting a superior class of purchaser to their estates.[66] No developer would have bothered with Fernham; no one but its curate, its rural dean, and its bishop gave much thought to it at all, or to the multitude of parishes like it. Wilberforce was ready to go to work for his Fernhams. His correspondence on the construction, decoration, and restoration of churches and rectories is voluminous and incredibly detailed. To one churchwarden he wrote that he could agree to his plan for restoration, but for the proposal to substitute slate for lead roofs. "This would be a great evil. It would make your Church *exceedingly cold,* no slating however good ever proving thoroughly impervious to air." [67] He urged clergymen to do all that needed to be done to make their churches what they should be and was ready to lend them whatever financial help he could. "Write to E. Street Esq. [the architect]. . . Tell him your difficulties, and ask him to give you a plan for making the interior of your Church fit for its purpose—at the least possible cost; we will all help you to raise this sum, so you shall be a restorer of the temple." [68]

The restored temple was to become a center of parish life. Wilberforce wasted no time in instructing his clergy in this regard. Only two months after he came into the diocese he was issuing orders and instructions like that sent to the rector of Great Marlow:

I am led to address you by the accounts which from various authentic sources I have received of the State of The Parish of Great Marlow, committed by God's providence to your care and government.
I. I find that you have only one sermon in your Church on Sunday.
II. That from your own age it is impossible for you to give the daily, hourly attention which such a parish needs; and
IIIly. That you have no resident curate. I beg therefore, Reverend sir, in the name of Christ and for the sake of his Church and in remembrance of that strict and fearful account which we shall both render before His judgement seat, to exort and beseech you to set yourself immediately to the due ordering of these matters.[69]

The better to see to it that parishes were given the attention they needed, and to lend his presence and his office to the efforts his clergymen were making there, Wilberforce traveled incessantly throughout the diocese. Bishop Bagot, in 1840, had nine centers for confirmation. Wilberforce by the 1860's had one hundred eighty-eight, each of which he visited tri-

66. Thompson, *English Landed Society in the Nineteenth Century,* p. 208.
67. To C. E. Barnes, September 1, 1848, Letter Book, BD, d.204. 64–65.
68. To the Reverend R. Rees, May 29, 1854, Letter Book, BD, d.148. 76.
69. To the Reverend T. T. Coxwell, February 10, 1846, Letter Book, BD, d.204. 40.

ennially.[70] In the years between 1848 and 1851 he took part in services in two hundred and sixty-three parishes, and he maintained the pace throughout his reign as bishop.[71] Clergymen did not spare him and would invent devices to make his appearances all the more effective. Burgon, for example, numbered confirmation tickets against a numbered list of names, and by each name wrote out a few words of biographical description. "The Bishop was pleased, for he was able to know *what to say*: and he told me afterwards that he *knew* the people almost before he verified their numbers." [72] Another clergyman reminisced to Canon Ashwell of the bishop's Sunday appearances: "Riding, with his servant on a horse behind him with his robes, he used to ask me as he washed his hands and robed whether there was anything I wished him to speak about. I always took advantage of his offer and whether it was about behaviour in Church, non-attendance at the Holy Communion, schools, swearing or any subject he always introduced it in a most happy and telling way; and I felt as he rode away after the service he had helped on my work in a most lasting manner." [73]

The most elaborate and impressive descents Wilberforce made upon a parish occurred during the Lenten missions which he originated and organized. The bishop, with as many as two dozen clergymen, would settle into a town for a week. Three and often four services would be held daily in the parish church, while others were conducted simultaneously in smaller, outlying parishes. Often, as at Banbury in 1850, the bishop would include an ordination among the services.

At ten o'clock [reads an account from the *Guardian*] a long procession, formed of sixteen candidates for holy orders, in surplices and hoods, followed by twelve clergy of the diocese, also in surplice, hood, and stole and lastly the Bishop, moved slowly and in silence from the vicarage to the church, preceded by the churchwardens. . . It was probably the first time that the great majority of the people present had witnessed an Ordination, or had any clear idea of the way in which the clergy of the Church receive their commission to teach and to minister Christ's sacraments. The holy communion was attended by more than one hundred and fifty persons and the whole service lasted five hours. Yet at three o'clock the Church was again full, when about one hundred and twenty young persons of Banbury were confirmed, the Bishop addressing them at some length and with much force and earnestness. And at seven another vast number, nearly three thousand, were assembled in the church, when the Bishop set before them a vivid heartstirring picture of the sinner in death and judgement, with earnest exhortations to repentance.[74]

70. R. K. Pugh, "The Episcopate of Samuel Wilberforce," unpubl. diss. in Bodleian Library, Oxford, 1957, p. 351.
71. *Charge*, 1854, pp. 2–3.   72. Goulbourn, *Burgon*, I, 202.
73. James Ashhurst to Canon A. R. Ashwell, September 18, 1874, Chichester, 25.
74. Ashwell and Wilberforce, *Life*, II, 31–32.

That was only the beginning. Wilberforce took his share of weekday meetings as well. At Henley in 1858 he preached in the parish church on six occasions, and at nearby parishes on fifteen. He saw these missions offering laymen a chance to "regard their clergy's words and work more as parts of a whole scheme, rather than the solitary sayings and doings of an individual." [75] As a symbol of that unity Wilberforce was linchpin at the center of all the sermons and celebrations. At Banbury, the *Guardian* noted, the Church had shown herself as a divinely ordered society; "her Bishop had become known to [the people] as a preacher of repentance and of the Gospel of Christ, warning, exhorting, pleading, with all earnestness, and ready to receive in private, and guide and encourage with ghostly counsel, the meanest sinner in his diocese." The mission, as Butler wrote to Keble, had represented "the assertion of a Bishop's right to deal with the souls of his diocese and not merely with his clergy." [76]

Often enough Wilberforce felt called to assert himself as ecclesiastical arbiter within the parish. Although his opportunities for legal intervention were not many, he constantly received appeals for advice and adjudication, and as constantly moved to take a hand in parish matters when he felt it his duty. Sometimes it was to recommend the solution of a difficulty that had arisen between rector and curate, which, if left to fester, might have stunted the life of the Church in the community. More frequently it was to try to settle disputes between clergymen and those to whom they were forced to look for support, whether squire or churchwardens. In the case of the former, even a bishop had to tread cautiously. The wife of one local personage took umbrage at her clergyman's insinuation that her servants had conducted themselves irreverently in church. Wilberforce was appealed to by the curate and replied:

After weighing carefully your letter I can see but one course for you to take. It is clear that Mrs. Jenney (than whom no one living would be more unwilling to encourage irreverence at Church) believes that you are deceived in supposing that her servants behave ill. This must be from her supposing that you cannot perfectly see what passes in your chancel *pew*. I therefore advise you to remove the pews on each side of the chancel and replace them by open seats, with open desks before them set Cathedral-wise. There will then be no shelter for irreverent persons and the matter in dispute will at once decide itself.

The Jenneys did not take kindly to this solution, and Wilberforce was obliged to tell Mr. Kelke, the curate, to give them a soft answer. To Mr. Jenney he wrote as well, expressing the "earnest hope that you will meet Mr. Kelke halfway in the reestablishing of that good understanding between the Manor House and the Parsonage which is so essential to the well-being of the parish." [77]

75. *Charge,* 1869, pp. 6–7.   76. Butler, *Life and Letters,* pp. 75–76.
77. To the Reverend H. Kelke, February 28, 1848; to —— Jenney, Esq., April 11, 1848. Letter Book, BD, d.204. 193, 212.

Churchwardens could make a good deal of mischief if so inclined. In many Victorian cities, Nonconformists ran for the office, won election, and once elected, voted to dispense altogether with the rates. Few parishes endured contentions as acrimonious or as prolonged as those that plagued Leicester, where the Tories determined to levy the church rate as political revenge for the Liberals' Corporation Act and the Liberals in turn elected a town councilor who had gone to jail for nonpayment of his rates.[78] Many fair-minded citizens argued that there was little sense in paying rates to support a church where all the seats might be privately owned. Even Hook, who was able to establish friendly enough relations with his Chartist churchwardens had to forego the rate and rely upon voluntary contributions. Wilberforce's difficulties were not usually on so grand a scale, but they were constant enough to vex him and his clergy. Butler, when he wished to restore his church, called a vestry meeting, not to ask for a rate but simply to explain to the parish what it was he had in mind. Extreme Protestants, however, saw to it that the meeting degenerated into an attack on Butler's supposed Popery. Finally, one of Butler's allies rose and denounced what he injudiciously called the rabble. "The word rabble set the whole meeting by the ears, and he ended his speech with much difficulty." [79] Three months later Butler assembled a few influential parishioners at the vicarage and won approval for the restoration. Often the vicar was not made of as stern a stuff as Butler and felt compelled to call upon his bishop. The rector of North Leigh was charged by his churchwardens with neglecting his duties and with a further catalogue of offenses large and small. Wilberforce asked him to account for himself and after he had done so, Wilberforce replied to the wardens in a tone suggesting his impatience with what he clearly considered a carping succession of criticisms, and his dismay at their own reputed negligence.

I lost no time in requiring from Mr. Gillam a reply to the articles alleged against him in your presentations. His reply admits only one. He allows that heavy beasts have occasionally been turned into the Church Yard. He alleges that the presence of pigs in it, is from your neglecting to repair the churchyard gate and the consequent straying in of pigs. He positively asserts that he is quite regular in beginning Service. He denies neglecting sick people or refusing to administer the communion to *qualified* persons: he asserts that he was diligent in attending the School till he was withstood in performing that duty. He denies having injured the Glebe or that any son of his pursues game during the hours of divine Service. He declares that he pays to the Clerk for the land a higher rent than Mr. Druce gave as its value. He further makes grievous complaints of his treatment by the late and present churchwardens: alleging—(1) their entire neglect of the duties of their office—neglect in supplying Sacramental Wine: in maintaining order in

78. A. Temple Patterson, *Radical Leicester* (Leicester, 1954), pp. 248–254.
79. Butler, *Life and Letters,* pp. 84–85.

the Church: in attending there themselves. (2) their disrespectful treatment of himself—amounting in the case of the ex-churchwarden to absolute insult, (3) permitted abuse of a Church Charity whereby bread left for distribution at the Church is given by a dissenting baker to parties at the school, closely adjoining his meeting house. In a word he alleges that opposition, unkindness, and ill-treatment have thwarted uniform and earnest efforts on his part to promote the welfare of his parish.

I must now request you to inform me whether you are prepared to tender legal proof of the Charges Mr. Gillam so absolutely denies: and which he attributes to that opposition which he asserts has withstood a faithful ministry for its fidelity.[80]

Wilberforce did not by any means stand out in all cases against the judgment of parish churchwardens. Several months after his letter to North Leigh, he received a memorial from the squire and churchwardens of Pudworth opposing the return to duty of their rector who had been on leave. Wilberforce wrote the man implying that it might well be better for all concerned if he stayed away.[81]

Without question parish disputes would have been less frequent and a good deal more well-mannered had it not been for the Church's never-ending worries about money. For years much of the Church's income had come to it from pew rents and rates. By mid-century, however, the Church itself was questioning the first while the country at large had debated and in many instances decided to oppose the latter. Clergymen were generally agreed that church accommodation should be free and open to all. Wilberforce had doubts as to the propriety and more pronounced reservations as to the effectiveness of abolishing pews altogether. But he could no more than any other bishop rely upon the traditional forms of clerical income, including both pew rents and rates, to support the expanded ecclesiastical activities he wished to promote in his diocese. His plans for the division of parishes meant that endowment money would often have to be stretched thin. Subdivision was certainly one explanation for the figures cited by Wilberforce in his 1860 Charge concerning the large number of poor livings under his care. The situation demanded either a clergy recruited from the ranks of the independently rich, or a vigorous public campaign to raise money for the further endowment of impoverished benefices. Wilberforce pressed for the second solution while relying heavily upon the first.

The diocesan papers illustrate the extent to which clergymen remained willing to undertake large-scale improvements within their parishes. Many used their own money to repair and maintain the parsonage and adjoining farm. Many more appear to have contributed in great measure to the restoration of their churches and to the foundation of

80. October 23, 1848, Letter Book, BD, d.209. 99–101.
81. To the Reverend G. Curtis, January 5, 1849, Letter Book, BD, d.204. 233–234.

parish schools.[82] Wilberforce kept his eye upon those whom he knew to be rich and pressed them hard. He recorded in his notebook in March 1855 that the vicar of Spelsbury had just come into a fortune and had talked of resigning. "I tell Casey [the curate] I shall remonstrate and try to get him to give some of the profit of his wealth to the parish." [83] For every vicar of Spelsbury, there was at least one other clergyman at a corresponding point on the other end of the financial scale. One such, the Reverend Edmund Peel, though by no means a poor man, found himself nominated by the bishop to an incumbency with a tiny endowment and no parsonage. Peel printed a circular requesting the aid of fellow clergymen and laymen.

The Parish of Toot Balden, near Nuneham in Oxfordshire, contains a population of 300, chiefly poor people. It is an incumbency with an endowment of £30 p. a., but with no house of any kind for the residence of the incumbent. The Bishop of the Diocese has kindly offered the living to me; and I am willing to undertake its duties if there is any prospect of a house being provided.

Peel reported that he could expect some help from the Diocesan Society (presumably the Society for the Augmentation of Small Benefices) and the Bounty Board, but that he would be forced to raise £700 privately. He pledged £210 himself; Wilberforce pledged £20. On the circular which is pasted into the diocesan records, a handwritten list of names and contributions totaling £638.15.0 is appended.[84]

That Peel could without much apparent difficulty come within £60 of his goal suggests what was true of nineteenth-century ecclesiastical fund raising: astonishing amounts could be collected once clergy and laymen set themselves the task. The device of the offertory was only just beginning to be generally used; many considered it a Papist custom. Instead, dignified begging letters went out, and rich individuals were none too discreetly dunned; sermons were preached and societies formed. Somehow the money was almost always forthcoming. Manchester raised £12,000, Glasgow £20,000 "in a few days" in 1836 following the announcement of a church-building scheme. A. C. Tait, when bishop of London, in nine months received over £100,000 with £92,000 more

82. For the repair, renovation and enlargement of the parish church of Drayton Paislow in 1865, for example: of the total of £734.15.11 collected, £300 came from the rector. The rest from ratepayers (£300), the Diocesan Church Building Society (£50), and miscellaneous contributions (ODP, b.72. 178). In Garsington three schools, with a total enrollment of about 130–140 children and infants, were supported by "the children's pence, a government grant, and subscription, the rector making up the deficiency" (ODP, c.335. 167).

83. ODP, d.178. 465.

84. ODP, b.70, 48. Wilberforce normally contributed £10 to every diocesan fundraising project. He appointed a special almoner to handle such requests (Ashwell and Wilberforce, *Life*, I, 354–355).

pledged, for a general course of church extension.[85] Wilberforce tapped a variety of financial sources in addition to official channels of governmental or national support such as the Ecclesiastical Commissioners and—for schools—the National Society.[86]

The Commissioners granted money to poorly endowed livings only if local contributors matched their funds. "Every £100 which our Association [the Small Benefices Society] could grant," its Report of 1864 states, "would as a common rule draw forth £100 from local funds, and the offer of £200 to the Ecclesiastical Commission would secure a like grant from them." [87] For more than particular parish needs, Wilberforce often canvassed outside the diocese, occasionally promising to allow donors or lenders the right to recommend for nomination to the livings they augmented.[88]

The major portion of the money raised came from the societies organized by Wilberforce for specific ecclesiastical purposes. He founded three major ones: in 1847, a Church Building Society; in 1857, a Spiritual Help Society, designed to augment the number of curates in the diocese; and, in 1861, a Society for the Augmentation of Small Benefices. All three burgeoned rapidly. By 1863 the expenditures of the Church Building Society had reached £104,081.[89] To aid the Society for Small Benefices, Wilberforce organized a large meeting in the Sheldonian Theatre in November 1864 and arranged to crowd the platform with a galaxy of diocesan notables. Spencer Walpole, Beresford Hope, and the Dukes of Marlborough and Buckingham attended, and Disraeli consented to speak.[90] Twelve hundred pounds was raised in one day, and more thereafter as the result of a circular sent out describing the successful meeting. The Society's report for 1865 records the Committee's belief that "this exceedingly satisfactory result is due to the earnest and active Bishop of the Diocese, who is both the founder and sustainer of this, as every other good work." [91]

85. C. J. Blomfield, *Proposals for the Creation of a Fund to be Applied to the Building and Endowment of Additional Churches in the Metropolis* (London, 1836), p. 9; R. T. Davidson and William Benham, *Life of Archibald Campbell Tait,* 2 vols. (London, 1891), I, 447.

86. Wilberforce was chary of too much government support, fearing that it might contribute to a move on the part of opponents to disestablish the Church. See his speech in the House of Lords, in *Hansard,* 3rd ser., CLIX (May 11, 1854), 133.

87. *Report of the Oxford Society for the Augmentation of Small Benefices* (Oxford, 1864), p. 2.

88. Samuel Wilberforce to Robert I. Wilberforce, December 23, 1851 (Wrangham papers). "I would propose further to give all lenders of £100 and upwards a right of recommending a young man at £60 instead of £70 charge in lieu of receiving this £10 p.a. back or £200 lenders, 2 young men."

89. *Charge,* 1863, pp. 15–17.

90. It was in this speech that he declared himself on the side of the angels.

91. *Report of the Oxford Society for the Augmentation of Small Benefices* (Oxford, 1865), p. 5.

There was truth behind the hyperbole. Wilberforce did unquestionably direct operations with extraordinary imagination, energy, and success. James Ashurst, at one time treasurer of the Church Building Society, recalled for Canon Ashwell a morning he once spent at Cuddesdon at work fund-raising with the bishop. Wilberforce had counseled Ashurst to press ahead with building schemes and not to worry if he ran out of money. Ashurst did just that and reported his consequent indebtedness.

I spoke to his Lordship and he told me to come to Cuddesdon Palace on a morning when he was disengaged. He then wrote with his own hand more than fifty letters—and added something to a good many more that I wrote and he signed. In most of the letters he reminded the gentlemen to whom he wrote of some act of kindness he had been able to do them—such as giving a confirmation, marrying a daughter, etc. and the result of that morning's work was over £2000.[92]

As an expert director, Wilberforce understood the importance of getting as much work as he could from his subordinates. A good many of the letters he wrote were to archdeacons and rural deans, passing instructions and advice, and asking for the sort of detailed information about particular parishes which only they could give. Wilberforce used his archdeacons as senior advisers. They examined at ordinations, conferred with him on general questions of diocesan policy, and often deputed for him. In this he followed the custom in other dioceses. He broke with tradition in his heavy reliance upon his rural deans, the men best qualified, in his opinion, to enrich and augment the role of the Church in the parish, and to keep him in touch with the daily loss and gain against which he measured his own failure and success. As soon as he came into the diocese, Wilberforce determined to put as much upon the shoulders of his rural deans as they could bear. He called them to Cuddesdon in January 1846 and went over their lists with them parish by parish "to get to know all the men and the wants of the places." To a clergyman whom he hoped to persuade to accept the rural deanship of Waddesdon, Wilberforce wrote a month later:

I would say that my great object is that the Rural Deans should form an easy and accurate medium of communication between me and the clergy of the Deanery, and still more that he should be a local centre of spiritual influence and brotherly union to his clergy: being himself a pattern of the true Spiritual Pastor's life, leading all around him into more zeal and more unity.[93]

Manning wrote Wilberforce to criticize him for commissioning the deans direct. He thought the plan "a bit informal in the ecclesiastical aspect," since it appeared to bypass the authority of the archdeacons, of which, of course, he was one.[94]

92. To A. R. Ashwell, September 18, 1874, Chichester, 26.
93. To ? February 7, 1846, Letter Book, BD, d.204. 33.
94. January 27, 1846, BD, I. C194.

Anxious to transmit his ideas and enthusiasm throughout the diocese as fast as he could, Wilberforce did not hesitate to remodel the hierarchy to suit his impatience. Nor is there any record of archidiaconal displeasure at the way he went about it. If he earned Manning's mild censure, he won praise from his brother, Archdeacon Robert. "I hear of you as giving quite a new example of Episcopal [illegible] as associating with your clergy and hearing their minds. I have just been at Bishopthorpe where they were very kind but did nothing. There were all my rural deans [Robert was the archdeacon of the East Riding] but there was no business. No one had any idea that the whole Diocese is asleep." [95] Cuddesdon, when the rural deans gathered for annual discussion and meditation, presented a different picture. Wilberforce wrote Louisa Noel of his satisfaction at the way his meeting for the Archdeaconry of Berkshire in January 1847 had passed off: "I did expound in chapel this time and I think got closer to them at many points. We have settled on 2 Diocesan Societies; considered rural deans duties, gone through the lay reader question, taken their parishes seriatem etc." [96] Careful attention to their particular problems encouraged the rural deans to unburden themselves to their bishop, as Wilberforce hoped that it would. He gave them direct assistance whenever he could:

I learn from your Rural Dean that your afternoon service has been disturbed by disorderly conduct and that you complain of your Churchwardens as having neglected their duty in interfering to prevent it. I have written to your Churchwardens for an explanation of this neglect. But I learn also that you intimate to the Rural Dean your intention (in consequence of these interruptions) of discontinuing your afternoon service. I am therefore obliged to call upon you to continue that service; since I cannot allow you to omit its regular performance.[97]

When Wilberforce asked to have his official residence enlarged, it was so that he could accommodate large diocesan gatherings. Regular meetings of the rural deans were just one in a series of annual convocations at the palace. Clergymen came on retreat; clergy and laymen came together for conferences. Wilberforce encouraged small and easily managed foregatherings at the palace where he could preside and gather information and ideas. Of anything larger, of a formally convoked diocesan synod, for example, he remained chary. In April 1864 at a meeting of Convocation he did suggest summoning all the clergy, the churchwardens, and other officially designated laymen for some sort of annual synod. A meeting of this kind might foster unity and would almost certainly increase lay support for the Church.[98] But when the question arose again four years later, he was far from enthusiastic. "I admit the great advantage

95. No date, Wrangham papers.   96. January 15, 1847, BD, II. F.
97. To the Reverend W. I. Baker, August 16, 1848, Letter Book, BD, d.204. 34.
98. *Chronicles of Convocation,* April 19, 1864, p. 1466.

of bringing together the Clergy and the laity, and the Clergy and laity and the Bishop, and my life has been spent inventing opportunities for that purpose, and I am happy to say with no inconsiderable success." But, he continued, what advantage did a synod have over those smaller meetings which he had already instituted? If they were to serve any purpose, they would have to be prepared to settle "small practical reforms, unifications, etc," and settle them by vote. "These external things"—the wearing of the surplice, for example—"are nothing in themselves, but they are valuable as indications. I want to ask whether questions of this kind could be discussed in the Synod, and whether the minority would take the declaration of the majority." [99] The answer implied is that they would not. Under those circumstances, better to remain content with a less all-embracing and more flexible system of deliberation, one centered not in some public meeting place like the Sheldonian but at the bishop's dining table or in the bishop's chapel, where the bishop was in better command of the situation.

Once every three years Wilberforce went forth formally into the diocese to deliver his Charge to the clergy. An Episcopal Visitation, as he undertook it, was a solemn and strenuous exercise. Forms were first dispatched from Cuddesdon to each parish, demanding a detailed tabulation of services, communicants, schools, general needs and special problems. The returned questionnaires formed the basis for the first portion of the Charge, a general accounting of the affairs of the diocese, the remainder being devoted to a discussion of ecclesiastical questions and affairs of the moment. Wilberforce delivered the Charge in a number of towns throughout the diocese, moving often very rapidly from point to point. A letter to Disraeli in October 1851, accepting his invitation to stay at Hughenden during a visitation at High Wycombe, reflects the bustle and commotion that accompanied the progress, and suggests the nervous apprehension that must have lodged in many clerical bosoms pending the arrival of such an entourage.

I shall gladly avail myself, if it is made with a full knowledge of what it is to receive a Bishop on visitation. For, imprimus, I come with my own horses for which, as essential to my progress, I must provide close to me; and secondly my chancellor Dr. Phillimore and my chaplain Archdeacon Clerke are of my party: both very agreeable men, but still men and so occupiers of chairs and beds. I think it probable that my secretary Mr. Burden will *not* be with me: but he constitutes also a part of my full 'tail.' [100]

Visitations were something of a strain on both clergy and bishop. "A Bishop's Charge is almost as fearful to him as a Regiment's charge is to

99. *Ibid.,* February 20, 1868, pp. 1220–1227.
100. October 22, 1851, Hughenden Mss. B. xxi, w.345.

it," he once wrote his son Herbert.[101] The work and worry seemed to
him well spent in return for the information and general sense of the state
of Christ's Church in the diocese which came to him through the questionnaires and through his traveling. Nor did he wait long to correct
whatever faults he might find. To one incumbent who had admitted to
celebrating communion less than monthly, Wilberforce replied with
dispatch: "I think that the fact of your having at this moment a young
curate resident makes it a good time for beginning this habit." [102] His
clergy looked upon a visitation as a chance to pass judgment of their
own on him, and were at least occasionally disappointed. "The Visitation here was spoilt by the dear Bishop's unpunctuality," wrote the Reverend William Bright, a Fellow of University College, to a friend. He
came too late for matins; there was no time to celebrate Holy Communion, "and the clergy, who were wearied with the waiting and the long
sitting were disappointed by the Bishop's only just appearing at dinner
and then hurrying away." [103]

That the criticism came in this instance from the Fellow of an Oxford
College is coincidental, yet it can stand as testimony that Wilberforce's
relations with the University were never particulary easy. As Jowett
once wrote of a proposal to make Wilberforce the College Visitor: "The
old master [Jenkyns] objected. He said he did not like having a doctor
who would be in the habit of coming in any morning, and feeling your
pulse! And indeed where the little finger of the Bishop of Oxford was
once admitted, the whole of his eminent person was likely to follow." [104]
Oxford wished to be free of all meddling fingers. Common rooms resented any interference and therefore resented Wilberforce, who felt
called upon to interfere a good deal. Much of the difficulty stemmed from
the Colleges' unwillingness to surrender to the bishop of Oxford any of
the ecclesiastical privilege or jurisdiction which they had once possessed
but which the reforming legislation of the nineteenth century was strip-
ping from them. B. P. Symons, warden of Wadham and vice-chancellor
in 1846, feared the newly drawn Clergy Discipline Bill would take from
the University its power to discipline its own clergy without regard to the
bishop. "It should be borne in mind," he wrote in February, "that the
authority of the Vice Chancellor is concurrent with that of the Bishop
in all the parishes within the precincts of the University, and has *within
a few years* even been exercised." Later he wrote to insist that the new
Act "should not be alleged as a reason for not continuing to the University its ancient spiritual powers and privileges." If, as it did, the Act took

101. October 18, 1854, BD, II. W.
102. To ? England, November 23, 1854, Letter Book, BD, d.148. 94.
103. To ?, December 7, 1866, in B. J. Kidd and P. G. Medd, *Selected Letters of William
Bright* (London, 1903), p. 266.
104. Geoffrey Faber, *Jowett* (Cambridge, Mass., 1957), p. 104.

them away, Symons added lamely that "this effect was not *intended* by those who drew the Act [and] probably not by those who passed it." [105]

Much the same sort of desperation marked the rector of Lincoln's refusal the following year to submit to an Order in Council which had abolished all peculiar jurisdictions in the diocese and therefore made necessary the licensing of all clergymen by the bishop. Radford, the rector, refused to believe that the chaplains of All Saint's and St. Michael's, appointed by the College, were subject to archidiaconal summons and visitation. Wilberforce, with the law clearly on his side, refused to give way, and Radford in the end was forced back upon the same strong rhetoric and feeble logic with which Symons had had to content himself. "Some . . . are so enamoured of uniformity, and the beau ideal of a Bishop's diocese, that they would carry out the system, cost what it may. But there are a few not altogether to be despised, who deprecate the unnecessary tampering with ancient Rights." [106]

These tangles with the ancient foundations of Oxford made Wilberforce a stout defender of the measures for University Reform introduced following the Commission Report of 1852. Jowett asked him to manage the reform bill in the Lords, but upon Gladstone's advice he refused. "In point of law," Gladstone wrote, "I do not imagine that the occupant of the See of Oxford has such a relation to the University as is held to invest him with any general charge of its concerns—and if there is no natural and historical reason for your intervention, then the prejudices of the House of Commons against the management of the question by a bishop would come into full play, and would I fear greatly complicate the question." [107] Wilberforce contented himself with several speeches during debates on the bill, denying particularly that its provisions challenged the union of Church and State. [108]

Wilberforce never found it easy to have his way with the dean and chapter of Christ Church. Henry Liddell, the dean from 1855 until 1891, was by no means unwilling to honor his bishop's requests to use the cathedral, but it galled the bishop that a request should be necessary at all. His exasperation expressed itself in a letter to Liddell in 1860 after having been denied the use of the cathedral for a visitation.

---

105. February 16, 1846; June 11, 1846, BD, I. C202.
106. Preface, *The Substance of a Correspondence between the Bishop of Oxford and the Rector of Lincoln touching his Lordship's claim to license the Chaplains of Lincoln College* (London, 1848). See also Green, *Oxford Common Room,* pp. 139–140. The year before, Eton had unsuccessfully opposed the transfer of the parish and collegiate church from the jurisdiction of the Bishop of Lincoln—whose diocese had, until 1845, included Buckinghamshire—to that of the Bishop of Oxford. In 1854 Wilberforce pressed a claim to the visitorship of both Eton and King's which he was eventually persuaded to drop. See letters to E. C. Hawtrey and Sir John Patteson, BD, I. C198.
107. December 6, 1853, Add Mss. 44343.
108. *Hansard,* 3rd ser., CXXXIV (July 7, 1854), 1357–1358.

I was well aware when I was appointed Bishop of Oxford that the Bishop's position had been almost from the foundation of the See an object of [illegible] jealousy to some members of the Chapter, and I carefully avoided taking any step which might keep alive a state of things so much to be deplored. For fifteen years I have claimed no right but accepted gladly all courtesies (and they have been many) from the Chapter.

Wilberforce argued that an agreement with Liddell three years before had placed the cathedral at his disposal for all services save confirmation. "Before, however, I am driven to enquire what are the legal rights of the Bishop of Oxford in his Cathedral Church I would make one more appeal to the Chapter." [109] Liddell replied that the agreement mentioned had been an informal one, to which the chapter was not privy, and that it had reference to only one specific visitation. He added, however, that since St. Mary's would not be available the chapter would permit the cathedral's use, and Wilberforce, in reply, asked him to "convey to the Chapter my acknowledgement of their courteous communication touching the use of the Cathedral Church of my diocese for my approaching visitation." [110] To Wilberforce, Cathedral ceremonies were an important expression of the dignity and power of the national Church. This constant dickering must therefore have seemed as demeaning to the Church as it was to his position as her bishop.

Behind the concern for his clergymen and their parishioners, driving him to work as visitor and missioner, was the single compelling conviction that had inspired Wilberforce from the beginning of his career in the Church, that all its work must be directed toward the saving of souls. The Church of England shared this conviction, and by mid-century was working for the same goal. The Census of 1851 suggested concern was by no means enough. The Church was failing to bring souls—especially working-class souls—into touch with the message it felt a mission to convey.[111] Churchmen could legitimately lay much of the blame for that

109. No date. [November, 1860], BD, I. C197.   110. *Ibid.*, n.d.
111. Wilberforce did not believe in the religious census as conceived, or in its results. Disparaging the efforts to enumerate the worshippers, he remarked in the Lords that "Mr. Canning once observed that nothing was so fallacious as facts except statistics." He objected to "nearly all" the questions asked, and believed the answers would prove to be very inaccurate. When the results suggested the Church's weakness, he refused to believe them, and demanded the census documents from Lord Granville *(Hansard,* 3rd ser., CXV [March 27, 1851], 632; CXXXV [July 11, 1854], 23). Two recent analysts have declared that the results were probably accurate enough. See K. S. Inglis, "Patterns of Religious Worship in 1851," *Journal of Ecclesiastical History,* 15:1 (1960); W. S. F. Pickering, "The 1851 Religious Census—A Useless Experiment?," *British Journal of Sociology,* 18:382 (1967).

failure upon the implacable rise of working-class populations. Though Longley of Ripon consecrated one church every two months during the twenty years of his episcopate, it was impossible to battle tides such as that which deposited an increase of 2,000 annually at Bradford. No one could hope to do more than keep abreast of waves that size. While numbers contributed to the Church's failure to evangelize the poor, attitudes played a part as well. K. S. Inglis has demonstrated the manner in which class consciousness kept the poor out of many churches that were being built for them, and prevented the clergy from finding a way to draw them in.[112] He notes that the men who founded settlements in the latter part of the nineteenth century did so not in the expectation of doing away with class distinctions, but in the more modest hope of bridging them. Despite their well-meant efforts, Establishment social workers like the Barnetts of Toynbee Hall offered their poor friends not so much a bridge as a series of hurried flights, away into a foreign world, then back again to the reality of a dirty slum. Meanwhile, the poor were certainly as conscious of class—and, in almost all cases, as willing to acquiesce in its orders and degrees—as were their betters.

With his fellow Churchmen, Wilberforce shared a sense of the need to draw workingmen to church. In the predominately rural diocese of Oxford, his task was not as great as that he had faced when archdeacon to the fast-growing suburbs of South London. The country poor may have been as ignorant of Christian doctrine as slum-dwellers; they were not as outright heathen. Squire and parson could more easily see that they came to church and sent their children to be catechized. If Oxford's problems differed in magnitude from those of the more urbanized of her sister dioceses, the attitude of her bishop toward the care and conversion of the poor resembled that of most of his brethren. Wilberforce had a social conscience, and believed a bishop's task in the House of Lords was to serve as guardian of the moral and social well-being of the people.

His humanitarianism did not lead him to disavow the English class structure, any more than it had his father or his own contemporaries. Any political philosophy which promised the abolition of class and the creation of a world of material prosperity he considered a delusion. Only the Church could unite society: "she who can stand between these two classes; who can bind both in a common unity; who can teach the rich man that all he has are talents; that man must hang on man; that the sin, ay, the robbery, begins with him, if he uses for himself what was but lent to him to use for others; who can tell the poor man that he is God's pensioner, and the rich that he is God's almoner." [113]

112. See K. S. Inglis, *Churches and the Working Classes in Victorian England* (London, 1963).

113. *Charge*, 1840, pp. 35–36.

In his early Charges, written when he was archdeacon of Surrey, he expressed his awareness of the tremendous tasks the Church faced in the cities. Cities forced men apart from each other: "The tendency of all things round us is to break our people into separate and unsympathizing classes"; "in all our great towns thin walls separate luxury from starvation. The two classes live in absolute ignorance of each other: there are no points of contact between them." [114] This separation was the Church's challenge, as reunification was her great task. And the poor remained the Church's particular charge. Unlike the dissenting sects, the Church of England was not compelled to depend upon popularity for its support. She possessed the power to interfere on behalf of her poorer members, a power she had too often failed to exercise, with the result that the poor had grown up "ignorant of their true redressor and thus easily befooled by the emptiest promise of deliverance from any quarter." [115]

Those best able to interfere were the bishops, and Wilberforce in a letter to Anderson in 1844 expressed the wish that they might be "more identified with the people in some way." [116] The year before, however, he had voiced reservations in response to a suggestion from Hook that the Church could best help the poor by divesting its bishops of their wealth. "Let Farnham Castle and Winchester House and Ripon Palace be sold," Hook argued, and the Church would have funds to establish other bishoprics. "Let the Church do something like this, and *then* the Church will live in the hearts of the people who now detest her." [117] To such a radical proposal Wilberforce could not agree. This was not the sort of identification he hoped the bishops might make.

It seems to me that your instances of rich men making *themselves* poor, living in *self*-denial for others, giving up well-nigh all for their brethren, as God gives them grace and opportunity—that these are the instruments by which to effect what you desire; but that to strip a class, to impoverish our Bishops and sell their palaces, would only be the hopeless career of revolution. There always has been, I suppose, poverty; always want; yet God has ordained differences of rank, and intended His Church to pervade all ranks, as she does with us. The (I repeat) voluntary labours, charities, and *self*-emptying of those specially called to them, seem to me to be *the* means of effecting your object.[118]

Voluntary work, home missions, and district visiting remained Wilberforce's answers to the problem of connection and identification. Only once did he bring forward a solution as radical as that proposed by Hook. In his Charge of 1844 he recommended an increase in the diaconate. In a letter to Louisa Noel the same year he referred to "getting a sort of

114. *Charge*, 1842, p. 19; *Charge*, 1844, pp. 15–16.
115. *Charge*, 1842, pp. 29–30.   116. May 30, 1844, BD, I. C191.
117. July 5, 1843, Ashwell and Wilberforce, *Life*, I, 226.
118. July 29, 1843, *ibid.*, I, 227.

Subdeacons Order instituted," the candidates to be drawn from a class outside the Universities, and to be admitted to the priesthood "when by faithful service for a term of years in the office of a deacon, they shall have 'purchased to themselves a good degree and great boldness in the faith which is Jesus Christ.' " [119] Such a reform, Wilberforce added, "would prove we are the Church of a nation and not a class." It might indeed have done so, but it was never instituted. Once translated to Oxford, where the problems of urban poverty and irreligion did not exist with the intensity of South London, Wilberforce appears to have dropped the idea and returned to more orthodox notions of a gentlemanly and University-educated clergy. From time to time he spoke of the necessity for some mighty effort to attract the masses to the Church. "I am deeply convinced," he remarked at a meeting of Convocation in 1857,

that while we are merely carrying on, for the most part, the old machinery of the Church, slightly increasing the number of our districts, there is really rising around us, at this time, a tide of unbelief and ignorance of Christianity leading to absolute godlessness, threatening destruction to everything that is dear to us in the land.[120]

All Wilberforce could suggest on this as on other occasions was more preaching and more fund-raising, and in this faint response he echoed that of his fellow Churchmen.[121]

Despite the Church's failure to win the interest and support of the poor, it remained for Wilberforce the one institution capable of drawing England's two nations together. When upper and lower classes could meet in church and offer prayers to a God who recognized no class distinctions, the country stood to gain. Wilberforce urged squires and businessmen to preach churchgoing to their employees and practice it themselves. "Your labourers would soon value the care for them which it would bespeak; more than anything it would tend to check that dangerous division of ranks, and insubordination of the lower, which is growing amongst us." [122] This last reflects Wilberforce's conviction that though ranks should not remain divided, men should remain in ranks. And in support of that conviction he continued less certain than many of his episcopal brethren of the desirability or indeed the efficacy of a pewless

119. *Charge,* 1844, pp. 28–29. Letter to Louisa Noel, November 19, 1844, BD, II. J.
120. *Chronicles of Convocation, 1847–1857,* February 6, 1857, p. 376.
121. Wilberforce was ready to approve special, *i.e.* shorter, services for the poor, but because he feared it might subvert the Church, heartily opposed Shaftesbury's Religious Worship Act Amendment Bill which permitted church services to be held in public meeting rooms (see *Hansard,* 3rd ser., CXXXIX [July 6, 1855], 513–515; [July 23, 1855], 1276–1278).
122. *Charge,* 1857, p. 26. Wilberforce suggested in the same passage that the best way to insure a laborer's appearance in church on Sunday was to pay him his wages sometime other than Saturday night.

or a completely unappropriated church. The ideal was a church in which there was place for the rich and place for the poor. Nor should the poor be herded into the corners or the galleries of their church; abuses of this sort—churches in which one found "all the best parts of the nave entirely engrossed by private pews . . . in each of which sit two or three straggling inmates nursing their separate dignity" [123]—these abuses were too frequent and should be stamped out. And yet free churches brought problems of their own. "I know," he remarked during a Church Congress in 1862,

> there are many churches in which *because they are free the poor* are wholly *thrust out*. That is the great danger. You may build a church, for instance, in London, with a very poor population near to it; you may have an admirable service, and you may let every seat be free and unappropriated, and let a very energetic man be at the head of it, and manage it to admiration—and what will follow? Why, the crinolines will fill the church.[124]

Churches should therefore reserve a large section of free seats for the poor, and in a location that would insure their ability to participate fully and devoutly in the services. A circular asking money for the rebuilding of St. Aldgate's, Oxford, and including a warm episcopal endorsement, catalogues the sort of conditions Wilberforce strove to eliminate. The population of the parish was two thousand, but the church held only 457, and of those sittings all but thirty-five were rented pews; for the rest there remained "a few loose forms, three uncomfortable benches fixed outside the pews, and the low seats for the children in and under the small gallery in the tower. . . The Church is very full on Sunday evenings, and many of the poor say to those most interested in their attending Church, 'when we do go, we do not know where to sit.' " [125]

Provisioning parish churches with free seats would not in itself bring the poor to church. Various other devices to attract and hold them were attempted. The notes Wilberforce made regarding St. Clement's parish, Oxford, in 1855 describe the nature of those attempts and their limitations.

> A few earnestly religious tradesmen. Moody [the rector] attempts to get men of this class to work for others. 6 or 7 tradesmen as a committee work with him in night school. As to the lads and daughters of the tradesmen. To these the Dissenters chiefly address themselves by belle [lettres?] classes etc. services for them. Moody has a Bible class for this class . . . 8–10 attend it going through St. Mark—catechetical lecture. Mainly taught by a serious undergraduate. For the girls M. takes a bible class of about 20 aged about 13 to 20. . . . Third rate shopkeepers he classes with poor. Not much professed immorality. No positive houses of ill fame but light girls residing with parents who do not like to drive them out. Spirit and beer drinking the great evil. . . A spirit of religion in an undefined way

123. *Charge,* 1842, p. 17.   124. *Church Congress Report,* 1862, p. 199.
125. ODP, b.70. 571. The year was 1862.

amongst the poor. Yet more amongst the tradesmen than them. Most useful 2 lectures, one on Thursday and one on Sunday from 7–8. . . *Night School* for working men from 7–8 one tradesman teaches and is paid. They pay 1d. a week towards books. 25 average age. It is worked in classes, reading, writing, and arithmetic, and the better readers read the Bible with M[oody] or some representative. Many amongst the poor and third class of tradesmen strongly disposed to Holyoake secularization. The main evil of the University in keeping the lower class of college servants irreligious.[126]

St. Clement's could offer something to those who had already made up their minds to improve themselves. To those who had not, Moody could only open his doors, make free his seats, and hope. To how many, however, did Wilberforce's insistence that the Church of England was the poor man's church ring flat, suggesting rather that it was a church for the poor man who was willing to stay in his place? Christianity, Wilberforce once preached, taught the poor man to carry his load.

It proclaimed for men a true equality, not by destroying the gradations of earthly rank, but by exalting the redeemed humanity which underlaid and overweighed them. It took away the rich man's arrogance. . . It took away the poor man's grudge, drawing the sting out of his poverty. . . teaching the poor to minister for Christ's sake unto the rich, and the rich to be for Christ's sake the helpers and defenders of the poor. So truly is the Church of Christ the poor man's church.[127]

When helping and defending, Wilberforce was prepared to demand a *quid pro quo*: help and defense for those who came to church, and for the rest, nothing from the Church. "If the distribution of alms is left to you as *clergyman of the Parish* to be made as you 'deem meet,'" he once advised a rector, "I do not see how you can conscientiously deem those meet who for any reason systematically absent themselves from the public worship of the Church." [128] Those who came to church thereby proved themselves worthy of their Church's support.

Hook, in speaking of the Church's role as educator for the community, was realistic enough to turn the proposition around. Two thirds of the children sent to Church schools went not for religion "but for the general information we give, the price we demand being that they shall also receive religious instruction." [129] Hook considered this all the more reason

126. ODP, d.178. 358. Compare with the Visitation return for Henley in 1869; answer to the question: Does church attendance bear a fair proportion to the population of the Parish. "As regards the higher class it certainly does. As regards the middle class it does not, 1st owing to the influence of dissent, 2 owing to a withdrawal to a neighboring church which began during the repairing of the Church some years back and it is suggested that a sudden introduction of the offertory three years ago helped to increase the secession. As regards the poorer classes, the indigenous poor do not seem undevout, but the families of those who have introduced themselves in later years are very careless of, and indifferent to all sacred duties" (ODP, c.335. 193).

127. *The Poor Man's Church* (Halifax, 1859), p. 13.

128. To the Reverend W. Lloyd, July 14, 1849, Letter Book, BD, d.209. 142.

129. Stephens, *Hook,* I, 420.

to continue to oppose a system of secular education. If a secular system were established, he argued "two thirds of the children will be brought up without any religious instruction, without any knowledge of their Saviour and their God." And that would not be right. On these grounds the Church continued to press for the right to educate the children of England, and the State continued to acquiesce in the Church's demands. Events of the 1830's had suggested that a lower middle class educated to political action but denied access to the steadying and restraining message of the Church might propel the country into revolution. Sir James Kay, later Kay-Shuttleworth, in an early pamphlet, was careful to recommend more than a merely utilitarian education. Religious training would insure a happy and prosperous populace. Denied religion, that same populace would remain a prey to all the evils which their gradually won political freedoms might otherwise help them to abolish. "Crime, diseases, pestilence, intestine discord, famine, or foreign war—those agencies which repress the rank overgrowth of a meagre and restless race—will by a natural law, desolate a people devoid of prudence and principle, whose numbers constantly press on the limits and means of subsistence." An effective system of education must therefore ensure that the "vast masses of our operative population" are "acted on by the ministers of an ennobling faith." [130] Responding to this assumption, shared by Churchmen and Dissenters, the government in 1833 granted funds to both the National Society and the interdenominational British and Foreign School Society for the support of an educational system grounded in religion. Parishes were encouraged to establish day and evening schools, and pupil-teachers often helped the schoolmaster—in many cases, the rector—to bring at least the rudiments of reading, writing, and arithmetic to all the children in the community.

With these straightforward tenets Wilberforce was in complete accord. In a sermon which he preached in 1838, he declared the ideal of education to be the instilling in every pupil "a high toned character, to make them brave, honest, and industrious, and unselfish; and then to add to this as much of knowledge upon other matters as will enlarge their powers of mind without diverting them from the peculiar duties of their several stations." [131] This was the message of a pamphlet he addressed to Brougham in 1840, opposing secular education and arguing the need for church schools which would "teach and mediate" a moral code throughout the country.[132] As bishop he continued to preach the same

130. J. Kay, *The Moral and Physical Condition of the Working Class in Manchester in 1832.* Quoted in Brian Simon, *Studies in the History of Education* (London, 1960), p. 169.
131. *The Power of God's Word Needful for National Education* (Portsea and London, 1838), p. 13.
132. *Letter to the Right Honourable Henry Lord Brougham on the Government Plan of Education* (London, 1840), pp. 34–35. The letter was a reply to Lord Russell's attempts

message. In his first Charge he expressed his mistrust of all schemes which did not teach Englishmen to fear God and honor the Queen, "which did not, that is to say, teach them to base upon serving God all their other actions; which did not set before them, as man's highest honour as well as his greatest happiness, the being under a true law of duty, and fulfilling its requirement towards their neighbour and their God." [133]

Education under a law of duty implied education according to class. Obligations to a particular station in life dictated the sort of education one received. Wilberforce believed that society set each class a certain task, and that a sound education was one which prepared a child to take up that task. Addressing himself in 1857 to the "out-cry against taking children away from school to the land," he declared to the Diocesan Association of Schoolmasters that he "did not want everyone to be learned men, or to make everyone unfit to follow the plough or else the rest of us would have nothing to eat." [134] He sensed a need for schools for the middle classes: "practically speaking," he remarked during a debate in the Lords, "the great improvement effected in the schools of the labouring class had a tendency to leave the class above the labouring class in need of considerable improvement in the schools suitable for them." [135] Upon the upper classes and upon the public schools charged with their education rested the burden of shaping the minds and the moral character of the nation's leaders. He cautioned young Etonians in 1847 to remember that they were the men who would "fix the tone" of the next generation. He urged them to beware "the luxurious and expensive habits" growing up there. "From a luxurious, expensive, self-indulgent youth, what deliverer can arise for England—for the world?" Rather than succumb to the habits that guarantee a "sickly, effeminate, timid manhood," he urged them to "seek by your example to stamp on those around you a tone of courage and manly temperance." [136]

Wilberforce considered it his responsibility to provide as many schools as he could for both the lower and the middle classes. He began to understand the magnitude of England's educational needs, as he came to learn so much else, while archdeacon of Surrey. He had written F. D. Maurice in 1845 expressing, Maurice reported, "entire concurrence in the views I had expressed to him about the Borough [Southwark?], and holding out the hope that they will not begin with raising wretchedly cold-looking

in 1839 to establish normal schools in which only the Bible would be taught, and to the Whig government's insistence that government grants be accompanied by government inspection.

133. *Charge,* 1848, p. 19.

134. *Report of the Annual Meeting of the Diocesan Society of Schoolmasters, 1857* (Oxford, 1857), p. 38. Quoted in McClatchey, *Oxfordshire Clergy,* p. 143.

135. *Hansard,* 3rd ser., CXXII (June 11, 1852), 497–498.

136. *An Address Delivered at a Confirmation* (London, n.d. [1847]), pp. 18–19, 22.

churches, into which no poor person will go, but will open schoolrooms in the worst courts and lanes, first for the children, then for worship." [137] In his first episcopal Charge Wilberforce catalogued the educational deficiencies and inadequacies within the diocese. Of a population of 478,773, one seventh were in need of charitable assistance to enable them to go to school. Of these, only one half were at present under direct training of the Church, and in many of those cases, the schooling received was sketchy at best.[138] Improvement could come only with efficient and enthusiastic local school boards. The 1847 Report of the Diocesan School Boards observed that success depended upon "completeness of organization." And the Report's authors admitted that "at no time since the formation of the Board has the local agency been less effective than at the present moment. In some districts, the Reports of the Board are very irregularly distributed; and in only three or four [rural] deaneries, during the past year, has the inspection of schools been thoroughly carried out." [139]

Inspection would prod the local boards into action as the Board itself recognized. Wilberforce, who was helping the National Society hammer out a compromise inspection scheme designed to retain Church influence while accepting government assistance, stood firmly in support of the campaign to introduce it into the diocese. In January 1850 he summoned all the diocesan inspectors to Cuddesdon "to consult upon the best means of making inspection more general and more effective." He offered inspection at diocesan expense to any board that wanted it, and assumed the supervision of the lists of examination subjects, and of the distribution of prizes and exhibitions.[140] The following year the Board reported itself gratified with the results of the bishop's intervention. Three hundred sixty-seven schools had been brought under the inspection system, eighty-five as a direct result of Wilberforce's offer. The Board agreed to a resolution expressing the need to bring pupil-teachers and monitors "into more immediate connection with the Bishop," and proposed to institute under the bishop's direction an examination in theology, open to all such teachers and monitors in the diocese willing to present themselves.[141]

Meanwhile school-building proceeded apace. The diocese spent £22,542 on construction between 1851 and 1854, all but £1475 of that sum contributed intramurally.[142] Attendance increased steadily through-

137. To Priscilla Maurice, May 17, 1845, in Frederick Maurice, *Frederick Denison Maurice*, I, 414–415.
138. *Charge*, 1848, pp. 25–26.
139. *Report of the Diocesan Board of Education*, 1847, p. 9. Hereafter cited as *Report*.
140. *Report*, 1850, p. 6.   141. *Report*, 1851, pp. 7–8.
142. *Charge*, 1854, p. 19.

out the fifties. By 1862, 482 schools in 330 parishes were inspected; 31,487 pupils were reported "on the books"; 23,032 were present at the time the inspections occurred.[143] Wilberforce was by no means satisfied with the results. According to the calculations of Horace Mann, he reported in 1854, one sixth of the population should be at school. In 1862 an average of only one in eleven attended an inspected Church School.[144] The curriculum, apart from the three R's, remained limited. About one tenth of the students studied geography, half as many grammar and singing. A handful did some map-drawing; over half the girls had instruction in needlework.[145] There was little time for much more; the average age of the students in the first class was ten. After that the children in these schools went to work, occasionally taking advantage of Sunday schools or night schools to continue their education.[146] Wilberforce, believing as he did that the poor could do without long years in school, did not consider a child of ten too young to earn a wage. He did think it important to bring the child to school before he went to work so that he might learn to read and write and, as important, to understand God's world and his place and duty within it.

To encourage good teaching Wilberforce founded a Diocesan Training College at Culham. The National Society had recommended teacher-training institutions in a report in 1838; a number were consequently established. Wilberforce had lent support to Kay-Shuttleworth's Battersea training school while archdeacon. As soon as he came into the diocese he determined to have one of his own. A small school at Summertown had existed since 1840, training between one and two dozen students a year. Wilberforce envisioned a far bigger and more generally effective institution. He reached an agreement in 1847 with Bishop Monk of Gloucester and Bristol whereby Wilberforce contracted to build a training college for men for the two dioceses, and Monk agreed to do the same for women. The college was designed to accommodate one hundred, making it, next to Cheltenham, the largest institution of its kind in the country. Wilberforce wanted it built at Cuddesdon, but the site was deemed inaccessible; land was found instead at Culham where Robert Walker, Wilberforce's mathematics tutor at Oriel, had been collated to the living by his former pupil in 1848. The school cost £19,700, £5,700 more than the original estimate. Parliament contributed £5000, the Na-

143. *Report,* 1862. General Summary.
144. *Charge,* 1854, pp. 44–45; *Report,* 1862. General Summary.
145. *Report,* 1862. General Summary.
146. A note in the Visitation Return from Hughenden in 1869: "The large number of Sunday School children (only) is to be accounted for by the demand for children's labour at lacemaking and straw plait for girls and agricultural and chair work for boys" (ODP, c.334. 182). The number of evening scholars in the diocese in 1862 was 2821 males and 309 females *(Report,* 1862. General Summary).

tional Society £1000, the University £1000, the diocese and private donors the rest—testimony to Wilberforce's abilities as a fund-raiser.[147] Culham opened in 1852. By 1854 there were sixty-eight scholars in residence, and although enrollment slumped in the next two years, there were ninety students in the college in 1860. The proposals of the Newcastle Commission embodied in a Minute in 1863, requiring entrance fees and certification of apprenticeship from candidates for admission, hurt the college but did not cripple it. Wilberforce picked able young administrators—A. R. Ashwell, the first principal, was only twenty-nine when chosen for the job—and the training was competent and thorough. In the certification examinations in 1869, Culham won a higher percentage of first-class places than any other training college; no one placed in the fourth class, and there were no failures.[148]

Most students remained at Culham for two years. The schedule was demanding: lectures began at six, students cleaned their own rooms, worked in the gardens and in a model school established nearby for practice teaching. The staff did not labor to produce clever teachers. As the Board of Education reported in 1856, there was some apprehension "lest the higher standard of attainments arrived at should breed an upstart class of teachers above the work of Village schools." But the report of the Reverend B. F. Smith, a diocesan inspector of the Canterbury Board of Education, contradicted the nay-sayers.

With great variation due to the difference of disposition and system of training, I give a decided preference to the class of duly-qualified teachers with whom I have been brought in contact during my inspection, even in the graces of humility and subservience; and in truthfulness and earnestness of character, I believe that education has already gained immensely by the change.[149]

Truthfulness and earnestness of character were the goals of the educational system the Church of England blessed and Wilberforce worked to spread throughout his diocese. Intellectual preeminence, even for those sons of the rich who would one day lead the nation, would be of little use to any scholar or indeed to his country, without a sense of the way in which God had endowed the minds of rich and poor with the need to work his will.

Wilberforce described the bishop's office as "the earthly centre of the Christian ministry, with all its risks and ventures for our souls, and for the souls of others for whom Christ died." [150] Without question he was a

147. *Charge,* 1851, p. 20; *Charge,* 1854, p. 4.
148. Leonard Naylor, *Culham: Centenary History* (Abingdon-on-Thames, 1953), p. 52.
149. *Report,* 1856, p. 10.   150. *Charge,* 1848, p. 6.

success in his own terms. It meant ceaseless work on behalf of the Church. "Let there be no interval of conscious self-allowance," he once warned a class of ordinands, "no earthly parenthesis in our ministerial life." [151] From service to the Church, Wilberforce permitted himself no interval of self-allowance save his family. With that exception, the Church was his master.

He divided his year into rough quarters, spending a fourth of his time at Cuddesdon, a fourth in travels about the diocese, a fourth in London, and a fourth at Lavington or on travels elsewhere. His work in London included attendance in the Lords, at the meetings of Convocation, following its revival in 1854, and speaking and preaching engagements throughout the city.[152] He worked to avoid entangling himself in social life. "I see the dear little boys every day, I think more than I did at Alverstoke," he wrote Louisa Noel from London in March 1846, soon after his appointment. "I generally go to any debate in the House of Lords and see what is going on and stay or not as seems promising. I have refused and avoided a good many dinner invitations and had several quiet evenings." [153] Entertainment, especially at Cuddesdon, was generally with the purpose of furthering the work of the Church. A visitor recalled a clerical open house at Christmastime.

The order of the day was as follows: First, prayers in chapel, and sometimes a short exposition of Scripture by the Bishop. Then breakfast, with general talk, the Bishop, as always, the leader; then shortly, an invitation to his study to certain of us, to discuss, perhaps, the subjects for the Lenten sermons, or to settle the preachers, or to make arrangments for a mission, the when, and the where, and the what. This might last till luncheon. Afterwards he would invite some of us to walk with him, himself, with a thick stick in hand, heading the party. Then he might start a subject and ask us to express our thoughts. They were serious ones. I remember one on the Blessed Sacrament, and his asserting his views; while – – – and some of us bore witness to another belief. But he was always patient with differences.

Returning home, some of us might be called into the study to write letters for him, he dictating to each, then signing, if necessary, and sealing; he always sealed his letters. Then, in due time, dinner, somewhat, though not over luxurious; and then his very remarkable conversational powers would come out. The ladies being gone, he would sometimes start some subject of the day and have it discussed. Then the drawing room, and easy talk, himself calling one or another aside, to speak more privately while resting on a sofa by his side.[154]

All who had anything to do with Wilberforce remarked on his ceaseless activity, and few failed to single out his dogged perseverance with di-

151. *Addresses to the Candidates for Ordination*, p. 222.
152. An additional duty, incumbent upon the Bishop of Oxford since the addition of Berkshire to the diocese, was the chancellorship of the Order of the Garter.
153. March 9, 1846, BD, II. F.
154. W. H. Hutchings, *Life of T. T. Carter* (London, 1903), p. 37.

ocesan correspondence. He tried to answer as many letters as he could in his own hand. When asked once why he did not employ secretaries to deal with the routine he replied that too many would be disappointed by a secondhand reply. "For instance, a clergyman at Huddersfield writes to me—at Cuddesdon—to go to the north to preach on four special occasions. Of course I cannot comply with his wish. But I write a refusal myself with a few kind words which make it less annoying. Whereas my secretary would say it was 'impossible' and the poor man would feel that he had made a mistake." [155] Often he found himself forced to press others into his service. Reginald Wilberforce records an occasion in 1867 when his father dictated four letters to four secretaries while writing a fifth himself.[156] In letters to Louisa Noel and other close friends he frequently alluded to a daily correspondence of from twenty-five to forty letters. His son Ernest, after inspecting letter books, estimated that he wrote an average of 6430 letters a year.[157] When he got behind, as he might during a confirmation week, it was no small task to catch himself up. "Some 100 pressing letters all unanswered and wrote none yesterday or the day before," he once confessed to Louisa Noel. "I was up between 4 and 5 this morning to write my sermon and tonight I am very tired having been always engaged ever since." [158]

Wilberforce's willingness to undertake every humanly possible commitment asked of him kept him moving about for weeks on end. Requests rained in: would the bishop preach for the schools of the parish; would the bishop lay the cornerstone of the church and speak upon the occasion; would the bishop honor the squire by performing the ceremony at his daughter's wedding. And if he possibly could he would, for he knew that his presence and his words might bring a sense of the majesty of the Church into the parish, to say nothing of an extra fifteen or twenty pounds into its funds.[159] These exertions, when added to the yearly round of confirmations and ordinations, set Wilberforce an exhausting pace. Though it wore him out, he relished it and felt it worth the exhaus-

155. ? to Reginald Wilberforce, n.d. BD, I. C206.
156. Ashwell and Wilberforce, *Life,* III, 222.
157. A note in the front of the book into which Ernest copied letters to him from his father (BD, I. C205). Disraeli once commented in a private notebook: "Bishop of Oxford said his average correspondence (letters he received) was nearly 100 per week. This exceeds the average of a Minister of State with a great department or that of the Leader of the House of Commons in the session" (Hughenden papers, A/X/A.45).
158. October 24, 1847, BD, II. F.
159. See, for example, an unmarked and undated newspaper clipping in the Diocesan Papers reporting the bishop's visit to Chalfont St. Giles to dedicate a new school. He spoke at the opening of the school on Saturday, preached again the following day, and raised £38.13.2½ of the £75 still needed. "He made one of the most impressive discourses that ever was heard, it being stated by some that it would never be effaced from them as long as they lived" (ODP, b.72. 96).

tion for the good it did his diocese. During his Visitation in 1848, he wrote Louisa Noel describing just one of the many halts during his progress, Great Hampden.

It is a beautiful spot on the Chiltern Hills amongst beechwoods. Rather like Lavington. I went to preach and administer the holy communion. A very good man officiates there. . . It was delightful to see such a church and congregation and community gathered among the Beechwoods. This p.m. I have preached at his other church of Great Kemble. I hardly ever saw a Church so full: all the labourers of the neighbourhood seem to have flocked together to hear their Bishop preach. It was very hot and gratifying.[160]

When he preached Wilberforce could be certain of a crowd. For many years after he began his ministry he preached from a manuscript. Once a bishop, the press of time as well as years of experience induced him to speak ex tempore. His style was elaborate, "a combination of eloquence, piety, sympathy and (above all) unction." [161] Bishop Handley Moule recalled a meeting in Cambridge on behalf of University Missions at which both Gladstone and Wilberforce spoke. "I see and hear them speaking now, a wonderful pair and a striking contrast. Gladstone, erect and dignified, was restrained and elevated in style and manner, while giving a grand impression of force in reserve. Wilberforce was life and fire personified. I hear still the thunder of applause he called down by a noble panegyric on Henry Martyn." [162] Listeners found his direct appeal compelling: "I ask every one amongst you, with that reasonable soul within you, has Christ never singled *you* out from amongst others;—has He never spoken to *you*—has there never been in *your* mind a drawing towards Him?" [163] People had the sense that he was talking to them because he was interested in them as individuals, that his speeches and sermons were composed with them in mind and no others. He collected facts about the histories of his parishes in a notebook: a passing reference, when at Ashendon, to the defeat of Alfred by the Danes there in 871 would please the locals and perhaps draw the dubious a bit closer to the Church.[164] A homely touch might also narrow the distance between the palace and the hearth. Much of what sounds more than a little condescending now went down well enough a hundred years ago. At the dedication of the National Schools in Newbury in 1860, he called attention to a portrait of Jack of Newbury in the hall.

That fine old fellow, who some persons had dared to tell them never existed; but they knew better—see how he rose to what he was by that honesty and uprightness and those good old English manners, taught by English Churchmanship,

160. October 8, 1848, BD, I. C194.
161. George Trevor to Reginald Wilberforce, July 22, 1881, BD, I. C206.
162. J. B. Harford and F. C. McDonald, *Handley Moule* (London, 1922), p. 25.
163. "Going Sorrowful from Christ," *St. Paul's Sermons* (London, 1859), p. 187.
164. These notes are interspersed throughout one of his parish notebooks (ODP, d.178).

which would do for the children of Newbury now what they did for the children of old. (Loud applause.) Some of the parents might be tempted to let their children come irregularly to school, but that would not do. No one ever got on in the world by fits and starts except grasshoppers; and if they brought up their children to habits of irregularity all that they might tell them about regularity would be to no avail. . . They should send their children to school neither smart nor slatternly—but tidy—that good old English word he so much liked.[165]

When Wilberforce encountered heckling or hisses, as he often did at the hands of Dissenters or High and Low Church partisans, he always tried to argue them down. Once at Bradford, when interrupted during a speech on missions by Dissenters' hisses, he stopped to praise the courage, if not the doctrine, of the Pilgrim fathers. Toleration was not understood then, he declared, as it is now.

Now, the absence of toleration confines itself to a few nasty articles in newspapers (cheers and laughter, followed by a storm of hisses); Yes, I am going to say, if you will wait a moment (hisses and interruption), to a few, very few (interruption), and to a few nasty hisses from nasty mouths (laughter, cheers, and hisses.) Well, I tell you that every one of such persons—and there may be some such here now—would burn us if they could (hear, hear, hear). But they cannot, thank God, they cannot; they must tolerate us.[166]

If Wilberforce eventually bested hecklers of this sort, as he apparently did, he perhaps had his general demeanor as an ecclesiastical personage to thank for the victory, as much as his ability as a debater.

The "personal" touch, which in public address might produce a sort of artificial heartiness, and so seem a device and nothing more, in private conversation conveyed a genuineness that reflected Wilberforce's fascination with humanity. He made notes of the physical characteristics of his clergymen—"tall, hook-nosed"; "dark, thin"—so that he would remember them and place them when he met them. He told the clergy that they must feel free to call upon him at any time with any problem. "Never think that you weary me with questions as to anything which can strengthen your hands or lighten your hands," he once wrote Butler.[167] His correspondence makes it clear that the clergy took him at his word. His replies to their entreaties and complaints were generally cordial, though if written in haste, as they often were, sometimes perfunctory. Only occasionally, and usually when he felt his judgment unfairly questioned, would he let loose his anger. In answer to a clergyman whom he had charged with misconduct, and who wrote to complain that he had been unfairly charged, he replied: "You *assume* that I have had '*secret*,' you imply anonymous, you say insufficient information; you sit in judg-

165. Account from the *Oxford Gazette,* July 21, 1860, ODP, b. 71. 391.
166. "Upon the Duty of England to Accompany Its Commerce and Immigration with Christianity," *Speeches on Missions,* ed. Henry Rowley (London, 1874), p. 78.
167. May 29, 1849, BD, I. C205.

ment on me and condemn me. Who told you my information was secret? How can you possibly know whether it was sufficient or not: You know only that I thought it sufficient and for so thinking it you proceed to condemn me." [168] Far more characteristic of his manner with clergymen was a note he sent H. H. Swinny, the principal of Cuddesdon, after some short and apparently unsatisfactory conversation with him.

I have been unhappy ever since I came away lest I should have *hurried* you in that short interview. I hope I did not. I know I did not, because I could not, show you any of the deep affection I bear you, or of my continual remembrance of you labouring on in your high calling in the midst of such weakness of the body. Believe me, it is a spur and incentive to my idleness you cannot dream of. May our loving Lord be very near to you in all your work and in all your soul.[169]

The busy life he led meant that Wilberforce would often travel away from one parish to the next—or from one problem to another—without having thought or heard all that there was to think or hear about matters at hand. His apology to Swinny is that of a man too busy to listen as he should have, yet too attached to the man he may have slighted to allow that slight to stand without amends. Wilberforce was often forced to make amends, as is any man who tries to accomplish so much. His charm and his unquestionable good will made men forgive him, much as they made men ready to do his bidding.

The effect of all the work—the efforts lavished upon clergy and parish, the time consumed in writing and preaching and traveling—is not easy to assess. Statistics offered an answer, and they were the answer which Churchmen, Wilberforce among them, invariably gave when the question arose. Figures became something of an obsession with the Church. At the beginning of each of his Charges, Wilberforce catalogued the achievements of the preceding three years: the number who came to church, the number confirmed, the number communicating, the number at school by day and on Sunday, the number of clergymen newly ordained, the number of clergymen recently deceased. During Wilberforce's episcopate, the numbers increased with every return. During the two-year period, 1846–1848, 9249 received the sacrament of confirmation; between 1851 and 1854, the figure rose to 14,057; between 1860 and 1863 to 18,570; between 1866 and 1869—his last year as bishop of Oxford—to 20,028.

168. To the Reverend John Fry, August 18, 1848, Letter Book, BD, d.209. 41. Fry was accused of having buried parishioners without a proper service. His accuser, as Wilberforce informed Fry in the same letter, had been Lord Curzon.

169. November 25, 1862, in Ashwell and Wilberforce, *Life*, III, 72–73. Swinny suffered from cardiac trouble.

Congregations increased throughout that period from 106,224 to over 181,879, keeping pace with the population of the diocese, which rose from 478,773 in 1845 to 550,329 in 1871. Although congregations increased in size during the twenty-four years that Wilberforce was bishop, the number of communicants remained constant in a period when most clergymen instituted monthly in place of quadrennial celebrations of the sacrament. Thus the figures provide a muddled answer. Wilberforce was content to use them as proof that the Church was gaining increased influence within the diocese, and as a sympton of a similar increase throughout the country. Despite setbacks and difficulties—self-satisfaction, mammonism, and doubt—he found in 1863 "on every side,"

marks of life and vigour which cannot be mistaken. At home these may be traced, not only in the churches increased in number and restored to a decent and comely suitability for worship, but also in the multiplied, better attended, and more devotional services; in more frequent celebrations of the Holy Communion, partaken of by larger numbers of worshippers, and these, so far as man can judge, more faithful and devout; in schools in which the number of the pupils is often more than doubled, and who are taught far better than they were of old.[170]

About the schools there is not much question that Wilberforce was right. Grants from the National Society and teachers and inspectors trained and supported by the diocese meant that a child had a better chance for a better education in 1863 than had his father or mother thirty years before. About the churchgoers, there is room for question. More churches and larger congregations might not mean "more faithful and devout" churchgoers. There is no yardstick by which faith and devotion can be measured en masse. Even if the figures recorded a vast increase in church attendance, which in terms of percentage they did not, they would still give only a rough idea of the depth of belief and hence the real strength of the Church throughout the diocese. That strength can be measured only in terms of the extent to which the Church affected the lives of the men, women, and children living in the parishes under Wilberforce's charge. One is left, not with the simple task of adding together the various gains advertised in triennial Charges, but with the far more difficult one of recounting an impression conveyed through the study of diocesan letters, notebooks, and returns.

When traced parish by parish across the years of Wilberforce's episcopate, that impression is of his own driving determination to make his office the generating force for a renewal of faith within the diocese, of his painstaking efforts to bring into being a group of clergymen as dedicated as he was to the task of making that renewal effective, and of the year-in, year-out patchwork success and failure of his efforts. Each parish had a

170. *Charge*, 1863, p. 37.

unique church history of its own, in some cases rich, in others, meager. Woven into them all, as into the few here given as illustration, was the common theme of episcopal attention and concern.[171]

Didcot, in Berkshire, had a meager history, befitting both its size and incumbents. A village of from 200 to 300, it offered its parishioners a rather sparse ecclesiastical fare throughout most of the century. In 1838 church services were held twice on Sunday, communion, as then the custom, four times a year. A dame school and a Sunday school, quantity and quality in each case unknown, provided the parish with its education. By 1854 a new incumbent had raised the number of communion services to nine per year, and estimated his congregation at 85. In other respects, the parish was as it had been sixteen years before. And fifteen years later, in 1869, it remained the same. The rector supported the day school himself and had restored the church with his own money. But Wilberforce lamented that he was "seen of none." He had arranged for no opening service to celebrate his generous restoration. He was "a very shy man; hardly sees anything of his neighbors." And one can assume that those neighbors felt only at a distance, if at all, the impress of their rector and the Church.

Olney, in Buckinghamshire, had a happier history. Though bothered by a large congregation of Dissenters, a hard-working rector, appointed by Wilberforce in 1856, managed to attract congregations of up to 600 on Sunday afternoons. He increased services, filled his schools, and, with his bishop's help, persuaded his patron, Lord Dartmouth, to restore the church. He was in all respects a model clergyman, and Wilberforce was pleased to have him. "A most marked and blessed improvement in the whole bearing of the people," he noted after a confirmation in 1856. "The Church, too, has been greatly improved. The chancel reseated by [George Gilbert] Scott. Pews cut down. Three decker abated etc."

At *Bicester* the returns were somewhat mixed. The incumbent J. W. Watts, rector since 1843, did not please an influential quarter within his congregation. Wilberforce heard complaints that he did not read the service distinctly, and in 1864 discovered from Watts himself that he and his wife were in severe financial difficulties, owing to the worthlessness of some East India properties. Despite his shortcomings, Watts assisted the town, which until 1859 had made do with three small day schools, by establishing a school system comprising a National School for 300, an infant school for 145, and a Sunday school for over 300.

Chinnor, in Oxfordshire, in the presentation of a family of Musgraves and presented regularly to Musgraves bore witness to the dangers of that practice. The Reverend Sir W. A. Musgrave, 10th Baronet, had

171. Evidence comes from the following sources: ODP, d.550; d.178; b.70; b.71; b.72.

held the living since 1816. Dissent was rife. In 1855 Wilberforce reported that parishioners "attribute the whole evil state of Chinnor to poor Musgrave. All the religious poor are dissenters. Musgrave a gentleman and with no evil, wholly I fear, irreligious. Seen working in his garden and mending his farm on Sunday after service." Musgrave was not so much irreligious as he was old and out of sympathy with his zealous bishop. He, at any rate, was conscious of his failings. In a note on his Visitation return in 1854 he attributed the state of the parish to "Dissent and my own weakness." The following year Wilberforce "after much inquiry and search" appointed a curate to assist him. Though apparently not as tactful as he might have been, the curate was able to pump a good deal of life into the parish, and particularly into the schools.

Henley remained a thriving parish throughout the years of Wilberforce's episcopate. The church, which had before 1854, accommodated only a few poor, reopened in that year following restoration, Wilberforce himself preaching on the occasion. Services were conducted daily and communion celebrated weekly and on festivals. J. B. Morrall, the incumbent for many years, and afterward Bishop of Edinburgh, contributed to the reconstruction and expansion of the Church's facilities, including a donation of £500 for the repair of the parish hall.

Of such histories, and hundreds much like them in general outline, was the history of the diocese of Oxford in the mid-nineteenth century. Difficulties varied from parish to parish less in nature than in degree. Irreligion and Dissent remained throughout the two major obstacles to Church influence. Successful confrontation depended in almost every case upon the abilities of the incumbent. A hard-working, devout man would probably advance the position of the Church within the parish. A wicked man might do the Church positive harm. A mediocre man would, in all probability, manage to see that the Church held its own. Yet the Church could no longer afford to stand still. If the Church in the diocese of Oxford played no larger role in the life of the community in 1869 than it had in 1845—if, as was probably the case, it had managed to hold its own and no more—that is not to say that the Church had not taken effective measures to strengthen itself as an institution and as a faith. It had had to move forward to stay where it was. And of its move forward Wilberforce had been both the force and the direction. He instituted no reforms that were not already being instituted elsewhere. Sumner had taught him a great deal, and Blomfield had set him a worthy example. His power was to turn the experience of others into action on all fronts at once, to descend upon the diocese by injunction, by persuasion, and by example and thereby to remodel not just the diocese but the episcopate as well.

CHAPTER V

Hampden

Renn Dickson Hampden, the extreme Broad Church Regius Professor of Divinity, received nomination in November 1847 to the See of Hereford, recently vacated by the translation of Thomas Musgrave to the archbishopric of York. Hampden held the living of Ewelme, in the diocese of Oxford, in conjunction with his professorship, and thus served under the ecclesiastical jurisdiction of its bishop. In this way Wilberforce found himself bound up in the fierce controversy which arouse from what was a most contentious appointment. Although he played out his role so as to bring down a stream of adverse criticism upon his head, he considered that he had acted throughout in a forthright and judicious manner, and maintained that an honest if belated *renversement* on his part had been misinterpreted by the public as an opportunistic maneuver. He agreed with most in blaming his conduct for his loss of favor at Court and consequent failure to succeed to an archbishopric. Whatever its consequences, the episode reveals a good deal about Wilberforce's abilities as an ecclesiastical diplomat and arbiter of doctrinal and theological controversy.

Hampden had done nothing outwardly to excite the wrath of his Tractarian and Evangelical opponents since his appointment as Regius Professor in 1836. A lengthy public debate had followed the University censure, for which Wilberforce had voted,[1] culminating in an attack by Melbourne upon those bishops who had opposed the appointment, and a response from Archbishop Howley, in which he argued that Hampden's latitudinarian pronouncements would mislead if not corrupt the students under his charge.[2] In 1842, upon the occasion of Hampden's *ex officio* appointment as chairman of the newly created Board of Examiners in Theology, the Heads of Houses attempted a repeal of the 1836 censure. The attempt failed, by a vote of 334 to 319, largely on the ground that Hampden had done nothing in the intervening years to recant or to clarify his supposedly heterodox views. Wilberforce did not vote at all, giving as his reason the belief that the issue had now become one of party, and that a vote against Hampden would be a vote for Tractarianism.

1. See above, page 67.
2. *Correspondence between The Rev. Dr. Hampden and The Most Reverend Dr. Howley, Lord Archbishop of Canterbury,* London, 1838.

The essays which had brought Hampden's orthodoxy into question were without doubt latitudinarian. The Bampton Lectures, delivered in 1832, and written in hurried consultation with Blanco White, attacked the words and phrases of Christian theology as a screen interposed by scholastic philosophy to separate Christian believers from the simplicity of the early Church. Hampden insisted that scholasticism was a blight upon the Church, and, in language which occasionally appeared to disown scholasticism by altogether disowning logic, he recommended that the Church purge itself of the crippling theological inheritance of its middle age. *Observations on Religious Dissent,* a pamphlet published during a campaign to abolish University religious tests, two years later, was a further and more generally intelligible expression of the same position expounded in the Lectures. Separation and division, Hampden claimed, had come about when men began to mistake theological and moral truth for religion. "No conclusions of human reasoning, however correctly deduced, however logically sound, are properly religious truths—are such as strictly and necessarily belong to the scheme of human salvation through Christ." [3] Difficulties arose only when religion was confused with dogma, and the confusion bred dissenting sects. As in the Lectures, Hampden pleaded for a sweeping aside of philosophy and scholasticism to uncover the beliefs of the early Church. Surely, he argued, "the false philosophy of former times" might be rejected without loss of vital truth.[4] Once back where they belonged, with the religion of Jesus Christ, Christians could enjoy the unity which would be theirs. As a first step toward that goal, Hampden urged the abolition of religious tests. "Tests are no part of religious *education;* if they were, I should think we were justified in retaining them: they are merely boundaries of exclusion." [5] These ideas seemed at the time to Wilberforce to come close to denying the Church itself, and on that ground he had gone to Oxford in 1836 to register a protest against Hampden's appointment as professor.

Eleven years had done nothing to change Wilberforce's opinion. Hence his dismay when he read of the appointment to Hereford. Although Hampden had supporters among Evangelicals and Latitudinarians,[6] many Churchmen considered him unsound, and thought Lord

---

3. R. D. Hampden, *Observations on Religious Dissent* (Oxford, 1834), p. 8.
4. *Ibid.,* pp. 26–27.   5. *Ibid.,* p. 59.
6. The Evangelical Shaftesbury, although he thought Hampden's appointment as Regius Professor "infamous," favored his appointment as bishop, since "during the last four or five years he has written and published very beautiful and orthodox discourses" (Edwin Hodder, *The Life and Works of the 7th Earl of Shaftesbury* [London, 1886], p. 388). The fact that Shaftesbury could change his mind in this way suggests the extent to which Hampden had become a party issue. As long as Tractarians opposed him, Evangelicals would find it hard not to give him their support.

John Russell's nomination an insult. Among the most outraged was Henry Phillpotts, the High Church Bishop of Exeter; it was he who first canvassed Wilberforce on behalf of the opposition, three days after the nomination. Phillpotts believed that Church interest demanded an episcopal address to the Queen opposing the election to the office of bishop of a professor still under censure by the University of Oxford.[7] Wilberforce quite agreed, and signed the Remonstrance. His position was much that of Bishop Blomfield, who had written soon after Phillpotts: "What say you to Dr. H.? His publications *since* the censure, as far as I have seen, are perfectly orthodox, but he ought to have retracted, or explained (if they were explicable) those papers which drew down on him the censure." [8]

This was to be Wilberforce's argument throughout the ensuing controversy: not that Hampden's appointment would under any circumstance be an unthinkable one, but that his appointment without prior recantation or at least explanation was an affrontery and a gross disservice to the Church. He was convinced, with all the bishops, that they could do nothing legally at that stage to stop the proceedings. *"We* cannot move in this," he wrote Robert, "because if the confirmation is stopped for alleged false teaching I am assured that the Archbishop has to assemble his comprovincials as assessors. And so it may come before us judicially." [9] He hoped, instead, to persuade Gladstone to lead lay opposition to the confirmation at Bow Church. "It is *your* business. . . I suppose the *continuous* act of publication of the Bampton lectures would suffice. But I need not go into details. It would be a relief to me to know that-provision is made for resistance at that point if unhappily it becomes needful." [10] Gladstone replied that he, too, felt his hands tied, since he expected the matter to come eventually before Parliament, where he could move more effectively against the appointment as Member for Oxford, if unconnected with "out-of-doors public agitation." [11] No one else volunteered to assume the leadership of a lay protest; the opposition was left with only one weapon, the episcopal Remonstrance. Duly signed by thirteen of the twenty-five incumbent bishops, it was presented to Russell on December 3.[12]

Meanwhile, agitation within the diocese of Oxford was drawing

7. November 18, 1846, BD, I. C200.　　8. *Ibid.,* November 24, 1847.
9. November 28, 1847, Wrangham Papers.
10. November 27, 1847, BD, I. C205.　　11. November 29, 1847, BD, I. C193.
12. Although Sumner of Winchester signed, his brother, J. B. Sumner, the bishop of Chester, did not. Bishop Kaye of Lincoln, in a letter to Wilberforce on December 1, 1847, asserted that he had written a private letter to Russell "in stronger terms." Phillpotts wrote Wilberforce on the 9th that Kaye had told him the same thing. Howley, the Archbishop, did not sign. He was at that time extremely feeble and died on February 11, 1848 (Ashwell and Wilberforce, *Life,* I, 432, 437).

Wilberforce closer to the center of the controversy. Charles Marriott, the Tractarian rector of St. Mary's, Oxford, backed by Mozley, Keble, Pusey, and other like-minded opponents of Hampden, proposed to bring suit against him in the Ecclesiastical Court of Arches. To do so would require Letters of Request from Hampden's bishop, as transmitter if not promoter of the suit. Wilberforce believed wholeheartedly in the necessity for some sort of hearing. He therefore did not oppose Marriott's attempt to bring a suit, although he informed him that he did not think he should himself serve as promoter of the action.[13] Hampden's adherents within the diocese had already heard that this was to be their bishop's position and one of them, W. H. Cox, a Fellow of Exeter College, had written charging Wilberforce with a desire "to see an agitation got up, and your name kept in the background." In reply Wilberforce remarked wryly that "if I thought it right to get up an 'agitation,' it would be far from my custom 'to keep my name in the background.'" He added that he had been canvassed as to his own course of action and that "I have always given one answer—that I can advise nothing upon a matter which may come before me judicially." [14]

Prepared though he was to forward the letters, Wilberforce delayed doing so for several days in the hope that Hampden might request a judgment in order to clear himself of suspicion. To further this end he undertook to write Russell on December 11, requesting a tribunal to weigh "the specific charges of disqualifying unfitness" which lay in the minds of some against Hampden. Russell had already sent the bishops a cool rejoinder to their Remonstrance, pointing out that many bishops had required certificates of attendance at Hampden's lectures from candidates for ordination, and that he could find nothing in the Remonstrance demonstrating a want of confidence in the soundness of his doctrines.

In these circumstances, it appears to me that, should I withdraw my recommendation of Dr. Hampden, which has been sanctioned by the Queen, I should virtually assent to the doctrine that a decree of the University of Oxford is a perpetual ban of exclusion against a clergyman of eminent learning and irreproachable life.[15]

In requesting the tribunal of Lord John, Wilberforce argued that Russell was wrong to assert that the bishops had asked that the appointment be set aside on the strength of a mere Oxford decree. He expressed utmost respect for the doctrine of the Royal Supremacy, "strengthened in me by that heightening of the common feelings of loyalty into the strongest and most dutiful affection for the Person of my Sovereign which must have been the effect of receiving from Her Majesty the un-

13. December 5, 1847, BD, I. C200.   14. December 2, 1847, BD, I. C200.
15. Ashwell and Wilberforce, *Life,* I, 439.

merited kindness of years." But "without trenching in the very smallest degree on the Royal Supremacy," he insisted that "the Church may reasonably expect that before its exercise in behalf of any person resting under specific charges of disqualifying unfitness, he should be required to refute before a competent tribunal those specific charges." Such an opportunity, he reminded Russell, had been afforded Prince Lee, recently appointed bishop of Manchester, when charges against his character had been filed by a Birmingham surgeon.[16] "Will your lordship apply to Dr. Hampden the rule you laid down for Dr. Lee, and require him to disprove before a competent tribunal the truth of these charges?" This assurance, Wilberforce insisted, would satisfy the Church.[17]

Wilberforce thought that Russell might well agree to this new proposal. He suspected that Hampden's "Letter to Lord John Russell" announced for publication on December 15 had been commissioned by the Prime Minister and would prove to be a request for trial.[18] He could not believe that Russell would rest his case upon the narrow logic of his reply to the bishops, and in this a good many agreed with him. "His Lordship has floored the Bishops, it is true," the *Times* remarked on December 13. "But *cui bono?* Why floor them? What if he should have floored the Church of England and himself too?" [19] But the same day Russell, in answer to Wilberforce, demonstrated that once he had the bishops on the floor he was not prepared to let them up again.

In the case of Mr. Lee specific facts of immorality were alleged which he could disprove. But the facts in Dr. Hampden's case are admitted.

It is obvious that this is a question which may lead to interminable controversy, the Bishop of Durham may think one way, the Bishop of Exeter another. The Bishop of London may think there is unsoundness, the Bishop of Chester may think there is none. So that Dr. Hampden may be kept suspended between the cap and the mitre for years, to the infinite amusement of the idle crowd, but to the detriment of the Church and of the Royal Supremacy.[20]

Hampden's "Letter," made public two days later, paid the bishops even less heed. Ignoring their Remonstrance entirely, Hampden concentrated his defense upon the vague wording of the censure of 1836— "nothing specific was ever alleged against me"—and blamed his persecution on the Tractarians.[21] Neither Russell nor Hampden appeared at

---

16. Thomas Gutteridge accused Lee of corruption during his years as headmaster of King Edward's School, and of general drunkenness. Lee brought him to court on charges of libel and won his case with ease. Newsome, *Godliness and Good Learning,* pp. 118ff.

17. December 11, 1847, BD, I. C200.

18. See his letter to H. Majendie, December 12, 1847 (BD, I. C200): "I have been all along expecting that Dr. Hampden's promised 'letter to Lord John Russell' was a *prescribed* publication, in which he *was to ask* for a trial."

19. *Times,* December 13, 1847, p. 4.   20. December 13, 1847, BD, I. C200.

21. *Times,* December 20, 1847, p. 5. The letter, written on the 9th and made public on the 15th, did not appear in the *Times* until the 20th. Hampden's opponents in 1836 had

all interested in Wilberforce's proposed tribunal; neither felt the need for one. The day after the publication of Hampden's reply Wilberforce therefore signed and forwarded the Letters of Request. In doing so he insisted that he was acting ministerially only. "This ministerial act," he wrote Hampden the same day, "I have not felt at liberty to refuse to perform." It pronounced no opinion on the truth or falsehood of the charges. Nor, Wilberforce insisted, did it arise from a spirit of hostility. It was no more than his duty, and "its hostile appearance has cost me, as has every similar step which has been forced upon me, the deepest pain." [22]

Wilberforce's reluctance to send the case to the Court of Arches was not feigned. On December 12th, when he still hoped that Russell would agree to his plan for a separate tribunal, he informed a clergyman in the diocese that he considered Sir Herbert Jenner-Fust, at that time the dean (judge) in the Court of Arches, "about the most unsatisfactory pronouncer possible of a judgment." [23] He gave no explanation for his distrust; it stemmed presumably from Jenner-Fust's reputation as a defender of the Supremacy. His distaste for an action in the Court of Arches manifested itself the day after he had forwarded the Letters of Request, when again he wrote to Hampden, suggesting a less formidable solution to the problem. "Before matters reach an extremity," he explained, he wanted to see "whether my interposition as Bishop of this diocese may yet save the Church the injury of this struggle, and you the pain and risk of its doubtful conclusion." He believed that if Hampden would avow his belief in sound doctrine, and withdraw the suspect language of his dissertations, all might yet be well. He proposed that Hampden subscribe to a set of propositions, eleven in all, which he framed in consultation with the promoters of the suit and set out in the letter.[24] Designed to bring positive reassurance to Hampden's Tractarian critics, these propositions taken together amounted to nothing less than a complete declaration of Christian faith, an orthodox gloss upon the doctrines of Holy Scripture, the sacraments, the Trinity, original sin, the incarnation, atonement, justification, and life after death.[25] In addition, Wilberforce asked Hampden

---

attempted to pass a more specific censure but had been prevented from doing so by the pro-Hampden faction.

22. December 16, 1847, BD, I. C200.

23. To H. Majendie, *ibid.*, December 12, 1847.

24. "[The promoters] suggested to me that now probably Dr. H. would give me privately the satisfaction the Court would require. I agreed to try, and worked hard with them to prepare the terms" (to Louisa Noel, December 29, 1847, BD, II. F).

25. For example, Wilberforce asked Hampden to affirm: "That you believe fully that 'the Son was begotten before all worlds, being of one substance with the Father,' and that it is 'necessary to salvation that a man believe rightly the Incarnation of our Lord Jesus

... to consent, for the peace of the Church, and in deference to the expressed opinion of your Bishop and others, to withdraw the 'Bampton Lectures' and 'Observations on Dissent,' *not thereby* admitting either that you intended in them to assert any doctrine contrary to those which you have since avowed, or that you now believe your language to contain any such assertion.

The same day Wilberforce wrote Russell of this latest attempt on his part to solve the dilemma, stressing that he was asking of Hampden no admission of "conscious error either now or heretofore" and that the concession he asked implied "no retraction of doctrine." [26] The day before, Marriott had declared himself willing to withdraw his suit "if Dr. Hampden should be willing to withdraw the Bampton Lectures and Observations on Religious Dissent from circulation and to make a full disavowal of the heterodox opinions they have been understood to contain." [27] What was to be for Hampden an avowal of orthodoxy would, Wilberforce apparently hoped, appear to his opponents as a disavowal of past errors.

Russell and Hampden both replied the following day. Lord John remarked that he thought Wilberforce's suggestion neither sufficient nor fit. Hampden had taught religion at Oxford for eleven years. Bishops had sent candidates to hear his lectures. Was it proper to question such a person in the manner Wilberforce proposed? "How is such a man to be interrogated upon articles framed not by the Church, but by one of its Bishops, as if he were himself a young student of divinity?" As for his request that Hampden withdraw the dissertations, Russell argued that it would require him "to degrade himself in the eyes of all men for the sake of a mitre." [28] Hampden himself complained that he was being unfairly used by his bishop. He remarked that had he not been convinced of Wilberforce's good will he would have "been justified in considering that an insult was not only conveyed but intended to be conveyed to me, by having such elementary tests applied to one who holds the position I do." Willing to do what he could to bring the matter to a close, he declared himself ready to answer "yes" to the declarations Wilberforce proposed, "in the sense in which they are the plain natural sense of our articles and formularies." He asserted that any talk of charges on the part of the Church against him was premature.

Christ.'"; "That you believe the Sacraments of the Church to be 'effectual signs of grace, by which God doth work invisibly in us'; and are 'means whereby we receive the same inward grace'" (December 17, 1847, BD, I. C200).

26. *Ibid.*

27. To Samuel Wilberforce, *ibid.,* December 16, 1847. Those who signed the suit were a group of four beneficed clergymen in the diocese of Oxford: W. H. Ridley, T. Stevens, E. Deane, and W. Young. Behind them stood Marriott, Mozley, Keble, and Pusey (Samuel Wilberforce to Louisa Noel, December 29, 1847, BD, II. F).

28. December 18, 1847, BD, I. C200.

Pardon me if I say that I have yet to learn that the Church at large has recognized any charges whatever... You speak of my 'forcing my way through all obstacles before me to a disputed seat.' [29] My Lord, I force my way nowhere. I know of no obstacles, legitimate at least, to my taking upon myself the office for which I am designated, which will not have their due weight and effect; and I do not admit that my seat is disputed by any who have a right to call it in question, and other disputants will doubtless be duly met and disposed of.[30]

To this declaration, which ignored the request to withdraw the publications, Wilberforce could only reply by reaffirming his devotion to the cause of ecclesiastical peace, and by reiterating his conviction that while he did not doubt Hampden's faith, he believed him "to have unconsciously used language at variance with it." [31]

This letter closed what might be termed the first stage of Wilberforce's attempts to deal with the Hampden controversy. At this point men with strong feelings on the matter ranged themselves in three main groups. There were those who considered Hampden in all respects a suitable appointment and who therefore saw no reason to challenge the authority of the Royal Supremacy by contesting his nomination. There were those convinced by what they had read—or what they had heard—that Hampden was altogether unfit, to a degree that warranted pressing the matter as far as it could be pressed. And there were those, among them Wilberforce, who had been upset by Hampden's former declarations, who resented the nomination as an affront to the Church, but who were willing to acquiesce provided Hampden could assure them of his orthodoxy. Throughout the early weeks of discussion and correspondence, Russell and Hampden had both shown themselves unwilling to understand how anyone might rightfully take offense—indeed, express surprise—at the suggested elevation of a censured professor of divinity to the Bench. They assumed that anyone challenging the wisdom of the appointment was challenging Russell's right to make it. But, as the *Times* remarked, "No one disputes the Royal Prerogative: no one denies Lord John's perfect right to take his stand upon it. The question is, 'Is it statesmanlike or patriotic to throw a fresh firebrand into our unhappy Church?' "[32] Those most convinced of Hampden's unsoundness might have denied Lord John his right. Wilberforce was not among them. To satisfy the militants he felt he must dissuade them from the belief that Hampden had long ago convicted himself by his own writings, and that nothing he said now would alter the fact of his fundamental and intolerable heterodoxy. Wilberforce saw a strongly worded affirmation as the key to compromise. He failed totally to perceive the effect his proposal might have

29. A reference to Wilberforce's letter of the 17th.
30. December 18, 1847, BD, I. C200.   31. *Ibid.,* December 20, 1847.
32. *Times,* December 14, 1847, p. 4.

upon a man like Hampden, a distinguished scholar some twelve years his bishop's senior. Believing that he had every right to a place upon the Bench, that his opponents were a Tractarian faction, Hampden naturally resented "interposition" of any sort, and especially peremptory, albeit well-meaning, catechizing by a young and seemingly inexperienced prelate. In his understandable eagerness to help the Church avoid an angry confrontation with the State, Wilberforce assumed that others were as anxious for some sort of private resolution of the quarrel as he was. Though, with the rest of the bishops, he professed a sense of the "depth of general feeling" upon the subject, he remained insensitive to the intransigence on both sides, and to the affront which Hampden had himself suffered.

On the day after Wilberforce sent what he believed to be his final letter to Hampden, he came in to Oxford from Cuddesdon for a confirmation, and went to lodge with Provost Hawkins at Oriel. While entertaining Wilberforce, Hawkins received a letter from Hampden, declaring that *Observations on Religious Dissent* was being sold and circulated against his wish; that he had sanctioned only a second edition, and that in 1834. Wilberforce believed that this admission changed the situation entirely. He considered that Hampden had now virtually disowned the *Observations,* and that he was thus compelled to reconsider the Bampton Lectures by themselves, to ascertain whether they alone would justify a case against their author.

During the next two days, Wilberforce read the Lectures, and solicited further legal opinion as to his role in forwarding the letters to the Court. The evidence suggests that until this time Wilberforce had not studied the Lectures in their entirety. Canon Ashwell, when writing his *Life,* had access to a manuscript account of the affair, no longer existing, written by one of the promoters—unnamed—of the suit against Hampden. The author recorded that before Wilberforce sent Hampden the request for an affirmation of faith on the 17th, he had, in the words of Ashwell's paraphrase, "been closely engaged, at Cuddesdon, with some of the most earnest and sober-minded of Dr. Hampden's opponents, in a minute examination and discussion of the objections to the 'Bampton Lectures.'" Ashwell continues: "The Bishop was unable to deny that the language was such as not merely to leave the Professor's own convictions doubtful, but such as might involve indefensible conclusions." Two pages later, however, Ashwell casts this examination in a different light. The consultations, he explains, took place "amid the pressure of business accompanying an examination of candidates for Holy Orders." The subject for discussion "was not so much the book of the 'Bampton Lectures' itself as the selected passages from it, and very especially from the 'Observations on Religious Dissent' upon which the promoters mainly rested the case which they desired to bring before the Court of Arches." [33] Wilberforce himself maintained that until December 22, he had not read the Lectures "as *judge*," nor "Dr. Hampden's other writings *with the explanations* (for these, and not the 'Bampton Lectures,' were new to me, not having voted in 1842, and so not required to read them)." [34]

Wilberforce fails to specify the nature of these explanations. Their sudden appearance comes as some surprise, since it was the lack of such explanations which Wilberforce had previously claimed as the great stumbling block to his acquiescence in Hampden's appointment. Whatever their nature, they convinced Wilberforce that the extracts from the Lectures which he had read, compiled by Newman at the time of the first censure, were "most unfair"—that is, taken out of context by Newman— "so unfair as scarcely to let one hope they were not consciously unfair." Again surprise, since in an undated draft in Wilberforce's hand he noted that "objections to them [The Extracts] were stated by me to Mr. Newman in 1836." [35] The welter of conflicting testimony suggests that Wilberforce read Newman's Extracts in 1836, and voted then in accordance with what he had read, despite his disagreement with Newman on particulars. There is no reason to suppose that he looked at the Lectures at all during the following eleven years. When he reconsidered them in early December 1847, it was in the company of the suit's promoters, men disposed to shed the most unflattering light possible on Hampden's words. Wilberforce may have re-read the less opaque *Observations* and Newman's Extracts as well. But it is hard to believe that he read through the whole of the Bampton Lectures before December 22, when he decided that the suit must rest upon them alone. On the basis of this reading, Wilberforce concluded that the Lectures "contained a good deal that was disagreeable, a great deal that was obscure, and nothing that was heretical." [36]

Meanwhile he was reconsidering his legal position with regard to the Letters of Request. Did the terms of the Church Discipline Act of 1840 commission him to forward the Letters without first determining the existence of a *prima facie* case? Could he, as he had until now assumed, transmit the suit as minister and not as judge? He decided that he had misunderstood his powers and that the evidence would have to satisfy him before he could send the suit to the Court of Arches.[37] Since he did not consider the remaining evidence—the Lectures—heretical, he de-

33. Ashwell and Wilberforce, *Life*, I, 463, 464, 466–467.
34. To Louisa Noel, December 29, 1847, BD, II. F; To ? Walker, January 25, 1848, in Ashwell and Wilberforce, *Life*, I, 500.
35. BD, I. C200.
36. To Louisa Noel, December 29, 1847, BD, II. F.
37. Wilberforce took the advice of a Dr. Addams, at the time counsel for Bishop Phillpotts of Exeter in the Gorham case.

clared himself legally unable to proceed further against Hampden and wrote to inform Hawkins of the fact on December 24th. But he could not leave it at that and attempted once more to play the role of peacemaker between Hampden and his opponents. He wished to use his office to obtain the "cordial concurrence" of the Bench—"which I think I can do"—and to remove "doubts, difficulties, suspicions and offence" by persuading Hampden to make "friendly concessions"—"and they are not many." Wilberforce proposed that Hampden should direct Parker, the publisher, to stop selling the *Observations,* and that he should, in addition, correct certain misapprehensions arising from the Lectures. With these concessions and "the assurance he has already given me of his personal soundness and what has already passed between us... I should be able to quiet many minds now greatly disturbed, and I *believe* that I could prevent all opposition at Bow Church and elsewhere." [38]

This letter produced a further series between Wilberforce, Hawkins, and Hampden. Hawkins explained to Wilberforce that he did not believe Hampden could commit himself to the sort of revision Wilberforce desired. "It is one thing to declare to me [as Hampden had] his intention of doing his best to *improve* his work in a future edition, taking advantage for that purpose of all objections that have been made to it, and quite another thing to engage so to *correct* it as to remove all objections." [39] In a second letter, written the following day, Hawkins urged Wilberforce to desist in his attempt to persuade Hampden to agree to specific revisions. Two days later, in an interview with Hampden, Hawkins discovered that upon the advice of his lawyers Hampden was now acknowledging nothing at all. "Even the facts to which I adverted in my conversations with your lordship," Hawkins reported to Wilberforce, "I have no permission to repeat *as from him;* I mean as to the 'Observations,' and his wish to improve the 'Bampton Lectures.'" [40] Hampden thus stranded Wilberforce without any sort of definite reassurance whatsoever, and Wilberforce considered briefly the possibility of resubmitting the Letters after all.[41] Instead, he published a lengthy letter to Hampden recounting in detail the entire history of his involvement in the controversy. In the course of it, he maintained that after he had received Hampden's "yes" to the affirmation of belief, and Hawkins' reassurance about the "virtual withdrawal" of the *Observations,* he felt that "there remained only the withdrawal of the 'Bampton Lectures' to fulfill every condition at first

38. December 24, 1847, BD, I. C200.   39. *Ibid.,* December 24, 1847.
40. *Ibid.,* December 27, 1847. In a letter of January 25, 1848, Hawkins explained that Hampden had withdrawn the *Observations,* but not as part of any bargain with Wilberforce.
41. Hawkins to Wilberforce, December 28, 1847 (BD, I. C200): "That there should be a very earnest desire on the part of the promoters of the suit to be entered, I can well understand. But how your Lordship can consent to their decision, after what you have told me, I confess I cannot understand."

desired for my own or the promoters' satisfaction." [42] With this assertion Hawkins could not agree. Many of Hampden's opponents, he wrote, held unsound theories which the Lectures had been designed to explode. "No revision which he can make without a sacrifice of truth can meet the views of such objectors." [43] Hawkins denied Wilberforce the right to claim major concessions from Hampden as a basis for the withdrawal of the suit, maintaining that Hampden had not in any sense recanted. If Wilberforce thought so and had acted accordingly, he had simply been mistaken.

Wilberforce, the self-appointed negotiator and peacemaker, had failed his mission. Most of the bishops who had signed the original Remonstrance were, by the end of December, ready to extricate themselves as quickly and quietly as possible from their entanglement. Blomfield appeared reluctant to allow Wilberforce to act on their behalf. "I doubt whether it will not be the fittest mode of providing," he wrote Wilberforce on the 24th, "for you to signify your own opinion to Dr. H. and to leave the other Bishops to adopt their own courses—but I am puzzled." The following day he wrote that after discussing the matter with the Archbishop, they had agreed "that it will be the safest plan for us to ground the withdrawal of our objections on Dr. H's letters to Lord John,[44] and (if deemed expedient) upon your being satisfied, as Dr. H's diocesan, with his explanation: and that this should be done in *general terms,* without entering into particulars." [45] Wilberforce could not resist the temptation to press this very vague commission to its limits. He wrote Hawkins on the 26th "that the Bishops for whose expressed opinion Dr. Hampden would feel most value, *are* ready, if I say to them as Diocesan, 'Dr. Hampden has given me as Diocesan a satisfactory explanation,' to adopt my judgment." [46] In the end, these bishops proved unwilling to do so. Though he claimed to act as their spokesmen, Wilberforce waited in vain for public expression of their support. He had shown a draft of his letter to Hampden to six of his fellow Remonstrants, and five had approved it. But, as published, it seemed to absolve Hampden of too much.[47] Blomfield objected in particular to the final paragraph—"en-

42. *Ibid.,* December 28, 1847.   43. *Ibid.,* January 1, 1848.

44. In which Hampden had stated that "I should be much concerned if, from any unskillfulness in the use of words, I should have given rise to misapprehensions. I would not assert, however, that I have always succeeded in conveying my thoughts exactly."

45. December 24, December 25, 1847, BD, I. C200.

46. *Ibid.,* December 26, 1847.

47. This point became a matter of controversy in February when The Reverend C. E. Kennaway, brother-in-law of Louisa Noel, wrote in defense of Wilberforce to the *Times.* Kennaway, who had followed the controversy closely, wrote with Wilberforce's consent, though without consulting him on what he planned to say. He maintained that Wilberforce had written with a "full persuasion" of the concurrence of the five bishops and with "an intimation of a similar character from the venerable primate himself. It was the illness of

tirely new to me" [48]—in which Wilberforce pledged himself to entreat those who had expressed alarm at the appointment "to weigh well the expression of my deliberate opinion, that you [Hampden] have given such explanations of what you personally believe on the points of suspicion, and what you intended as your meaning, as may well suffice to quiet all just alarm at your consecration to the office of Bishop." This asked a great deal on the basis of very little. Wilberforce was making bricks without straw, and the bishops declined to endorse his well-meant but insubstantial effort.

Only Phillpotts of Exeter, among the original Remonstrants, criticized Wilberforce for failing to forward the Letters and prosecute the suit.[49] He objected particularly to the wording of Wilberforce's public letter to Hampden, in which he had remarked that the purpose of the original Remonstrance was to represent to the government "the inconveniences" which might arise with the appointment of Hampden. "When I concurred in [the Remonstrance]," Phillpotts declared, "I did not deem . . . nor do I believe that you yourself then deemed, that it was an apprehension of 'an inconvenience' which arrayed us in an attitude, not of hostility, but of friendly, indeed yet earnest expostulation against a grave and very dangerous act of ministerial power." Phillpotts was unquestionably right, but his fellow Remonstrants, Wilberforce among them, were prepared to leave militant rectitude behind, if by so doing they could withdraw from the fray in more seemly order.

The controversy sputtered on in the newspapers for another month. Hampden denied that he had made concessions of any sort to Wilberforce. Wilberforce considered publishing a "Letter to a Friend," explaining once more his role in the proceedings, but was persuaded not to do so by Peel among others.[50] Most of the correspondence between Wilberforce and Hawkins eventually found its way into print, Hawkins assuming that Wilberforce was surreptitiously supplying the *Times* with

---

one, combined with one or two other circumstances, which delayed the public expression of this concurrence to so late a period that it was then thought better to let the matter rest" (*Times*, February 9, 1848, p. 8). This was not so, and Wilberforce worried lest the bishops think he had supplied Kennaway with this story. He wrote off immediately to one of the bishops (the name of the addressee is omitted on the copy; it was probably Denison of Salisbury): "I looked with great anxiety to the part which concerns my expectation of concurrence from the other Bishops; and though I should (especially since our conversation) have expressed the matter differently, yet I trust that taken in its context Kennaway's statement will not appear to you to be otherwise than substantially correct. I write in extreme *haste*. Will you communicate the substance to the Bishops of London and Winton and write to me?" (February 9, 1848, BD, I. C200). To Kennaway he wrote that there was *non*concurrence, grounded "on the difference between my draft letter and my actual letter. I see quite enough to account for their fully justifying to themselves their silence; I do not see any *material* difference" (February 11, 1848, Letter Book, BD, d. 204. 172).

48. February 8, 1848, BD, I. C200.   49. *Ibid.*, January 1, 1848.
50. January 25, 1848, BD, I. C194.

his side of the correspondence and insisting upon presenting his half as well. Wilberforce admitted that he had shown the letters to friends, but protested, genuinely enough, that he wished to see an end to the entire matter.[51] A group of Hampden's opponents had meanwhile attempted to bring the matter legally before the Archbishop, but their plea was denied. Hampden was consecrated on March 26 in Lambeth Chapel and went off to commence a long and completely uneventful episcopate in Hereford.

Without doubt Wilberforce was ready by that time to hear no more of the matter. The controversy had been much discussed and written of. The Oxford Heads of Houses had come publicly to Hampden's defense, voting twenty-four to fifteen in support of his nomination. The *Times* had throughout urged an examination of the Lectures and *Observations* by some sort of public tribunal, not necessarily the Court of Arches. The *Guardian,* the leading Church newspaper, hoped for something of the sort as well, and berated Russell for his willingness to ignore the Church's demand to have the dispute resolved to its own satisfaction.[52] Papers partisan to Russell argued his right to proceed as he had; in the process they lectured the bishops for their protest and singled out Wilberforce for particular abuse. The *Morning Chronicle,* in listing the Remonstrants' names, remarked upon that one "to whose Christian name men are profane, and have read of Sam Slick, and will add the epithet of 'sly,' and it was a bad sign of the success of the movement that men wondered very much that his name should be there." [53] When Wilberforce announced his intention to withdraw the Letters of Request, the Tractarian press turned upon him, now joining the very Low Church papers in jeering at his inconsistencies. The Evangelical *Record* quoted with delight from the High Church *Morning Post:* "An epithet more familiar than courteous has frequently been applied to Dr. Wilberforce, both before he became Bishop and since. So far as we can judge of the probable effect of his conduct in the Hampden affair, upon His Lordship's general repu-

---

51. Hawkins to Wilberforce, February 12, 1848; Wilberforce to Hawkins, February 12, 1848, BD, I. C200; Letter Book, BD, d.204, 182.

52. *Times,* December 25, 1847, p. 4; *Guardian,* December 8, 1847, pp. 728–729; December 29, 1847, p. 777.

53. *Morning Chronicle,* December 25, 1847, p. 2. On January 1 the *Chronicle* (p. 2) printed the following verse:

> "So you've watched the flying crow,
> Sam of Oxon—Sam of Oxon!
> Sniffed the way the court winds blow,
> Sam of Oxon—Sam of Oxon.
> Trimmed your sails and turned your coat.
> Sam of Oxon—Sam of Oxon.
> Thank ye, thank ye for your vote.
> Sam of Oxon—Sam of Oxon."

tation, he is likely for the future, as in former times, to be best known by
the designation of 'Slippery Sam.'" [54] Greville's opinion tallied with the
Post's. "Sly Sam of Oxford," he recorded in his diary, "has covered
himself with ridicule and disgrace. The disgrace is the greater because
everybody sees through his motives: he has got into a scrape at Court
and is trying to scramble out of it; there, however, he is found out, and
his favour seems to have long been waning." [55]

The Court had been much in Wilberforce's thoughts throughout the
controversy. The day after he wrote his first letter to Russell, he confided
to Louisa Noel that the "whole Hampden business is *very* painful to me.
It is so like hunting a man down that I am at times sick at heart, and feel
I could do anything to show him how I hate persecuting him. Then it is
painful to me to feel how probable it is that it will cost me that kindly
trust of the Queen, which, for no *end,* but for *itself,* I do, now God has
given it me, value highly. But one cannot *act* on these things." [56] He
believed that the signing of the Remonstrance had lost him royal favor
for good. That the loss galled is manifest in the subdued rancor of remarks in another letter to Louisa Noel, this one written while attacks
against him were at their height. "I know little about the news of the
Queen. I know that *early* she was as I believe very much displeased
with *me* about it. No leaning to Hampden, but *prerogative*. That I foresaw but could not help. I do not suppose the end will better it. I think
if I had stood out it would indeed so far have been better. Great people
can't afford to be abased by their friends." [57] To those who charged he
had tempered his initial judgment to win back the favor he had lost,
Wilberforce complained that justice, not self-service, had compelled him

54. *Record,* January 3, 1848, p. 4. No one apparently had yet begun to call him "Soapy."
The *Record* attacked Wilberforce as a Tractarian persecutor of Hampden. It charged that
Wilberforce had been behind the original proceedings, that the clergymen initiating the suit
were acting under their bishop's orders. "Everyone knows, who knows anything of the
matter, that Dr. Wilberforce's captivating manners, insinuating address, and bland deportment, quickened and carried home by great talent, extensive reading, and pious expression
have secured for him the confidence and approbation of his clergy in an unusual degree.
They move as he wishes them to move. Their act, in effect is his" (December 23, 1847,
p. 4). When Wilberforce subsequently withdrew the Letters, the *Record* was forced to admit
that he was less of a Tractarian than they had thought him. "It may be said, we presume
with truth, though somewhat invidiously, that the melioration of Tractarian views which
he at one time held, was indispensable for his advancement in the Church" (December
30, 1847, p. 4).
55. Greville, *Memoirs,* ed. Strachey and Fulford, VI, 3. Entry for January 7, 1848. Greville had been astonished to receive a visit from Wilberforce in 1846, while Wilberforce
was attempting to arrange the transfer of the parish and the collegiate church of Eton from
the diocese of Lincoln to Oxford. Greville believed that Wilberforce was trying to win his
influence. Wilberforce insisted, however, Greville wrote, "that he had heard I had been
dangerously ill, and that he had called to tender his spiritual advice and aid" (*ibid.,* V,
340–341).
56. December 12, 1847, BD, II. F.   57. *Ibid.,* January 9, 1848.

to admit his error and change his mind. "What mean the insulting epi-thets of 'courtly,' and such like," he asked indignantly in a letter to an Oxford clergyman.

Anything contrary to Christian honesty is equally bad at Court or away from Court: and if God were pleased, as I believe for my sainted father's sake, to give to one so unworthy his Sovereign's favour, surely that gift alone, unless it be misused, is not a warrant for the abuse of Christians. . . Such checks may be—it has been my prayer many times a day for this last week that to me it may be—an especial blessing. . . And if at times I can realise His 'Blessed are ye when men shall say all manner of evil against you falsely, for My sake,'—it is enough to turn all these sharp stings of natural pain at men's representations into joy it-self.[58]

Wilberforce did not resort to prayer alone in order to remove the stings. Early in January, while at Drayton, he managed to have "a long, private talk, and a satisfactory one, with Sir Robert as to *my* affairs." He reassured himself that Peel "entirely sees through the hollowness of all the charges of insincerity which have been urged against me so falsely, and this is a comfort to me." [59] Wilberforce hastened to defend his con-duct to Albert's secretary, Anson. "As I know the honesty of my own conduct, and am convinced that saving human errors, my judgment on dismissing the suit, was *just* to Dr. H. and *wise* for the Church, I hope for the best final issue." [60] Wilberforce remained convinced that for him the final issue was to be governmental and royal disfavor. He believed that had it not been for the Hampden controversy he, and not Sumner of Chester, would have acceded to Canterbury upon the death of Arch-bishop Howley in February, 1848. "Now when I think this I have rather a sad feeling," he confessed to Louisa Noel, "as If *I* had made a great mistake, and thrown away a great means of usefulness. But this is only a *feeling*. I *know* that God has ordered all, and I really do not believe I would have it otherwise, and I am sure it would have been a most *trying* position for me." [61] The rationalization cannot conceal the disappoint-ment. Nor could it then have kept Wilberforce from wishing that he had managed his role in the Hampden affair more adroitly. He had blundered badly, and his blunders, whether well-intentioned or not, did a great deal subsequently to keep him off the archepiscopal throne. Doubtless his signing of the original Remonstrance had been enough to prevent his advancement in 1848. Yet that misstep might have later been forgiven him had he not immediately followed it by a series of unskillful negotia-

58. To Edward Bickersteth, January 8, 1848, Letter Book, BD, d.204. 127–130.
59. To Louisa Noel, January 12, 1848, BD, II. F.
60. February 11, 1848, Letter Book, BD, d.204. 168–169.
61. February 20, 1848, BD, II. F.

tions which suggested to many that, slippery or not, he had neither tact nor judgment enough to be an effective archbishop.

Wilberforce was not without supporters and defenders. A. P. Stanley thought he had handled the situation ably, and could see "no interested motive" which might have dictated his behavior.[62] Keble defended his intentions in a letter to J. B. Mozley. He believed Wilberforce had felt "an earnest desire of peace joined to a fancy that he was the person to make it, as by a kind of special mission, which all must allow." [63] In this sentiment Keble was joined by Manning and by Robert Wilberforce. Both had hoped that Samuel would be able to stop the appointment. Both thought Hampden's writings dangerous to a degree Samuel did not. Yet Robert wrote that he did think Newman's Extracts unjust, and Manning, from Rome, expressed sympathy with the burdens Wilberforce had been compelled to bear.

> . . . Every one can imagine from their lesser experience how harassing are the weighings of a case pregnant, either way, with public and future consequences. One thing I am sure of, that what you have done, you believe to be just and right. And I can see how the points on which in our brotherly conferences we have varied in judgment make the line you take consistent with previous views.[64]

Although Wilberforce shouldered a difficult task with the best of intentions, he misjudged its nature and therefore the role he should play in its resolution. He treated Hampden as he might have treated any other parish clergyman, with no apparent thought of the offense Hampden would take at the manner of his interference. Anxious to save the Church the embarrassment and strain of a public trial, he failed to realize that the case had attracted too much attention to warrant the sort of private settlement he promoted. One of his critics pointed out that opponents of Hampden who might have accepted the verdict of an episcopal synod were not by any means prepared to acquiesce in the judgment of a junior bishop, following "an inquiry in his library by means of a mutual friend [Hawkins] communicating between him and the accused party." [65] In his self-confident determination to settle the matter himself, he allowed his natural impatience to draw him into a controversy without a complete understanding of his legal position and without a thorough knowledge of Hampden's own theological views. Believing doctrinal disputes served only to split the Church apart, he was more willing than others to interpret Hawkins' reports as concessions. His letter to Hampden, when published, therefore satisfied few. He seemed in fact to have delivered

62. A. P. Stanley to Mary Stanley, in Prothero, *Stanley*, I, 352–353.
63. February 18, 1848, J. B. Mozley, *Letters*, p. 191.
64. January 14, 1848, BD, III.
65. W. J. Trower, *The Hampden Controversy* (London, 1848), pp. 60–61. Trower was rector of Wiston, Sussex, and a former Fellow of Oriel.

himself into Hampden's hands, and the Church along with him. Pusey called the letter "more injurious to the Church than Hampden's appointment." [66] And Bishop Denison of Salisbury, like Wilberforce a moderate, questioned "whether, in your wish to avoid all unnecessary unfavorable language, and to do full justice you have not exposed our position more to attack in return than need have been the case." [67] Wilberforce agreed up to a point. "I ought to have been far colder," he wrote Charles Anderson. "And I do not think my letter expressed what I meant it to in more than one point: partly because I was anxious, as far as possible, if there was *not* legal ground for resistance to lead others to a peaceable acquiescence: partly as I was rather freshly indignant at the unfairness of the extracts of which I had of old complained to Newman." [68]

Wilberforce allowed himself to assume that his fellow bishops would welcome his public statement and would subscribe to it. When they did not, he considered himself unfairly treated.[69] The bishops, in turn, thought Wilberforce had compromised them behind their backs by discovering major concessions where none existed. He believed that his public declaration of Hampden's orthodoxy would serve the Church by "smoothing the way" to his appointment. So it would, had it been believed. But Hampden had conceded almost nothing, and Wilberforce had constructed his letter from air. By persisting as mediator, once legal proceedings appeared unjustified, Wilberforce chose the most challenging but also the most dangerous of alternatives open to him. He maintained, correctly, that it would have been simpler and far less damaging to his reputation to have forwarded the Letters of Request as he had originally intended, with the suit's promoters left to carry its burden through the courts.[70] When convinced he must drop the suit, he need not have entangled himself further by seeking to solicit reassurance for the Church from Hampden himself. In the face of Hampden's distrust and the bishops' reluctance Wilberforce declared himself ready to undertake the task. He had no doubts about his fitness for it. If he expected that his efforts might in the end redound to his credit, he hoped as well that they might bring a measure of peace to the warring factions of his Church. In the event they did neither. Wilberforce suffered public ridicule and private chastisement,

66. H. P. Liddon, *Pusey*, III, 162.   67. December 31, 1847, BD, I. C200.
68. January 30, 1848, BD, I. C191. If he had complained "of old," there is no record of it.
69. To Louisa Noel, January 9, 1848, BD, II. F. "Certainly I think my brethren have acted rather unfairly to me. I hear today from the Bishop of London that they are about to speak. High time, I think."
70. To Charles Anderson, January 1, 1848, BD, I. C191: "It is very easy for people to think I shrink from sending it into court, but the real shrinking as to that was *first* doing it and it was far more easy afterwards to stick to it when others were to carry it on, than to avow that a careful study of his work *with his explanations* had convinced me there was not matter for a criminal suit."

while to the eyes of already disaffected Tractarians the Church showed itself the captive of ruthless and ungodly Erastianism.

During the early years of his episcopate, Wilberforce allowed himself only one diversion from his work as a bishop. He had determined that much as he might suffer from Emily's death his children would suffer as little as possible. To that end he vowed to show them the affection he felt for them and give them all the time and attention he could. Fortunately for him, Mary Sargent, his mother-in-law, agreed to live with the family and help Samuel raise the children.[71] She was sixty-three at the time of Emily's death in 1841 and in the past twelve years had watched at the deathbeds of her husband and four of her children. She undertook her new position, not because she wanted to, but because she felt it her duty. Her tranquil acceptance of new burdens marked the depth of her simple faith.

Always I have declared I would not live with any of my sons-in-law, but would have an independent home, and above all that I could not live in dear SW's family as it would be too bustling for me; and especially I could not bear to live with his children as notwithstanding my love for them they were from delicate health, irritable temper, and fidgetting noisy habits more troublesome and required more attention than any children I had ever known excepting *two* of my own beloved seven. I felt that having gone through much fatigue with my own family I could not bear to begin again the labour and turmoil of life with all its sweets to be taken away. And yet this has been allotted to me and God has preserved my health, and I am sure I am in an ungrateful state of mind not to accept willingly all he appoints and to receive thankfully the many blessings which surround me. . .

I admire the wisdom and love which has ordained this change for me—I quite believe I was settling down in an easy, indolent, selfish state; enjoying my little quiet amusements and having enough occupation with the poor to satisfy my conscience. The sudden wrench from everything I had admired and liked has been a useful weaning from earthly enjoyments, and I hope to benefit by it. Everything but the dear children is perfectly uninteresting to me and I can take no pleasure in them. I am too old to find it in the company of children but I will try (God helping me) to be useful to them and to give up my own comfort for their sakes.[72]

Mrs. Sargent had hoped to spend a good deal of time at Lavington, which had passed into Wilberforce's hands upon Emily's death, but she went willingly with him to Cuddesdon when he was made bishop, and lived as much there and in London as she did at her former home in Sussex.

71. Wilberforce's mother lived with her son Henry, after Robert moved north, until her death in 1847.
72. Reflections, September 5, 1841, Chichester, 63.

The children were well looked after and did not lack for affection. Wilberforce was an attentive father. He took the boys on rides and to the zoo. When they were sick he fretted over them. When they left for school he pined for them. Often when he watched them he thought of the pleasure they would have given Emily, and then he mourned her loss afresh. "Christmas is a time at which I searchingly feel my baseness," he wrote in 1846 to Louisa Noel, his closest confidante in family matters. "Those times of nestling together, of creeping into the closest family life, are very trying: a sword seems to run into the soul." [73] He naturally concerned himself with the state of his children's souls and reported a conversation with Ella when she was thirteen. "Oh I do long beyond expression, dearest sister [Louisa] to see in her a real choice. It is curious but Garton [Reginald], seems to me *far* more accessible to religious feeling than either of the others. I think dearest Ella the least." [74] He hoped, as she grew up, that she would not fall prey to the world. After a visit to the Bishop of Gloucester: "How little I should like my darling Ella to be like the Bishop of Gloucester's daughters. Poor Mrs. Monk seems so entirely worldly: and *how* shall *I* guide her. Oh my dearest sister, it seems then to me, as if *her* blessed motherly instincts would have done all." [75] Ella's own instincts proved up to the task. She determined to marry a country clergyman and in 1851 did so, taking as her husband the sober-sided rector of Clifton, Henry Pye. A "thorough English High Churchman," Wilberforce described him at the time,[76] though Pye was to prove him wrong by taking himself and Ella with him into the Church of Rome in 1868.

The boys attended a succession of public schools and left behind them a general tradition of lawlessness.[77] Only two of the four went to University. Herbert left Eton and at twelve went to sea. Reginald (called Garton by the family) joined the army and began his service in India. Ernest and Basil, after a spate of private tutoring, were able to gain admittance to Exeter College. None of them were scholars, nor got much pleasure from books. And all of them upon occasion sorely tried their father. "I often doubt," he once wrote plaintively to his brother Robert, "whether we gave our parents quite as much anxiety as our boys do us. I do not mean that I think *I* was any better, though you were, because I know I was not. But somehow or other I do not think our dear father was anxious about us." [78] William Wilberforce was anxious for his children but not in the way his son was. Both worried lest their sons and daughters

73. December 26, 1846, BD, II. F.   74. *Ibid.,* August 30, 1843.
75. *Ibid.,* May 22, 1845.   76. To Charles Anderson, April 10, 1851, BD, I. C191.
77. Herbert to Eton; Reginald to Radley and Rugby; Ernest to Radley and Harrow; Basil to Eton.
78. March 28, 1852, Wrangham papers.

grow up without a consciousness of God and of his message. But Samuel concerned himself as well with their way in the world to a degree his father would have thought unnecessary and in a manner that he would have found hard to understand.

Herbert, the eldest son, was his father's favorite. Like his brothers, he got himself into scrapes and relied on his father to get him out. Only after repeated difficulties at school did Wilberforce consent to his joining the Navy. As usual he communicated his worries to Louisa Noel. "Unless there comes some great change he will never do more than reluctantly pass through school and college exercises," he wrote in 1845. Even with a university education, his prospects were dim. "He will not have fortune enough to live as a country gentleman at Lavington: it might be his home when he came on shore and his anchoring ground when his character was made and he had added something to his inherited means." [79] In June 1846 Wilberforce saw Herbert off at Spithead. "He was most beloved: talked a great deal to me and would remember all I said to him: and what his uncle HEM [Manning] had said: that he should not be unhappy and hoped we should not... He is gone under Captain Meresly the father of Mrs. James Prevost who has a great affection for all of us and will I think look after H. a little." [80] The chance that Herbert, young and far from home, would acquire the bad habits of a sailor preyed on his father's mind. When the boy wrote home for £5 behind his captain's back, Wilberforce, fearing "it is some gambling or cards," sent the money sealed with a covering note to the chaplain, asking that it be given Herbert if deemed necessary.

All went well enough with him until April 1852, when he was sent home for acts of insubordination. "This is not being dismissed the service," Samuel reported to Robert, "but it amounts to the same thing." Herbert had claimed his first lieutenant had treated him unjustly. The captain backed the lieutenant, and Herbert refused to accept the captain's decision. He came to England in the summer, "in a most gratifying state of mind: affectionate, thoughtful with a new desire to educate himself, and altogether turned from a thoughtless boy into a thoughtful man." Wilberforce went to work on his behalf and reported to Robert in August that he had successfully "arranged dearest H's matters at the Admiralty." [81] Not for the last time. Two years later he persuaded Sir Richard Dundas, a junior Lord of the Admiralty under Sir James Graham, to bring Herbert home on the sly to Portsmouth to take his examination for a lieutenantcy. "I would give anything to get him made Lieutenant," Samuel confessed, again to his brother, "but our friends are all so con-

79. January 14, 1845, BD, II. F.   80. June 14, 1846, BD, I. C194.
81. December 30, 1851, April 28, 1852, August 13, 1852, Wrangham papers.

scientious that nothing can be got *from them* by friendship."[82] In the end, and by dint of his father's hard work Herbert got both the lieutenantcy and an appointment on the *Trafalgar,* a ship of 120 guns about to depart for the Crimea. Tenacity and connection had paid off. "Here I am," Samuel had reported to Herbert in June,

sitting in Captain Hamilton's room, hoping to hit Sir Jas. Graham between wind and water as he comes out of the Board Room. I have got Lord Aberdeen to speak very strongly to Sir Jas: Sir Jas. objected to the scrape you had got into in the Daedalus, 'there was really bad conduct etc.' Ld. Aberdeen pressed hard, 'a single instance, good conduct before and since etc.' and at last Sir Jas. [said] it should be so and Ld. A. advised waiting at present to see whether Graham did it of himself. But now comes this appointment to the Trafalgar just in the nick of time and Hamilton advises me to go to Graham and try what I can do with him.[83]

Three weeks later Wilberforce wrote Herbert a long instructional letter, encouraging him to make the most of his new opportunities, while revealing a good deal of himself in the process. He urged him to pursue the practice of reading and writing, promising to return, corrected, any themes he might send home.

Then the second thing I want to say is this: Rise up to your new position. Put away the narrowness of the midshipman's mess. Do not allow yourself to *think* of your Captain as being your enemy etc., but throw yourself into the spirit of your noble profession. Remember how everything now depends on yourself. As a midshipman you were thought of as a boy. Tempers, passions, and any other faults were *punished*—your leave stopped, etc; and then they passed away. It will not be so now. *Now* you can stand alone in the great life struggle. I can help you far less than before. You must help yourself. I could not get you through another scrape as that of the 'Daedalus.' Watch your temper; pray against giving way to it; you will find a great help against it in the self-education I have spoken of before. As your mind opens, and takes a greater interest in other things, you will be less tempted to irritation by those round you. I have only two things more to say—First make the men under you love you, and they will serve you well; show them that you care about *them,* about their *feelings,* and they will soon serve you for love: There is a man's heart at the bottom of the worst of them. Secondly, remember God's Eye, Christ's Cross, and the free pardon for sin which it has brought for you; and that God's holy Spirit *will* help you against all temptations if you will pray. May God Almighty bless you.[84]

Herbert Wilberforce did not live to follow the course his father was so assiduously charting for him. Although he survived the battle of Sebastopol and returned to England in 1855, the strain and exposure of active duty induced the disease his mother had died of. In February 1856 Wilberforce, accompanied by Mrs. Sargent, took Herbert to Torquay.

82. *Ibid.,* March 2, 1854.
83. June 20, 1854, BD, II. W. Wilberforce was a close friend of Arthur Gordon, Aberdeen's son.
84. July 10, 1854, BD, II. W.

Thoughts of his son's impending death intensified his thoughts of Emily. "Up early and found dearest Herbert looking on the sea from his bed and enjoying it," he wrote in his diary. "I walked on the rocks where I had walked of old with my beloved wife, and saw the same sea swelling into the same caves as when we used to watch it in 1826–7." [85] Herbert died on the night of February 28, "with a firm, humble hopeful confidence in Christ's blood which was remarkable. All this is *full* of mercy," he wrote to Anderson, "but oh, my very dear friend, it is a stroke which cuts to the very quick of my soul and opens all its agony afresh. He was so bound up with the memory of his blessed mother in my heart of hearts." [86]

As he had at the time of Emily's death, Wilberforce smothered his grief in work. He buried Herbert at Lavington on March 2, and remained there to mourn for two days. Then he swung into a round of confirmations with an energy that astonished his archdeacon, James Randall, who recounted the bishop's activities to R. C. Trench. "If I had not been prepared for something wonderful by what you told me at Cuddesdon about the Bishop's conduct under a still more bitter bereavement, I should have been perfectly amazed at his self-command and self-possession under his present loss." The exertions made him fear for "the heavy wear and tear upon the inward man. But what an astonishing creature he is! What is he made of? What is he made *for?* Surely there must yet be some great purpose for him to fulfill." [87]

85. February 14, 1856, Ashwell and Wilberforce, *Life,* II, 305.
86. February 28, 1856, BD, I. C191.   87. March 10, 1856, Chichester, 26.

CHAPTER VI

Ritual and the Church of Rome

Ritualism and the fear of Roman aggression upset and divided the Church of England more than any other issue during the early years of Wilberforce's episcopate. From 1845 until about 1860 he endured pressures and, when he refused to yield to them, vituperations from both Tractarians and Evangelicals, while attempting to establish some sort of Anglican *modus vivendi* in the parishes under his jurisdiction. Newman's secession and the ritualist enthusiasms of a second generation at Oxford had intensified Evangelical opposition to the Tractarian movement. Many sensed a further hardening of parties and positions and charged older Tractarians, such as Pusey and Keble, with allowing themselves to be led on by others willing to countenance the mutilation of the Church. "Instead of controlling the ebullitions of the young wrongheads," a friend had written Pusey in 1841, "you have suffered yourselves to be inoculated with their frenzies." [1] Young clergymen, inspired or inoculated as the case may be, went out from the University in the late 1840's as anxious to revive the spiritual life of their parishes as their earlier counterparts had been, and insisting in a way those older men had not upon ritual as an indispensable means to that end. The Tractarians of the 1830's, as one biographer has put it, "sat lightly on the niceties of worship. With them, the main business of a celebrant was simply absorption in the awful presence of God." [2]

Not so their successors, who pressed ritual innovation, often upon unwilling congregations, and thus stirred parishes into dispute. Men like Hook deplored this newer sort of Anglicanism. "I am quite sure of this," he wrote a friend in 1842, "that the wrongheadedness and tyrannical disposition of many of our young clergy who dare to make alterations in their Churches, and to restore ceremonies which they consider old, without consulting the wishes of the people, or applying for the direction of their bishop, have set more persons in opposition to the Church than

1. From E. Churton, December 9, 1841, in H. P. Liddon, *Life of Edward Bouverie Pusey,* 4 vols. 2d ed. (London, 1893). II, 269.
2. B. A. Smith, *Dean Church* (London, 1958), p. 179.

all the violence of Papists and Dissenters." [3] On the contrary, the Ritualists insisted, their attention to the outward forms of religious life was drawing people to the Church who would otherwise have remained indifferent to its message. The only way to bring a slum parish to life, they argued, was to reintroduce the solemn and colorful pageants which puritanism had successfully repressed for over three centuries. Zealous priests did attract new worshippers with strenuous revivals in such London parishes as St. Paul's, Knightsbridge; St. Barnabas, Pimlico; and St. George's in the East. But in the process they attracted violent and abusive opposition.

Church newspapers began to reflect the increasing division brought on by the aggressive campaigns of ritualists and antiritualists. The Evangelicals had their *Record* and their less vociferous *Christian Observer*. The ritualists were forced to rely upon the relatively moderate *Guardian* until in 1860 and 1863, the *Church Union* and the *Church Times* were founded in their defense. Without doubt the papers furthered faction and disunity. Wilberforce, a frequent target, bemoaned their influence and effect. "Can any one read these habitually," he asked in a sermon on Church unity, "without finding them specially distinguished by angry assertion of merely party distinction, and this supported by frequent personal slander, by insinuations of evil motives in others, by the aggravation of every error, by the infusion of the worst suspicion, by audacious assertions, reluctant retractions, themselves armed with poisoned stings, that they who have been once injured by the false assertion may now be doubly harmed by the faint denial." [4]

Wilberforce had tried to stand clear of factionalism before coming to Oxford, and tried even harder thereafter. With the Evangelicals he hoped to maintain at least a truce. He continued to preach at annual May meetings of Low Church organizations such as the Church Missionary Society and the Pastoral Aid Society. He took pains to appoint an Evangelical to his staff of chaplains, "lest he be criticized for Tractarian leanings." [5] He nevertheless found it difficult to support the sort of Evangelicalism which seemed to him to deny the importance of the Church. He expressed the difficulties he felt in a letter to Hook.

We may unite and I long to unite with them in aggression against sin and absolute deadness of the soul because as to these things we agree with them: but as to these Church matters we have not a common object and our union would be untrue and unblessed. They do not believe in what you have been spending your

3. W. F. Hook to ? Bellairs, February 16, 1842, in Stephens, *Hook,* II, 144–145.
4. "Unity in the Church," *Sermons Preached on Various Occasions by The Right Reverened Father in God Samuel Wilberforce, late Lord Bishop of Winchester,* ed. J. R. Ely (Oxford and London, 1877), pp. 125–126.
5. He chose E. M. Goulburn, later dean of Norwich.

life to prove: that God the Holy Ghost dwells with the Church of Christ and makes his sacraments his means of working on souls.

Agree to cooperate with them, he warned, and then watch them "turn round on you and hunt you out." [6] Wilberforce wrote this letter in 1858, after having suffered a number of attacks at Evangelical hands. Try though he might to maintain a middle ground he failed to convince Evangelicals he was not a High Churchman. Middle ground seemed indefensible in the eyes of ecclesiastical partisans. Thus an Evangelical, writing to criticize Wilberforce's appearance at a confirmation in the parish of St. Paul's, Knightsbridge: "It is the contradictory position, the insincere profession, the trimming so as to be on with the new love yet not off with the old, that forms a principal ground of offence, not only of the Protestant public, but really of all who regard such conduct in its proper light." [7]

Ritualists were no more satisfied with Wilberforce's conduct than Evangelicals. Once a bishop, he softened his criticisms to suit his self-imposed role as mediator, but his personal views remained much the same. He felt Bennett of St. Paul's, Knightsbridge, had done "unspeakable mischief," and supported decisions taken during the 1850's restraining the more extreme Ritualists.[8] His concern remained throughout that ritualist and antiritualist partisanship would split the Church apart. "That of which I complain above all," he wrote to the *Record* following a series of attacks upon him in 1853, "is your increasing efforts to divide my own clergy of all schools allowed within our Church—whom I desire to unite, quicken, and help in their ministerial work—in habitually striving to render these men suspicious of their brethren and their Bishop." [9] Wilberforce, who had expressed the hope when he became a bishop that he might be "Father in God to all my clergy" complained that dissension and division between parties in the Church was not allowing him to do so. A bishop was charged with the duty of binding together the clergy into a community as wide as the Church allowed yet obedient to the bishop as final arbiter and authority. The charge put to young ordinands that they strive for the quietness and peace of their parish was, Wilberforce once declared, a charge peculiar to the Church of England, and

6. August 14, 1858, BD, I. C194.

7. *The Bishop of Oxford's Reception in Belgravia* (London, 1857), p. 12.

8. To Charles Anderson, January 25, 1851, BD, I. C191. See *Charge*, 1857, pp. 50–51, where he supports the banning of embroidered linen and lace—"the tawdry and tinsel trappings of Rome"—from the Communion table.

9. November, 1853, Ashwell and Wilberforce, *Life*, II, 221. In 1862 Hook encouraged Wilberforce to buy a provincial newspaper himself: not a religious journal—"a religious newspaper is a nuisance—I speak of a common newspaper which shall be liberal on points of social reform, and as you like in politics. What we want are clever newspapers which will state the truth about the Church; which will not engage in petty polemics, etc." (Stephens, *Hook,* II, 415). Nothing came of this interesting idea.

based upon the divergent rituals and doctrines it accommodated. Divergence necessitated tolerance, and Wilberforce never ceased preaching it, urging his clergy to remember that "what we deem errors in others are often but different views of the same truth, imperfect on the one side as our own very probably are on the other." A bishop, though unable to reconcile such divergences, was charged with the maintenance of quiet and peace by ruling firmly and fairly, "allowing the full license the Church allows, without ever compromising what seems wrong." [10]

So Wilberforce had hoped it might be. As he himself lamented frequently, it happened much differently. While still bishop-elect he began a long disputation with Pusey that proved one of the most taxing of his career. When, in 1843, Pusey preached the sermon on the Holy Eucharist that led to his suspension from University preaching for two years, Wilberforce defended him from charges of heresy, although he thought the tone of the sermon exaggerated and un-Anglican in its "misty exaggeration of the whole truth." [11] Bishop Bagot had tolerated Pusey; Wilberforce was prepared to do the same, but made it clear that toleration was to be on his own terms. Pusey's recent interference on behalf of Tractarians in the parish of St. Saviour's, Leeds, and his sympathetic pronouncements at the time of Newman's conversion, had disturbed Wilberforce and warned him of the difficulties he might be forced to face in the near future.

Believing as he did that Pusey's pronouncements represented a threat to the Church, and recognizing full well the influence he could exert as canon of the cathedral, professor of Hebrew, and acknowledged leader among the Tractarians, Wilberforce responded coolly to Pusey's proffered good wishes upon his succession. In his reply he wrote of the pain he had felt when reading Pusey's remarks concerning Newman's conversion, and although he closed with thanks for the prayers and intercessions Pusey had promised on behalf of his new bishop, he left no doubt of his deep disagreement with the fundamentals of Pusey's belief. In a second letter, he expressed himself more strongly and more fully. He deplored the readiness of Tractarians to consider themselves a party, and accused Pusey of harboring "a subtle and therefore most dangerous form of self-will; and a tendency to view yourself as one in, if not now the leader of, a party. This seems to me," he continued, "to lead you to judge the Church which you ought to obey; sometimes to blame, sometimes almost to patronize her; and hence to fall into the further error of undervaluing the One inspired Revelation of God's will given to us in His perfect Word." These were hard words to address to a distinguished theologian;

10. To Charles Anderson, November 15, 1845, BD, I. C191; *Addresses to the Candidates for Ordination,* pp. 229–232; *Charge,* 1848, pp. 37–40.
11. To R. Walker, July 16, 1843, in Ashwell and Wilberforce, *Life,* I, 229–230.

Wilberforce thought them necessary. "Should you admit even the possibility of this being true, you will agree with me that not to take any new step, but to watch most earnestly against self-dependence and the spirit or acts of party, is at this moment your especial duty." [12]

Pusey, whatever his opinion of Wilberforce himself, was less likely than most to accept the advice of his bishop. He had little regard for episcopal authority. When Keble had complained to him several years before that he found it hard to accept his bishop's word, Pusey had replied that Keble had no cause to worry. "In whatever degree he is really speaking against you, he is speaking against the truth, and therefore I should not think that I had any responsibility. It is everyone's duty to maintain Catholic truth, even if unhappily opposed by a Bishop." [13] Pusey would never surrender to any authority save that of Catholic truth. His self-reliance cost him his bishop's trust. He sensed that his position as canon *ex officio* compounded the tenuousness of his relationship. "I hardly know what my relation to yourself will be; we seem in such an un-episcopal state," he wrote Wilberforce. "Electing you, it seems, in a very effective and solemn way, as our Bishop, and then, in no relation with the Bishop, when elected, except privately or in concurrence with the Ordinations." [14] With this analysis Wilberforce could not agree. A bishop exercised authority over all those in any way under his charge. He might privately attend to any who came to him for an expression of theological opinion. "Such . . . I would always be ready to listen to, and if possible to aid, not by controversy, but by a true sympathy and by any practical counsels which God may enable me to offer." At the same time a bishop could not shirk his public responsibilities. And should those same disturbed people express to the world the doubts—perhaps the heresies—they had confided to their bishop in private, the bishop might be compelled to move against them. Private communications, he warned Pusey, "stand wholly apart from any judgment or step which I may be compelled to pronounce or take by any public act, in which these same persons may embody the difficulties or errors which they have communicated to me, and from which I have sought by private counsel to withdraw them." [15]

Both men had made their positions clear. Both continued to disagree, and a public clash of some sort was probably inevitable. It came five years later. The grounds were Wilberforce's conviction that Pusey's

12. December 5, 1845, Ashwell and Wilberforce, *Life,* I, 308–309.
13. February 14, 1842, Liddon, *Pusey,* II, 238.
14. November 27, 1845, Ashwell and Wilberforce, *Life,* I, 306. Pusey was technically correct. Neither as canon of Christ Church nor as Regius Professor of Hebrew was he subject to the bishop, as Ordinary.
15. *Ibid.,* December 5, 1845, I, 307.

preaching, while in no way heretical, led men to embrace the Roman Catholic faith; specifically, that his use of devotional books, supposedly of Roman origin, and his readiness to encourage the practice of confession carried men away from the Church to Rome. Wilberforce opened his correspondence with Pusey in consequence of a pamphlet, written by a London clergyman, William Dodsworth, accusing Pusey of distributing dangerous devotional books among his followers. Wilberforce insisted that he was not suggesting Pusey intentionally proselytized for Rome; "nay, I know that you have often fruitlessly striven, in the last stages of their course, to retain in the Church of England those who under you, as I believe, had learned to distrust her. But giving the fullest credit to your intentions, this, I am convinced, is the actual result of your teaching." The recent pamphlet merely confirmed what Wilberforce had long suspected. Had Pusey been directly under his jurisdiction, he declared, he would have brought the matter before him sooner. "Your occasional exercise of your ministry in my diocese, with my conviction of its results, forces me now to address you, and to call upon you to give some public and distinct answer to Mr. Dodsworth's charges." Without such an answer and assurance of Pusey's intention to alter his present habits of instruction and devotion, Wilberforce declared he would remain convinced that the diocese would continue to be dangerously exposed "to the corruptions or the communion of the See of Rome." [16]

Pusey replied with a long letter in which he complained that Dodsworth had represented the books unfairly, that he encouraged no practices that the formularies of the Church did not themselves countenance, and that those who persecuted Tractarians—"Lord John Russell, Presbyterians, and all who hate the Church"—did so because they did hate the Church, and saw the Tractarians as its major bulwark.[17] Wilberforce was unmoved, and though shrinking from a formal inhibition, expressed the wish that Pusey no longer preach within the diocese until he could satisfy Wilberforce as to the soundness of his beliefs. In an ensuing exchange of letters the dispute centered upon a discussion of confession. Wilberforce drew a distinction between confession as occasionally sanctioned by the Church of England and as habitually practiced by the Church of Rome. He insisted that Pusey, ready to "guide" any who might come to him, had become a confessor in the Roman Catholic sense. The Church of England might countenance confession "as a special remedy for a special disorder." Rome regarded it as "the only safe, habitual state," and invested it with a sacramental character. Pusey's letter, Wilberforce wrote, convinced him "that your system is in this matter more nearly allied to

16. *Ibid.,* November 2, 1850 [probably misdated and in fact sent November 20], II, 80.
17. November 21, 1850, Liddon, *Pusey,* III, 303.

Rome than to England." Pusey's motives may well have been pure; "and yet the fact remains: you seem to me to be habitually assuming the place and doing the work of a Roman Confessor, and not that of an English clergyman." [18]

Pusey found it difficult to respond. "I can only say generally that I have sought honestly to act as a priest of The Church of England." Wilberforce insisted that confession must not appear compulsory; Pusey agreed. But, he added, "What ought I to do as an English priest, if persons ask me from time to time to allow them to open their griefs, and would not be at peace without so doing?" He explained that in these cases he saw nothing wrong in assuming the role of director. Wilberforce could not understand how distraught the worried souls were who came to Pusey for help, about to declare themselves unable any longer to withstand the blandishments of Rome, yet pathetically anxious to grasp at any straw to keep themselves within the Church of England. "Your Lordship has probably not seen such cases, when people are so panic-stricken that all reasoning is useless, but they can feel 'you know better than I, and if you think it safe and right for me, I can stay with a quiet conscience.'" Absolution, Pusey believed, did have a sacramental character—"as a means of grace with an outward sign"; such, he insisted, was the teaching of the Homily on Common Prayer and Sacraments. He realized that Wilberforce might well disagree with him, but asked only for a chance to explain his views to him in person.[19]

There could be little discussion between the two as long as Wilberforce's language remained as vague as it was. "Influence" and "tone" were difficult to assess objectively, and Wilberforce ignored Pusey's request for an interview. Meanwhile, Pusey agreed to respect Wilberforce's injunction, a private one known only to a few. There the matter rested until Pusey had prepared a written answer to Bishop Blomfield, who acting on Dodsworth's evidence, had leveled similar accusations against him in his Charge of 1850. Again Pusey asked for a chance to talk with Wilberforce, to discuss the draft of his letter; again Wilberforce ignored the request. Pusey despaired and turned to Keble for advice. "What is to be done, if the Bishop continues this quasi-suspension? To wait quiet, until this tyranny be overpast? One may say, 'Lord how long?' . . . Is it best for me to go on thus, doing what work God gives me, yet secretly disowned and crippled." [20]

Keble replied that it would be better to act than to wait, and undertook to write Wilberforce on Pusey's behalf. He deplored the "similar proceedings elsewhere," but this particular one "most especially, be-

18. November 30, 1850, Ashwell and Wilberforce, *Life,* II, 89–90.
19. *Ibid.,* December 6, 1850, II, 91–93.
20. March 1, 1851, Liddon, *Pusey,* III, 310.

cause I say to myself, here are two persons who really ought to understand one another; and it seems quite a judgment upon us that they
cannot act together on our behalf." [21] Wilberforce replied that though he
welcomed Keble's advice, he would be unable to accept it. "To *answer*
Dr. Pusey's writings as you suggest, seems to me the duty of those who
have leisure for theological writing. My call is to action. I see a great
danger of a very peculiar form, if young men, some very slightly instructed, some struggling out of gross sin, some loving novelty and
excitement, were brought under his spiritual guidance." [22] He informed
Keble that he was "far advanced" in a study of Pusey's recent statements
on doctrine and ritual and of his "adaptations" of Roman Catholic books
of devotion, and pledged himself to write Pusey once he had decided his
own course. For a time, Wilberforce contemplated addressing a public
letter to Pusey. He sent it to Bishop Denison of Salisbury, who approved
it, and to Pusey who passed it on to Keble. Both Pusey and Keble contended that Wilberforce could not continue his inhibition without bringing
Pusey to court on specific charges. Neither side could acknowledge the
other's argument. Pusey demanded a trial on the grounds of preaching
false doctrine. Wilberforce argued that the matter was not for the courts
but for him to decide. He had never accused Pusey of heresy. He believed
that Pusey's "tone and tendencies" led on to Rome men whom he, as
bishop, was particularly charged to protect from that temptation. If such
was the case, would he not be doing less than he should, if he did not
strive with all his power to halt the contamination? [23]

Here the matter rested and was bound to rest until someone came forward with some sort of compromise solution. Friends of both men worked
to prevent a public clash. Gladstone cautioned Pusey against bringing
the matter to a head. The bishop's "marvellously acute and rapid mind,"
he advised, was immature. A crisis might "precipitate in fixed form his
cruder ideas and check the free growth of those which, but for that
crisis, may be destined to correct and overrule them." [24] Wilberforce
finally consented to an interview. The two agreed that Pusey should
continue to abstain from preaching within the diocese until Wilberforce
could speak in his forthcoming Charge generally against the threat of
Roman aggression and specifically against the sort of devotional books
Pusey had been adapting for Anglican use. This Wilberforce did in November 1851, condemning the books as dangerous, morbid, and alien to
the teaching of the Church. Pusey began a public reply, but eventually
contented himself with a private letter to Wilberforce in April, setting

21. March 11, 1851, Ashwell and Wilberforce, *Life*, II, 95.
22. March 14, 1851, Letter Book, BD, d.204, pp. 277–279.
23. July 18, 1851, Ashwell and Wilberforce, *Life*, II, 111–112.
24. Liddon, *Pusey*, III, 324.

out once again his defense and renewing his request that he be allowed to preach. He covered no new ground, but put his case as fervently as he could.

It has been one of the greatest wearinesses I have, to go through the Roman question again and again, until I turn almost sick at the very first words in a letter which tell me of perplexities about the Church, knowing what a weary labour there is before me, what great fears of its fruitlessness, how much it will hinder what I wish to do of solid work for the Church in exposition of Holy Scripture. I wish, my dear Lord, I could send these cases to you and that you could satisfy them. But if for the Church's sake and for their souls I undertake a very weary and often thankless labour, which often brings on me ingratitude and misrepresentation, it is really hard that this is made a ground of suspecting me, that I fail where no one can succeed.[25]

Wilberforce, though still concerned that Pusey encouraged devotional excesses—invocation of saints, use of the rosary—which went contrary to the teaching and practice of the Church, replied that having himself now pronounced against those excesses, and having convinced himself that Pusey did indeed mean to keep as many within the Church as he could, he felt himself able to set him free as he requested.[26]

The long controversy had not been a happy one for Wilberforce. Though he could not get close to Pusey, he had a good deal of respect for him, and the reluctance he professed when he moved against him was genuine. His fear for the Church was undoubtedly just as real. He had received word that Pusey was prepared, if necessary, to undertake the secret counseling of young people against the wishes of their parents and deplored his readiness to do so.[27] He despised the sort of perfervid adorations catalogued in the books of devotion Pusey edited and recommended. Convinced that he must act, how was he to proceed? He did not believe Pusey a heretic and could not take him into court. J. T. Coleridge, the Tractarian justice, wrote Wilberforce advising him against a suit and urging him to do his best to avoid controversy of any sort.[28] Wilberforce replied that he was anxious, too, to prevent a public confrontation. That none occurred was due far more to Pusey's forebearance than to Wilberforce's pious hopes. Wilberforce, unable to issue a command, instead made a request. Pusey, determined not to aggravate where he could not heal the divisions in the Church, agreed to heed the request, and this despite his general antipathy to episcopal jurisdiction of any sort. His agreement suggests the length to which he was ready to go to preserve the body of the Church. It suggests, too, an appreciation

25. *Ibid.,* April 18, 1852, III, 340.
26. May 6, 1852, Ashwell and Wilberforce, *Life,* II, 115–116.
27. Letter from T. T. Carter, April 17, 185(?) [probably 1851], BD, I. C193.
28. July 16, 1851, Ashwell and Wilberforce, *Life,* II, 112.

of the fact that Wilberforce, despite those "cruder ideas" which Pusey along with Gladstone might deplore, was working for the same important goal.

Relations between the two men improved rapidly after 1852. Both could join together to deplore "Germanism," and soon did so. Wilberforce invited Pusey to preach Lenten sermons and Pusey accepted gladly. Wilberforce continued a strong opponent of confession as anything more than a temporary and very occasional aid to faith. Burdened souls must be permitted this relief, he argued in his Charge of 1851, and for such souls the Church did prescribe confession. But, for most, such drastic measures were unnecessary. The Church believed that it could rely upon "the instructed conscience" of each member to direct his own spiritual life. "She knows that no soul can hand over to another its own fearful gift of individual responsibility. She uses, therefore, every part of the ministry not to supersede, but to awaken, quicken, restore, strengthen and direct that internal supremacy of the individual conscience which she believes to be the voice of God in man." [29] This remained his belief. When sufficient cause presented itself, when consciousness of sin could not be removed with general confession and absolution, or "when there is some real question as to duty which another can help us solve," only then were confession and absolution God's ordinance.[30]

In controversies over doctrine and ritual Wilberforce was seldom blessed with opponents as patient and forebearing as Pusey. Most proved at best argumentative, at worst defiant. One such, the Reverend T. W. Allies, had plagued Wilberforce during the course of his very early years as bishop. Allies, a High Churchman and friend of Henry Wilberforce and Henry Manning, had been rusticated to the parish of Launton after serving without much effect as a chaplain to Bishop Blomfield. There he determined to impose his own views upon a parish unwilling to accept them. The result was a battle into which Wilberforce was bound to be drawn. In July 1846 Allies bridled at marrying couples in his parish who seemed to him to have left the Church altogether. Wilberforce wrote to inform him that he must marry anyone unless excommunicated by sentence of court. The following year Allies attacked the vicar of Bicester for preaching contrary to the Church's teaching on baptism, in language so violent and abusive as to bring a sharp rebuke from his bishop.

---

29. *Charge,* 1851, pp. 66–67.

30. To Mrs. Sidney Herbert, August 16, 1855, Letter Book, BD, d.148, pp. 158–60. In 1858 Wilberforce found himself embroiled in the so-called "Boyne Hill case," in which the subject of confession raised itself again. This time a young curate was accused of extracting confession from a dying woman. The affair received a good deal of attention, especially from the *Times* (September 6, 1858), which criticized Wilberforce for tolerating confession and for supporting a church which encouraged it. Wilberforce appointed a commission which cleared the curate of the charges brought against him.

You are very little aware of the Spirit which is in you. There is a self-sufficient bitterness running through your former and your present letter. In that you undertook to excommunicate a brother presbyter, your elder in the ministry; in this you insult your Bishop; insinuate that he has been guilty of advising one of his presbyters to act against his conscience; as well as of a gross dereliction of duty; and threaten, as the consequence of your opinion not being adopted, separation from the Church of your baptism. Do you believe that Christ reigneth? That you are a presbyter in His Church? and that you have in me one set over you in Christ's stead? [31]

Allies had pondered these very questions himself, and without the rhetorical assumption that he would answer in the affirmative. Distraught by opposition, he published the following year a *Journal*, written while a traveler in France in 1845, and filled with descriptions and discussions that left little doubt of his sympathy with Rome. He meant his action as a challenge, and Wilberforce lost little time in responding to it as such. A week later he addressed himself to Allies, remarking that the *Journal* seemed to him to reflect a "complete alienation" from the Church of England and "addiction to the Roman Communion." He asked for either an explanation or a retraction.[32] Allies replied, but in a manner that failed to satisfy Wilberforce, who tried once more to bring Allies into line. "Nothing but Truth," he wrote, "is dearer to me than Peace; and I shall therefore be heartily rejoiced by your freeing yourself from the imputation which your published words seem to me to cast upon you." [33] Allies, who had less reason than Wilberforce to hold peace dear, continued recalcitrant. Wilberforce consulted Dr. Stephen Lushington, judge of the Consistory Court of London, as to the advisability of an ecclesiastical suit. Lushington's reply, phrased with the caution characteristic of all legal opinion, warned Wilberforce of the inevitable agitation such an action would arouse, yet encouraged him in the belief that a case could be made and won. The *Journal* was mischievous, it had come to the bishop's knowledge, and he had taken notice of it. "If evil consequences should arise there are some certainly who would attach blame to your Lordship, and as this undoubtedly would be a mishief, so ought care to be taken to avoid such a result." [34] Others whose advice Wilberforce sought recommended less drastic action, among them both Blomfield and Howley, the Archbishop of Canterbury. He proposed finally that Allies submit his book to the judgment of either the Archbishop or the professors of Divinity, Pastoral Theology, and Ecclesiastical History at Oxford. To this plan, Allies refused consent. At the instance of a friend, Baron Alderson, he agreed to sign a letter expressing regret at

31. May 22, 1847, Letter Book, BD, d.204. 61–62.
32. March 17, 1849, Letter Book, BD, d.209. 104–107.
33. *Ibid.*, March 27, 1849, 113–116.
34. April 8, 1849, Ashwell and Wilberforce, *Life*, II, 22.

the pain the book had incurred, proposing to forsake the publication of a second edition, and undertaking to declare his adherence to the Articles of the Church in their "plain, literal, grammatical sense." This he did, and Wilberforce consequently wrote a public letter to Allies' archdeacon, declaring himself satisfied that the charges could now be laid to rest. But Allies was either dishonest with himself or with his bishop. On June 2, less than a month after Wilberforce had cleared him, he declared in the Roman Catholic *Tablet* that he believed Christ present "personally and substantially" during the celebration of the Eucharist. An Oxford newspaper reported the letter in late August, and Wilberforce again wrote off to Lushington for an opinion.[35] By this time there was little point to further inquiry. On September 3 Allies resigned his living, and soon after received communion in the Roman Catholic Church.

In the course of his proceedings against Allies, Wilberforce had received counsel from his brother-in-law and Allies' close friend Manning. Defending the *Journal,* Manning declared that it in no way contradicted the Thirty-nine Articles. But he worried lest it receive an adverse judgment in an ecclesiastical court. He hoped that Wilberforce would not think himself compelled to press for any sort of legal pronouncement. He urged a voluntary reconciliation, by which he meant an end to the correspondence. A statement of retraction on the part of Allies would inflame rather than quell controversy. "The two sides," Manning wrote, "will make each its own outcry—that you have done too much, and that you have done too little. And their 'peace-makers' will say that you have done *enough* because Allies has been *made to retract all his statements.* This will light up the whole flame again." Voluntary reconciliation would allow the entire issure to remain untried.[36] Manning wrote this letter in May. By June he had concluded that the best solution would be a statement from Allies saying, "These were and are my honest convictions. I believe them to be not inconsistent with the Thirty-nine Articles. Nevertheless in deference to you I will publish no second edition." He stressed the importance, whatever the final statement, of distinguishing between exterior obedience and interior belief, "Allies' interior belief being left to his conscience." Misunderstanding would arise, he warned, "if the full nature of the arrangement were not to be clearly stated to all who have any need to know it." [37] Wilberforce was spared the danger of public misunderstanding by Allies' rapid conversion. Yet he relied upon the statement as something more than a mere declaration of "exterior obedience." Perhaps he put too much faith in declarations. The Hampden controversy might have led him to mistrust them more. Still, Manning's

---

35. August 27, 1849, Letter Book, BD, d.209. 157.
36. May 16, 1849, Chichester, 96.   37. *Ibid.,* June 23, 1849.

argument appeared to grant clergymen unwarranted license to declare one thing publicly while secretly believing another; and few would have expected bishops to sanction distinctions of that sort.

Manning's almost frantic insistence upon private settlement was a sympton of uncertainties that by 1849 were at the front of his own mind, and reflected the strained and confused state in which the Church of England found herself as well. Hampden's appointment had offended Tractarians and ritualists. Their offense upon that occasion was nothing, however, to the anger they felt as a result of the Gorham judgment, another seeming manifestation of the doctrinal impurity and Erastian insensibility of their Church. At issue were questions of belief and of ecclesiastical jurisdiction. Was a Calvinistic interpretation of baptism— one which treated regeneration as a devout hope but not a certain fact— tolerable within the admittedly broad limits of the Church of England? G. C. Gorham, a clergyman nominated to the living of Bramford Speke, in the diocese of Exeter, insisted that it was tolerable. Bishop Phillpotts insisted that it was not and refused to institute Gorham.[38] Tolerable or intolerable, who was finally to decide the case? Ecclesiastical law demanded that any complaint be heard first in the Court of Arches, and to that court Gorham duly brought his action, demanding that Phillpotts justify withholding the living. Sir Herbert Jenner-Fust found for Phillpotts, but Gorham insisted upon appealing the case, as was his right, to the Judicial Committee of the Privy Council. The Council, generally unconcerned with matters of dogma but ready to allow the widest possible latitude,[39] in March 1850 reversed Jenner-Fust's judgment. This second decision, rendered by a lay court, had dismayed all sensitive High Churchmen and swept the less moderate of them to the brink of communion with Rome.

Wilberforce tried to stifle the alarm and to make the best of things. Along with most Anglicans he believed that the sacrament of baptism washed infants clean of original sin. We educate children, he had once argued in a sermon, because we know the life of the spirit is in them. "If we did not know this, it would really be as senseless to strive to educate the true humanity in the child, as it would be to strive to bring natural life into the dead by feeding and cherishing them." [40] He maintained that the Gorham judgment did not impugn the doctrine of baptismal regeneration, shutting his eyes to what he did not wish to see and arguing in-

38. Phillpotts accused Gorham of two heresies: first, that he maintained that "remission of sins, which depends upon an act of prevenient grace, must precede Baptism, if that sacrament was to be received worthily, and second, that Regeneration and Adoption must likewise precede Baptism" (see J. C. S. Nias, *Gorham and the Bishop of Exeter* [London, 1951], p. 112).

39. See A. O. J. Cockshut, *Anglican Attitudes* (London, 1959), p. 41.

40. "Sons of God," *Sermons,* 5th ed. (London, 1849), p. 47.

stead that the dispute was jurisdictional rather than doctrinal. "The rejected clerk," he explained in his Charge of 1851, "appealed to the Crown, not to declare the orthodoxy of his teaching, but to call upon the Archbishop [a member of the Judicial Committee] to exercise a jurisdiction which had lapsed to him. . . The decision was that the Archbishop ought to have exercised this jurisdiction. Consequently the sentence of the court below was reversed, and the matter remitted to the Archbishop, not to institute the rejected clerk, but to see that right was done in the case." [41] The consequence of such an interpretation—which appears to have been his alone—was to deprecate any attempt to stir up undue controversy. Gladstone encouraged Wilberforce to circulate an episcopal declaration of adherence to the doctrine of baptismal regeneration. Wilberforce went so far as to send a draft to Archbishop Sumner, who returned it with the comment that it would serve to limit the latitude sanctioned not merely by the judgment but by the Church,[42] and the declaration died aborning. As in the case of Allies, controversy seemed likely to further separate the already divided sections of the Church.

Instead of public protest, Wilberforce, urged on by the importuning of his Anglo-Catholic friends and relations, proposed a reform of the system of ecclesiastical review. Almost alone among the bishops he supported a bill introduced by Blomfield which would have removed all cases affecting doctrine from the Judicial Committee to a revived Upper House of Convocation. When the proposal failed he canvassed for a procedure which would have placed similar authority in the hands of an archbishop's court. In his discussions Wilberforce made himself take a sanguine view of the judgment. "I do *not* see that this leaves us in *any way* tainted with heresy," he wrote W. J. Butler. "It is very likely to mislead and we must of course strive for a better state of things. But I cannot say that it wounds." [43] Meanwhile, the Church might console itself with the hope that harmful division was but an aberrant symptom of the diversity which was its greatest strength. "We must feel that where, even with verbal differences, our great common truths are held implicitly, that there, far more than in mere verbal agreement, the true ground of unity is present." [44]

His determination to find consolation of some sort in the decision grew from his awakening realization that it had driven his brothers Robert and Henry, along with Manning, to despair. He tried to make them believe, as he himself believed, that all might still come right. What had not wounded him, however, had struck them a heavy blow. All three signed a declaration, in company with eleven other Tractarians of high repute,

41. *Charge*, 1851, pp. 46–47.   42. April 28, 1850, BD, I. C195.
43. March 15, 1850, BD, I. C197.   44. *Charge*, 1851, p. 48.

condemning the judgment as a denial of the Nicene Creed—"I believe in one baptism for the remission of sins"—and urging the Bench "acting only in its spiritual character" to reaffirm the doctrine of baptism, "impugned by the said sentence." [45] Robert, in his Charge of 1850, maintained that the entire sacramental system of the Church had been undermined. Gorham's victory meant "a denial of the reality of those channels of grace whereby divine gifts are communicated to men." If the efficacy of infant baptism is denied, "unless it can be accounted for on some principles which rest it on the faith or feelings of the receiver, how can we doubt that these, and not the external agency of the unseen cause, are the true basis on which the result of less distinctive ordinances is rested." [46] In May, Robert, together with Manning and W. H. Mill, the Regius Professor of Hebrew at Cambridge, addressed a letter to 20,000 clergymen, asking their support of a statement declaring that the Royal Supremacy extended no further than temporal matters. Both Keble and Pusey had advised against a widespread canvass of this sort, and Samuel had written Robert that "if you put anything forth, I hope you will strongly assert the advantage of the Supremacy of the Crown properly administered. I am very anxious that in every move this *just* Supremacy of the Crown should be maintained." [47] To Robert and his Anglo-Catholic allies, the Gorham decision suggested that any sort of Church-State affiliation could lead only to injustice; the State, through the appointment of bishops if not through the jurisdiction of its courts, would inevitably have final say in matters that were in no way its concern.

The government offered further proof of the proposition by introducing the Ecclesiastical Titles Bill the following year. Designed to counter threats of papal "agression" in the form of a reestablished Roman hierarchy in England, it did little more than feed the general anti-Roman appetite of Protestant Englishmen. Wilberforce shared with a majority of the clergy a resentment at the presumption of the Pope to divide England into ecclesiastical territories. He chaired protest meetings in the diocese and sent out copies of an Oxford Remonstrance, signed by 393 of the 507 active incumbents in the diocese, to every bishop of the Anglican communion throughout the world. He took a middle ground, and tried to focus resentment upon Catholics and away from Tractarians. He sensed correctly, as he wrote Robert, that "Lord John will do nothing but try, like a cunning little fellow as he is, to puzzle the scent of his own trail, by turning out Tractarianism as his bagged fox." [48] As a result of his

45. Nias, *Gorham and the Bishop of Exeter*, pp. 123–124. Other signers included Keble, Pusey, and W. H. Mill, Regius Professor of Hebrew at Cambridge.
46. *Charge*, London, 1850, pp. 31–32.
47. Undated letter in Ashwell and Wilberforce, *Life*, II, 40.
48. November 19, 1850, Ashwell and Wilberforce, *Life*, II, 55.

restraint, extreme Protestants within the diocese accused their bishop of softness. In reply, he objected to their demand that the Remonstrance include a condemnation of "Romish leanings among ourselves," insisting that their task was not to publish a history of causes, but a simple protest of "agression from without." [49]

The aggression seemed to Wilberforce a plague upon both the High Church and the Low, brought about by their own partisan shortsightedness. He supported Russell's Bill outlawing Roman Ecclesiastical Titles on the ground that the establishment of a Roman hierarchy meant "the introduction of false and fallacious religious doctrine into the land, and secondly, because it is a systematic intrusion of a rival Church, into the ground already occupied by the Protestant Church of England as by law established." But he found it hard to believe that the Bill could achieve anything worthwhile. The real purpose of a Roman hierarchy was not the administration of ecclesiastical affairs, but the conversion of souls, and this Bill would do little by itself to slow that unhappy process.[50]

The Bill proved a dead letter as Wilberforce feared it would. Nor did it do much to assuage anti-Roman fears. The clamor against Tractarians and ritualists, as well as Romanists, continued as loud as ever. In the face of it, Wilberforce outlined to Gladstone the moderate course he felt compelled to take

to show unmistakably that I do not believe Romanizing doctrine to be a necessary accompaniment of Anglican teaching. That a man may now be all that R. Hooker was as a believer in the Sacramental System, and yet all that he was against Rome. Here then, not from any truckling to the rampant Latitudinarianism of the day, but because I will not see our only stronghold against it beaten down, I myself, feel bound to act.[51]

Wilberforce was acting now under an almost unbearable double strain. His concern to defend the spiritual welfare of his diocese from Rome increased as he awoke to the impending secession of his own brothers. Henry and Mary Wilberforce traveled to Belgium in the summer of 1850, Mary already a Roman Catholic, Henry still struggling to decide where to lodge his faith. By September the struggle had ceased; on the 15th he too was received. He had kept both Robert and Manning informed of his final doubts and his ultimate decision, since they too were suffering much the same agony. Samuel learned of Henry's conversion a week after the fact. The blow, he wrote Robert, was a heavy one. "I love dearest H. just as much as ever but I feel that our *lives* are parted in their purpose, aim and association." [52]

49. January 21, 1851, Letter Book, BD, d.210. 48–52.
50. *Hansard,* 3rd ser., CXVIII (July 29, 1851), 1646ff.
51. May 27, 1851, Add Mss. 44343.
52. September 23, 1850, Wrangham papers.

So their lives had always been, and though the news naturally upset him, it did not cut into his heart. He had loved Henry, and claimed that he now "loved him just as much as ever." But Henry had found it impossible, after 1845, to think or to work apart from the agonizing fact of Newman's departure, and this kept the brothers at an increasing distance from each other. Samuel had attempted to advise Henry when he ran afoul of the Protestants within his parish. He could not help but despair at the manner in which Henry had allowed himself to become a fierce partisan in the Tractarian cause. He warned him that he must work to reconcile differences among his parishioners, not inflame them. When Henry quarreled with his curate, Samuel counseled conciliation, and when parishioners complained of his Romish intonations, he repeated the advice.

Henry's principles permitted little toleration. Samuel complained that they were not Henry's principles at all, but Newman's, second-hand. "I know Newman's absolute command over your mind almost deprives you of free agency, and that he uses it unsparingly." [53] He feared that once Newman defected, Henry would follow him. "Henry is here. We have had much furious arguing," Robert informed Samuel in October 1845. "He is sadly upset by Newman's going. I think he should suspect intercourse with him, but I fear that he will not." [54] The fears were justified. Newman continually pressed Henry to join him. "I wish I could bite you with my madness," he wrote to him in 1850, "though I know you dread large dogs and small." [55] By that time Newman himself probably realized that Henry was on the brink of submission. The conversion of his sister-in-law Sophia Ryder and her husband in 1846 and the strain of family sickness and death, heightened by an outbreak of cholera in the hopfields around East Farleigh, prepared the way. The Gorham decision proved the final straw. "This Gorham case ends all," he wrote Robert. "I can't for the life of me feel that it makes personally *to me* much difference which way it goes. The fact that such a cause is to be decided by such a court is the one great symptom which seems far to outweigh the consideration *which way* they may decide it." [56] Opposed by parishioners unwilling to grant him license to worship as he felt he must, chained to a church that was itself chained to the State, he could tolerate the situation no longer. Samuel believed his lack of steadying self-discipline had made the decision inevitable. Many years later, at the time of Henry's

53. September 15, 1844, Letter Book, BD, d.208. 150.
54. October 24, 1845, Wrangham papers. Henry had written Robert earlier in the month: "I cannot say how bewildered I feel by this awful event, tho' I have contemplated it (more or less) for six years. . . Only think of the man who admits Newman! What will he dare to do afterwards" (October 8, 1845, Sandwith papers).
55. January, 1850, in Wilfrid Ward, *Life of John Henry Newman* (London, 1927), p. 237.
56. December 15, 1849, Sandwith papers.

death, he recalled that it was that very fault that had made him so charming as well:

That tendency to give the reins to any high and noble feeling and let the panting steeds dash where they would: the way he, every now and then at a sudden turn, reminded me of my dear father—not when the swell of my father's soul was on, and the diapason sounding, but at some rather curious note of the 'Vox Humana' —was wonderful.[57]

Manning, who had held tightly to the reins of his life, was the next to go. David Newsome has rightly credited Manning with much of the success enjoyed by the Anglo-Catholics in their campaign of parochial evangelism after 1845. He was, as Newsome points out, a far "safer," and for that reason a far more successful, leader than the ascetic and at times fanatical Pusey.[58] Yet the Hampden and Gorham decisions disillusioned him as they had others, and his conviction that the sacraments, and especially the sacrament of penance, were relevant to true religion in a way the Church refused to acknowledge drove him away to Rome. Unlike Henry Wilberforce, Manning did not follow after someone else into conversion. At the time of Newman's departure, he criticized the sort of personality cult which he felt had done a great deal to damage the Tractarian movement.

To rely on individual minds has been a strong temptation to many of late, and the design of the Head of the Church may be to correct this dangerous inclination. We have perhaps all been too intellectual, too much related to persons, and to a school of opinions; too little to the Church and to the Person and Presence of our only true Master. I trust that this sorrow may humble us and turn us back to Him with a firm and fervent attachment.[59]

This was a statesmanlike appraisal of mistakes and miscalculations, and one suggesting Manning's continued allegiance to the Anglican communion. Wilberforce believed him trustworthy and called often for his advice during the first years of his episcopate. He knew Manning's views about the sacraments varied from his own, yet felt no reason to doubt his loyalty to the Establishment. Manning's sympathetic letter to Wilberforce during the Hampden controversy cloaked the fact that he was sickened by Hampden's theology and by the State's assumption that it could appoint whomever it chose to the Bench. A year later he was writing to deplore the latitude which, to Wilberforce's mind, gave a national church its strength. "Our whole theology is without order," he complained. "We have not one 'theologica' of any system, unity, or completeness. And this which is true of dogmatic theology is still more true of all moral, spiritual and ascetical theology." [60]

57. To Marianne Thornton, April 30, 1873, in Ashwell and Wilberforce, *Life,* III, 412.
58. Newsome, *The Parting of Friends,* pp. 317ff.
59. To Edward Coleridge, October 28, 1845, Chichester, 94.
60. January 8, 1849, Chichester, 96.

Manning refused to acknowledge to Samuel the direction his thoughts and convictions were taking him. "My last visit to Italy has in no way weakened the grounds of my abiding faith in the English Church," he wrote in February 1850. His remarks in that same latter on Hampden and Gorham gave the lie to his own insistent disclaimers. Both cases had, he admitted, "disturbed me by rendering all but untenable the grounds on which I have been resting." So much held him back: "My heart and life are bound up with such a multitude that to be out of [the Church] would be as death." But heart and life no longer had the strength to stop his pressing forward. "If in its divine office it should fail, what remains?" [61] Wilberforce, realizing now how near to the edge Manning had come, worked and prayed to hold him back; Manning in turn urged him to take the lead against the Gorham judgment. "We seem to me to be at a crisis where a man—and none more than you—may do a work for which their people may hereafter count him blessed. . . How gladly would I work by you and under you in such an appeal to the Kingdom of Christ. But I have no hope if this crisis is to be eased over, or compromised, or hushed up, or harnessed to details and schemes such as the Bishop of London's bill." [62] Gladstone echoed Manning's own plea the following September, with Manning still apparently wavering. He begged for a strong statement from the Bench, "that the doctrine of Baptism will be by them maintained as the doctrine of the Church." [63] But Wilberforce recognized that Manning was lost to them. Writing to Gladstone from Lavington, where he had been staying, he reported that it was upon "the broad ground of historical inquiry where our paths part." Manning was unwilling to dispense with any of the usages of the ancient church, no matter how corrupted. And Hampden and Gorham set the seal on a conclusion already reached.[64]

Wilberforce, who had known Manning so well, could understand that his change of heart had been a long and a gradual one. What he could not understand was why he had not before this recognized it for what it was. Vexed and downcast at the thought of Manning's inevitable secession, he charged him with having concealed his true beliefs through the years by dishonestly representing his position to his parish and his friends. Manning replied that it was not so. If there was dishonesty, it was in the "false-hearted compromise" between Catholic and Protestant elements within the Church of England. "If you mean by dishonesty that I have knowingly and intentionally used my place and office in the Church of England to advance ends of the Church of Rome as such, I 'answer noth-

61. *Ibid.,* February 26, 1850.   62. *Ibid.,* February 18, 1850.
63. September 8, 1850. In a letter of September 17, Gladstone declared himself "sure" that such a statement would have kept Manning in the Church (BD, I. C193).
64. September 14, 1850, Add Mss. 44343.

ing.' I should be too deeply wounded by a sense of unutterable wrong, and turn to Him who will judge us both." [65]

Wilberforce was too distraught to know just what he meant. He felt robbed of a friendship and a confidence, and he allowed his angry sorrow to dictate his words for him. A friend lost to Rome was a friend lost forever. He did not simply leave one church for another; he stepped across a boundary as real and in many ways more frightening than that which separated life from death. He no longer saw those he had loved and who loved him. Often as not he abandoned his profession and left the country. Wilberforce anguished over the partings as he watched first the Ryders, then Henry and Mary Wilberforce, now Manning drawing away from him. "Few," he wrote Gladstone, "can at all understand what his [Manning's] and my brother's present state are to me.

I believe you can: the broken sleep, the heavy waking, before the sorrow has shaped itself with returning consciousness into a definite form; the vast and spready dimensions of the fear for others which it excites; the clouding over of all the future; it has quite pressed upon me; and I owe I believe to it as much as anything the sharp attack of fever which has pulled me down a great deal.[66]

Wilberforce went away from Lavington in September and did not return until June, two months after Manning was received into the Roman Catholic Church. The sight of the church where Manning had preached for so many years depressed him. "The glory of our beloved little church is departed," he wrote his friend, Richard Cavendish. "The heavens weeping over us, and the trees dropping round us, seem acted parables of our thoughts." [67]

There still remained Robert, the favorite brother. Though aroused and heavy-hearted at the course the Church had taken, he continued willing to serve as her priest, and Samuel clung hard to that willingness. On a trip to the continent in the late summer of 1851, Samuel wrote the sonnet for Robert which David Newsome has made the text of his book on the Wilberforce brothers, *The Parting of Friends.*

> Oh Brother! Thrice beloved, who from those years
> When, as with common heart we lived and shared
> Childhood's keen griefs and joys, hast ever bared
> Thy breast to every storm of woes and fears
> Which beat on me, and often with thy tears
> Has staunched mine; who in dark days hast dared
> All questions to explore—Since it has fared
> So sadly with our house that careless ears
> Of passers-by with the wide severance ring
> Of four who at one altar vowed to serve—

65. October 20, 1850, Chichester, 96.
66. September 14, 1850. Add Mss. 44343.
67. June 10, 1851, Ashwell and Wilberforce, *Life,* II, 51.

How closer to thy faithful love I cling;
How pray we two may yet endure, with verve
Strung as of iron, and beneath the wing
Of this our Mother Church hold fast and never swerve.[68]

Samuel's hope sprang irrationally from his love for Robert and from the love he knew Robert bore him. He could not believe that this brother "thrice beloved" would be taken from him, too. Robert's gentle affection had often led him to spare Samuel the pain of his own doubts and misgivings; he was nearer to Rome even in 1851 than Samuel realized. They had differed and had debated their differences for years. Disagreement had done nothing to weaken the bond between the two. After hearing of Samuel's nomination to the bishopric, Robert wrote "how happy it was that we two, who had been so much brought up together, were so united as we are in all matters of feeling and in so many matters of practice. Among all the confusions of the world I cling to the feeling of concord and unity with one to whom I am bound by a tie which cannot be divided." [69]

But Robert was a Tractarian and his brother was not. Samuel wrote asking him to preach the sermon at his consecration, yet implored him to do nothing to arouse suspicion that he, too, was a Tractarian sympathizer. "I who know my own deep aversion from that whole scheme, know of course that in time all such misapprehensions must clear off; but it would be a needless hindrance to my well starting to have such a suspicion aroused." [70] Robert replied that he would be willing to speak as Samuel hoped he would, on the calling and responsibility of bishops. "As far as I can tell," he added, "we do not differ much in what we aim at and desire, but I think that you take a different view of the persons who have moved toward the medieval church and I cannot but feel that the popular feeling against them is founded in a deep tendency towards unbelief." [71] Samuel's elevation set the lives, if not the aims, of the two brothers apart. While he went to work to reorganize and revitalize the diocese of Oxford, Robert, still an archdeacon in the north, devoted his time to scholarly theological investigation and synthesis: *The Doctrine of the Incarnation* (1848), *The Doctrine of Holy Baptism* (1849), and *The Doctrine of the Holy Eucharist* (1853). Like Manning, Robert had sympathized with Samuel's attempts to resolve the Hampden muddle, but had deplored the result. It offered conclusive proof of a fact already obvious, that the State, with Socianians, Roman Catholics, and non-believers in its Parliament, had no longer the right to demand the Church's obedience. "The only thing, therefore, which the Church can rightly ask from Parliament is to be left alone." [72] Gorham served only to con-

68. In a letter from Samuel to Robert, September 9, 1851, Wrangham papers.
69. *Ibid.,* October 18, 1845.   70. *Ibid.,* October 25, 1845.
71. *Ibid.,* October 27, 1845.   72. *Charge,* London, 1848, p. 20.

firm his convictions. Samuel tried to persuade him that the decision meant nothing theologically, but Robert was not to be persuaded.

By this time Samuel, who had watched Henry and Mary depart from the church and saw Manning before him in the act of leaving, began to have active fears that Robert would soon follow them. He had always recognized the danger. In 1847 he had written Louisa Noel that he believed the worst had passed. Robert was, he reported, "more firmly established in the true faith, although there is still a certain dash of what pains and grieves my very heart." [73] And so it would be until Robert finally did convert to Roman Catholicism in 1854: the fear that all was not right, the hope against hope that fear was groundless. As Robert drew nearer to conversion, Samuel argued less and pleaded more.

Never for months has a day passed that I have not earnestly prayed for you, that you may be kept from this most fearful sin. Of course in comparison with this aspect all other things are light. But it is heartbreaking to me to think of losing you, my brother and friend—my friend, guide, and aid since boyhood, and with whom I do believe, there does still exist an unity of feeling which has perished (though affection survives in all its strength) between Henry and myself. May God evermore bless you, my beloved brother; I think you so much better a man than I am, that it is marvelous you should be ensnared by such a painted hag as that Roman Jezebel.[74]

Pleas of this sort simply made Robert's life more painful without helping him decide what he should do with it. His studies had led him in 1853 to affirm the doctrine of the Real Presence in his book on the Eucharist, in words that seemed as unequivocal as words could upon that very equivocal subject. Unequivocal or not, Samuel worried lest it appear heretical. He was himself involved at the same time in the prosecution of Archdeacon G. A. Denison, examining chaplain to Bishop Bagot, who had deliberately preached the doctrine of the Real Presence in the hope of forcing a judgment. Bagot, too feeble to undertake the proceedings, had entrusted them to Wilberforce, who wrote off for Robert's advice and interpretation. He hoped that Robert might use his influence to persuade Denison to reaffirm his belief in the Articles. Although the case did not then come to court, as Samuel had feared it might, he took the opportunity to question Robert closely as to his own beliefs. He argued that one could not, in true faith, suppose the Presence to be real,

subject to the ordinary laws by which the presence of a material body is governed. Now if on the other hand, without defining anything as to the *mode* of Presence, we merely assert that the Presence is supernaturally effected to the salvation of the worthy receiver, and the condemnation of the unworthy, how is truth endangered? Do, my most beloved brother weigh this. I find the deepest minds, and the best read men I know differing from you on this point.[75]

73. January 22, 1847, BD, II.F.   74. September 5, 1850, Wrangham papers.
75. *Ibid.,* March 25, 1854.

Robert's answer did not put his mind at rest, and Samuel wrote again:

The point in your kind letter as to which I am in doubt seems to me this:—Do you mean that you worship the *Person* of Christ as having revealed to us that He is very specially really present after the Consecration of the Elements? or do you worship a *part* of His Body? or what? as locally present.[76]

Robert replied:

It seems to me, my dearest brother, that those who fell down and worshipped our Lord—'held his feet'—worshipped GOD as manifest in His Body. GOD was personally and therefore throughout manifest in Him; now the Holy Eucharist, as to its inward part is His Body—not a part of it but His Body as a whole is there supernaturally. That Body therefore I worship, as they it. I should worship a part of it, of course, but it is present *whole* as the Holy Eucharist, and His Godhead along with—by means of—it. For His manhood is the organ or instrument through which His Godhead is bestowed.[77]

Samuel was apparently content. The relatively peaceful resolution of the Denison inquiry had helped put his mind for the moment at rest. He could not enthuse, as Gladstone and other Anglicans had, over Robert's *Doctrine of the Holy Eucharist.* Samuel continued to argue that the Presence existed in the Sacrament only to the degree its recipient was disposed to receive it in a godly manner. "Viewed irrespective of the receiver," he had written Robert, "there is no warrant for adoration, etc.; whilst to the intending receiver you may use the strongest words as to the Real Presence." [78]

Gladstone's extravagant praise for Robert's scholarship marked the general esteem in which he was held by thoughtful High Churchmen. As David Newsome has demonstrated, his was a highly prized soul; the battle for it, when it came, was correspondingly intense.[79] Samuel realized by this time that Robert had not opened himself to him as he had to others. "You know why it is that he says more to me," Gladstone wrote Samuel after they had both spent time with Robert at Lavington, "it is because of the tenderness of the relation between you which makes him dread the pain you would feel from even the appearance of conflict with him on subjects pertaining to the history and attitude of the Church." Gladstone believed there was "room for fear as well as hope—but I think more for hope than for fear... He never so much as glances at going into the Church of Rome while he feels but ill at ease in an official and public position." [80] Robert's discomfort was inclining him to resign his preferments. Samuel, who appreciated more than most the consoling steadiness hard work could bring, despaired at this suggestion. "To stand

76. *Ibid.,* March 31, 1845.   77. April 1, 1854, BD, II. C.
78. June 24, 1851, Wrangham papers.
79. Newsome, *The Parting of Friends,* pp. 382–383.
80. October 20, 1853, BD, II. K.

off intermediately from the fullest carrying out of the work of the present station, because you may change, seems to me to be inviting doubts.[81]

While Robert's Roman Catholic friends pressed him hard, he remained undecided throughout the spring and summer of 1854. He questioned Manning and a former curate, William Henn, now a Catholic, and they answered by driving home the inconsistencies of the Anglican position. He appealed to Gladstone, to Hook, and to Keble, and they in turn responded with evidence they hoped would pull him back the other way. Restless and miserable, Robert spent months suspended between the arguments of those he trusted and the blandishments of those he loved. "It is very sad that he cannot rest at the age of fifty," Charles Anderson wrote Samuel. "I cannot understand his not considering the effect upon his boys, as well as the clergy over whom he is set, and that consideration being weighty enough to settle him. I know this, that the constant worry and fidget which one sees around are liable to act very injuriously on my own mind by giving a kind of reckless don't care turn to it." [82] At last, in early September, Robert put his mind at rest and resigned his preferments. Samuel blamed the constant pressure of Manning and of Henry Wilberforce. Keble, more accurately, surmised that Robert had been driven by "his constant longing to have everything made theoretically square and neat." And so, he wrote sadly to Pusey, "he takes up with those who make most profession of supplying the want, without too nice inquiry into the truth of their profession." [83] No doubt the drift of Anglo-Catholicism was toward the logical and comprehensive—holiness, authority, and obedience—and at a time when the Church of England was foundering on its apparently fragmenting and illogical relationship to the State. This question of Church authority in the end apparently decided Robert. In October, a month before he was received into the Roman Catholic Church, he published an *Inquiry into the Principles of Church-Authority* in which he declared that authority in the English Church had given way to private judgment. "Indeed, we may be surprised that men were so much agitated when they found that the Church of England would allow error to be taught in respect to one of the two great sacraments; since in respect to the other it has never been alleged that she does more than tolerate truth." [84] A state might be erected upon a base of toleration. A true church could never be.

Robert's conversion, though Samuel had come to expect it, fell heavily upon him nonetheless. "If ever . . . you were seduced from us I think

81. November 5, 1853, Wrangham papers.

82. August 31, 1854, BD, I. C190. Robert's sons were William Francis, born 1833, and Edward, born 1834.

83. September 18, 1854, Liddon, *Pusey*, III, 289.

84. *An Inquiry into the Principles of Church-Authority* (London, 1854), p. 280.

all my work would be at an end," he had written in a moment of despair in 1853. The thought of yet another separation, and from one whom he loved as he had loved Robert, had drained him almost beyond endurance. "He is *the* one brother who is as my own soul, and we shall soon be parted, perhaps opposed, for two weary lives." [85] For a time he considered resigning his bishopric, not so much from an unwillingness to work any longer at the job, but for fear that with two brothers Roman Catholics, his usefulness would be compromised.[86] Blomfield wrote to dissuade him, urging him to stay at his post to fight against the error that had seduced Robert. "The Church cannot afford to lose one of its rulers, and its ablest defender in Parliament." [87] The plan was born of temporary dejection and Wilberforce did not consider it for long. Robert, alone on the continent, longed to see him and wrote to reassure him that if he came to Paris he need not fear embarrassment or unpleasantness of any sort.

I will go with you just as much and no more than you desire. There are some less public and more rural objects to be seen near Paris where we might go together with less difficulty than to the Champs Elysées. But you shall do just as you prefer. You need never be afraid of distressing me by doing as you find it suits you.[88]

Robert's quiet puzzlement at Samuel's astonishing public success never left him. Samuel, in turn, admired in Robert a humility and an intellect he realized he did not himself possess. He paid tribute to both in a review of Newman's *Apologia* in 1864.

In the theological literature of our Church his name can never be forgotten; nor of all who left us was there one who took with him a truer, purer, more loving or more humble spirit. It has indeed always seemed to us without, as if that very humility had led to his yielding up his post to the imperious pressure of minds of far lower quality than his own.[89]

Robert died in Rome, where he was preparing for Orders, in February 1857. When Samuel heard the news he conveyed it to Charles Anderson. "His end was what the end of a life of such purity, humility, self-sacrifice, and through all the superstition of his new creed, true and living personal faith by Christ would lead us to look for. It was entire peace. . . Dearest Fellow! There was a childlike humility about him such as I never saw in so able a man." [90]

To those who had seduced Robert away to Rome Wilberforce refused

85. Diary, October 18, 1854, in Ashwell and Wilberforce, *Life,* II, 266.
86. William Wilberforce, Jr., was received into the Roman Catholic Church in 1863.
87. September 14, 1854, BD, I. C193.
88. October 5, 1855, Wrangham papers. Samuel did go, but was forced to return to England soon after his arrival upon the news of Herbert's illness.
89. "Dr. Newman's Apologia," *Quarterly Review,* 116:536 (1864).
90. February 11, 1857, BD, I. C191.

the same generosity. They had brought him pain unlike any he had suffered since Emily's death. He had long since ceased to have anything to
do with Newman. They had last met at the funeral of Sophia Ryder,
Samuel's sister-in-law, in 1850. "I thought it best not to see him," Samuel
had reported to Robert. "I heard that unmistakable voice like a volcano
tamed into the softness of the flute stop: and got a glimpse (may I say it
to you?) of the serpentine form through an open door. 'The Father
Superior'!" [91] Of Manning he saw almost nothing. Once, in 1866, he
encountered him on a visit to St. Albans. "At first he seemed not to know
me; but I went and shook hands, and he returned it cordially." [92] A smile
and a handshake could not efface the damage done. Two years later
Wilberforce was pleased to record a grotesquely unflattering description
of the Cardinal at the Court of the Pope, relayed by Odo Russell. "He
is more Papal than the Pope. . . creeps on hands and knees to kiss his toe,
and, even when bidden to get up, remains prostrate in awe." [93] Given
Wilberforce's passionate nature and his anguish at the loss of his brother
Robert to Rome, the enmity is not difficult to explain. What is remarkable
is that his bitterness remained private; that hatred of Rome did not become hatred of anything faintly "Romish"; and that Wilberforce continued as sympathetic to the sensibilities of the ritualists and Anglo-
Catholics under his charge as he did.

Wilberforce set his course to accord with those principles of latitude
which had finally driven Robert from the Church. The Church was a
living body and "life implies, of necessity, change.

Death only secures immutability. In any normal condition of the Church, the
spiritual necessities of the body necessitate changes. Every varying phase through
which it is passing renders some change expedient, perhaps essential to life. The
bark-bound tree, the hide-bound animal, must suffer, and too often die. The
rigid clasp of an unalterable ritual may fatally repress zeal, generate formality,
or nourish superstition.[94]

Growth meant change and experiment, and Wilberforce was prepared to
sanction both. In 1849, at the behest of W. J. Butler and a rich and devout
laywoman, Elizabeth Crauford Lockhart, he consented to the founda-

91. March 26, 1850, Wrangham papers.
92. To Ernest Wilberforce, April 23, 1866, BD, II. W. Manning had sent Wilberforce
a long and tender letter at the time of Herbert Wilberforce's death.
93. Diary, June 13, 1868, in Ashwell and Wilberforce, *Life*, III, 248. Odo Russell
subsequently denied having reported as Wilberforce claimed he did, at the time of the
publication of the third volume of the *Life*. See his letter to the *Times*, January 2, 1883,
pp. 5–6.
94. *Charge*, 1866, p. 52.

tion of a sisterhood for the reclamation of fallen women at Wantage. A home was opened in February 1850, a chapel licensed, and a small group of women, living under common rule, began work with six penitents. Two years later the rector of Clewer, T. T. Carter, established a similar House of Mercy there. Almost immediately the sisterhoods became the target of Evangelical outrage. The departure of Miss Lockhart herself and then of two of her protégees for the Church of Rome provided grounds for public protest. Henry Wilberforce had sent women into the community; Manning had, for a time, been its spiritual director. To many it seemed little more than a center for the cultivation of Romish perversions. Wilberforce, who had allowed Butler a free rein, moved quickly to expunge whatever taint there might be. "I am more and more convinced," he wrote Butler, "that to give it the Church of England character without which neither you or I will or honestly can have anything to do with it we must unsparingly exclude everything Romish and cultivate the Church tone of R. Hooker, Bp. Andrews, etc." [95] This remained his attitude toward both sisterhoods. In 1854 the *Record* attacked Clewer for its use of devotional manuals. Typically, the paper failed to cite specific passages, "yet the whole book, from beginning to end, is so close to an imitation of Romish forms and services, that any reader accustomed to them only wonders why the Litanies to the Virgin and the Invocation to Saints have been omitted." [96] Wilberforce refused to allow pressures to dictate his instructions to the sisters. He wrote Carter that he realized a stringent rule would be "definite and clear and sure from some difficulties." On the other hand it might "cramp life and alienate sympathies and hamper one in a way that brings in other hindrances." [97] But he refused to condone continual confession, "spiritual directors," or specifically Roman Catholic books of devotion. "If Sisterhoods cannot be maintained except on a semi-Romanist scheme," he warned, "with its *direction,* with its development of self-consciousness and morbid religious affection, with its exaltation of the contemplative life, its perpetual confession, and its un-English tone, I am perfectly convinced we had better have no Sisterhoods." [98] In the end he continued to grant the sisters a large degree of discretion, and with specific reference to confession, to hold them to no promises. "Yet I must press upon every one of you that in granting this license, I must trust to your sensitive Christian integrity not to seek to establish bona fide evasions of the spirit of that rule which is the rule of Clewer." [99]

Wilberforce could support Anglican sisterhoods only as long as they were content to exist in a sort of ecclesiastical limbo. They could not

95. September 27, 1850, BD, I. C205.   96. *Record,* January 19, 1854, p. 3.
97. April 7, 1854, BD, I. C193.   98. *Ibid.,* May 18, 1854.
99. To the Sisterhood of Clewer, *ibid.,* May 19, 1854.

ascribe to their membership any special purity or holiness. They were to be a means of usefulness but in no way a means to grace. A married woman, in the midst of her family, might lead a life as Christian, "every whit as holy and acceptable," [100] as a spinster sister. Vows which pledged their maker to a life of perpetual devotion and service were out of place and indeed dangerous in a church which refused to acknowledge one calling purer than another. Even the term "religious order" struck Wilberforce as inaccurate and distasteful. "I think it was adopted at a time when the standard of lay piety was very low." It seemed to imply "that God can be better served in the unmarried sisterhood than in the blessed and holy state of matrimony." [101]

Anything tending to set people apart by leading to "self-exaltation" received his emphatic condemnation. He opposed the establishment of a Contrafraternity of the Holy Sacrament under Carter's direction in 1862. And for this same reason he kept pressing the men who directed Cuddesdon College to discourage exaggerated expressions of devotion among their students. He encountered particular difficulty once he had agreed to the appointment of Henry Parry Liddon as vice-principal of the College in 1854. He had required Liddon to make Keble rather than Pusey his confessor, and asked that Liddon never insist upon a confession from the students in his charge. He had recognized in Liddon a remarkably devoted and talented man, and had accepted him on those grounds. He differed with him on questions of doctrine and ritual and remained alive to the possibility of disagreements. When founding the College he had assumed that he would have time to superintend and control the course of events there. As Owen Chadwick has shown, he was too busy to keep in touch as he had hoped to. After the illness of Alfred Pott, the principal, in 1856 and 1857, Liddon for a time assumed virtual management of the College.[102] And from that point, Wilberforce was bound up in a running controversy which lasted for the next two years. Liddon supported and encouraged ritual variations in chapel services of which Wilberforce did not approve. Liddon celebrated the Eucharist from the eastward position—that is facing the altar; Wilberforce celebrated at the north end. Liddon decorated the chapel with painted figures and adorned the altar with colored cloths. When the Bishops of Glasgow and London visited the College as Wilberforce's guests in the spring of 1857, they were upset by the innovations, and Wilberforce instructed Liddon to discontinue them, which he did. A public impression remained that Cuddesdon had become a center for the teaching and practice of ritualism. Charles Anderson confided his concern to Wilberforce in the fall: the

100. *Charge*, 1854, pp. 14–15.   101. *Church Congress Report*, 1862, p. 149.
102. Chadwick, *The Founding of Cuddesdon*, pp. 51–52.

College was encouraging "effeminacy and sentiment repugnant to English taste"; the governors were taking advantage of their bishop's good nature and forbearance.[103]

By that time, the Reverend Charles P. Golightly, a persevering High and Dry Anglican controversialist, had written Wilberforce to call his attention to the "Romish leanings" he had detected in the ceremonies and practices at Cuddesdon. Wilberforce replied that although, as Golightly must know, "everything Romish stinks in my nostrils," he could not accept his account as an accurate one. "Men have come there with strong Romish leanings and left it cured, but I do not believe anyone has there acquired any Romish tastes. There are, it is true, little things that I should wish otherwise, but men must work by instruments of the greatest possible excellence in fundamentals." [104] Golightly remained unsatisfied. He pressed to know what those little things were to which Wilberforce objected. Liddon shrugged off the inquiries; Wilberforce worried that Golightly might write a pamphlet or make some other public protest which would undermine the work of his College.

The protest came instead from an unexpected quarter. In January 1858 the editor of the *Quarterly Review,* Whitewell Elwin, wrote an article criticizing theological colleges for encouraging a cloistered and unmodern attitude toward clerical life. Elwin drew his examples almost entirely from Cuddesdon, which he had visited briefly the preceding fall. In the special, private atmosphere of the College, extravagances flourished, he reported, and students were encouraged to indulge tastes for indiscreet ritualistic practices which would serve to alienate them from the parishes to which they would eventually be called.[105] It took Golightly little time to call the article to the attention of any in the diocese who might have overlooked it. In a public letter to the clergy, he made four distinct charges against the College, all drawn from the evidence in the article: the chapel was fitted out with an altar, with flowers and lights; Eucharistic vessels were washed in a piscina; genuflections were permitted; and a service book drawn from a Roman model was used in conjunction with daily worship. Wilberforce thought it best to issue a commission to investigate the charges and for the purpose appointed his three archdeacons. Golightly considered the commission absurd, since he believed the men would be inclined to report only what their bishop wished them to.[106] He also objected to the hurried way in which the in-

103. October, 1857, BD, I. C190.
104. September 23, 1857, Ashwell and Wilberforce, *Life,* II, 359–360.
105. "Church Extension," *Quarterly Review,* 103: 139ff, esp. 163ff (1858).
106. Charles Anderson was also critical, though for a different reason. "What is the use of a Commission when the Bishop must from being on the spot know all about it" (to Samuel Wilberforce, February 3, 1858, BD, I. C190).

quiry was put into motion. "Though you are no stranger to the Napoleonic rapidity with which our wonderful Bishop 'moves to his design,'" he wrote A. C. Tait, "I think you will be astonished to learn that a commission has already set upon Cuddesdon College." He had, he claimed, been summoned to the College, but without any prior knowledge that he was to be questioned officially.[107]

Wilberforce received the completed report as a vindication of Cuddesdon, and crowed to the extent of reminding Anderson of an old charade on Golightly:

> My whole does my first when he walks,
> My second pours down from the sky,
> My whole does my third when he talks,
> And himself is a very Paul Pry.[108]

The crowing was premature. The archdeacons had, by and large, found nothing to substantiate charges of Romanizing, but they had not found everything to their liking. Though they "saw no reason to impute a party meaning" to any of the decorations in the chapel, they nevertheless considered the chapel overdecorated in a way that would serve only to discredit theological colleges in general and Cuddesdon in particular. They found no evidence of genuflection, and the use of the piscina had been abandoned for some time. While the service book in use contained nothing that did not appear in either the Bible, the Prayer Book, or the hymnal, it had "been cast in a form which bears an unfortunate resemblance to the Breviary of the Church of Rome." The commissioners recommended that it be recast.[109]

Wilberforce forwarded the report to the principal, Alfred Pott, remarking that he was "rejoiced to see that it negatives completely every charge brought against you by my gossiping friend, Mr. Golightly." He added that he expected Pott to see to the redecoration and the remodeling suggested by the archdeacons.[110] Those suggestions were enough to convince Golightly that he had been right. When the College removed the decorations, and to a small degree altered its service book, opponents took this as further proof of guilt. Letters from clergymen attesting to the orthodoxy and suitability of curates trained at Cuddesdon, solicited by the principal, also proved of no avail. Golightly claimed to have won his battle. As Wilberforce himself surmised, it would probably have been impossible to satisfy him. "The habit of his mind makes him quite unable to form an unbiased judgment on any matter which appeals to his in-

---

107. February 9, 1858, LPL, Tait Correspondence, pp. 79, 161.

108. February 13, 1858, BD, I. C191.

109. *Correspondence Relating to Cuddesdon Theological College* (Oxford, 1858), pp. 6–8.

110. *Ibid.*, February 15, 1858, p. 9.

veterate prejudices. I doubt whether any Diocesan College would satisfy him. I am sure that none could which simply embodied in its conduct the full teaching and practice of the Church of England." [111] There the matter would have to remain. Wilberforce prevailed upon Gladstone to obtain a retraction from the *Quarterly,* and the *Review* obliged with a paragraph which stated only that its author had not meant to imply that Roman doctrine was being taught at the College. The question at issue was not one of doctrine, but of ritual. "Though we retain the same sentiments we expressed in the article, we entirely acquit the authorities of entertaining any ulterior or covert designs." [112]

Wilberforce labored to make the best of it. He thanked Gladstone for his trouble and declared that "nothing could have been better than the settlement you have made." [113] He was reassured when his rural deans at a meeting on April 7 voted by a large majority to express their confidence in Cuddesdon. Yet, as Gladstone had written Wilberforce, the impression left by the episode was "controversial." [114] And that meant that Golightly and his party would continue their campaign, as for over a year they did. Owen Chadwick has remarked upon the manner in which Wilberforce deflected the attack from the College to himself. It was his College. If it had faults, they were faults for which he and not the College was responsible. Though he protected his assistants, and by shouldering blame for them in all likelihood saved the College, he did not approve of all that Liddon had done and was continuing to do. He worried because he disagreed with his vice-principal on confession and on the Eucharist. He believed Liddon lived too closely tied to the College, with no perspective and little appreciation of the need for latitude and fresh air. He wrote Anderson he hoped the quarrel with Golightly had at least knocked some common sense into Liddon. "People live in one atmosphere till they don't know that others don't breathe comfortably in it." [115]

He respected and admired Liddon greatly and had no doubts as to his general soundness. But could he continue to assume the over-all direction of the College, while disagreeing in so many respects with its vice-principal? For some time he believed he could. Then when Pott resigned for reasons of health in 1858 and Henry H. Swinny, vicar of Walgrove, was chosen to succeed him, the question raised itself in a manner that demanded immediate answer. Liddon had opposed Swinny as a Latitudinarian. If there was now to be disagreement between the two, demanding the bishop's intervention, Wilberforce wondered if he could tolerate a point of view so far from his own. More and more it seemed to him that

111. *Ibid.*   112. *Quarterly Review,* 103:574 (1858).
113. April 14, 1858, Add Mss. 44344.
114. April 12, 1858, Ashwell and Wilberforce, *Life,* II, 365.
115. June 4, 1858, BD, I. C190.

Liddon would have to go. Liddon had tendered his resignation at the very beginning of the controversy. Now many pressed Wilberforce to accept it for the good of the diocese, while Liddon's devoted admirers argued that for the sake of the College he should be kept on. To one of these, Butler of Wantage, Wilberforce wrote explaining that the College was his responsibility to a degree that precluded his toleration of attitudes so far at variance from his own. If, he argued, he preached his own mild High Churchmanship throughout the Diocese while Cuddesdon continued all the while to turn out men "of the *most* sacredotal type, it cannot it seems to me but happen that I am counted for deceiver, professing one thing in my own words and conduct to the Diocese and then sending out from my own Training College men of a different shade as my best men." [116]

On these grounds Wilberforce reluctantly concluded he must accept Liddon's resignation. Swinny concurred, though his reason was simply that he thought he could not work closely with a man who disagreed with him so markedly on matters of doctrine. Liddon left the College in February 1859 to become vice-principal of St. Edmund's Hall. He went with Wilberforce's blessing and his thanks for the undoubted good work he had done. [117]

He had not done it just as Wilberforce had hoped, however. Liddon wanted to show men how to lead a holy life. Wilberforce wanted him to train parish priests. In a letter written shortly before Liddon left, Wilberforce described the sort of men he did not want the College to produce.

Our men are too peculiar—some, at least, of our best men. I shall never consider that we have succeeded until a Cuddesdon man can be known from a non-Cuddesdon man only by his loving more, working more, and praying more. I consider it a heavy affliction that they should wear neckcloths of peculiar construction, coats of a peculiar cut, whiskers of peculiar dimensions—that they should walk with a peculiar step, carry their heads at a peculiar angle to their body, and read in a peculiar tone. I consider all this as a heavy affliction. First because it implies to me a want of vigour, virility and self-expressing vitality of the religious life in the young men. It shows that they come out too much cut out by a machine and not enough induced with living influences. Secondly, because it greatly limits their usefulness and ours by the natural prejudice which it excites. Then there are things in the actual life I wish changed. The tendency to crowd the walls with pictures of the Mater Dolorosa etc., their chimney pieces with crosses, their studies with saints, all offend me and all do incalculable injury to the College in the eye of chance visitors. The habit of some of our men of kneeling in a sort of rapt prayer on the steps of the communion table, when they cannot be *alone* there; when visitors are coming in and going out and talking

116. January 22, 1859, BD, I. C205.
117. Wilberforce continued to show his confidence in Liddon by writing him to participate in Lenten services and missions in the diocese throughout the 1860's. A number of his letters of invitation are preserved at Liddon House in London.

around them: such prayers should be 'in the closet' with the 'door shut'—and setting apart their grave dangers, as I apprehend them to be to the young men, they really force on visitors the feeling of the strict resemblance to what they see in Belgium, etc., and never in Church of England churches. [118]

To charges of this sort Liddon replied that theological colleges should be places apart from the world. He freely admitted that his students had more control over "mere animal spirits and energy" than other clergymen. So they must.

When a young man clearly *sees* God he *must* have a different bearing, outward and inward, from the man who perhaps only catches glimpses of Him or talks of Him. There is Christian manliness, doubtless; but it differs in kind from the animalism of Kingsley and it is consistent, I submit to your Lordship, with . . . a grace which may be mistaken for effeminacy—which will certainly provoke criticism from those who do not profess or understand it.[119]

Wilberforce realized that he and Liddon understood Cuddesdon's purpose in different ways. Nor could he hope to bring Liddon to share his views. Work, vigor, usefulness—these meant a clergyman in Wilberforce's own image; scrupulousness and grace mattered more to Liddon. "I want to turn out the established English clergyman with a more awakened heart," Wilberforce wrote. "You want to get *more* of a reformed seminary priest." [120] The College could not very well turn out both, and the choice as to which it would be lay ultimately with Wilberforce.

Usefulness remained the criterion against which every man was measured. A useful clergyman avoided party labels and party controversy. Parochial contention over ritualism and "Romishness" exasperated Wilberforce, because of their debilitating effect upon the Church. To a man who had come uninvited to Wantage to preach in that High Church parish for the Evangelical Church Missionary Society he wrote that he must think of the good of the parish as well as the good of the Society. "It is a question whether that 'cure and government of souls' which in the name of Christ I have solemnly committed to Mr. Butler at Wantage is to be violated by a brother clergyman on the plea of promoting the interests of the C.M.S." [121] To another Evangelical who had refused to

118. Ashwell and Wilberforce, *Life,* II, 367–368. Reginald Wilberforce gives no date for this letter and says it was written "to a friend." The fact that Liddon's letter of November 19, 1858, to Wilberforce seems to answer these charges so directly suggests that the letter was written to him. I have not been able to find the original among the Wilberforce correspondence.

119. November 19, 1858, BD, I. C194.   120. November 26, 1858, BD, II. R.

121. To S. Bricknell, October 4, 1848, Letter Book, BD, d.209. 87. Evangelicals, in turn, accused him of misrepresenting their real concern as mere factiousness. One objected to charges "such as that we are Puritan; that we cherish a dislike to the Surplice; that all disquietness which exists arises from 'a small knot of persons who have been sending round inflammatory pamphlets'" (J. Tucker, *A Letter to The Lord Bishop of Oxford* [London, 1859], pp. 16–17).

march in processional with the bishop into a church service at Reading on the grounds that such a procession was Roman, Wilberforce could only reply that he believed the man to have "sacrificed the real to the imaginary. . . Few things weaken us more than suffering needless scrupulosities to engender divisions and sunder hearts which the love of Christ ought to unite together." [122] Willingness—readiness—to discover Romish perversions behind every change in liturgy or ritual introduced in the diocese turned Evangelicals into bothersome tale-bearers and tried their bishop's patience sorely. He wrote in sympathy to one clergyman who was criticized for allowing his curate to pray with his face toward the cross. "Some of our good people seem to me to feel about the instruments of our dear Lord's passion as they would about juggernaut." [123] In a weary moment in 1856 he recorded a visit from another agitated Low Churchman: "I wanting to write, [he] bored me horribly about some unhatched scheme of anti-Roman action. I sorely tried, worn, and tempted to be uncourteous, but I hope was not. He very deaf too, so that I could scarce make him hear." [124]

Exasperation with Evangelicals by no means led Wilberforce to cast his lot with the ritualists. Any innovation that might lead to misunderstanding and lessen a clergyman's effectiveness instinctively upset and repelled him. When he encountered what he considered mannered or peculiar ceremony of any kind, honesty compelled him to raise objections. After a visit once to Lavington, he wrote at length to the rector, R. W. Randall, complaining of the damage he was doing by incorporating affectations into the services. Mannerisms upset his own worship, injured Randall's ministry with the people, and might be leading him toward Rome further than he himself suspected.[125]

He worried for the clergyman and for the parish, and the worry was with him from the beginning of his episcopate until the end. In a letter to Butler written fifteen years before his letter to Randall, Wilberforce expressed exactly the same concern. With Manning's recent conversion a painful fact before him, he warned Butler to guard himself against a first step that might carry him off in the same fatal direction. "I dread anything which may entangle a reverential and somewhat ritual-loving mind like yours in even the beginnings of such a delusion. Whatever therefore looks however distantly that way I would avoid, and hence new and uncommanded acts I would not begin." And the danger lay not just in what they might do to Butler himself. His parishioners would suffer as well the consequences of his incautious experiments. Some might find

122. To C. D. Goodhart, October 25, 1850, BD, I. C197.
123. To P. Jacob, August 28, 1848, Letter Book, BD, d.209. 52.
124. Diary, May 31, 1856, in Ashwell and Wilberforce, *Life,* II, 317.
125. December 31, 1866, Letter Book, BD, d.211. 121–123.

themselves attracted Romeward; others, "startled and offended," would simply be driven "to lower depths and greater unwillingness to learn the truth." [126] Butler, the parish of Wantage, and the Church of England would be the losers. No one—unless Rome—would gain a thing.

To the degree a priest allowed ritual to come between himself and his parishioners he failed in his task to serve the men and women whose souls were in his care. Refusal to attempt a resolution of differences, unwillingness to listen to dissatisfactions, would blight the spiritual life of a community and drive congregations away from the Church. Wilberforce was constantly urging reconciliation. A ritualist who had kept "farmers and others who have taken offence" at arm's length received his bishop's exhortation to "at once and heartily really alter all this. Otherwise, it will be impossible for me to retain you at Piddington unless by such alterations you can gain the confidence and affection of your flock. For great as is my feeling for you, the souls of the people must have my first thought." [127] The people, too, had a charge upon them to understand and to forgive. Wilberforce took Anderson to task when he left his parish church in disagreement with his rector over ritual. The quarrel was harmful to his soul, and, because of his position in Lea, harmful to the parish as well. "All this tends to stir up your own sense of injustice and to provoke you against the man and it is so very easy to mistake gratifying this personal feeling for standing up for a principle." [128] To another discontented squire he once wrote that although the new rector might "in manner and demeanour" not quite suit the parish, he was nevertheless a decent and hardworking man who deserved support. He had made concessions—he no longer wore a surplice—and it behooved the squire to do likewise.

You might have had, as a successor to your late beloved pastor, a wordly-minded man, or a cricket-playing, smoking clergyman; you have one earnest to win souls to Christ, loyal to the Church of England, and ready to devote himself entirely to his work. If there be blemishes in such an one, if he be more strictly Church than your parish was ripe for, if in anything he has given occasion to those who seek occasion, still my dear sir, it is your duty . . . to stand by him.[129]

When pressed upon another occasion to establish guidelines for settling disputes over ritual, he responded with an argument for "a large liberty," and with three rules which set the limits of the toleration he prescribed:

1. There must be on all sides an entire obedience for Christ's sake to the law of the Church.
2. When the letter of the law seems to an individual to be against long-established

126. March 4, 1851, BD, I. C205.
127. To R. Matson, October 28, 1868, Letter Book, BD, d.211. 136.
128. July 20, 1868, BD, I. C192.
129. To Maj. ? Court, January 19, 1852, Letter Book, BD, d.210. 102.

custom, there should be no revival of the obsolete without the allowance of living authority.

3. Where long tradition has linked the religious sympathies of a parish to a lower, but lawful use, there should be no arbitrary alteration for the pastor's pleasure to the wounding of the flock.[130]

Though most within the diocese would have expressed agreement with this moderate stand, some, of course, did not. They objected that Wilberforce's plea for limited liberty disguised a willingness to welcome ritualistic perversions. Only when the public was aroused, one pamphleteer charged, would he take steps, and those of a showy, but ineffectual sort. "Quietly and 'on the sly,' Catholic practices are not only permitted, but approved; but as soon as public opinion is aroused, principles are flung to the wind: wordy addresses, or anti-Roman claptrap, are published, and some person or thing is readily sacrificed." [131]

Toleration appeared to extremists a sort of slippery and devious opportunism. They claimed that Wilberforce had no real position at all. He knew this, and in his final Charge to the diocese in 1869 he tried to make those men understand once more the message he had tried to preach as bishop for twenty-five years. Diversity and variety meant life, and, for that reason, he welcomed it.

Life, even with certain eccentricities, seems to me, after all, to be so much better than death; the sparkling stream, even though it does brawl, is so far more lovely than the reek of a stagnant pool, that I have always joyfully associated myself with living workers of the diocese, whether in their fear of change, they sought as to ritual observances, to maintain a somewhat starved and unpicturesque simplicity of manner; or in their desire of acting by all lawful instruments upon the souls of men, they adopted a more ornamented style of worship...

Better, surely, it is to run the risk of some occasional excess in development, than to bind down the rising temper of the Church to the almost obsolete poverty of a doubtful life.[132]

The message was life, and not a surprising one, coming from a man who loved life and people as Wilberforce did. The "sparkling, brawling steam" was his delight. And he prayed for a Church which would course with vitality through the lives of his fellow Englishmen. Any man who prayed as he did became his ally. At the time of his death the *Guardian* complained that Wilberforce had "too often accepted the cooperation of men who he believed to be earnest and loyal in the main without calculating whether there might be something in their teaching of which he did not

130. To W. R. Fremantle (a Low Church rural dean), February 10, 1866, in Ashwell and Wilberforce, *Life*, III, 197.

131. *The Position of The Right Reverend Samuel Wilberforce, Lord Bishop of Oxford in Reference to Ritualism*, "By a Senior Resident Member of The University of Oxford [Golightly?]" (London, 1867), pp. 25–26.

132. *Charge*, 1869, pp. 24–25; 27–28.

approve." [133] Wilberforce would willingly have pleaded guilty. "Earnest and loyal in the main": these were the men he looked for, these the "good Churchmen" he so wished to send into the field. Ritualist or Evangelical, if through their work they brought the Church to life, they were doing all he could ask of them, and for this he would be thankful.

133. In a review of vol, II of the Ashwell and Wilberforce *Life,* in the *Guardian,* May 25, 1881, pp. 760–762.

CHAPTER VII

Faith and Orthodoxy

The toleration Wilberforce preached did not generally extend in practice to the growing school of Broad Churchmen. Earnest though they might be, their theological attitudes appeared to him to cast doubt upon their loyalty not only to the Church but to Christianity itself. During the 1850's and 1860's, Wilberforce stood forward to defend orthodoxy against the double threat of higher criticism and evolutionary theory. The defense, conducted both in sermons and reviews and in the revived assemblies of Convocation, won him a wider reputation than he had ever known. At the time his was probably the position of a majority of English Churchmen, who welcomed the appearance of a doughty, unyielding champion. Among many of the more thoughtful, his responses often seemed hasty and rather shallow. While hailed in some quarters as an ecclesiastical statesman, in others he was dismissed as the advocate of a position that was somehow irrelevant to the difficult challenges the Church was experiencing.

From about 1850 on, the Church sustained attacks from all directions—attacks powered by an optimism the Church itself no longer felt. As A. O. J. Cockshut has remarked, if one is searching for a serene and confident statement of doctrine during the mid-Victorian period, "by a man certain that his opponents are in retreat, one does not go to Archbishops Longley or Tait, but to an agnostic like George Eliot or T. H. Huxley, or a Roman Catholic like Newman, or an Anglican rebel like Jowett or Colenso."[1] In spite of the difficulties engendered within the Church by the Tractarians, their movement and even their defections had been something with which Anglicans of Wilberforce's theological persuasion had felt capable of dealing. Their arguments lay within the bounds of ecclesiastical history, and the debate more often than not went forward in terms of degree. Tractarianism had as its goal the enrichment of religious life. Its aim was fulfillment. If Tractarians or, later, ritualists, went too far to suit the feelings of other Anglicans, their fault was simply virtue in excess.

Broad Churchmanship, on the other hand, dealt not in terms of addition but subtraction. Here the aim was not enrichment so much as it was a

1. A. O. J. Cockshut, *Anglican Attitudes*, p. 12.

casting aside of irrelevancies and accretions which seemed to have all but obscured a simple faith. It appeared to many a basically destructive movement, aiming to rip irreverently through layer after layer of precious and most holy mysteries to perceive a truth which, in the orthodox view, could be understood only when veiled in the manner God intended. Moreover, its methods—research and criticism—made it a more professionally academic movement than Tractarianism had been. Natural scientists and philologists measured evidence with a competence denied the average University-trained clergyman, who in turn often dismissed as blasphemous an argument he was not equipped to understand. Bewildered by criticism, Churchmen took to blaming their new difficulties on "Germanism." Few High Churchmen were as perceptive as R. W. Church, who wrote in 1857 after reading the *Memoirs* of Frederic Perthes that although unreconciled still "to their ways of going on . . . it does make one feel how very much without real knowledge has been a great deal of the broad abuse of Germanism that goes on; and how much real goodness, and often strong religious feeling there has been in quarters among them, where it has been a *priori* assumed to be incompatible with their speculative opinion." [2]

The root of the difficulties lay not so much in acceptance of imported philosophical speculations as in the readiness of the Church of England to allow its members to think through their religion for themselves. The injunction to believe—as well as to act—in accordance with one's own conscience had been one of the two simple tenets of the eighteenth-century revival. The other, faith in the literal truth of the Bible, had insured the orthodoxy of first- and second-generation Evangelicals. But once the research of others induced them to pronounce the Bible allegory, the more sensitive heirs of Evangelical individualism felt the compulsion to discover for themselves the truth or error of this alarming contention. It could be a lonely, wracking process. Markham Sutherland, the hero of Froude's *Nemesis of Faith,* lamented: "With what absurd childishness one goes on asking advice of people, knowing all the while that only *one's self* can judge, and yet shrinking from the responsibility." He condemned Bible societies for "cramming" the Bible into the hands of the people without making them understand that they were to read it for what they could learn from it themselves. Sutherland found himself condemned for a time to a life without either of the two things he believed one must have to live at all:

either sufficient respect for oneself to take whatever comes, *aequo animo*, even though it be what is called damnation, I mean so great an honouring of oneself or confidence in oneself, that nothing external can affect one—, or else, sufficient

2. B. A. Smith, *Dean Church*, p. 177.

faith in an all-powerful, external Being of qualities which ensure His preserving us on both sides of the grave.[3]

Sutherland escaped his unendurable limbo by becoming a disciple of Carlyle. His dilemma was that of many a sensitive Victorian, profoundly disturbed in spirit yet willing to take counsel with no one but himself. Most eventually found a way to resolve their despair, if not their doubts. Some left the Church, and those who remained stayed on their own terms. Their presence forced the more orthodox to address themselves to the questions they had raised and at least partially answered for themselves.

For many years Wilberforce felt no particular compulsion to respond to this challenge. The straightforward and simple cast of his own beliefs held him back from a confrontation with the subtle and demanding arguments of scholar-theologians. He remained willing to accept the evidences of the Bible and the beliefs and doctrines of the primitive Church. Belief erased the inconsistencies and doubts which troubled so many. Christian doctrine and belief, he once cautioned a group of young ordinands in a sermon on the "Sufficiency of the Holy Scriptures,"

does not aim at answering speculations, questions, doubts, and difficulties, though it does resolve them. It reveals the person of the Father, the Son, and the Holy Ghost, speaking at once to the highest reason; to that which apprehends by faith and not by the mere exercise of logical faculty; to the will in its most secret excesses; and to all the affections in their highest sealed fountains.[4]

Religion must comprehend reason and then transcend it as well. The affections must receive instruction not just in morality but in the nature of God's will. Only revelation could respond to these imperatives, and only the Church, the repository not simply of knowledge but of faith, could act as keeper and witness of holy truth. This uncomplicated creed seemed to Wilberforce a stalwart one. He believed not that the Bible contained the word of God but rather that it *was* the word of God.[5] He had difficulty in understanding why others could not take religion, as it should be taken, on faith. Investigation often seemed to him blasphemous prying, reinterpretation no more than purposeless speculation. As the scientific and philological attacks grew in their intensity, so did Wilberforce's determined defense of orthodoxy.

All the more surprising, then, his admiration and support for F. D. Maurice, a speculator and Germanizer of the sort to whom Wilberforce customarily gave short shrift. In this case, long-standing friendship and an appreciation of Maurice as a devoted if confused Christian, led Wilberforce to stand by him when he found himself accused of preaching heresy.

3. J. A. Froude, *The Nemesis of Faith* (London, 1849), pp. 24, 72–73, 94.
4. *Addresses to the Candidates for Ordination,* p. 49.
5. J. R. Woodford to A. R. Ashwell, in Ashwell and Wilberforce, *Life,* I, 334.

Wilberforce had ordained Maurice a priest and had exchanged infrequent visits and letters with him throughout the 1840's. In the "Advertisement" for his 1839 edition of University Sermons, he acknowledged a debt to Maurice for ideas incorporated in one of the sermons reprinted there.[6] Though his theology soon grew apart from Wilberforce's, Maurice continued to look up to the bishop, while Wilberforce, in his turn, remained convinced of the worth of the work Maurice and his friends in London were doing.[7] Yet he could not pretend to understand, let alone agree with, much that Maurice was trying to say. "Read a great deal of Maurice's Essays," he noted in his Diary in August 1853. "Many striking things in them but I think a great deal of obscurity. I really hardly can discover in what sense he holds the Atonement—set me thinking much."[8] It was the conclusion of one of these essays, declaring an unwillingness to dogmatize on the subject of eternal life but pronouncing the hope that punishment might not be of endless duration, that led to the dismissal of Maurice as Professor of Divinity at King's College, London. R. W. Jelf, the principal, troubled by Maurice's activities as a Christian Socialist and alarmed by a letter from Bishop Blomfield declaring himself unable to accept candidates for ordination from the College as long as Maurice remained on its faculty, instituted a formal examination of the book. Wilberforce wrote immediately to Jelf, expressing his belief in Maurice's orthodoxy and his hope that the proceedings against him could be halted. He acknowledged that if the *Essays* were made to stand alone "I should think him so unsafe a teacher of youth that I should acquiesce with great pain in his removal." But viewed together with his previous writings, and as an attempt to resolve the doubts of "partial unbelievers or men in error," they ought not to cause the College particular concern. He argued that the Church encouraged the sort of latitude Maurice had allowed himself. "Maurice has in these 'Essays' dealt with difficult and unsettled questions; or with the difficult and unsettled side of settled questions. Now on such matters as these it seems to me that the whole temper of the present day is alien to persecution, or the arbitrary infliction of merely stereotyped phrases." To proceed would be to encourage the Low Church *Record,* in the vanguard of the attack and a constant persecutor of Wilberforce as well as of Maurice, to find other victims. "The first

6. "Many of the Thoughts [in the sermon "Doing All to The Glory of God"] may be traced to the 'Letters on the Kingdom of Christ' by The Reverend F. Maurice, which he [the author] had recently been reading when that sermon was written" (*Sermons Preached Before the University of Oxford* [1839], "Advertisement").

7. "I forgot to answer your questions about Politics for the People. I have only yet seen the first number. That I like exceedingly. I do not *know* who Parson Lott is but I guess at Kingsley the writer of Elizabeth of Bohemia" (to Louisa Noel, June 13, 1848, BD, II. F).

8. August 18, 1853, Ashwell and Wilberforce, *Life,* II, 208. Maurice's *Theological Essays* were published in 1853.

act of persecution will entail a second and a third, which may take the very opposite directions, till we are all in confusion." [9]

Jelf refused to be persuaded. He pressed on, and in late October along with the College Council declared that Maurice's teachings were "calculated to unsettle the minds of the theological students of King's College," and that the continuance of his connection with the College would be "seriously detrimental to its usefulness." [10] Previous to the Council meeting Wilberforce had asked Maurice's leave to prepare a gloss on his *Essays*. He attempted to state Maurice's views on damnation in a manner compatible with the Church's teachings, reiterating the contention that because of the impossibility of transferring earthly notions to God, dogmatizing on the subject was not only useless but dangerous, and insisting "that in any contemplation of its horrors we must always contemplate God's exceeding love." [11] Maurice was touched by Wilberforce's concern for him. "I wish I could show you a statement which the Bishop of Oxford . . . drew up, of what he conceived to be my doctrine," he wrote Julius Hare. "It was as lucid and beautiful as anything I ever read. I accepted it unreservedly, but at his request, I returned him his letter that he might make use of it." [12] Though he accepted the gloss, he insisted, as he wrote Wilberforce, that it should not be read as "modifying the account in my Essays, but merely as making [them] clearer and more distinct." [13]

Wilberforce wrote as well to Gladstone and Blomfield, both on the College Council, suggesting that three theologians sit in review upon Maurice's writings. Gladstone moved such a commission but was voted down. Blomfield replied that he had found it impossible to reconcile Maurice's own words with the explanation of them Wilberforce had offered, and argued that by appointing three theologians the Council would have been forced to dogmatize, something it had tried hard to avoid.[14] Wilberforce insisted that the Council had nevertheless pronounced a theological opinion. Had it declared that it could not support a professor "of so speculative a mind and whom so many distrusted," it would have acted properly and Wilberforce believed that Maurice would have reluctantly but without protest resigned. Instead, the Council, by its pronouncement against the particular offensive passage, had declared its right "to decide on doctrine to the injury of the Church of England" and "to require its Professors to accept on matters not defined by the

9. August 27, 1853, BD, I. C200.
10. F. Maurice, *Life of Frederick Denison Maurice,* II, 191.
11. To F. D. Maurice, October 24, 1853, BD, I. C200.
12. October 28, 1853, F. Maurice, *Frederick Denison Maurice,* II, 194.
13. October 24, 1853, BD, I. C200.
14. *Ibid.,* November 5, 1853.

Church of England the Principal's definitions as the condition of their
continuing to teach," [15] a right which Wilberforce could not allow. Yet
by asserting that the Council could very well dismiss professors for distrusted speculations, he was countenancing a proceeding far more dangerous to academic communities because far less specific than that instituted against Maurice. His anxiety was to preserve to the Church the
right to dogmatize. Colleges had no business meddling in that important
and sacred task. But if the College wished to protect itself from speculation, to shut out opinions it considered in some way dangerous, it, like
the Church, should be allowed to do so. The temper of the times might
oppose needless persecution, but Wilberforce believed that speculative
freedom had its boundaries, and one suspects that had Maurice not been
his friend, Wilberforce might well have decided he had strayed beyond
those bounds. As it is, his defense of Maurice must be read more as a
testament to his loyalty, than as an indication of his belief in the virtue
of unrestricted theological exploration.

Those divinely ordained limits beyond which man had no right to go
were rudely trespassed by Darwin with the publication of *Origin of
Species* in 1859. Wilberforce was asked by the *Quarterly* for a review,
not a surprising choice in view of his lifelong interest in natural history.
He was a vice president of the British Association and had served on the
Council of the Geological Society. He was acquainted with both Buck-
land and Lyell, and a friend and admirer of Richard Owen. These were
an amateur's credentials, substantial enough, however, to reassure
Wilberforce of his ability to handle the job. He had in a sermon three
years before discussed "the relation of man to the natural world," and
his conclusions then made the framework in which he would cast his
review of Darwin's book predictable. God the Creator was his theme,
and he preached of the wonder of his manifold works. "Everywhere such
foot-prints of the course along which it has pleased the creator to walk
are left marked on the world which He has made; such notes and indications are fixed everywhere in material things, of the wise, designing, and
all-powerful working of the immaterial Intellect." [16]

God left man to discover the message of nature on his own. That
message was in harmony with revelation. If, on occasion, it seemed instead in conflict, man was not to worry:

his faith is too firm to let him waste his strength, and perhaps perplex the truth,
in a fidgety anxiety to reconcile apparent discrepancies. He receives revelation,
and he searches into nature: nature becomes, to such an one, a glorious parable,
evermore declaring and illustrating the revelations of the Lord.[17]

15. November 8, 1853, Letter Book, BD, d.148. 19–20.
16. "The Relation of Man to the Natural World," *Sermons,* ed. J. R. Woodford (Oxford
and London, 1877), pp. 189 190.
17. *Ibid.,* p. 192.

The secrets of God's natural world were not a code of laws unto themselves. They were a reflection of God's purposes for man, there for man himself to discover and understand, so that he might better discover and understand God. Nature encouraged man to teach himself, but the lesson, if properly taught, would only draw him closer to the God who had revealed himself as creator both of man and of the world he lived in.

Wilberforce's critique of Darwin's theory echoed these themes, but not until the end. Relying heavily on Owen's work, he first took Darwin to task on scientific grounds. Although he had attempted to illustrate "the wonderful interdependence of nature . . . the golden chain of unsuspected relations which bind together all the mighty web which stretches from end to end of this full and most diversified earth"—although this was Darwin's purpose, he had failed. Natural selection was a law in which all could believe. Yet Darwin had assigned limits to its actions for which he had not offered sufficient proof. True enough that it prevented the overpopulation of the world and thereby displayed a "merciful provision against the deterioration, in a world apt to deteriorate, of the works of the Creator's hand." To assume, however, that natural selection resulted in variation through survival was an assumption "opposed to all the facts we have been able to observe." Darwin's attempt to rest his case upon the experiences of pigeon breeders flew in the face of evidence demonstrating that there had never occurred "the faintest beginning of any such change in what that great comparative anatomist, Professor Owen, calls 'the characteristics of the skeleton or other parts of the frame upon which specific differences are founded.'" Any relaxation of the breeder's care and the pigeon reverted to the character of its simplest ancestor. The same held true for dogs and horses. To prove that natural selection brought changes in species, Darwin would first have to demonstrate that natural selection could raise individuals within a species to a higher form than ever before attained, and that a power existed by which favorable variations might be passed on to successive descendents. Rather than strain to support Darwin's untenable hypotheses, Wilberforce declared he would remain content to accept Owen's theory of creation. Fossil evidence, far from substantiating evolution, suggested clear breaks in the development of species. In Germany an unbroken record of evidence from the Permian and Triassic periods revealed "an entire separation" of the various forms of animal life.

Once he had, as a naturalist, discovered Darwin's arguments to be fantastic and unsound, Wilberforce addressed himself as a Christian to their implications for those revelations disclosed by God to man in the Bible. It would be wrong, he insisted, to argue the truth or falsehood of the theory on religious grounds. "But this does not make it the less important to point out on scientific grounds scientific errors, when those errors tend to limit God's glory in creation, or to gainsay the revealed relations of that creation to Himself." Wilberforce contended that Darwin had unintentionally done both. By denying the laws of sterility a place in his argument [18] Darwin had denied that "the difference between various species was a law of creation." Instead, he had declared that difference "an ever-varying accident." Far more distressing, he had suggested that man himself was only a part of this long evolutionary chain, thereby reducing him to the level of a beast. Free will, reason, responsibility, redemption, the Eternal Spirit, all these attributes a Christian must attach to man's nature if he is to believe and to partake in God's glorious plan for his salvation—"all are equally and utterly irreconcilable with the degrading notion of the brute origin of him who was created in the image of God and redeemed by the Eternal Son assuming to Himself His nature." Evolution and natural selection took from God his omnipotence and from man those divine attributes God had willed him. Far from reflecting God's design, nature moved at the behest of chance; random accident denied divine purpose.[19]

The argument was deft enough. Owen's reputation made it no disgrace to side with him; he had himself treated the *Origin* far more severely in the *Edinburgh*.[20] Wilberforce had no first-hand knowledge of the subject. He accepted Owen as a respectable and thoroughly creditable scientist and a man whose theories tallied most closely with his own preconceptions. Much of the Origin was speculation; Wilberforce simply took hold of Darwin's doubts to suggest that he had bent fact to theory. Darwin himself wrote wryly to J. D. Hooker that the article by Wilberforce was "uncommonly clever; it picks out with skill all the most conjectural parts, and brings forward well the difficulties." [21] The fact that Wilberforce did not possess the sort of mind that feels a compulsion to penetrate to the heart of a problem, to test for itself the conclusions reached by others, allowed him to continue to accept Owen, and kept him from understanding the tremendous challenge Darwinian evolution would

18. Owen rested many of his conclusions on this theory of parthenogenesis. He had sent Wilberforce a copy of his treatise on the subject in 1849, which Wilberforce acknowledged as enabling him to study further "the ideas which your lectures suggested so profusely to me" (June 29, 1849, Add Mss. 42584. 217).

19. "Origin of Species," *Quarterly Review,* 108:226 (1860).

20. For an account of Owen's work and theorizing, see Roy M. MacLeod, "Evolutionism and Richard Owen, 1830–1868: An Episode in Darwin's Century" (*Isis,* 56:259 [1965]). MacLeod demonstrates that Owen's personal animosity toward Huxley, and his desire to remain on good terms with politicians and Churchmen, led him to disguise from himself the fact that he was more of a Darwinian than he confessed. He was influenced by the work and thought of Cuvier, Oken, and Goethe, and formulated an evolutionary theory of his own—"derivation."

21. July, 1860, in Francis Darwin, *Life of Charles Darwin,* 3 vols. (London, 1887), II, 324.

present to Christians more disposed to probe and investigate than he was. He could dismiss the *Origin* as bad science, deal with it in an "uncommonly clever" fashion, and remain generally unaffected by its implications.

This unwillingness to recognize the book's significance and to treat it with respect and attention resulted in Wilberforce's inept performance during his famous debate with Huxley at Oxford—the incident in his life for which he has generally been best remembered. The encounter occurred on Saturday, June 30, 1860, at the meeting of the British Association. The preceding Thursday the assembly had heard a paper "on the final causes of the sexuality of plants, with particular reference to Mr. Darwin's work on the *Origin of Species*." Huxley, though called upon, declined to speak, fearing that the scientifically uneducated and generally anti-Darwinian audience would give him neither a fair nor intelligent hearing. After Owen had objected, however, that the brain of the gorilla bore less resemblance to that of man than to that of "the very lowest and most problematical of the Quadrumana," Huxley, who had recently investigated that very subject, rose briefly in contradiction, promising to support his contentions with published evidence in the near future.[22] On Saturday, Dr. J. W. Draper of New York was scheduled to read a paper on the "Intellectual Development of Europe Considered with Reference to the Views of Mr. Darwin." Huxley had no intention of staying to hear him, but a chance encounter with Robert Chambers, the geologist, and Chambers' plea that Huxley must not desert the ranks of the evolutionists, convinced him to change his mind. Huxley, knowing that Wilberforce expected to speak, told Chambers that he did not see the point of "giving up peace and quietness to be episcopally pounded." But he declared himself willing to come "and have my share of what is going on."

The meeting room was crowded—it had already been changed to accommodate a crowd of about 700. Most accounts mention the large number of clergymen and ladies present, disposed to deprecate the small group of Darwinians who had gathered about Professor Benjamin Brodie, by whose side Huxley managed to secure a seat. Dr. Draper

22. He did so in the *Natural History Review* the following year. When the article appeared, Huxley wrote Wilberforce:

"Believing that his Lordship has as great an interest in the ascertainment of truth as himself, Professor Huxley ventures to draw the attention of the Bishop to a paper in the accompanying number of the *Natural History Review* 'On the Zoological relations of Man With the Lower Animals.'

"The Bishop of Oxford will find therein full justification for the diametrical contradiction with which he heard Professor Huxley meet certain anatomical statements put forth at the first meeting of Section D, during the late session of the British Association at Oxford" (January 3, 1861, in Cyril Bibby, *T. H. Huxley* [London, 1959], p. 73).

spoke for more than an hour, and his speech was followed by several short remarks from the floor. Wilberforce then rose to make almost the same points that were shortly to appear in his *Review* article. His love for a telling phrase had led him in the article to make light of Darwin's ideas in a foolishly bantering way, referring at one point, for example, to "our unsuspected cousinship with mushrooms." Now he adopted the same tone. Referring to an additional vertebra found in a North of England sheep and produced as evidence for Darwin's theory, he jokingly asked: "What have they to bring forward? Some rumored statement about a long-legged sheep." He contested, as he had in his article, the assertion that distinct changes could be bred permanently into any species. Then, wishing to deny the derivation of man from the ape, he wondered aloud "if any one were willing to trace his descent through an ape as his grand-father, would he be willing to trace his descent similarly on the side of his grandmother?" It was a silly mistake, but in keeping with his inability to understand that Darwin might be right. Huxley saw his chance and, turning to Brodie, declared, "the Lord hath delivered him into mine hands." He waited until called upon and then, in the course of a thorough refutation, remarked that he saw no reason to be ashamed of having an ape for an ancestor. "If there were an ancestor whom I should feel shame in recalling, it would rather be a *man*—a man of restless and versatile intellect—who, not content with success in his own sphere of activity, plunges into scientific questions with which he has no real acquaintance, only to obscure them by an aimless rhetoric, and distract the attention of his hearers from the real point at issue by eloquent digressions and skilled appeals to religious prejudice." The sally met with a great burst of applause, and Huxley concluded his remarks in an atmosphere far friendlier to him than that which had prevailed when he began.

Though much of his support undoubtedly stemmed from his having scored off a man who had treated him unfairly in debate, Huxley concluded that it had been worth his while to stay and speak. "Hooker and I walked away from the meeting together, and I remember saying to him that this experience had changed my opinion as to the practical value of public speaking and that from that time forth I should carefully cultivate it, and try to leave off hating it. I did the former but never quite suc-ceeded in the latter effort." [23] Huxley's determination to engage in public

23. Leonard Huxley, *Life and Letters of Thomas Henry Huxley,* 3 vols. (London, 1900), I, 179ff. Leonard Huxley based his account upon a number of sources, all of which agreed as to the main facts: reminiscences of J. R. Green and A. G. Vernon-Harcourt, Francis Darwin's *Life* of his father, an article in *Macmillan's Magazine* of October 1898, and letters of T. H. Huxley himself. The account of Huxley's reply is taken from the remi-niscences of J. R. Green. Huxley wrote Francis Darwin that he considered it the most accurate transcription. Reginald Wilberforce did his best to mask his father's embarrassing experience, and his account, as a result, is a false one: "In the course of this speech, which

debate on the subject of evolution—to become Darwin's bulldog—was therefore a direct consequence of his encounter with Wilberforce. A second was the realization that science might challenge the assumptions of religion in public debate without fear of public censure. If there had been misconduct at Oxford, it had been on the part of the champion of the Church, who by making light of his opponent, had helped bring his opponent's cause to the thoughtful attention of his audience.

If Wilberforce had not fully comprehended the threat posed by Darwin's *Origin of Species, Essays and Reviews,* published a year later, struck him immediately as a book destined to poison the work of the Church by perverting the doctrines of its faith. He at once set to work to refute and condemn it. The essays were the joint product of seven men, six of them clergymen. The volume was the inspiration of two of its authors, Benjamin Jowett and Frederick Temple, who had felt the need for a serious yet popular discussion of recent biblical scholarship, and had agreed to undertake the project on the stipulation that "nothing should be written which was inconsistent with the position of ministers of our Church." [24] None of the essays was original, some were muddled and unnecessarily obscure. Taken together they presented to the educated English reading public for the first time the results of over a quarter-century of theological research and rethinking.

Temple's essay, "The Education of the World," discussed the manner in which mankind had received its knowledge of God's laws and purpose. The childhood of mankind was a period of law, when knowledge came by instruction from God himself. Youth—the period of God the Son—saw mankind learning by example. Manhood—the period of God the Holy Spirit—encouraged man to think for himself, to learn by precept. The Church, too, had passed through similar developmental stages and had along with mankind now come of age. In her adulthood she would naturally perceive more clearly than before the holy purposes God had set for her, and she would discard what no longer helped her to achieve those purposes. Man would feel a confidence in his judgment which would help him in sorting through his own aids to faith, a task which every devout Christian was duty bound to undertake.

Rowland Williams, Professor of Hebrew at Cambridge, contributed a review of Bunsen's biblical researches. He argued that no one could any longer ignore the fact that the Bible was the product of many hands,

made a great impression, the Bishop said, that whatever certain people might believe, he would not look at the monkeys in the Zoological as connected with his ancestors, a remark that drew from a certain learned professor the retort, 'I would rather be descended from an ape than a Bishop'" (Ashwell and Wilberforce, *Life,* II, 451). In the third volume Reginald corrected Huxley's riposte, though not the Bishop's own remarks.

24. *Memoirs of Archbishop Temple,* ed. E. G. Sanford, 2 vols. (London, 1906), I, 223.

composed by men inspired by their faith in God, but writing with a passion that made them liable to error. Reiterating Temple, Williams emphasized the role of individual reason and personal faith in biblical interpretation. Man himself possessed a "verifying faculty" which it behooved
him to use. He need not hesitate at the task before him, nor fear the
consequences should he feel compelled to read the Bible in a new and
more rational light. "There is no antecedent necessity," Williams wrote,
"that the least rational view of the gospel should be the truest, or that
our faith should have no human element and its records be exempt from
historical law."[25] Charles Goodwin and Baden Powell made the same
point in their essays on miracles and the Mosaic cosmology. Goodwin,
who wrote baldly and spoke plainly, and was the one layman in the lot,
insisted that the account of the creation had not been written mystically
or symbolically, but simply incorrectly, by a poetic but ignorant scribe.
Men must not strain, therefore, to explain away biblical inconsistencies;
rather they should accept the book on its own terms, which were the most
sensible and, ultimately, the most meaningful. Baden Powell insisted
that miracles could not be proven. Paley's "evidences" were beside the
point. Instead, the Bible's evidence must be allowed to speak for itself,
in different ways to different individuals. "In whatever light we regard
the 'evidences' of religion, to be of any effect, whether external or internal, they must always have a special reference to the *peculiar capacity*
and apprehension of the party addressed."[26]

Mark Pattison, in an historical essay on recent tendencies of religious
thought, also criticized the Palean tendency to seek proof of biblical
mysteries. Religion, if it was to be vital, should turn outward, toward a
solution of man's problems, not inward, in a useless attempt at self-
verification. Unless it did, it would die out, as the "great speculative
movement" in Germany had, by neglecting the world for useless scholarship. H. B. Wilson, formerly Rawlinsonian Professor of Anglo-Saxon at
Oxford, insisted in his essay that the Church of England was in danger of
meeting the same end. A national church, if it was to survive, "should
undertake to assist the spiritual progress of the nation and of the individuals of which it is composed, in their several states and stages."[27]
It should not remain static; it should impose no tests or subscriptions
to articles of belief. To set barriers of this sort was to infringe upon the
birthright of its citizen-members. Especially must it insure that "those
who distinguish themselves in science and literature" remain cordially
attached to it. For if they were not, "they must sooner or later be driven
into a position of hostility to it."[28]

25. *Essays and Reviews,* 2d ed. (London, 1860), p. 83.   26. *Ibid.,* p. 125.
27. *Ibid.,* p. 173.   28. *Ibid.,* p. 198.

Jowett's essay on the interpretation of Scripture, the last of the seven, touched upon all the major themes contained in the others. He insisted that the Bible be treated as imperfect history; that the only base upon which a sound religion might be raised was one that recognized its limitations. Nothing suggested that the Bible was "inspired," at least in the traditional meaning of that word. Instead, each writer and each age had a character of its own which the reader must penetrate to obtain the real worth of the Bible's literature and message. "The true use of interpretation," therefore, "is to get rid of interpretation, and leave us alone in company with the author." [29] Once in that company, the individual must be allowed to find his own way, to read as nearly as possible with the sensibilities of the author, to understand that the Gospels and Epistles, especially, were written to be read "like a man talking to a friend." [30]

And here the Church must play its all-important role. As Wilson had suggested, it must give the Bible meaning by showing its relevance generally to the life and worship of individuals, and not by searching its every chapter and verse for constraining laws and precepts. It must remember Christ's injunction: "My kingdom is not of this world," and suit its actions to his words. "That is the real solution of questions of Church and State; all else is relative to the history or circumstances of particular nations." [31] To pontificate upon original sin, to legislate against divorce, using the Bible as an authority, was to make use of "the chance words of a simple narrative" in ways for which they had never been intended. Sectarian "interpretation" had generated division. Now, perhaps, a new and more sensible interpretation might lead to union. Nor need the gain be accompanied by sacrifice. The Bible would still remain unique and "unlike any other book; its beauty will be freshly seen, as of a picture which is restored after many ages to its original state; it will create a new interest and make for itself a new kind of authority by the life which is in it." [32] Man would just as easily hear Christ's call to pick up the Cross and follow him. "Christian duties may be enforced, the life of Christ may be the centre of our thoughts, whether we speak of reason and faith, of soul and body, or of mind and matter, or adopt a mode of speech which dispenses with any of these distinctions." [33] The danger lay not in the pursuit of knowledge and understanding but in the denial of that pursuit. Jowett spoke for all the essayists, and sounded the central theme of their book when he declared:

Doubt comes in at the window, when inquiry is denied at the door. The thoughts of able and highly educated young men almost always stray towards the first principles of things; it is a great injury to them, and tends to raise in their minds a

29. *Ibid.,* p. 384.   30. *Ibid.,* p. 367.   31. *Ibid.,* p. 358.   32. *Ibid.,* p. 375.
33. *Ibid.,* p. 403.

sort of incurable suspicion, to find that there is one book of the fruit of the knowledge of which they are forbidden freely to taste; that is, the Bible.[34]

Theologians commenting today upon Essays and Reviews are generally quick to point out how small the commotion would have been had it been published twenty to thirty years later. Published when it was it generated controversy and unpleasantness, not all of it as unwarranted as later critics have suggested. Judged on the basis of what they did not say, the essays were attacked for having cut the depth and thus the meaning from Christianity. As once recent commentator writes: "All seven writers spoke as if Christianity came naturally to the man of reasonable education and culture. They all considered its moral code, instead of being as Christians had always supposed, difficult, exacting, and contrary at many points to natural instincts, to be only a sublime statement of the normal feelings of a gentleman." [35] Their readiness to dismiss questions of sin and atonement, damnation and salvation, as unimportant if not irrelevant transformed Christianity from a religion into a system of ideas, appealing to them as precepts for living a good life, but unsatisfying to those who had accepted Christianity as a rich if irrational explanation of the ways of God to man.

Reaction to the book was immediate and direct. Evangelicals read it as an attack upon the Scriptures; High Churchmen resented its insinuations concerning Church authority. For the first time the two factions combined and condemned the book as ungodly. Shaftesbury declared war on it; Archdeacon Denison pronounced against it as containing "all the poison which is to be found in Tom Paine's Age of Reason, with the additional disadvantage of having been written by clergymen." [36] Nonconformists objected that they subscribed to more of the Prayer Book than did the Anglican authors of the essays and wondered aloud why State revenues, withheld from them, should continue to support men who had all but renounced the faith to which they had subscribed. Pusey, who had already opposed an increase in the endowment of the Regius Professorship of Greek on the grounds of the incumbent Jowett's infidelity,[37] headed the opposition in Oxford and found himself the ally of his former antagonist Wilberforce.

Essays and Reviews was published in the fall of 1860. By the following February, Wilberforce was agitating for condemnation of the book and

34. Ibid., p. 373.   35. Cockshut, Anglican Attitudes, p. 64.
36. Davidson and Benham, Tait, I, 302.
37. Liddon, Life of Edward Bouverie Pusey, IV, 10ff. Wilberforce supported Pusey's compromise solution, which would have taken both nomination and endowment out of the exclusive hands of the government, vesting the former in a Board composed of both University and government representatives, and the latter with both the University and the government (ibid., IV, 16).

of its authors in Convocation.[38] The previous month the *Quarterly* had afforded him the opportunity to express his opinions in a review which most took to be the orthodox, traditionalist Churchmen's reply to the essayists. He began by lamenting the fact that the book had been written by men of such ecclesiastical prominence and general ability. Their "earnestness of character, piety of spirit, and high moral object" would make especially the younger minds who read their essays all the more susceptible to their arguments. Their disclaimer of joint authorship he considered valid only in part; though some essays were less pernicious than others, all seven men had to bear equally the blame for the damage that would be done by the volume as a whole. Had any one of them "entered on such a copartnership without first ascertaining how far the 'freedom' of the hands he united with his own would reach, he would have evinced a levity and unconcern from which we honestly believe that many of these writers are altogether free." He found the style generally cloudy and difficult to comprehend. Grappling with the authors' meanings was like "grasping at a nebulosity or seizing upon a sepia." Nevertheless, Wilberforce contended that their main intentions remained starkly apparent. First, they aimed to demonstrate that the Holy Scripture could be treated like any other book. Here biblical evidence showed them up as wrong, and proved the Bible to have been divinely inspired. How else but by God's will could one explain the Mosaic cosmology? It was certainly more difficult to suppose, with Wilson "that the writer of the Book of Genesis, without divine enlightenment, rose so far above his age as to invent the cosmology which he is hinted to have fraudulently palmed upon mankind as a revelation, than to suppose that the higher discoveries of science will manifest to all the essential truthfulness of the Mosaic account of the creation." Here, as in his previous discussions of nature and revelation, Wilberforce continued to insist upon their ultimate fusion to the glory of God. The doubts that prevented resolution were the fault of Germanism. Englishmen were being asked to adopt "weapons forged in the workshops of German criticism against the faith," weapons seized upon by these fledgling English critics "with such a blind greediness that they often come to the attack with weapons which have been already shattered upon German battlefields of theological discussion."

Resolution would not come if faith were abandoned to reason. Those who asked the orthodox for a theory of inspiration must accept the fact "that no perfect theory is possible unless we could first fathom the infinite and reduce to definite proportions the hidden nature of the unfathomable Godhead." Were man to do so, he would be assuming the mantle of God

---

38. The history of this attempt, involving a discussion of Wilberforce's views of the relationship between Church and State, appears in Chapter VIII.

himself, something the essayists, with their craving to know everything, to answer all questions, to understand all things, appeared ready to do. Because man could not be all-knowing, he must accept the limitations both faith and dogma placed upon his investigations. Wilberforce argued that Wilson, by his insistence upon Latitudinarian tolerance, was denying the dogmatic basis of the Anglican religion, the Thirty-Nine Articles. *Tract XC* had asked for no greater latitude in interpreting the Articles of the Church than had the equally Jesuitical authors of the *Essays and Reviews*. He complained that the essayists, by arguing away all dogma and revelation, had ended by dismissing Christianity itself. "The whole central idea of Christianity is that it is a revelation of God's truth, which is not a philosophical abstraction capable of leading men away from holy living, but is the very power of God unto salvation, which, brought home and applied by the covenanted aid of the Holy Spirit, is the efficient cause of the Church's holiness—the central power of attraction which holds in its own separate orbit every reconciled Christian will." The essayists ignored the fact that "the articles of the Christian creed are in truth as much the basis of Christian morals as of Christian faith." They equated Christian morality with the morality of right-thinking men of the world. Faith must mean more to a Christian than mere acceptance of the principles of reason and right. God had inspired Abraham to prove that very point. These clergymen appeared to insist otherwise. Wilson, writing of life after death as a final "refuge in the bosom of the Universal Parent" might as well be describing "the poor Buddhist dream of re-absorption into the infinite." Neither Wilson nor Jowett had contended with the problems of the darker side of man's nature; neither understood that Christianity meant atonement as well as forgiveness, and that a Christian's faith had to incorporate the severity of the first as well as the gentleness of the second. In both Wilson's and Jowett's essays, Wilberforce found "an absolute lack of all perception of what sin is, and so of what atonement is"; instead, "a dreamy vagueness of pantheistic pietism, which is but the shallow water leading on to a profounder and darker atheism."

One could not chip away at Christian faith and Christian revelation and not see Christianity itself fall to pieces. Once one began to deny miracles, once one tried to explain away the inexplicable, one was left in the end with nothing at all. Give up the fall of Adam, Wilberforce argued, as Temple seemed prepared to do, and we give up Christ's redemption of man. "All surely pass away together amidst the mists of this rationalizing ideology." Deny Christ his miracles, and you deny Christ himself. "If He wrought the works, the whole rationalistic scheme crumbles into dust; if He wrought not the works, claiming as He claimed to work them as the very proofs of His mission, He was, in truth, the deceiver that the chief priests declared Him to be." Wilberforce believed that if man did not wish to lose his faith altogether, he would need to rid himself of the illusion which he saw correctly as the "great principle" of the Latitudinarian school. Reliance upon man's own "verifying faculty"— the "power of each man of settling what is and what is not true in the Inspired Record"—had led the essayists to demand for each man the right to judge religion for himself. Their reliance upon individual conscience represented the apotheosis of the Evangelicals' insistence upon a "thinking through." But, as Wilberforce had realized, the Church could no longer tolerate this simple rule of faith. Conscience alone could no longer decide a man's religion for him. It could, so long as the Bible stood unchallenged, and Germanism kept its distance. Once challenged, a Christian needed the Church and the dogmas the Church preached to protect him from ideas which, if received unfiltered into his conscience, might in the end lead him off into unhappy disbelief. Only with the Church to guide him to an understanding of God's revelation could man achieve what all Christians understood to be his truest greatness—"that he can acquaint himself with God and be at peace." [39]

Wilberforce's was by no means the only answer to the *Essays*. A group of orthodox Churchmen issued a collection of *Replies to Essays and Reviews,* to which Wilberforce contributed a fervid preface, declaring his conviction that the controversy had brought the first drops of that "last and mighty tempest which shall precede the restoration," and that it was this fact which invested the discussion "with an almost fearful importance." [40] Individual bishops treated the subject in their Charges during the three years following publication of the *Essays;* Wilberforce's remarks in his Charge of 1863 reflected the position he had already established. He condemned the one book as a symptom of the general spread of rationalism, "an endeavour to get rid of all belief in the personal acting amidst us of any supernatural power, whether in the realms of matter or of spirit." [41]

By 1863 the battlefront had widened. The Church had been forced to notice the writings of Wilberforce's former friend and protégé, Bishop Colenso, who, in his commentary on Romans, had insisted that redemption was universal and who had argued that the Pentateuch, analyzed as it should be—historically—proved nothing but a collection of unbelievable fables.[42] Nor had Wilberforce himself gone unanswered. A. P.

---

39. "Essays and Reviews," *Quarterly Review,* 109:250 (1861).
40. *Replies to Essays and Reviews* (London, 1862), vi.   41. *Charge,* 1863, p. 45.
42. See below, p. 253. Wilberforce had supported Colenso's appointment as Bishop of Natal in 1853 and had preached the sermon at his consecration. Colenso was led to undertake missionary work after hearing a sermon preached by Wilberforce during his tour for the S.P.G. in 1839. In the Cuddesdon Visitor's Book, at the time of his consecration, he

Stanley, dean of Westminster, chose to reply to him in the *Edinburgh Review,* defending not so much the positions adopted by the essayists as their right to make their positions clear. He charged that the *Quarterly* reviewer, while accusing the essayists of inaccuracy and confusion of thought and expression, was himself prey to the same deficiencies; he had failed to understand the extent to which the essayists had declared the Bible a book like no others. But, at the same time, it was written by men as men write all books; "and therefore, in exact proportion to our belief in its divine inspiration and authority, in exact proportion as we wish to understand its real meaning, and not to substitute for it our own or other men's fancies,—in that proportion we must 'interpret the Bible as we would interpret any other book.'" [43] The authors had attempted to put Christianity "beyond the reach of accidents whether of science or criticism," by resting its claims on moral and spiritual truths.[44] If they had contradicted any of the formularies of the Church, no one had yet proved that they had done so "in a degree at all comparable to the direct collision which exists between the High Church party and the Articles, or between the Low Church party and the Prayer Book." [45] The difficulty, Stanley maintained, was that in trying to achieve their goal, the essayists had been forced to adopt so negative a tone. Nor had they understood what an impact the essays and reviews would make when published together; hence the general and generally unwarranted commotion they had aroused. Stanley insisted the ideas in the book represented nothing new at all. "The principles, even the words of the Essayists have been known for the last fifty years, through writings popular amongst all English students of the higher branches of theology." [46]

Stanley's tone seems deliberately aimed at damping down the controversy: the book says nothing new; the authors, if occasionally harsh or offensive,[47] nevertheless write with pure motives and a worthy goal. Yet Stanley deliberately overlooked the fact that what to a Broad Churchman like himself might appear merely harsh and offensive, would strike a more conservative Anglican as heretical. Words could be weighted to give one meaning or another. Stanley could insist that the essayists considered the Bible a "clear representation of the mind of God." Wilberforce believed this was what they were working to deny. Debates about the book itself therefore proved fruitless then and sound even more so

---

wrote: "In memory of words spoken in Cornwall, fourteen years ago, which first awakened in the writer's soul a lively concern for the spiritual distresses of our colonies; and of the solemn charge delivered by the *same* lips, in the name of Christ and His Church, at Lambeth, on November 30, 1853" (Ashwell and Wilberforce, *Life,* III, 118).

43. A. P. Stanley, "Essays and Reviews," *Edinburgh Review,* 230:484–485 (1861).
44. *Ibid.,* p. 486.   45. *Ibid.,* p. 491.   46. *Ibid.,* p. 480.
47. Stanley thought that Goodwin's article was offensively written, Williams' tone unpleasant, and Wilson's argument extreme ("Essays and Reviews," p. 479).

now. They did rouse Churchmen to discuss with more point what Wilberforce had recognized as the book's central tenet, the insistence upon man's right to question his beliefs, the insistence upon his right to doubt. Throughout the 1860's Wilberforce continued to search for some satisfactory way to define the limitations of man's "verifying faculty." In a short series of sermons published in 1861, *The Revelation of God the Probation of Man,* he argued as he had in the *Quarterly* against the pride which induced man to look beyond revelation—perhaps "the greatest indignity" man could put upon God. "If God has given to us a revelation, He must have given it in His love for the receiver." [48] For man to turn his back upon this loving gift and to assume for himself the right "to decide whether its separate proportions, however distinctly they may be stated, are or are not such as they ought to be," [49] was to presume to act in place of God himself. God intended revelation to train the heart, not to gratify the intellect. Man had to forsake doubt and argument; he had to stop asking questions and believe.

If he insisted upon poking and probing where God had not intended him to, and if he thereby ended by thinking himself out of Christianity and into some sort of rationalistic limbo, he should at least, if a clergyman, have the decency to declare himself a nonbeliever. In his Charge of 1863, Wilberforce disparaged an unthinking clergy. But he insisted that bishops had a duty "to prevent the dishonesty of a man engaging to teach one thing and then under that pretext teaching its opposite," [50] as he believed at least some of the essayists had done. A clergyman should remember he is a teacher. "He may think as he will, but he must teach both what he thinks and what he is pledged to teach, and if this cannot any longer be, he must lay down his teacher's office." [51] Wilberforce served on a commission in the 1860's to investigate the problems of the latitude of clerical belief. He defended the assumption that the Church of England must not unduly inhibit its members. "The assertion of an absolute unity of view, which is really incompatible with the inalienable freedom of the human mind, must introduce either conscious falsehood, which swallows the whole declaration at a gulp, or a latitude in the use of the common words, the limits of which, being left to the conscience of each individual, are practically wholly unrestricted." [52] Yet though absolute unity was not only impossible but undesirable, the Church had to remember that it taught "not as an inquiry into philosophy but as revealed truth, a positive set of doctrines." [53]

Wilberforce's difficulty was that he was attempting to distinguish between varieties of inquiry and doubt, a hard and for him an almost im-

---

48. *The Revelation of God the Probation of Man* (London and Oxford, 1861), p. 16.
49. *Ibid.,* p. 27.   50. *Charge,* 1863, p. 66.   51. *Ibid.,* p. 68.
52. "Clerical Subscription," *Quarterly Review,* 117:452 (1865).   53. *Ibid.,* p. 463.

possible task. Reviewing *Aids to Faith,* another book written in rebuttal to *Essays and Reviews,* he commended those ready to undertake "the fullest religious inquiry into Revelation, from which Christianity has nothing to lose," while condemning others willing through biblical investigation and criticism to promote "the sinfulness of encouraged doubts." Doubt was not in itself a sin; "it is the allowance and the encouragement of doubting which are sinful." [54]

To Broad Churchmen this argument made little sense. Wilberforce seemed to recommend the stifling of doubt at the expense of a mature faith. Goldwin Smith, writing as "a layman," replied to Wilberforce's sermons on revelation with a pamphlet entitled *The Suppression of Doubt is Not Faith.* He argued that Wilberforce had adopted an indefensible position. He had asked Churchmen to shun doubts, much as the Roman Catholic Church did. Still, he would have Anglicans question the seven Sacraments and transubstantiation, doctrines the Roman Catholics took on faith, but which an Anglican would insist upon questioning. What in the end save reason, Smith asked Wilberforce, was to be the judge of truth? "The human reason, like the human eye, to which you compare it, may, as you say, be 'diseased' in a particular person. But if the 'eye' is not to be 'the judge of the existence of colour,' what is?" [55] Another who found Wilberforce's responses to *Essays and Reviews* inadequate was his old friend Maurice. He wrote Stanley that although he did not have much sympathy with the book, he disapproved highly of attempts such as Wilberforce was making to suppress it. They seemed to him fruitless struggles to avoid unavoidable questions. Every Christian, "the bishops included," would have at some point to face: "What dost thou believe? dost thou believe in anything?" If, as he had heard, the bishop of Oxford was author of the *Quarterly* article, he found it shocking to think that he would attack fellow clergymen anonymously, and that he would jokingly disparage the work of Bunsen, a man "whom he knew, and for whom he professed esteem." [56] He considered Wilberforce's readiness to see Christ's miracles as evidence of his power rather than his love, "the most fatal denial of His revelation of the Father." He argued that man had to search everywhere himself "for that which is not denial, for the faith which is hidden under ever so much apparent contradiction." Only by searching within themselves could Christians halt the spread of unbelief.[57]

54. "Aids to Faith," *Quarterly Review,* 112:451 (1862).
55. "A Layman" [Goldwin Smith], *The Suppression of Doubt is Not Faith* (London, 1861), p. 15.
56. To A. P. Stanley, February 12, 1861, in F. Maurice, *Frederick Denison Maurice,* II, 382–383.
57. *Ibid.,* p. 390, to Bishop Ewing of Argyll, Lady Day, 1861.

In one of his *Tracts for Priests and People,* written specifically, as Smith's essay had been, to refute Wilberforce's sermon on revelation, Maurice insisted that Church formularies were not by themselves of sufficient strength to combat doubt and sustain faith. They might proclaim a God, but it would be their God. "He must reveal Himself to me; they cannot reveal him." Doubts helped a man strengthen his faith by forcing hard questions upon him. Maurice asked: might not "these doubts have been cast into [my mind] by a gracious spirit who wishes to break down its pride and self-sufficiency." [58] A second essay in the same Tract, by J. M. Ludlow, challenged Wilberforce for his "hardness and want of sympathy with one of the most acute, I would almost say the most sacred of human miseries"—doubt. Quoting Tennyson in praise of "honest doubt," Ludlow insisted that it was just this that Wilberforce refused to tolerate. Doubt was not, as Wilberforce had insisted, the "result of a peculiar constitution," "the fruit of unhappy training," the "bitter consequence of past sin." Far from an aberration, it was "an agony of human nature, in its noblest, most typical embodiments." Wilberforce might have looked to his Bible before speaking as he had. "You must erase the Book of Job from the Bible, and the remembrance of it from human speech, before you can prove that the honest doubts of a man are to be quelled by any means short of that of raising his troubled spirit into the higher sphere of a wisdom, and justice, and power in which he and all the universe lie folded." [59]

Though it would be wrong to call Ludlow and Maurice in any sense typical Churchmen, they were saying in this instance what a great many Churchmen were saying as well. Doubt had come to threaten the existence of the Anglican religion. Was it best met, as Wilberforce seemed to meet it, by calling it a perversion, by scarcely admitting its existence? Or was it to be faced as a sign of man's noble fragility and dealt with in the open light of reason? The most thoughtful would give the second answer, and would find little of use in what Wilberforce had to say. In the spring of 1863 the *Times,* reviewing a recent collection of his University sermons, made the point that he was having little effect upon the young and the intelligent. He was not and never had been a leader at the University. A few undergraduates might journey to Cuddesdon to pay homage; "but the clever boys who have distinguished themselves at public schools, and rejoice in the *éclat* of open scholarships, never, as a class, catch the Bishop of Oxford's views at all. They go to hear him as a great preacher, but they do not think of him as a guide, or accept him as a theological authority." Wilberforce, the *Times* continued, worried more

58. "Morality and Divinity," *The Sermon of the Bishop of Oxford on Revelation and the Layman's Answer,* in *Tracts for Priests and People,* VI (London, 1861), 29–30.
59. "A Dialogue on Doubt," *ibid.,* pp. 3–4.

than most about loss of faith among the young. A reading of his sermons had convinced the reviewer that his gifts were "not precisely fitted to regulate the workings of youthful minds of more than average cultivation and power, and that he does not quite know how to remedy the disease which has developed itself under his eye, and in spite of his energetic treatment." Undergraduates were "curiously sensitive" to rhetoric, and disliked exceedingly "being carried away unawares into the high sentimental latitudes." That was where Wilberforce, his particular talents being what they were, would try to transport them. "Clever men, who have felt at the time the effects of his eloquence, have been angry afterwards, either with themselves or with him, because they could not find on a retrospect that he had really said anything which ought to have disturbed their repose of mind or raised unusual emotions." As to doubt: "The Bishop very nearly says we may inquire about natural phenomena but not about religion. . . Cannot theology train and reward investigation; and cannot physical knowledge, if rightly received, in some way or other affect our moral and spiritual training? But how, then, is Christian revelation the very opposite of nature?" [60]

Wilberforce never contended that it was. Yet his insistence that physical nature could be assumed in some fashion to harmonize with the biblical revelations of God, and his own readiness to accept this assumption on faith, was as unsatisfying as was the *Times*'s unresolved hypothesis. In an age that pressed desperately for the answers to all sorts of questions, Wilberforce believed they were better left unasked. Frederick Temple, in his famous letter to Bishop Tait after the publication of *Essays and Reviews,* complained that Tait, having once instructed him to undertake the critical study of the Bible, was now prepared to admonish him for having reached conclusions in his studies that would disturb the orthodox. "Such a study," Temple argued, "so full of difficulties, imperatively demands freedom for its condition. To tell a man to study and yet bid him under heavy penalties come to the same conclusions with those who have not studied is to mock him. If the conclusions are prescribed, the study is precluded." [61]

Wilberforce, although prepared to countenance religious inquiry, would have argued that the fault was as much Tait's as Temple's. Secure in his own faith, he could not appreciate the force with which doubts might trouble and upset the faith of others. Never pushed by doubts himself to the brink of agnosticism, he failed to understand the power that freedom might lend to a yound man's struggle back from the edge. Anxious as he was to save souls, this failure inevitably thwarted his

60. *Times,* May 2, 1863, p. 9.
61. February 26, 1861, LPL, Tait Correspondence, 80.37.

mission. Tait himself had declared that there was "scarcely a Bishop on the Bench, unless it be the Bishop of St. David's [Thirlwall], that is not useless for the purpose of preventing the widespread alienation of intelligent men." [62] Wilberforce, with his often declared admiration for an active "doing" clergy, had little rapport, as the *Times* had suggested, with the "intelligent men" about whom Tait worried. By recommending investigation to them, Tait had inevitably encouraged doubt in their minds. That in so doing he might have strengthened their faith was an idea Wilberforce did not stop to consider. Instead, he continued to preach, as he had all his life, unquestioning devotion to a loving, all-powerful Father. In a sermon before the University in the 1830's he pronounced a solution to the problem of doubt that was to serve him the rest of his life:

Whilst irreverence and doubt are the object of your greatest fear; whilst you would gladly retain a childlike and unquestioning reverence by abasing, if need were, your understanding, rather than gain any knowledge at the hazard of your reverence; you are doubtless in God's hands, and therefore safe. . . Fly, therefore, rather than contend; fly to known truths; shelter yourselves, above all, under the shadow of His love and power, who is, in compassion, Father of your spirit, yet is the Lord God Almighty.[63]

Wilberforce's personal faith underwent little change as he grew older. His continued trust in the authority of the Bible only strengthened his belief in a personal God. What man most needed was "to meet with God in this our life, to meet Him for ourselves, to hear His voice, to know His presence, to stand before the personal God; to hear Him speak to *us,* to us apart, to hear that solemn 'I AM' 'hath sent thee.'" [64] Man need have no fear that God would work his will upon him in an arbitrary way, for he was holiness, wisdom, and love, as well as power. Though each soul stood before God "in its singleness as if no other existed," [65] and in so doing revered God's superintending providence, God, in turn, by recognizing the priceless value of that soul, acknowledged man's right to act out his life as he chose. God had set man on earth that he might cultivate and perfect his own intellectual powers. In return, God asked only that man labor to keep from sin, which Wilberforce once defined as "the willing revolt of a reasonable creature against the perfectness of his Al

62. Davidson and Benham, *Tait,* I, 325.

63. "The Temper of Mind in Which to Receive the Christian Mysteries," *Sermons Preached before the University of Oxford,* (1839), pp. 81–82.

64. "The Revelation of the Personal God," *Sermons,* ed. Woodford, p. 45.

65. "The Victor in The Counsels of Eternity," *Sermons Preached During the Season of Lent, 1867, in Oxford* (Oxford, 1867), p. 10.

mighty Creator." [66] Sin was the work of the devil, to Wilberforce far more than an allegorical abstraction. Both experience and revelation suggested his existence. To suppose that God had not created an intermediary galaxy of spirits between himself and mankind, "to suppose that here the series stopped abruptly, that between ourselves and the immaterial, self-existent, necessary Creator were imposed no higher order of created beings, would be to contradict all our precedent experience of the laws of gradation in His world." [67]

Sin was as real as the devil that brought it. "You are in conflict," he warned in a Lenten sermon. "It is raging around you, in you. It is NOW raging. It is not, as the enemy would whisper, something that must be hereafter. Now it rages round you; now it rages in you." [68] What awaited the sinner hereafter was therefore a terrifying matter to contemplate. If the expectation of Judgment Day was enough to strike terror in the hearts of believers, how much more dreadful the thought of what lay in store for the unrepentant. A belief in the reality of this everlasting punishment made it all the more imperative to lead the demanding life of a devoted Christian. One either spent eternity in the blessed presence of God, or in perpetual banishment from Him. Wilberforce insisted that "real" Christianity, the sort that had been practiced by his father, was all that could keep men from damnation. His complaint against the theology of a man like Maurice was that not withstanding its "high aspirations" and "noble instincts" it failed to provide any real answers to the practical problems of religious life, hiding instead, "in the puzzling involutions with which their impalpable wreaths invest them, some of the greatest truths which were plain to us before." [69] To dispel "the cobwebs of sophistry" one had only to live "the reality of Christian life." This was his message to a convocation assembled in 1861 at Reading on behalf of foreign missions.

If they would preserve the inheritance of the faith which they had received, and would hand it down to their children in its magnificance, they must not only argue the faith, but must live the faith. Emphatically that was the case with regard to the spread of the Gospel. . . Each generation, as it handed down its tradition to its successor, removed the successor further from the original facts themselves; but God's Providence had appointed that, as the evidence diminished, there was the other which should increase in weight.[70]

66. "The Nature of Sin," *Sermons Preached During the Season of Lent, 1859, in Oxford* (Oxford, 1859), p. 14.

67. "Our Spiritual Adversaries," *Sermons Preached During the Season of Lent, 1866, in Oxford* (Oxford, 1866), p. 3.

68. "The Church Ordained by Christ to Maintain His Conflict with the Special Corruptions of Every Age," *Sermons Preached During the Season of Lent, 1865, in Oxford* (Oxford, 1865), pp. 8–9.

69. "Aids to Faith," *Quarterly Review*, 112:446 (1862).

70. Ashwell and Wilberforce, *Life*, III, 41–42.

Nothing appeared more contemptible to Wilberforce than a half-hearted Christian, "letting his religion cloak a sin, be an excuse for sin, instead of the means of destroying it." [71] In an introduction to a catechist's manual which he wrote in 1865, he remarked that there was "in too many quarters a tendency to substitute religiousness of temper and feeling for faith; to treat error as comparatively unimportant if the life be blameless and amiable; to obliterate the stern declarations of God's word, and to paint over the broad outlines which it presents to us of heaven and hell." [72] On the Day of Judgment motives would matter, nothing else. Outward actions were of value "only because they indicate and help again to form the inward habit of which they spring. The most unblemished outward life *may,* therefore, be nothing more than a robe of dazzling spendour cast over corruption and a loathsome grave." [73] In his review of *Aids to Faith,* Wilberforce, reiterating this point, noted that for this very reason, a humble and uneducated person stood just as much chance of salvation as any other. "Real" religion often flourished among simple folk—"the poor Greenlanders," "the rustic inhabitants of the hundred thousand cottages of England." [74] Certainly the straightforward, Bible Christianity of sin and redemption which Wilberforce believed and preached would have been as intelligible to the rustic cottager as it was intellectually unpalatable to many Oxford undergraduates.

Wilberforce continued to believe as fervently as he always had in the centrality of the Church to the faith. The danger lay in its being treated not as a true but merely as a useful instrument of divine will. "God having given to man a revelation of Himself," had appointed the Church "a living body, constituted by Himself as—'the pillar and ground of the truth' to be its keeper and witness." [75] He remained a champion of the Church as the institution best able to hold the country to a righteous purpose. When the Church itself began to divide more and more he felt the need to search out the reason for its disunity. His compulsion to bring together its factions led him to propose a solution that his father might have offered. The reason for present disunity, Wilberforce declared, was "a want of true personal love to Christ our Lord." If Churchmen could learn to love each other by first remembering to love Christ they would better understand how the truth in their possession might add with other truths into one that was greater than the sum of its parts. Then there would be an end to factions and a renewed strengthening of the Church's purposes and accomplishments. He urged Churchmen to sit again "beneath His cross"; "let Him teach thee to love Him, and to love thy

---

71. "The Character of Balaam," *Sermons,* 1849, p. 182.
72. *The Catechist's Manual* (Oxford and London, 1865), v.
73. "The Revealing of Motives," *Sermons,* ed. Woodford, p. 65.
74. "Aids to Faith," *Quarterly Review.* 112:456 (1862).   75. *Charge,* 1851, p. 82.

brethren, and thy hard, suspicious, unloving nature will be melted and purified, until it, too, glows with the radiance of thy Lord." [76] The solution, appealing though it sounded, would be no solution at all unless men like Wilberforce recognized that there might be value in what the essayists were saying, that far from destroying the Church, their theology, too, contained truth that could play a part in its renewal. Until then, his call would remain only a rhetorical exhortation to espouse a limited system of beliefs, with meaning for him, but no longer of particular relevance to the concerns of a great number of devout yet doubting Churchmen.

76. "Unity in the Church," *Sermons,* ed. Woodford, p. 123.

PART III
The English Church

CHAPTER VIII

The Church, the State, and the Nation

Bishop Tait's readiness to disparage the Bench belonged to an ancient tradition, endowed with fresh impetus when the bishops opposed the Reform Bill of 1832, and strengthened at the time of the Gorham controversy and the Papal Aggression. Men might be devoted to the cause of the Church, yet distressed by the bishops' apparent inability as a body to lead it with imagination and intelligence. If Wilberforce did not share Tait's sensitivity to the particular needs of the more intellectual members of the Church, he nevertheless participated actively in the criticism that was being leveled against Church leadership during these years, and attempted to improve the quality of that leadership.

In these attempts he was encouraged and upon occasion prodded by Gladstone, whose opinion of the Church during the 1840's and 1850's was low, and whose remedy was a revival of Church unity under more effective episcopal leadership. He complained to Wilberforce in 1844 that a lack of discipline had kept the Church from exercising an influence upon the country. "Men are told to do right and if they do right it is all well for them; but those who do wrong are practically treated in a manner so nearly identical that the reality of the distinction is scarcely traced and vice loses a great part of the ordained means of correction, and faith of support." Methodism and Dissent, he added, had a discipline from which they had drawn "nearly all that is respectable and spiritually solid in their strength."[1] He was making the same point seven years later, and with the added evidence of the bishops' unwillingness to condemn the Gorham decision. Wilberforce replied in this instance that the appointment of Low or Broad Church divines to the Bench—Samuel Hinds,

---

1. December 29, 1844, Add Mss. 44343. Manning, at this time an ecclesiastical ally of Gladstone, saw the problem in much the same way. Writing to Wilberforce a year and a half later, he remarked of the episcopate that "if the truth must be told, it is morally and spiritually in abeyance as a Government." He recommended an increase in the number of bishops as the one way to set matters right. "Nothing but multiplying its power by multiplying itself will, I believe, ever restore to the Episcopate the Government of the Church. At present in all things except *legal functions* the Church is not even Presbyterian; it is governed by the likings of the laity" (July 15, 1846, Chichester, 96).

suspected by High Churchmen of Unitarianism, had recently been elevated to the See of Norwich—would inevitably induce "every conceivable evil." He hastened to exculpate himself, but in doing so was
forced to fall back upon his record as a diocesan administrator, without
reference to his part in the silence of the Bench as a whole.[2] When, at the
end of 1851, Lord Richard Cavendish forwarded a letter to Wilberforce
from Gladstone reiterating his disappointment, Wilberforce replied directly and at length to Gladstone, complaining again that much of the
fault lay in the caliber of Russell's new bishops and in recent newspaper
attacks which tended to degrade the Bench in the eyes of the public.
Though admitting the need for improvement, he once more defended his
own administration and that of others—Denison of Salisbury, particularly
—against Gladstone's charges.

    Gladstone replied in turn that he had not meant to direct his criticism
toward the bishops' intramural conduct of diocesan affairs. "It is the
conduct of the body out of the Diocesan relationship—as to the representatives of the entire Church in the face of the State and the country,
and as guards of the precious deposit of her faith as well as of her authority—that fills me with gloomy apprehension." The bishops had failed to
act together in the best interests of the Church and of the faith. Until
they found a way to do so, Gladstone suggested that it would be better
"for each bishop who feels all this to take his own line, to leave off
measures which belie the true state of the case by putting the face of
unity upon this divided body, to recognize the facts which are staring
every man in the face, and to join with those among his brethren who are
of convictions similar to his own."[3] This letter produced an invitation
from Wilberforce to come to Cuddesdon for further discussion of the
subject. The visit, in turn, strengthened a conviction in Wilberforce's
mind that the probable remedy for the ills Gladstone had so bluntly
exposed to him lay in a revival of Convocation, the official synod of the
Church, which had not met to conduct business for over 130 years.

    The conviction had been born of the difficulties and contentions of the
late 1840's. Before that time, when the subject of revival arose, as it did
periodically, Wilberforce had given less than warm support to proposals
for the convening of the Houses for more than the routine business of
receiving petitions and addressing the Throne. While a goodly number of
pamphleteers, among them Vernon Harcourt, were urging restoration,
Wilberforce remarked to Hook in 1836 that with the Church as weak as
it was, Convocation would be unable "to resist the necessary divisions
which must always spring from the shades of individual opinions, and we
should fight in the presence of our enemies."[4] Now in the aftermath of

    2. May 27, 1851, Add Mss. 44343.   3. December 31, 1851, BD, II. K.
    4. April 12, 1836, Ashwell and Wilberforce, *Life*, I, 98.

the Gorham decision, and with Gladstone's admonitions in mind, he was prepared to move for more. When Bishop Blomfield introduced his bill to remove ecclesiastical questions from the Privy Council to a revived Upper House of Convocation, Wilberforce was one of a very few to support him. In a speech the following year, on the same proposal, Wilberforce argued that although a revived Convocation might not insure peace, the peace the Church had known for the past several years was assuredly an uneasy one, and one that had not always remained consistent with the truth. "Peace in error was not peace; it was death instead of peace." Strife could be prevented by the expression of differences in a national synod. "It is only by mutual explanations and definitions, by united acts, by the incidents of a common life, by the self-assertion of possessing a spiritual being, that such evils can be warded off."[5]

Wilberforce insisted in his Charge that same year that Parliament was no longer qualified to legislate for the Church. "The laws of party, so tyrannous in England, will force the head of the Government to use such an instrument of power for its support, rather than for the edification of the Church, whenever these two objects are apparently or really opposed." If Convocation were restored, those in the House of Commons who now claimed to represent the Church, but were ignorant of her needs, "would speak in the future their own opinions: she would speak for herself, and be misrepresented neither by well-intentioned but incompetent advocates, nor by those (possibly an increasing class) who seek for popularity and power for themselves by assuming the easy and attractive character of reforming Churchmen."[6] In the months immediately following the Gorham decision, High Churchmen like Gladstone, who saw little but a bleak future for their Church, began to make this same argument. Might not a revival of Convocation restore to the bishops that power and dignity which Gladstone believed they so sorely lacked? Encouraged to legislate for themselves, might they not prevent a repetition of the recent debilitating proceedings in the Privy Council and rid themselves of bondage to the State? Low Churchmen and others anxious to preserve a strong connection between Church and State, answered "yes" to these questions as readily as High Churchmen, and consequently stood vigorously opposed to any scheme for revival.

Revival was by no means generally popular. Archbishop Sumner opposed the idea with the half-hearted conviction he brought to most matters. Of the cabinet, only Derby and Spencer Walpole were known to favor the scheme. The *Times* disparaged the notion, reporting that the Queen as well as the Archbishop disapproved, and arguing that in such

---

5. *Hansard*, 3rd ser., CXVIII (July 11, 1851), 554–555.
6. *Charge*, 1851, pp. 53–54.

bodies as Convocation moderate opinion had continually been stifled. "Experience has shown," a leader on October 25, 1852, declared, "that [the scheme] has been fatal to the unity of the Protestant Churches which have adopted it, and a nearer examination of the project will, both on political and on religious grounds, lessen the number of its supporters."[7] Despite opposition, Wilberforce continued to defend Convocation's power to act on its own. He had a valuable ally in his old schoolfellow, Henry Hoare, who organized a Society for the Revival of Convocation. By the fall of 1852 these protagonists had together managed to breech the Archbishop's defenses. At the November meeting the bishops amended the Address to reflect their contention that they had a capacity for internal self-government. Wilberforce secured, as well, an agreement insuring that the Archbishop would not prorogue a session without the consent of his suffragans. Finally he proposed and won approval for a committee to confer with one similar to it from the Lower House on the subject of clerical discipline.

This was real progress, but a concurrent setback occurred with the fall of the Derby Government and the accession of the less sympathetic Lord Aberdeen. Arthur Gordon, Aberdeen's son and a friend of Wilberforce, reported early in the new year that his father had no wish to assist in the work of reviving Convocation. He did, however, declare himself ready to allow the Houses to convene for one day. "They may talk till mid-night on the 16th if they like and pass the address [on clerical discipline] if they can, but they must not adjourn again."[8] Wilberforce, naturally downcast, obtained an interview with Aberdeen at which he was reluctantly forced to agree to limitation of the session to one day. "It would be most undesirable for us to have the new Cabinet forced to consider as a Cabinet question the revival of Convocation," he reported to Archbishop Sumner. "This *would* be forced on by questions in Parliament or direct motions if we adjourned for further business on the 16th; that anything we could *complete* on the 16th he thought we might do safely." Meanwhile, he prodded Sumner to call the bishops together so that they might consider at least the heads of a bill on clerical discipline which could later be introduced by the Archbishop in the Lords.[9]

Wilberforce used an opportune invitation to preach at Windsor to sound out royal opinion: "Long talk with the Prince in his room on Convocation. Tried to set plainly before him our needs, and internal action the only remedy. He spoke, as always, kindly and plainly, and paid great attention to my view."[10] He also spoke at length with Baron Stockmar and recorded that "he, as always, very sensible; promised to talk thereon

7. *Times,* October 24, 1852, p. 4.
8. January 10, 1853, Ashwell and Wilberforce, *Life,* II, 161.
9. January 14, 1853, Letter Book, BD, d.204.353–355.
10. Diary, January 19, 1853, Ashwell and Wilberforce, *Life,* II, 165.

with Lord Aberdeen." Gordon reported subsequently that Stockmar was by no means favorably disposed; presumably his views echoed those of his master. Wilberforce was further distressed to discover that though Aberdeen was contemplating a commission to inquire into the advisability of revival—a commission never issued—his name was not to be included among its members. Consequently, his role in the day-long meeting on February 16 was a minor one, and the meeting itself inconsequential.

Shaftesbury and other Low Churchmen meanwhile did what they could to confirm Aberdeen in his opposition. Apparently they overplayed their hand. Gordon reported his father "quite disgusted" at the abuse Shaftesbury poured upon Wilberforce. Aberdeen did nothing to prevent the meeting, which took place on February 1, 1854, at which a good deal was accomplished. Committees on discipline, Church rates, Church extension, and constitutional reform were approved. In the course of the discussion Wilberforce urged his fellow bishops to remember the purpose of their meetings. There were abroad in the Church anomalies and evils that cried out for reform. "They were all agreed as to the great evils that were to be remedied. But whether the remedy was to be found by an increased number of preachers, or by an alteration in the present machinery, or in the laws by which the machinery was carried out, was a very different question." This was the question Convocation had been summoned to settle. Reform of its constitution would insure that when the answer came it would be representative of the Church as a whole. They must not forget that their primary charge was to improve the Church's ministry to its people. During a debate upon the legality of enfranchising licensed curates, Wilberforce rose to remind them that their time was precious and that they must not waste it on nonessentials. "Those who felt above all things, the pressing needs of the population to which the Church of England had to minister, and that the most important matter was to settle how those wants might be supplied, were often pained by hearing it said that these were the idle frivolities in which Convocation would waste its time if it were allowed to sit." [11]

In his Charge of 1854 Wilberforce defended the beginnings that had been made and attempted once more to confound those who argued that the calling together of High and Low Churchmen would lead to nothing but further strife. The move to revive Convocation was not in itself a party maneuver. "This is only so far true, as that it is the movement of that party which believes in the Church's life, and seeks for its perfection." [12] His enthusiasm led Wilberforce to expect more from Convocation than it could achieve. As Bishop Thirlwall wisely pointed out in

11. *Chronicles of Convocation,* 1847–1857, pp. 134, 117.
12. *Charge,* 1854, p. 74.

his Charge of the same year, the business of a revived Convocation would not be to infuse a new spirit into the Church, but

to regulate that which has already awakened, and to prepare channels into which it may usefully be directed. It is a mischievous exaggeration to treat this as a question of supreme or vital moment to the being or the well-being of the Church. At the highest it can only be considered as relating to one among a variety of means toward the common end; one neither of indispensable necessity, nor comparable in importance to some which we have at our undisputed command.[13]

Despite his misgivings, Thirlwall was content to get what could be got from Convocation. Another critic, S. R. Maitland, who wrote a pamphlet directed against the remarks in Wilberforce's Charge, spoke for the goodly number who continued to believe that what could be got was very little. The argument that councils should convene when there was strife to be settled would make more sense if this particular council had authority behind it.[14] Behind a judge was a police force, a Parliament, and a constitution, but behind Convocation there rested nothing but a neutral, if not hostile government, while at its head sat an Archbishop who continued to hope, if not to work, for its downfall.

These reservations did little to daunt Wilberforce, and with some reason; in January, 1855, he was able to record in his diary that the Archbishop, apparently tired of being pushed, had of his own accord asked Aberdeen for permission to prolong the February session for two or three days, in order to consider the reports of the various committees appointed the previous year. "I feel as if the stone we had so hardly rolled up the hill was beginning to roll over. May God direct it aright." [15] The meetings in February encompassed discussion on some, though not all, of the committee reports, and were most noteworthy for the fact that Wilberforce, on behalf of the committee on Church extension, proposed the creation of a sub-order of deacons, such as he had recommended in his Charge as Archdeacon of Surrey in 1844.[16] No vote was taken on that particular recommendation or, for that matter, on any of the other items on the agenda. On June 28, 1855, on the advice of Richard Bethell, the Solicitor-General, and Robert Phillimore, Convocation addressed the Crown for permission to reform itself. The Government, with Palmerston now at its head and no doubt influenced by the Archbishop's opposition to so positive a step, refused its assent. Wilberforce at the meeting the following February resigned himself to a Convocation acting,

13. Connop Thirlwall, "Charge" [1854], *Remains, Literary and Theological,* ed. J. J. S. Perowne, 2 vols. (London, 1877), I, 219–220.
14. S. R. Maitland, *Convocation: Remarks on the Charge Recently Delivered by The Right Reverend The Lord Bishop of Oxford* (London, 1855), pp. 9–10. Maitland had been librarian to Archbishop Howley and was keeper of manuscripts at Lambeth Palace.
15. Diary, January 19, 1855, in Ashwell and Wilberforce, *Life,* II, 267.
16. See above, p. 130.

for the time being, as a consultative body only. He did not quit the fight without a parting shot. He remained convinced, he declared, that the Church needed "greater elasticity in the whole human side of her framework and machinery." He would far rather run a risk of danger "than that we should sit still, knowing that our Church needs those adaptations, and yet did not venture to attempt to begin the course which might safely lead to their being safely made." [17]

This was the first and by no means the last of such pleas Wilberforce would make. He lamented in 1859, during a debate on the advisability of special services for the urban poor, that "the feeling with respect to Convocation is not what it was. An impression existed that Convocation was going to do some terrible things. Now it is said we are all talkers, that we can do nothing, and that every spring we spend two or three days which might be much better spent in our dioceses." [18] Eight years later, in a call for a decision about diocesan synods, he complained that further delay would incur "the reproach of dilatoriness if not insincerity," and added the tactical objection that refusal to act would give opponents of the idea time to marshal their arguments against it. "It is reasonable to afford time for turning the weapons on it—but it is not reasonable to require time for the weapons to be forged, when the subject has been placed before you three times already." [19]

The ill-defined structure of Convocation continued to make action difficult. Wilberforce insisted that the Upper and Lower Houses could speak out as the official voice of the Church of England. Others disagreed. Bishop Baring of Gloucester and Bristol contended during the debates on *Essays and Reviews* that although "some few of the clergy and some few old ladies who are readers of the *Guardian* will say that when the Houses of Convocation have condemned *Essays and Reviews* the matter will be settled forever, that no heretical dog will ever dare to bark again after the utterance of this voice of the Church of England," this view was nonetheless preposterous. He declared himself opposed to the bishop of Oxford's statement "that what will go forth as the act of Convocation will in any way express to the Church of England the opinions of that Church." Convocation, "constituted as it is of large numbers, easily influenced by temporary excitement, and by one or two eloquent popular members," was not "a fit body to sit in judgment on questions of heresy." Wilberforce retorted that Baring—an Evangelical for whom he had little regard—"seemed to have been led to take up the cant cry of some people and to have repeated it in a manner which in his graver moments he will be ready to regret. . . There never was a doubt," he maintained, "that the

17. *Chronicles of Convocation,* 1847–1857, pp. 254–255.
18. *Chronicles of Convocation,* February 11, 1859, p. 29.
19. *Ibid.,* June 4, 1867, p. 861.

synods of Canterbury and York form together the sacred synod of the Church of England." [20] Yet when Convocation debated the remarriage of divorced persons, to which practice Wilberforce stood adamantly opposed, he turned about face and took pains to make it clear that he did not, after all, conceive of Convocation as a sort of supreme legislative body, above the jurisdiction of individual bishops. He seemed to want it both ways. "While our acting here together, consulting together, and coming to resolutions in common is of incalculable value . . . nothing can be much more injurious than that we should attempt to interfere with the individual responsibility and individual management of the several dioceses of the Church." [21]

Certainly without reform of the membership in the Lower House, the claim that Convocation as a whole represented the Church would remain a somewhat hollow one. As constituted at the time of revival, the Lower House contained ninety-nine nonelected representatives from Cathedral Chapters, and forty-four elected from the parochial clergy. An increase in the latter group seemed a sensible proposal to most, but not until 1871 did elected members equal the nonelected. Wilberforce was a member of the committee recommending this reform, and endorsed it wholeheartedly. His attitude toward a much more drastic innovation remained equivocal. Laymen who had worked with Wilberforce during the early 1850's to resuscitate Convocation believed that it could not be a truly effective body until it contained lay as well as clerical representatives. Wilberforce agreed that some procedure whereby lay opinion might at least be received would be useful. During the period of Russell's government he was constantly lamenting the fact that the House of Commons should be thought to represent that opinion, since it contained men of various religious beliefs and of no religious beliefs whatsoever.

But even had Convocation the license to recommend an innovation of this magnitude, Wilberforce was not at all certain he would support it. Much as he despaired at the treatment Anglicans received at the hands of the House of Commons, he recognized that their quarrelsome connection with Parliament sustained the venerable and cherished link between Church and State. If Church denied to State all power of intervention, it might as well deprive itself of power to work its will within the nation. He reluctantly concluded that lay representation, however theoretically desirable, remained incompatible with the idea of an Estab-

20. *Ibid.*, March 14, 1861, pp. 564–566; 571–572; Archbishop Musgrave of York had refused to summon Convocation because he believed it did not have authority to sit without special license of the Crown. The Convocation of York, therefore, did not sit until the Archiepiscopate of Longley (1861) and did not conduct much business until that of his successor Thomson in 1862 (H. Kirk-Smith, *William Thomson* [London, 1958], pp. 75–83).
21. *Chronicles of Convocation*, June 16, 1871, p. 436.

lished Church. "While we remain the Established Church," he remarked during a debate in 1872, "the Houses of Parliament must be the lay representative in the sense of the legislative body of the Established Church. The clamour to obtain laymen to legislate in Convocation is really in my judgment only another mode of asking for the disestablishment of the Church—to remove its legislation from the National Council, and to substitute a private lay council for it." [22]

Meanwhile, Wilberforce remained more than willing to throw his support behind the recently organized Church Congresses, annual meetings of clergy and laity designed to strengthen the Church through discussion of such topics as "Church Extension" and the "Agencies for the Revival of Spiritual Life." The aim was to keep the sessions as uncontroversial as possible. Nor were the Congresses expected to do more than talk. Wilberforce presided over the second meeting at Oxford in 1862 and took the occasion to give the Congress a well-meant but nonetheless wan benediction. "It is a body perfectly unfit to come to any . . . decision; perfectly fit to discuss matters; but the very thing that makes it fit to *discuss all things* makes it unfit to *decide* anything except the one question of where they will meet next year." [23]

Despite the revival of Convocation the Church remained without any strong, official voice. Though Convocation itself occasionally spoke out on issues, and though in the sixties it obtained for itself the power to revise certain Canons, it remained sitting still, reporting and recommending, but without the power to support what it had recommended, and without real determination to effect reforms for the Church which Wilberforce and others did recognize as necessary.

Credit for whatever limited successes Convocation did enjoy during the first decade of its revival must go in large measure to Wilberforce. Until Archbishop Sumner died, Wilberforce acted as its president, and spoke in the manner of one. "My object has been throughout," he addressed the Upper House in 1856, "gradually and in the safest way, to accustom and teach the present generation of the Church to exercise that, its inalienable function, of consulting together, as allowed by the law of the land, upon points needful to enable it to carry out its one great object of saving the souls of men." [24] He did not hesitate to instruct the Archbishop publicly as to how to conduct the affairs of the assembly. During discussion of a motion to appoint a committee of the Lower House on clerical discipline at the same session, he suggested that

your grace should, in the exercise of your prerogative, direct the Lower House of Convocation to appoint a Committee of their own body to report upon it, that

22. *Ibid.*, July 5, 1872, p. 734.
23. *Church Congress Report*, 1862, p. 227.
24. *Journal of Convocation*, February 1, 1856, p. 77.

your Grace should grant sufficient time for that committee to carry on their consultations . . . that when the Lower House has assembled to receive the Report, your Grace should direct them to consider it; that they should then proceed to consider it with the advantage of knowing beforehand what they are about to discuss, without which no body of men can be expected to come to a deliberate and valuable conclusion.[25]

Apparently Sumner, who was seventy-six, was either too old or too indifferent to the fate of any committee report in Convocation to bridle at this sort of treatment. Nothing in the Chronicles indicates that he was prepared to put up much of a battle at the meetings, and his eventual willingness to come at least part way with Wilberforce on the matter of revival itself suggests, as his critics declared, that he could be pushed one way or another by anyone willing to take the time and trouble to do so.

Sumner's successor Longley was a far stronger man, a man for whom Wilberforce had a good deal of respect, and with whom he could work naturally. When Longley was succeeded in 1868 by Tait, Wilberforce surrendered his preeminent place in the Upper House. Not only did Tait have a will of his own, but it was one which moved in an opposite latitudinarian direction from Wilberforce's on such matters as doctrine, ritual, and discipline. The two recognized that to avoid splitting Convocation apart they would have to support each other as much as possible. Wilberforce promised to do his best. "We have (as you said in your letter) differed," Wilberforce wrote following Tait's appointment. "Perhaps on some points we may yet differ. But placed where you are my strong personal regard only combines with a sense of duty in making me most anxious to support you and remove difficulties out of your way." [26] C. J. Ellicott, Baring's successor as Bishop of Gloucester and Bristol, immediately appointed himself go-between, and attempted in the officious manner that appears to have been typical of him to bring the two men into harmony. "I had a very long conversation with Oxford when in London," he reported to Tait. "I found him most warm in his feelings to you, and (as I judged) most willing to help loyally in these ritual difficulties. [At the time Evangelicals were pressing for anti-ritual legislation.] My feeling is that if you and he—possibly allowing me to be a third—were to confer on the heads of a measure, we might go very far to agreement. . . It is now a critical time with him and I do frankly want to secure him and his pleasant as well as great powers for us, rather than half against us." [27] Nothing suggests that Ellicott exercised influence of any particular kind on Wilberforce, who remained unsympathetic to the sort of Broad

25. *Ibid.,* p. 76.   26. November 28, 1868, LPL, Tait Correspondence, 85.243.
27. *Ibid.,* 85.241, November 26, 1868. Wilberforce had hoped he would be appointed Bishop of London to succeed Tait, and had not been (see below, pp. 286ff).

Church temper that Tait and a good many of the younger bishops now displayed. Nor did Wilberforce himself enjoy the power he had possessed in the early days of Convocation, though he may not himself have realized the fact. Still as hard-working and as concerned as he had always been, he nonetheless deliberated in the company of men who were unwilling to be dominated as he had dominated their predecessors during the ineffectual reign of Archbishop Sumner. Ellicott reported in 1871 to Tait, who was recuperating from a severe illness in France, that

there is a junior party that pull a great [deal] together, and are very much inclined to make their influence felt, greatly dislike the Bishop of Winchester's predominance in our councils [Wilberforce was translated to the See in 1869], but yet are too raw and undisciplined for us, the older party, to make much use of. They would soon acquire a power that, as their acts and speeches show, they would use very imprudently.[28]

No one, not even Wilberforce who set such store by its revival, expected Convocation to resolve all the Church's problems. He hoped it might serve, as eventually it did, to extend the influence of the Church and the effectiveness of its mission. Another means to the same end, and one, again, for which Wilberforce worked, was an increase in the episcopate. Russell's ministry in 1847 had promised to add four bishoprics to the existing twenty-five. In the end, only Manchester was created, and that after prolonged debate. Evangelicals opposed an increase in the Bench on the ground that bishops tended to discriminate against the Low Church. Wilberforce spoke then and thereafter in favor of an increase wherever it might be deemed necessary. He served on a Royal Commission in the 1860's which recommended the division of the huge diocese of Exeter, and supported a proposal which would have subdivided Lincoln and brought relief to the overtaxed diocese of London.[29] Responding in 1865 to a speech by Shaftesbury, who had argued that an increase in the episcopate would work to the detriment of the parish system, Wilberforce declared in the House that

the efficiency of diocesan management did not depend merely on the multiplication of clergy or of churches, important as were these elements of success. It depended more on the spirit in which the parishes were worked, in which the pulpits were filled, in which the cottages were visited; and it is the Bishop who

28. This "strong, restless, and not very prudent juniority," as Ellicott further described it, consisted, according to him, of Wilberforce's successor at Oxford, J. R. Mackarness, Bishop Fraser of Manchester, Bishop Temple of Exeter, Bishop Hervey of Bath and Wells, Bishop Goodwin of Carlisle, and Bishop Magee of Peterborough (C. T. Ellicott to A. C. Tait, April 7, 1871, LPL, Tait Correspondence, 89.178).

29. This latter diocese, to be named St. Alban's, was to be composed of parts of Middlesex, Hertfordshire, and Essex, and would have made the management of the See of Winchester, to which Wilberforce went in 1869, far less arduous (*Chronicles of Convocation*, May 4, 1866, p. 351; Wilberforce to Gladstone, April 30, 1869, Add Mss. 44345, in which Wilberforce discusses in detail a plan for financing the new See.)

must be the main instrument in encouraging the zealous, in stirring up the faint-hearted, in animating the despondent; he must be to his clergy the example and the mainspring of holy living and dying for the people committed to their care.[30]

All true enough, but to Wilberforce an increase in the number of bishops would serve the equally important purpose of providing the Church with a stronger voice when challenged, as increasingly it seemed to be, by an unconcerned and even hostile State. His hopes for the success of Convocation had stemmed, likewise, from his fears lest the prayers and petitions of the Church be drowned out by noisy Erastianism. Over and over, in the Lords, he rose to defend ecclesiastical interests from what he believed to be unwarranted depredation: charitable trusts and capitular estates should be left, when usage provided, to the management of the Church. Ecclesiastical Commissioners, though a necessary evil, should be held at bay.[31] The task of defense was neither pleasant nor easy, but it was a bishop's duty to perform it, and to look for ways to make its performance easier and more effective.

Events in the 1850's and 1860's led champions of the Church to conclude that success in their battle with the State would remain limited without a drastic reform of their appeal procedures. The Gorham decision, and the battles over *Essays and Reviews* and Colenso's books, made it plain that the State intended to reach its own verdicts in ecclesi-

30. *Hansard,* 3rd ser., CIV (June 23, 1865), 180. Wilberforce opposed any move to create suffragan bishops within the larger dioceses. He believed the scheme would jeopardize the entire process of succession and make the bishops themselves little more than Parliamentarians (*Hansard,* 3rd ser., CLXXXVIII [June 21, 1867], 251–254.) He was willing, however, to see an aged or infirm bishop's duties discharged by a coadjutor, appointed after negotiation between the bishop and the Government, who would have the right to succession when the present bishop died. "The chief difficulty," he remarked in a debate on the proposal in Convocation, "is that of an outgoing government taking advantage of the opposition to appoint its political partisans, but I do not apprehend that this difficulty would be found insurmountable" (*Chronicles of Convocation,* February 26, 1869, p. 174).

31. On Charitable Trusts see his speech in the Lords (*Hansard,* 3rd ser., C [August 4, 1848], 1142), in which he worried lest "a shrewd dissenting attorney, holding the office of judge, might, under [the operation of the proposed measure] divert Church property from its proper object and apply it to objects not contemplated, on the ground that he thought the new application would be beneficial." On Capitular Estates and the powers of the Ecclesiastical Commissioners see debates in *Hansard,* 3rd ser., CXVI (May 22, 1851), 1230–1233; CXXXIII (May 23, 1854), 783; and CL (May 4, 1858), 15–16. He continually opposed any weakening of Cathedral Chapters. "Instead of making chapters worthy of preserving to the Church by securing the proper performance of the duties for which they were founded," he complained in Convocation, "the miserable remedy has been adopted of cutting them down to a very small number, and trusting to them in their comparative uselessness" (*Chronicles of Convocation,* July 3, 1863, p. 1388).

astical matters and that it was prepared in doing so to overrule the Church. Church partisans insisted that Church, not State, must have the final say in matters of doctrine and discipline. During the 1850's Wilberforce hoped that the controversy might be settled on some middle ground. He wanted to reform procedure in a way that would preserve the Church's right to pronounce upon doctrine. At the same time he had no desire, as he wrote Robert during the Gorham controversy, to deny "the just supremacy of the State." During debate in the Lords on a Church Discipline Bill in 1856, he declared he was ready to leave "the entire settlement of every case of doctrine, as far as it concerned an individual, to the Privy Council." He argued that archbishops and bishops ought not to mix with laymen as judges as they did at present. Far better that the Council send them cases to hear and respond to, "deciding—not whether A. B. was guilty or not guilty—but whether certain doctrine was or was not in accordance with the formularies of the Church of England." This solution should please both Church and State. "It would preserve the Crown as the supreme arbiter, and would keep the doctrines of the Church from being tampered with by judgment given in individual cases." [32]

The more thought Wilberforce devoted to the Court of Appeal, the more convinced he became that the Church would suffer less confusion and retain greater freedom by withdrawing itself from the judicial review process altogether. He wrote Gladstone the following year that lay members of the Privy Council should be forced to decide cases as lawyers, calling upon ecclesiastical experts if they felt the need. "Let the Privy Council adivse the Queen about us as it would about a Wesleyan or a Roman trust deed." [33] Gladstone replied that to suggest that a sentence "might take effect and yet not in any real sense commit the Church" was both "vain in logic" and "demoralizing in practice." The Church, he argued, must retain its membership in the Court of Appeal. Without defenders present in court to declare the truth of Anglican dogma, the Church would soon find herself acceding unwittingly to the Erastian claim "that the business of an Establishment is to teach all sorts of doctrines and to provide Christian Ordinances by way of comfort for all sorts of people, to be used at their own option." [34]

Litigation proceeding from the publication of *Essays and Reviews* did little to resolve the question of final appeal, although it did strengthen Wilberforce's own mind on the subject. He acted throughout on the conviction that the book's dangerous fallacies demanded some sort of conclusive condemnation of its authors. In the preface to the series of published replies to the *Essays*, he declared the need for an authority "to

32. *Hansard,* 3rd ser., CXLI (April 21, 1856), 1321.
33. October 31, 1857, in Ashwell and Wilberforce, *Life,* II, 352.
34. *Ibid.,* November 2, 1857.

prevent the very idea of truth, as truth, dying out amongst us. For so indeed it must do if once it be permitted to our clergy solemnly to engage to teach as the truth of God a certain set of doctrines, and at the same time freely to discuss whether they are true or false." [35]

The bishops, assembled in London for the winter, met on February 1, 1861, to decide what action to take in response to the numerous complaints about the book they had received. Thirlwall of St. David's argued that an episcopal declaration against the *Essays,* unless followed by action, would be an admission "that we had no means of repressing prolate heresy." [36] He counseled caution, as he had in a letter to Wilberforce a few days before. "I should think it dangerous to do anything merely because we have affirmed that something ought to be done." [37] Tait, supported by Archbishop Sumner, favored a declaration of doctrine; Wilberforce agreed with Thirlwall that a declaration would be unwise; it might put the bishops in the awkward postion of originating an action, and it would be condemning the essayists unheard. The bishops adjourned for the day; three of them, Wilberforce, Waldegrave of Carlisle, and Wigram of Rochester, went for the night with Tait to Fulham Palace. There, according to Wilberforce's diary, "at the entreaty of Bishops," he drafted an answer to one of the addresses of complaint, intended undoubtedly to indicate general episcopal dismay at the publication of the *Essays.* The draft went out to the bishops for their approval and was published, under the Archbishop's signature on February 12, with the names of the Archbishop of York and twenty-three of the twenty-six bishops appended. The letter pronounced that the opinions "concerning which you have addressed us" seemed at odds "with many of the fundamental doctrines" of the Church. It did not commit the bishops to any further action, declaring that both a suit in the Ecclesiastical Courts and synodical condemnation were alternatives "still under our gravest consideration." [38] The letter did not mention *Essays and Reviews* specifically, nor had the address, which may have been singled out for reply on that account. But few who read the Archbishop's answer believed that it had been drafted without that specific book in mind.[39]

35. *Replies To Essays and Reviews,* p. x.

36. From a book in which Wilberforce occasionally recorded his notes of informal episcopal meetings (BD, I. C186.109). R. T. Davidson and William Benham, in their biography of A. C. Tait, criticized Reginald Wilberforce for having printed these notes. Yet the opinions credited to Tait by Wilberforce do not vary markedly from his general position on the subject (Davidson and Benham, *Tait,* I, 283).

37. January 28, 1861, BD, I. C195.

38. Ashwell and Wilberforce, *Life,* III, 4–5. Geoffrey Faber thinks it contemptible that the Archbishop allowed someone else's letter to go out in his name. Sumner was accustomed to allow others to speak for him, and very often Wilberforce assumed the role of spokesman (Faber, *Jowett,* p. 249).

39. This impression was fortified when the answer, without the address, appeared,

By the time Convocation met formally Wilberforce had come to believe that it should issue a direct pronouncement. He did not argue that Convocation should take the place of the present final court. He did believe that it might exercise a kind of judgment denied the State-controlled Judicial Committee, and, in so doing, better protect doctrine from the unwanted interference of uncommitted laymen. He had in mind a judgment that would be extra-legal in the sense that it would derive not from the authority assigned the Church within the State but rather from the Church's role as defender of Christian truth. The book, and not its individual authors, were the Church's concern. If the Courts should decide for the authors, he explained to Bishop Ollivant of Llandaff, the Church would nevertheless be saved the "intolerable scandal of such a book being justified, and the just distinction between the condemnation of the writing and the punishment of the writer will be preserved." In the same letter he argued that Convocation would be wiser to act immediately rather than await a judgment from the Privy Council. "For, if R. W. is condemned [Rowland Williams was being prosecuted by Bishop Hamilton of Salisbury], there would be a certain appearance of trampling on the fallen, in a synodical condemnation; and if he were acquitted, it would certainly be held to be an appeal from the Court of Law to the Synod." [40]

The Upper House could not agree, and decided, against his plea, to do nothing until the case had passed through the courts. That process occupied the better part of three years. Rowland Williams and H. B. Wilson were tried for denying the divine inspiration of the Bible in its entirety and, in the case of Williams, for denying the doctrine of eternal damnation. They were found guilty in the Court of Arches by Dr. Stephen Lushington; they appealed and were acquitted by the Judicial Committee of the Privy Council, the two Archbishops voting to uphold the lower court, Tait siding with the unanimous lay lords for a reversal. The judges demarcated the limits of their jurisdiction with care, making it clear they had passed judgment on "a few short extracts," and were expressing no opinion on the book as a whole.[41]

This argument echoed Wilberforce's presentiments, expressed in Convocation in 1861: that even if the Court condemned the essayists, it would leave the book untouched. As he had at the time of the Gorham judgment, Wilberforce went to work to persuade offended High Churchmen that they could live with a judgment even he found unpalatable. To his

previous to its official publication, in the *Times,* with the sentence: "We cannot understand how their opinions can be held consistently with an honest subscription etc." "Their" had been mysteriously substituted for "these" (Faber, *Jowett,* pp. 251–252; Davidson and Benham, *Tait,* I, 284).

40. July 3, 1861, Letter Book, BD, d.210.198–201.
41. Davidson and Benham, *Tait,* I, 315.

son-in-law Henry Pye, who had preached disestablishment as the one remaining honorable course for the Church, he wrote reassuringly that the judgment in no way interfered with Church doctrine. It insisted only "that there may be in [the Bible] *e.g.* as to science and history things which God did not directly inspire but as to which He left the human element to itself guiding supernaturally all that was for man's spiritual teaching. Now *this* it would I imagine be very difficult to show that the Church had at any time categorically condemned." [42]

Whether or not the letter succeeded in reassuring Pye, it implied Wilberforce's conviction that the Church was in no sense in thrall to the State, that it was her right and duty—as he had insisted three years before —to condemn the entire book as pernicious. At the April session of Convocation, he declared it Convocation's "legal and special function . . . to be able to condemn books, leaving the question of the treatment of the writers of these books to the criminal courts." [43] Not all the bishops believed with Wilberforce that the matter could be made to resolve itself that simply. Convocation had not pronounced synodically upon a question of doctrine since the early eighteenth century; there seemed little precedent for such a declaration now. Even if the mandate could be proved, would the country accept it? Tait, in a speech in Convocation the previous year, had wondered if it had won enough respect to make its writ run very far. "I would wish to speak, of course, with the deepest respect of this body. . . Yet it is a simple fact that it does not command (so much, perhaps, as we might desire—at all events, as many of our body desire) the unhesitating respect of the whole of the Church." [44] Under such conditions would it not be wiser to instruct individual bishops to act as they saw fit in matters of this kind? Wilberforce did not believe so. He pressed for a committee to consider condemnation, and won his point after Archbishop Longley broke a tie vote in his favor. The Upper House constituted itself the committee. Wilberforce presented its report in late June. Lengthy, and comprising in the main extracts from the essays, it not surprisingly recommended condemnation. The report carried, as did the condemnation. Only Tait and John Jackson of Lincoln voted nay.

The condemnation once more fanned flames of the controversy now almost four years old. Wilberforce continued to insist that quiet acquiescence in the Privy Council judgment would have betokened heretical complacency. When defending the action of Convocation in the Lords, Wilberforce contended that it had served to quiet men's minds and bring peace to the Church. Westbury, the Lord Chancellor, had earlier in the

42. March 7, 1864, Letter Book, BD, d.211.96–100.
43. *Chronicles of Convocation,* April 19–20, 1864, p. 1461.
44. *Ibid.,* February 13, 1863, pp. 1092ff.

debate declared that Convocation had no right to pronounce in the matter, since the condemnation, resting outside the law, allowed for no appeal to the Crown. Wilberforce considered the accusation irrelevant. Convocation was not trying to act independently of the Crown. It was attempting to set its own house in order. "And I am satisfied," he concluded, "that if you would avoid the recurrence of such a state of things as you have witnessed, you will find that the best way in which that can be done is by allowing the Church in her authorised manner to pronounce for her followers, as she has done in this instance, that she disclaims for her living ministry this erroneous teaching." [45] In this appraisal Wilberforce did not stand alone. Gladstone wrote the following September: "It is not necessary to *oppose* the judgment [of the Privy Council]. Taking the ground of the judges themselves, that of legal interpretation, and assuming theirs to be a fair specimen, it is plain that they are disqualified by their own confession from looking to the preservation of the Christian faith—and consequently they leave that to others who must use other means." [46]

The Church required authority of its own distinct from that guaranteed by its alliance with the State. Defenders of the faith could continue to support establishment, as Wilberforce did, yet argue that establishment could not secure the Church from pernicious attack. *Essays and Reviews* had proved it—and the thorny and exasperating Colenso affair proved it doubly; for in this case the threat to doctrinal purity was coupled with what ardent Churchmen believed an unwarranted interference on the part of the State with the administration of missionary Sees.

Missionary bishoprics raised problems which the Church did not fully resolve for more than twenty years. Wilberforce labored for a solution because of his concern to define the relations between Church and State, and as a result of the commitment to missionary endeavor he had inherited from his father.[47] From the time he had first begun to preach on behalf of missions, Wilberforce had urged the establishment of missionary bishoprics. Without episcopal authority and diocesan organization within the colonies and beyond, the English Church, as distinct from the Christian religion, would never flourish overseas. This had been his quarrel with the C.M.S. in the 1830's and 1840's: they had refused to

45. *Hansard,* 3rd ser., CLXXVI (July 15, 1864), 1563–1565. During this debate Lord Westbury made his famous attack upon Wilberforce, calling Convocation's judgment, for which Wilberforce had been responsible, "a sentence so oily and saponaceous that no one could grasp it—like an eel, it slips through your fingers and is simply nothing."

46. September 7, 1864, BD, II. K.

47. Wilberforce conducted missions for the S.P.G. in 1858 and 1859, in addition to preaching constantly on behalf of various missionary schemes. He was instrumental in bringing Queen Emma of the Sandwich Islands to England for the purpose of raising money for the Anglican Churches there.

understand the need to live up to their name of *Church* Missionary Society. But if Anglican bishops went out among the heathen, into territories beyond the British flag, from whom were they to receive their commission and to whom would they be ultimately responsible? Could the State expect to nominate to Sees outside the realm? High Churchmen, anxious to sever Erastian bonds whenever possible, argued that the appointment of missionary bishops was a function of the Church, acting upon its own initiative and taking counsel only with itself. Wilberforce had raised the issue in 1837 in a sermon commemorating the founding of the S.P.G. and the S.P.C.K. Before he wrote it, he had apparently consulted Newman, who replied that perhaps missionary bishoprics lay outside even the jurisdiction of Canterbury.[48]

Wilberforce grew to believe that without power to appoint missionary bishops of its own, the Church would be bound in an unseemly—and indeed an unholy—way to the State. In 1853 he undertook to pilot a Missionary Bishops Bill through Parliament—"The Archbishop left it very much to me to arrange," he confided to Arthur Gordon—a Bill which would have allowed the Church to head missions to the heathen, with English bishops of English consecration, and without the commission of the Queen. In territories where the State's writ did not run, Wilberforce argued, the Church was compelled to act on her own. Many refused to see the problem in those straightforward terms. Like most of the ecclesiastical disagreements during the 1850's, this one arose over Low Church suspicions that High Churchmen were acting for their own ends. Most missionary societies sent out Low Church missionaries. Might not their work be undermined by High Church episcopal henchmen dispatched to preach and practice offensive sacerdotalism among the heathen? The Evangelical *Record,* which at this time could say nothing good of Wilberforce, put the case with characteristic acerbity: "The Church of England does not stand in need of Bishops with a roving commission, to put down or impede missionary exertions. The Church of England does not believe in the Ultramontane doctrine of Bishop Wilberforce or hold that but for the not very apostolic resident of Cudworth [Cuddesdon] Palace the Church of Christ could not exist in the counties of Berkshire or Oxford." [49] The Bill passed in the Lords, but was defeated in the Commons, the opposition having outmaneuvered Wilberforce, who tried to arrange for its passage with Government support.[50] In the fall of 1861, when the

48. May 12, 1837, BD, III.
49. August 4, 1853, p. 8.
50. At the same time a Colonial Churches Bill, which would have allowed bishops, clergy, and laity in colonies to meet in synods to pass necessary ecclesiastical legislation, was defeated as well. Wilberforce favored its passage, as he favored most measures granting the colonies a measure of home rule in Church matters. In the winter of 1853 he voted

King of Hawaii pressed the Church to send him a bishop, the matter came to a head. Wilberforce insisted that should the appointment originate with the Crown, such an act would be tantamount to territorial usurpation. "If what [the Queen] grants is that power of jurisdiction which in the realm we receive from the Church for the better carrying out of the power which we receive from God, how can the Crown of England grant *it* in a foreign territory without usurpation?" But if this was not the jurisdiction granted, one was left to assume that the Queen was asserting the right to bestow "the pure spiritual power of the Word and Sacraments which the Crown does not grant in England and cannot grant abroad." [51] In the end, a compromise permitted the consecration of Thomas Staley as bishop of Honolulu by means of a royal license. The solution left Wilberforce and many others unsatisfied. They believed that the Church must be allowed free reign to deal with territories beyond Her Majesty's dominions. To grant the State a role there was to grant the State the power of spiritual as well as temporal authority.

With matters in this tangled state, the Church found itself without any certain understanding of its rights when attempting to press a case against Bishop Colenso of Natal. In spite of his former friendship with Colenso, Wilberforce led the attack against his writing in Convocation, as he was at the same time leading the attack against *Essays and Reviews*. At first he hoped to persuade Colenso to retract the most advanced of his interpretations. "Surely," Wilberforce pleaded, "the separation of Colonial life and the autocracy of a Colonial Bishop's position cannot be, with any gifts of intellect, the most favorable position for the discovery of religious truth. And if this be so, it must be a duty to review all conclusions so reached with others, if you have the opportunity [Colenso was at the time in England], before you irrevocably adopt them and run the risk of advocating error, of clouding truth, or of risking the usefulness of a life." [52] Colenso declined the offer to recant. Wilberforce thereupon moved successfully to persuade his fellow bishops to inhibit Colenso from preaching in their dioceses and to urge him, in the interests of peace, to resign. In May 1863 Wilberforce asked the Upper House of Convocation to officially condemn Colenso's *Pentateuch Critically Examined*. He brushed aside Tait's contention that the book ought no more to be dis-

---

to allow the Canadian Parliament the right to dispose as it wished of its Church Reserves, despite the fact that Canadian Churchmen opposed their government's intentions. Wilberforce argued that although he would like to see the endowments of the Church remain intact, the British Parliament had already granted the Canadian Parliament power to act on her own. Under the circumstances, England could only "use all legitimate means, all affectionate influences, all wise advice . . . but I will be guilty of no act of injustice" (*Hansard*, 3rd ser., CXXIV [February 28, 1853], 719–727).

51. To Roundell Palmer, November 18, 1861, Letter Book, BD, d.210.214.
52. August 8, 1862, Letter Book, BD, d.211.1–4.

cussed than the *Essays,* prior to a possible trial for heresy. "I think this House has to consider whether this is evil or dangerous teaching, leaving to other courts to settle the question as to whether the man had condemned himself as a teacher of heresy." [53] The next day the House passed a resolution declaring the Church's right to pronounce on matters spiritual, regardless of the decision of a temporally dominated ecclesiastical court, and pronouncing the book full of "errors of the gravest and most dangerous character."

The uncertain status of missionary bishoprics meant that no one could be sure just how temporal justice in such a case might be administered. When Colenso received his appointment in 1853, his bishopric of Natal was detached from the sprawling diocese of Capetown, whose incumbent, Bishop Robert Gray, was issued new letters patent for his altered See. The new letters granted the Bishop of Capetown metropolitan jurisdiction over the subordinate bishoprics of Grahamstown and Natal; Colenso duly swore an oath of obedience to Gray. In 1863, however, just as Gray was about to summon Colenso on a charge of heresy, the Privy Council delivered a judgment which seemed to deny him the right to do so. On June 23 the Judicial Committee, after hearing a case brought against Gray by a clergyman in his diocese, William Long, declared that the Bishop of Capetown had no coercive jurisdiction over a clergyman in his own diocese, let alone a fellow bishop in an adjoining See. Before Gray had received his second letters patent in 1853, the Crown had granted away his powers by bestowing representative government on the Cape Colony. Gray could exercise jurisdictional authority over his flock— and over the flocks of Natal and Grahamstown—only after entering into some sort of contract with them.[54] The Crown might make a bishop, but it could not continue to bestow upon him a temporal jurisdiction in disregard of its agreements with colonial legislatures.[55]

This judgment placed Wilberforce in an awkward predicament. On the one hand it asserted the sort of freedom for colonial and missionary churches for which he had long contended, by setting a limit to the Crown's ability to interfere in their affairs. At the same time, it restricted Gray's episcopal authority, declaring that he was essentially powerless to act coercively as matters then stood between himself and his clergy. Gray saw no dilemma. He proceeded with his plans to try Colenso for heresy in Capetown, declaring to Wilberforce that in doing so he would be

---

53. *Chronicles of Convocation,* May 19, 1863, p. 1163.

54. Long had objected to Gray's attempt to establish a synod at Capetown. Colenso had maintained in 1858 that Gray was not an independent metropolitan, but that both he and Gray were bishops together within the province of Canterbury.

55. See the opinion reprinted in C. N. Gray, *Life of Robert Gray,* 2 vols. (London, 1876), II, Appendix.

exercising a "purely spiritual function" with which the secular courts had no right to interfere. If Colenso refused to heed the sentence of his court, Gray intended to excommunicate him and appoint another in his place.

For the next year and a half, while the heresy trial proceeded in South Africa and the Privy Council sat in judgment in London on Colenso's petition that Gray had no jurisdiction whatsoever over him, Wilberforce tried to act as Gray's agent in England. He did not find it an easy role, since Gray remained throughout the proceedings as intractable as ever, refusing to appear before the Privy Council and bombarding Wilberforce with less than constructive criticism of bishops, judges, and lawyers. On March 20, 1865, the Privy Council pronounced judgment in favor of Colenso, declaring that Gray had no power to pronounce coercively in a colony where a legislative body already existed. Wilberforce could not help but regard the judgment as a "charter of the freedom of the Colonial Church." [56] "I am disposed to agree with the former parts of the judgment," he wrote cautiously to Gray—"jurisdiction, ie all external power, is not of the Apostles—must be of the Christian State and cannot be granted except by the Christian State—and that the Church in Africa is only capable of holding jurisdiction when given by the State there." He hastened to assure Gray that he did not believe the judgment meant that the deposition was null and void. "It can only really mean that the law does not contemplate these acts at all, they being the acts of a voluntary society, not that the law sets them aside." [57]

Deposition was one thing; excommunication another. Although Wilberforce had once favored the more extreme measure, that had been at a time when he assumed that Gray's letters patent gave him jurisdiction over Colenso. Now he urged caution. "My advice . . . would be—ignore him; inhibit him from doing any act, get clergy and laity to stick by you in rejecting him, but do *not* excommunicate. It would, I think, *here* tend to turn the tide again in his favour." [58] Wise enough words, but without effect upon the zealous Gray, who proceeded with the excommunication forthwith. Wilberforce had little more to do with the affair. He helped Gray look for a new bishop of Natal, certain of Gray's right to do so, and he persuaded Gray to refrain from disrupting the first Lambeth Conference in 1867 by demanding general recognition of the excommunication.

The Colenso business, complicated and drawn out as it had been, resolved itself much to Wilberforce's satisfaction. It had reaffirmed the Church's right to pronounce in defense of orthodoxy; and it had helped

56. To Lord Richard Cavendish, March 25, 1865, in Ashwell and Wilberforce, *Life*, III, 126.
57. March 24, 1865, BD, I. C199.   58. *Ibid.*, April 3, 1865.

free the Church—in the colonies, at any rate—from the overbearing and unwarranted interference of the home Government. Wilberforce could look to the future with a complacent regard denied his more Erastian peer Tait, to whom he wrote in 1866:

I most heartily agree in your object of holding the infant Colonial Church close to us; our *only* difference could be as to when the state hold was or was not gone. I have no doubt that it is altogether gone never to be replaced. But I firmly believe that if we use our own advantage of position wisely and heartily that we may by the spiritual bond hold the Colonial Church to us for the next century.[59]

Satisfaction with the outcome of the Colenso controversy did not lead Wilberforce to alter his attitude toward the Court of Appeal. The issues in the case had touched the temporal and not the spiritual power of the Church and were a matter for the decision of lay rather than clerical judges. More than ever, therefore, it seemed to make sense to divest the Court of its ecclesiastical members. Throughout this period, which saw the Court ruling first on Colenso and then on *Essays and Reviews,* Wilberforce mooted various schemes of reform. In 1861 he lent support to a plan of Gladstone's which would have seated the two English archbishops, eight English bishops, and the two Irish archbishops together as a separate court, passing judgment on questions of doctrine or discipline for the better information of the Court of Appeal, without prejudice to prerogative or discretion of the Crown.[60] He pressed constantly for such a solution. In his review for the *Quarterly* of *Aids to Faith,* he argued that the Church must pronounce doctrine, must "fix as to all fundamental questions" the true sense of the Gospel. But where no such pronouncement was required of the Church, it was unfair of the State to demand one from an ecclesiastical judge; "it would far transcend [his] power . . . to attempt the discharge of such a function as the fixing of its true meaning." [61] The State had no right to expect the Church to do work that was not rightfully hers to undertake. The Court of Appeal was constituted to decide legal matters; the presence of Anglican bishops on the Court only muddled matters and obscured the nature of the decision. "In fact," he declared in Convocation in 1865,

instead of the matter being discussed purely and simply by lawyers, and a simple legal decision being given, the accident of the single spiritual voice going with them will often be that which has caused the decision; so that that which gives to the decision its apparently spiritual character, and thereby disturbs the consciences of thousands, does also in fact injure the severity of the Church's voice in declaring doctrine for the time to come.[62]

59. May 17, 1866, LPL, Tait Correspondence, 82.167.
60. January 11, 1861, BD, II. K.
61. "Aids to Faith," *Quarterly Review,* 112:495 (1862).
62. *Chronicles of Convocation,* February 17, 1865, p. 1984.

Not all Churchmen agreed with Wilberforce. In Tait's opinion, there was something altogether fitting about a high court which included both laymen and clergy. The Court as constituted insured that ecclesiastical appeal cases would be heard not only sympathetically but intelligently. "I do not believe any other plan of judicature, very different in its general principles, can be suggested which so well unites the individuality of the Church in its maintenance of its own ecclesiastical law and the proper controlling power of the sovereign."[63]

Thirlwall's objection to the idea of a separate court of ecclesiastical advisers was more pragmatic. He did not believe that their advice would be asked. Recent experience suggested, he wrote Wilberforce in 1862, "that there never will be a reference made by the Judicial Committee in a question of doctrine to any body of spiritual 'experts.'" Lushington, the Dean of Arches, had stated that he would be guided as a judge "by nothing but judicial authority."[64] Wilberforce's rejoinder to this argument was that what Lushington did or did not do was of no fundamental consequence to the Church. His proposed advisers would function less as counselors of State than as defenders of the faith. They would insure that whatever a temporal court might decide, Church doctrine, reaffirmed in an "opinion" rendered in the name of the ecclesiastical authority, would remain untainted.

By 1866, chances for reform seemed slight. Gladstone had decided two years before to abandon his plan for a board of reference, and was at work on a proposal to strengthen the present Court of Appeal by the addition of further bishops. Wilberforce, in his Charge, could declare only that the question was one "the issues of which are so important that, provided only it is not let to fall asleep, I would rather see it wait the gradual clearing away of difficulties, than risk the danger of a too hasty settlement."[65] The resolution came sooner, perhaps, than Wilberforce expected it would—in July of 1873, when as part of the Judicature Act, ecclesiastical members were excluded from the Supreme Court of Appeal.[66]

Wilberforce's campaigns against what he considered the hampering interference of the State had implied a belief in the Church's ability to manage it's own affairs intelligently and circumspectly. Others began to

---

63. *Charge,* 1866, pp. 30, 45.   64. July 1, 1862, BD, I. C195.
65. *Charge,* 1866, p. 25.
66. Wilberforce had little to do with the winning of the battle at that time. His work within the large bishopric of Winchester, to which he had moved in 1869, kept him from participating as much as he had formerly in campaigns outside the diocese. By the time the Bill was debated in the Lords, on July 24, Wilberforce was dead.

have doubts, as quarrels over ritual spread throughout the Church. Wilberforce had long opposed any sort of legislative attempt by the State to dictate a set of rules limiting a priest's right to conduct services as he wished. He held no brief for the extremists; he believed extremists would refuse to heed the rules, while more cautious innovators, attempting to breathe new life into the forms of the Church, would find their efforts stifled by restrictive pronouncements. The most sensible way to handle ritualist controversy, Wilberforce declared in his Charge of 1866, was to place the dispute before the bishop "and act absolutely on his direction. He will, no doubt, consider well and lovingly the special circumstances of each church, the difficulty of suddenly abandoning all to which a congregation has become attached, and, so far as he deems he lawfully can, will seek to meet such difficulties by a just and comprehensive settlement of the questions referred trustfully to him." [67]

Wilberforce had reckoned without Lord Shaftesbury, whose Low Church convictions led him to introduce a bill in 1867 inhibiting all ritualistic innovation. The bill was defeated in the Lords on an amendment by the Archbishop. Lord Derby then proposed instead the establishment of a Ritual Commission to consider recent innovations and to recommend changes that might be wisely and safely adopted. Wilberforce wanted a narrow inquiry, one touching ornaments only, but the mandate eventually settled upon sanctioned investigation into all the rubrics which prescribed the mode of celebrating public worship. Though he had opposed such a Commission, Wilberforce was ready enough to serve as a member once it had been established. "Without you," Spencer Walpole, the chairman, wrote him, "it would be the drama of Hamlet without Hamlet himself." [68] Believing the Commission a lesser evil than immediate parliamentary legislation, he worked with a small group of moderately High Churchmen to protect innovations already introduced. At one point he went so far as to propose a test court case to determine which vestments, if any, could be considered illegal. Apparently willing to trust that

67. *Charge,* 1866, p. 48. In the Convocation of February 1867, Wilberforce joined Tait in moving that "no alterations from long-sanctioned and usual ritual ought to be made in our churches, until the sanction of the Bishop of the Diocese has been obtained" (*Chronicles of Convocation,* February 13, 1867, p. 711).

68. May 20, 1867, BD, I. C194. Shaftesbury, who had declined to serve on the Commission because he declared he held the extreme Protestant position on the matter of ritual, had urged Spencer Walpole to exclude extremists of the other school as well and had named Wilberforce as one of these. Wilberforce replied in the Lords to this charge: "I challenge the noble Earl, in the face of the House, to produce one single element of proof for the assertion that he has made, that I am, or ever have been, an extreme man in this matter. My actions and words are before the Church. I have done all in my power to repress these extremes, and I have in my Charge published the reasons why I have endeavoured to repress them: nay, I have done more—I have been successful in repressing them; and, whereas in other dioceses they have broken out, in the diocese of Oxford there has been a remarkable absence of them" (*Hansard,* 3rd ser., CLXXXVIII [June 20, 1867], 123–124).

lawyers would prove as unwilling to declare against ritualists as against Broad Churchmen, Wilberforce brought down upon him the wrath of Bishop Ellicott, who, with Tait, was anxious to proceed with legislation.[69] The first report, which Wilberforce had a hand in drafting, and which dealt exclusively with the matter of vestments, declared that though many found meaning in the use of copes and chasubles, none regarded them as essential. Then followed the report's operative paragraph:

We are of the opinion that it is expedient to restrain in the public services of the United Church of England and Ireland all variations in respect of vesture from that which has long been the established usage of the said United Church, and we think that this may be best secured by providing aggrieved parishioners with an easy and effectual process for complaint and redress.[70]

Reginald Wilberforce credits his father with substituting the word "restrain" for an inelastic "abolish" or "prohibit," and calls the report a triumph of moderation. Evidence from Wilberforce's diary suggests he had a part in the wording;[71] he defended it in a letter to his son Ernest, now a clergyman, on the ground that it represented no surrender of principle and had protected the ritualists from almost certain prosecution. "I was most anxious for the sake of the Ritualists, that there should be no making of the vestments in themselves illegal; because (1) this would, to a certain degree, have altered the standing of the English Church. (2) It would have prevented any use of them where the people do not object. (3) It would have stood in the way of any such gradual return to a higher class as alone can, I think, be useful."[72] Though it may have saved the ritualists for a time, the first report of the Commission did not solve so much as it hedged. Ellicott called it a "glossing give-and-take report."[73] The fact that vestment wearing was to be "restrained" rather than "prohibited" merely veiled the threat of eventual legislation of some sort, to which Wilberforce remained opposed. The words were vague enough to bear the gloss Wilberforce imposed upon them; they could hardly disguise his failure to hold the Commission together and keep parliamentary legislation at bay.

The clamor for some sort of limitation continued unabated following the publication of the first report. Charles Anderson complained to Wilberforce that doctrine was not "incense, and a chasuble with tassels."

69. To A. C. Tait, July 29, 1867, LPL, Tait Correspondence, 83.165.

70. *Parliamentary Papers,* XIX (1870), 1.

71. August 19, 1867. "Ritual Commission; long debate on draft report I had drawn up on Tuesday the 13th and given [J. G.] Hubbard [one of the Commissioners and patron of the High Church parish of St. Alban's, Holborn] to circulate—substantially adopted" (Ashwell and Wilberforce, *Life,* III, 217).

72. *Ibid.,* September 14, 1867.

73. To A. C. Tait, August 9, 1867, LPL, Tait Correspondence, 83.208.

Ritualists were bringing the clergy into contempt, "a very serious evil, for we of the laity tho' we do not intend to be priest ridden, we do not wish to despise our clergy; we desire to respect them." [74] The second report, issued in May 1868, and treating the subject of lights and incense, pronounced against ritualistic excesses in a much more specific manner than had the first. In addition to condemning unwarranted innovation, it recommended legislation permitting parishioners to make formal application to their bishop against clergymen who sanctioned practices that ran counter to general usage. Wilberforce, although he signed the report, entered a *caveat* along with five other commissioners against that particular provision. [75] "I cannot but believe," he wrote in explanation of his position to Longley, "that our common aim would have been better promoted by an united advice that the Bishop and Archbishop should be *empowered* to stop these things, than by a divided Report advising the compelling the Bishop to act, and so, in my judgment abrogating his office." [76] Wilberforce's case against the recommendation was threefold, and a consistent reflection of three of his most cherished beliefs. Legislation would mitigate against the doctrinal latitude so necessary to a national Church; it would hamper Church unity, equally necessary, by surrendering to Low Church partisans; and it would undermine episcopal authority, without which the Church could claim to be no church at all.

These arguments could not withstand the strident anti-ritualist sentiment that took hold of an increasing number of Churchmen. Wilberforce might succeed in resolving controversy within his own diocese; others, including Tait in London, had not been so fortunate. The parishes of All Saints, Margaret Street, and St. Albans, Holborn, had been subjected to continual and notorious disruptions as a result of disagreements between determinedly ritualistic incumbents and disgruntled and dismayed patrons and parishioners. [77] Tait had struggled to abate the controversies during his episcopate. Once elevated to the primacy, he announced his intention to press for legislation to put an end to such distractions once and for all. Disraeli was prepared to support a bill, but left office before one could be drawn. Gladstone did not share Tait's conviction, and the Archbishop was forced to wait for his Public Worship Bill until Disraeli's return in 1874. Meanwhile, the Purchas judgment delivered by the Privy Council in 1871, declaring vestments, the eastward position, wafer-bread, and the mixed chalice illegal, had further stirred the parties in the Church. Wilberforce deplored the decision for the same reason that he deplored any doctrinaire pronouncement on ritual: it only served to deepen the

74. December 3, 1867, BD, I. C190.
75. *Parliamentary Papers,* XIX (1870), 9.
76. April 17, 1868, LPL, Longley Correspondence, VIII. 98.
77. For an account of Tait's difficulties see Davidson and Benham, *Tait,* I, chaps. X, XV.

divisions within the Church. "We are in sad trouble as to this last decision of the Privy Council," he wrote Tait,

and I greatly fear the result. The mere suppression of Vestments would have passed quietly enough, but the imperative injunction to consecrate at the north end cuts far deeper and will not be obeyed. Men feel the one-sidedness of the judgment. . . They feel the separation from antiquity, the break through a custom which has prevailed always in some churches: the narrowing of liberty: the unfairness of attempting to prevent this while copes are not enforced or surplices. It is a very distracting time, and unless God hears our prayers will end in a great schism.[78]

When the Public Worship Bill became law, Wilberforce was dead. Had he lived, he would have opposed it. He was willing to recognize that, established as she was, the Church was bound into an indissoluble partnership with Parliament, inconvenient though that might be. "Life is a compromise, and I cannot see how the Church of England can, whilst she remains established, look for power of internal legislation apart from Parliament." [79] And yet, as he had written Anderson when commencing his work with the Ritual Commission, he had no patience with attempts to tie up "the future expansive power of the Church of England by new Acts of Parliament, destroying the liberty of congregations and the restraining and directing power of the Bishops." [80] He would have seen the Public Worship Bill as such an attempt. The Church's dilemma was that she did not know where to look for authority. As A. O. J. Cockshut has perceptively remarked, the Thirty-Nine Articles, the only standard of Anglican doctrine recognized by the law of England, were of little help in defining and safeguarding the Church's position.[81] Made, as Thomas Fuller said, "like children's clothes of a larger size so that the children might grow into them," [82] they allowed almost any interpretation. If limits were to be set, Parliament would have to set them. Tait, beleaguered by the constant fighting in London, was prepared to ask for such limits. Wilberforce, less severely pressed, did not feel compelled to seek that authority which only the State could provide.

Wilberforce's desire to protect the Church from State interference did not prevent him from insisting that the Church had a right to impose its teachings and its will upon the nation. He believed that the Church had a duty to see that Sunday remained a day of rest and religion, not a day

78. March 9, 1871, LPL, Tait Correspondence, 89.157.
79. *Chronicles of Convocation*, July 5, 1870, p. 446.
80. March 10, 1867, BD, I. C190.
81. *Anglican Attitudes*, p. 17.
82. Owen Chadwick, *The Mind of the Oxford Movement* (Stanford University Press, 1967), p. 16.

for amusement. "While we preserve it for rest and religion," he wrote one of his rural deans, "we are, I believe, upholding one of the main defences of religion and morals: if we let it be secularized, we throw away that defence." To open museums and exhibitions on Sunday would only set a precedent that would lead to the eventual destruction "of all reverence for and religious employment of the day. At the same time," he added, "I am very sensible of the mischievous exaggeration of the puritanical view of the subject; and greatly fear that through it occasion will be taken to loosen what hold the English, or more properly the Christian Sunday still retains upon the minds of the people." [83]

Upon all attempts to alter the laws of marriage and divorce Wilberforce turned a wrathy eye. Marriage with a deceased wife's sister would produce nothing but social evil. "No instance could be found," he argued in an 1858 debate, "of the tone of a nation's morals having been raised by relaxing a prohibition at the demand of those who wanted a greater license, for that would be contrary to the whole of God's dealings with man." [84] Social evil or not, such marriages defied God's laws and deserved prohibition on those grounds alone. Wilberforce had refuted the argument, advanced in a debate two years before, that Mosaic law sanctioned the practice. The fact was "of little weight when contrasted with the long and uniform current of authority arising from the constant practice of the Christian Church in its early and purest ages." [85] For divorce, and even more, the remarriage of divorced persons, Wilberforce had even less tolerance. He introduced clauses in the Divorce and Matrimonial Causes Bills of 1856 and 1857 prohibiting the remarriage of guilty parties, but before the second of the bills became law, the clause was struck out.

What particularly upset him was a provision permitting Church marriage of divorced persons, and further stipulating that if a parish priest refused to officiate at the service, another might be summoned into the parish by the couple to act in his stead. Wilberforce aired his distress in his Charge for that year. The law struck at the root of the union of Church and State by declaring that the State need not attend to Church law if it chose. From now on, the laws of Church and State would stand in opposition. "It is allowing that the State possesses the right of dictating what we, as the authorized clergy, shall or shall not teach as the truth of God; a concession absolutely subversive to the claim of the Church to have received and to set forth a revelation from God Himself." The insistence that the Church be a party to remarriage was the final and most ignominious stroke. If the Church was to have its doctrines flaunted in this

83. To the Reverend C. Barter, February 18, 1850, in Ashwell and Wilberforce, *Life,* II, 46.
84. *Hansard,* 3rd ser., CLIII (July 23, 1858), 517.
85. *Ibid.,* CXLI (April 25, 1856), 1507.

way, better to solemnize such unions with a civil contract only. "Whether or not we think that the innocent party ought to be set free from an adulterous union, and suffered to marry again is not the question, it is whether . . . we can permit the Church of this land to be degraded from being a witness for God, to being a mere earthly machinery to speak the words which from time to time, the State may be pleased to put into her mouth." [86]

The Church could hope to impress its moral sentiments upon the nation in many places; nowhere did it believe its mandate stronger than in the area of education. Here, surely, Churchmen insisted, they had the right as a national Church to be heard and to make their beliefs felt. Wilberforce, who worked in his diocese to bring Church-sponsored education to every parish, worked to make certain the State did not ignore its duty in this regard. The duty demanded that the State leave to the Church the direction and management of the nation's education, assisting when necessary with financial aid, while forebearing to establish any system founded upon the principle of secularism. The message of his published *Letter to Lord Brougham* was that "before *teaching* can be moulded and quickened into *education*" the government would have to summon the Church to its aid.[87]

Although the government might underwrite the Church's efforts with grants, such as those it had made since 1833 to the National Society, Wilberforce at first saw no reason why this should entitle the government to the right of inspection. When Russell insisted otherwise, as he did in a Council Minute in June, 1839, Wilberforce, rather than condone interference, declared to Anderson that he would prefer to refuse the money. Any sort of inspection scheme would "certainly throw [education] soon into the House of Commons," he wrote, "and *religious* education is our duty." [88] This conservative intransigence did not survive Wilberforce's first years as a bishop. He soon recognized that the country's desperate need for schools would necessitate some sort of compromise, given Russell's continued determination to press for a comprehensive educational program. By 1848 a full-scale confrontation between the government and a band of National Society diehards seemed inevitable. Wilberforce declared in the Lords that he was ready to permit inspection of Church schools by a committee of elected laymen, provided they were *bona fide* Churchmen, and provided, as well, that the bishop would have

86. *Charge,* 1857, pp. 56–57, 61.
87. *Letter to The Right Honourable Henry Lord Brougham,* p. 17. In 1862, Wilberforce declared in the Lords that England had taken the lead in education amongst all European nations except Prussia, "where elementary education is inflicted as a legal penalty instead of being conferred as a paternal boon" (*Hansard,* 3rd ser., CLXV [March 4, 1862], 1006.)
88. December 6, 1839, BD, I. C191.

appellate jurisdiction in any dispute arising from the committee's reports.[89] The opposition refused to acknowledge the State's right to insist upon any inspectors other than those approved directly by the Church.[90] At the annual meeting of the National Society in June 1848, G. A. Denison, the most outspoken conservative, declared that "the smallest concession, or compromise—the slighest wavering now or hereafter," was sure to bring nothing but disaster upon the Church.[91] He moved "that it is the opinion of the meeting that no arrangement which should involve the compulsory imposition of any management clauses whatsoever as a condition of state assistance . . . can be satisfactory to or ought to be accepted by the Church."

Wilberforce had already determined to oppose such a motion. He believed that a compromise along the lines he had outlined in Parliament could be achieved, without undue damage to the authority of either Church or State. He made it clear that he did not advocate secularism. "Perish all attempts to stuff the heads of children with undigested secular intelligence, instead of training them as baptized members of Christ's Church." The question was not secularization but rather specific conditions. "Are we to meet the government and endeavour to obtain safe terms for all, or to leave each one in detail to bind his school to conditions which we should altogether dislike and disavow because we say at once rather a rupture with the government than any settlement whatever, however satisfactory to the Church." Wilberforce worried that, left to strike their terms with the government, individual parishes would sell the Church short in order to insure themselves of a school. He worried even more that to turn away from compromise would be to admit that Church and State could no longer work together. They would be saying to the government "that the time has come when there is an irremediable rupture between the State and the Church on the matter of education." He proposed an amendment to Denison's resolution declaring confidence in the officers of the Association to continue their negotiations with the Committee of the Privy Council. Denison, realizing he was beaten, withdrew his motion, and Wilberforce the amendment. It was an important victory, and one for which Wilberforce could justifiably take credit. As he wrote Robert: "The meeting of the National Society was very strong; and I believe it is true as I am told that five-sixths of the meeting were prepared when I rose to carry D's motion and that I got five-sixths to be ready to reject it. For this I thank God."[92]

89. *Hansard,* 3rd ser., XCVII (March 3, 1848), 155–157.
90. A compromise in 1840 had established the Archbishop's right to approve all inspectors.
91. The following account is from the *Guardian,* June 7, 1848, pp. 371–374.
92. June 9, 1848, Wrangham papers.

The following year Wilberforce, joined this time by the bishop of Salisbury, brother of the as yet unabashed G. A. Denison, and by Henry Manning, fought and won the same battle. By 1851 Wilberforce was able to urge acceptance of a system providing inspection by Churchmen and by State-approved committees, a system he took the lead in instituting in his own diocese.[93] To any suggestion that the State construct schools of its own from rate money and exclude from them all special instruction in Christianity, he continued adamantly opposed. Rather than fill gaps in the Church's present system, such a scheme would discourage voluntary contributions and thereby eventually destroy that system entirely. He could see only one solution to the problem. The present shortage could only be met by increased individual effort on behalf of Church schools; "by setting about with renewed energy; by more personal service in our schools; by providing, as far as possible, efficient Church Schools for the different classes of society; by cooperating in all lawful ways with all lawful schemes for the improvement of our present system of religious education; above all, at this moment . . . by stirring up those who can, to aid us in providing a set of school-masters fit to work with us in this great undertaking." [94]

If Dissenters and others outside the pale of the Church felt uncomfortable with a system which imposed a particular creed upon their children, Wilberforce believed their discomfort beside the point.[95] Any attempt to accommodate the present system to their beliefs could lead, again, only to eventual secularization. Give Dissenters the right to dictate what doctrine was or was not taught in Church schools, he wrote Gladstone, and "Churchmen will not build and support schools. Then we [would] come to national education on an education rate—you sever charity from the work—you freeze up your whole system—you put the settlement of the doctrine to be taught into the hands of the rate payers and you will have most speedily schools with no doctrine and your teaching alone helped by public grants." [96] Wilberforce reasoned from a first premise that education, distinct from mere teaching, must include instruction in the doctrines of the Church of England. If the heterodox State could not directly and fully endow this sort of education, endowment would have to come instead from private, voluntary agencies, which could be relied upon to impose proper religious and educational

93. *Charge*, 1851, pp. 28–29.   94. *Ibid.*, pp. 26–27.
95. Dissenters were not enthusiasts for State-controlled education. Edward Miall, although worried about ignorance among the working classes, wrote that he deprecated "the intervention of the government in the matter. I have no faith in its happy issue. I feel convinced that however just at first it may spur on exertion, it will degenerate in the end into a system of patronage and jobbing" (*The British Churches and the British People* [London, 1848], p. 243).
96. August 7, 1860, Add Mss. 44344.

standards. Government grants could be accepted only if they did not compel the schools, their directors, and their benefactors to compromise principle. A "conscience clause," excusing Dissenters from instruction in Church doctrine, was such a compromise, and therefore posed a serious threat to the future of English education.

When conscience clauses were adopted in 1865, Wilberforce spoke out to his clergy, not to urge disobedience of the law, but to show that he was prepared to obey only under duress. Such clauses were "absolutely at variance" with a system of denominational education as adopted by Parliament. Enforcement would be "full of danger to the present efficiency and future character of our schools." A conscience clause was "simply a provision for compelling the clergy of the Established Church to give a secular education to the children of Dissenters."[97] The year before, Wilberforce had set down "that at which a conscience clause can fairly aim": in communities too small for more than one school, Church schools aided by public money might, "extraneous to their own education to their own children" teach reading, writing, and numbers to others. But in such cases the teaching would need to be "distinctly marked as not being education but as provision for unschooled children."[98]

The unsympathetic would have called this intransigence as short-sighted as Denison's. Wilberforce would have argued a difference. Denison had declared the interests of Church and State incompatible. Wilberforce believed they need not be—that ideally they were identical. Any reconciliation, however, was to be on terms set by the Church. She might negotiate details, as she had in the matter of inspectors, but she must never cease to fight against a compromise of principles, nor sacrifice what was sacred for mere secular advantage.

By the time Forster's Education Bill of 1870 became law, circum-stances had persuaded Wilberforce to admit as negotiable—or perhaps to accept as inevitable—that which a few years before he would not have surrendered without a struggle. Evidence of his attitude is scrappy, and there is no record as to how he voted. References in letters show him ready to acquiesce in some general scheme of reorganization, while con-tinuing to plead the best case he could for the Church. He hoped that the bill might retain its original form, with voluntary schools, aided by rates, given freedom to conduct religious education as they saw fit. When the Cowper-Temple clause forbade the teaching of formularies, he declared

97. *Charge*, 1867 (written and delivered in 1866), pp. 29–30.
98. To G. H. Fagan, June 9, 1865, BD, I. C197. Not surprisingly, Wilberforce opposed relaxation of the Universities' subscription rule. He agreed with Pusey that one came to a university for religious as well as civil training (Liddon, *Pusey*, I, 308) and defended his beliefs when attempts were made to relax the rule (*Hansard*, 3rd ser., CXXXIV [July 7, 1854], 1361).

that he saw "the danger of schools on the modified Christian instruction principle to be exceedingly great." [99] But he was in no fighting mood, and at the time worried far more as to the fate of a bill which he was piloting through the Lords enabling aged and infirm clergymen to resign their livings. His willingness to spare himself a battle sprang from his reading of the results of the 1868 election as a mandate for change which it would be wrong any longer to oppose. On these grounds he had reluctantly swallowed the bitter draught of noncompulsory Church rates and Irish disestablishment; [100] this further swallow, though as distasteful, followed in the wake of the others. Nor does his conduct seem unnatural when one remembers that Gladstone had only the year before translated him from Oxford to the See of Winchester. An outspoken opposition crusade, waged in that truculent tone he had so often employed in the sixties, would undoubtedly have struck Gladstone as both ungracious and ungrateful.

Gladstone had been no admirer of that tone. Twice he had written Wilberforce to criticize him for his attitude toward matters of Church and State. In 1862 Wilberforce had asked Gladstone if he would suggest his name to Palmerston as a successor to Longley as Archbishop of York. This Gladstone did, but he took the occasion to suggest why Palmerston might not see in Wilberforce the ideal candidate for the position. He remarked that one of the major tasks of an ecclesiastical statesman was redefinition of the relationship between Church and State. And he asked Wilberforce to agree that "the State has a right to expect from the Church that its episcopal rulers, at least that the leading and governing spirits among them, shall contribute liberally and sometimes boldly to the solution of these questions. . . You have opposed many changes which you thought injurious," Gladstone continued,

and, as regards many of those you have opposed, I certainly am in no condition to find fault with you.

But I think I should be puzzled were Lord Palmerston to say to me 'I will not dwell on the question which of the changes asked for he has opposed, but I will desire you to tell me of which of these problems he has, as a leader of the clergy, publicly and at his own risk, supported the solution.'

99. To W. E. Gladstone, April 17, 1870; "Holy Thursday," 1870, Add Mss. 44345.
100. With regard to Church rates, Wilberforce urged acquiescence in Gladstone's bill of 1868. He had, he said, always believed in the principle of Church rates and would continue to do so. "But the question now came to them under wholly different circumstances. It came with what they could not mistake as the declaration in 'another place' of the representatives of the people of this country that they would not continue the system of Church rates." He therefore advocated the present measure, which at least retained the rates. "The question to be decided was whether their lordships would wait to see Church rates abolished altogether, or whether they would accept some such provision as was offered in the present bill" (*Hansard,* 3rd ser., CXCI [April 23, 1868], 1134–1136). For Wilberforce's attitude toward Irish disestablishment, see below, pp. 291ff.

Now you may be able to furnish me with the materials of a reply for the satisfaction of my own mind as well as in case of need—which God send—for that of Lord Palmerston.

I seem to observe that the character you have got with politicians among whom I live is that of a most able Prelate getting all you can for the Church, asking more, giving nothing.

Now in my eyes there are certain limits of principle beyond which you cannot give. But the State, when it is strong and masterful, cares nothing as a State about those limits. It is partly to save them from transgression at a time of danger, that I want concessions of what can be conceded in the hour of comparative and apparent safety.

I know of certain things which you have, as I believe, been ready to concede. Bu the question put to me, if any were put, would be has he not, in his place in Parliament and with his great power there and elsewhere, been in all (ecclesiastical) things obstructive? What help has he given us, which part of his enormous labours has he spent, in bringing the mind of the clergy, even with difficulty and with risk, to anticipate the time in this or that, and to make, while they are still of some value, the sacrifices which it requires.

If I seem to arraign you, you will understand why it is. And if you ask me to point out a case in which you simply resisted and assailed, where we might have hoped for at least a more qualified course, I will point for the sake of example to the measures of the present year respecting national education [a reference to conscience clauses].[101]

A year later Gladstone took Wilberforce to task once more, this time for his refusal to support a bill to abolish the oath sworn by mayors that they would use their office to oppose the Established Church. The oath had for years been a sore point with Dissenters, and one that might without danger to the Church have been removed. Wilberforce refused to countenance its withdrawal, and this refusal Gladstone believed endangered the well-being of the Church.

In proportion as you insist upon retaining—I must say 'clutching'—every temporal prerogative, every assertion, in whatever form of rationality as such, you enhance the right and the disposition of the mixed mass of the community to say, this institution, which clings thus tenaciously to all legal preferences, and exacts a moral tribute from out of the very mouth of Dissenters, like the fish in the Gospel, as a condition of their holding office, must at least have her rough places made smooth and her mountains laid low within, that the nation which by the uttermost of her power she insists upon possessing, may really possess her in return.[102]

The contrast between Wilberforce's two replies is an interesting one. To the first letter he could only respond with a denial that he had never made constructive attempts to bring Church and State together, citing his support of the bill to reform Oxford—not surprising in view of the troubles the unreformed corporations were always giving him; and his campaigns for moderation within the National Society. He admitted that

101. October 2, 1862, Add Mss. 44344.   102. *Ibid.*, March 21, 1863.

"these are not much to point to," but argued that Palmerston's aggressive Low Churchmanship made cooperation difficult.[103] Chastened and—more to the point—convinced by Gladstone's lecture the following year, Wilberforce answered with a promise not to oppose the bill, convinced that "we should not obtrude needlessly our objections on the sore places of Dissenters." The promise was conditioned upon his bringing "the Church party and especially the Bishops to act together in that sense." [104] To this Gladstone replied with a reminder that "there is a point at which it becomes their interest that you should in case the need arise, act differently from them: not that that is not in itself an evil, but that it may be the avoidance of a much greater evil and the means of attaining a positive good." [105] When the Bill finally became law in 1865, Wilberforce had reconsidered and was ready to vote against it; a dinner engagement with Bishop Ellicott prevented him from doing so.[106]

Although political events of the late sixties were to temper his zeal to do battle for the Church, neither they nor Gladstone's lectures could convince Wilberforce that it was not the task of the Church to speak for the nation in matters of faith. His conviction dictated a course of action that Gladstone considered limited and shortsighted, a course that seemed to mark Wilberforce as a Church politician when he might so easily have become an ecclesiastical statesman. Wilberforce, in turn, believed that Gladstonian statesmanship involved compromise with heterodoxy, the sort of compromise a true Churchman was bound to oppose.

Throughout the world God had charged the Church with a two-fold mission. "Her banner," Wilberforce had written in his *History of the American Church*, "must be indeed 'Evangelical truth with apostolic order—the Gospel in the Church'." [107] In England, where the Church was by law established, her charge demanded more: to bring the State into harmony with her and together to hold aloft that banner of truth and order. There was but one truth; the Church possessed that truth; and the State, for its own sake and for the glory of God, must help her proclaim that truth across the land. The State might tolerate dissent, but the logic of its connection with the Church meant that it must never encourage it. "The notion that any State can do its work of making a people virtuous and happy by teaching them all dissonant views as to eternal truth is one of the greatest misconceptions which can flit in the misty imagination." [108]

103. *Ibid.,* October 4, 1862.   104. *Ibid.,* March 29, 1863.
105. *Ibid.,* April 2, 1863.
106. Diary, June 26, 1865, in Ashwell and Wilberforce, *Life,* III, 85.
107. *A History of the Protestant Episcopal Church in America,* 2d ed. (London, 1846), p. 454.
108. *Chronicles of Convocation,* February 17, 1865, p. 1983.

It was a misconception that made a mockery of establishment, whose essence was the acknowledgement by the State of a particular religion as true, and the encouragement of ministers "of that particular form to teach in the name of the State as well as of the Church." [109]

Spiritual vitality could of course exist independent of State support, as it did in Episcopal communions around the world. But the State which took upon itself the responsibility of an establishment could expect to be amply rewarded. An established religion, supported by devout citizens in countless parishes, would "raise the whole department of government from the low Dogberry and Verges level up to the high ministration of God's will." [110] Wilberforce could never surrender that vision. When political democracy forced him to give ground, he did so with the melancholy conviction that the State, by making the Church pay a price to stay alive, was itself committing a slow sort of spiritual suicide.

109. From a speech against Irish disestablishment, *Times,* May 6, 1868, p. 7.
110. *Ibid.,* p. 7.

CHAPTER IX

Politics and Appointment

Samuel Wilberforce never ceased to be ambitious. His appointment to the bishopric of Oxford at the age of forty seemed to promise the eventual gratification of that ambition with elevation to an archiepiscopal throne. When he found his advancement thwarted he inclined to lay the blame not upon himself but upon other men and circumstances; upon politics and political animosities.

He had vowed when made a bishop that he would not become a partisan in the House of Lords, but would try to speak out in the interests of the people as a whole, as it befitted a churchman to do. His first major speech, defending repeal of the Corn Laws, had urged the clergy not to look at the measure in terms of what it would do to them, but in terms of what it might do for the country. He afterward wrote Louisa Noel that he hoped always to adopt such a line, "of our being there as special guardians of the moral and social well-being of the English *people*." [1] If he failed to do so, he nevertheless supported a variety of measures which accorded with the dictates of a humane conscience. He opposed public hangings and transportation. [2] He could not enthuse over Britain's entrance into the Crimean War. He believed it a grave mistake on England's part to force a war upon the Chinese as a result of their boarding of the lorca *Arrow*. To attack a heathen country with such fragmentary provocation was, he declared, to misuse the gift of power God had granted Christian England. [3] And he worried that Britain, by opening Japan too rapidly to western trade, might permanently destroy the internal processes of Japanese government. [4]

His most persistent campaign was on behalf of the cause his father had sanctified in his eyes—the abolition of slavery. Although he favored

1. June 18, 1846, BD, II. F. Wilberforce's speech is in *Hansard,* 3rd ser., LXXXVII (June 12, 1846), 320ff.
2. He served on Select Committees investigating both questions, although he attended only one of the seven sessions of the Committee on transportation. Parliamentary Papers, 1856, VII, 14ff; 1866, XVII, 566ff.
3. *Hansard,* 3rd ser., CXLIV (February 26, 1857), 1377ff.
4. *Ibid.,* CLXXVI (July 1, 1864), 599–604.

free trade he spoke and voted again and again against the importation of slave-grown sugar from Cuba and Brazil. "My objection is that this Act is a direct bonus on that which we, as a nation, have declared to be so great a crime that we brand it as piracy on the high seas." Any move made to exterminate slavery and the slave trade from Africa won his support.[5] As for the institution of slavery in the southern United States, he had written in bitter tones against it in 1845 in his *History of the American Church,* castigating American Episcopalians for their unwillingness to stand against it. "No motives of supposed expediency, no possible amount of danger, can justify her silence. . . It is a time for martyrdom; and the Mother of Saints has scarcely brought forth even one confessor."[6] On the eve of the Civil War he gave his support to a motion by Lord Brougham that the government work to promote the cotton industry in free territories—Wilberforce recommended portions of Africa—so as not to rely any longer for raw material upon the slave-owning South. Once the war began, Wilberforce banked the fires of his conscience and accepted the generally help upper-class view that the war was the mistaken fault of the North. To an American acquaintance in the north he explained that

nothing can be more untrue than the supposition that we have rejoiced or that we have not deeply lamented over your sorrows: or more certain than that we long for your peace from no selfish motives but because we cannot bear to read of this bloodshed and misery amongst nations our nearest of kin.

He maintained that the North had mistaken the temper of the South, that at first a "violent handful of traitors," and not the "true states" had urged treason. Now, because of northern intransigence, the entire South was in arms. Should they win the war, how would the North hold the South in subjection? "We have too high an idea of our brethren in America to believe that they *will* be so held. They may be exterminated; they will never be white slaves to their northern conquerors."[7] The argument exposed him to charges of inconsistency. "The Bishop, as usual, swung with the tide," recalled one critic after his death, "with fashionable and aristocratic society, whose plaudits were always so dear to his heart."[8] Certainly he had ceased to call for martyrs; without direct evidence we can suppose that Wilberforce's reappraisal resulted from a belief that bloodshed was worse than slavery, or from a willingness to

---

5. *Ibid.,* LXXXVIII (August 13, 1846), 650. See also XCVI (February 7, 1848), 211–218; CVI (June 12, 1849), 29–39; CXXII (June 10, 1852), 380–382; CXXVII (May 30, 1853), 774–775; CL (June 17, 1858), 2195.

6. *History of The American Church,* pp. 424, 436.

7. To ? Coxe, August 10, 1862, Letter Book, BD, d.211.12–15.

8. G. D. Haughton in the *Spectator,* November 27, 1875, pp. 1487–1488. Haughton wrote in response to a sermon preached in memory of Wilberforce by H. P. Liddon.

fall in with the generally accepted opinion of leading statesmen, or from both.[9]

The attitudes toward political issues expressed by Wilberforce in the Lords were those any right-thinking bishop might have been expected to adopt. They certainly cannot be blamed for the fact that he failed to receive the advancement he believed he deserved. Instead, his understanding of the Church's role within the nation and of the right relationship between the Church and the State made him enemies within the governments of the 1850's and 1860's. After Peel's death, only Gladstone among politicians of the first rank came close to sharing Wilberforce's views on the matter, and Gladstone, although in and out of office, had little say in the matter of ecclesiastical appointments. Wilberforce took a natural interest in Gladstone's political career. He relied upon him to put forward the "Church" view, and as bishop of Oxford played an active and not surprising part in Gladstone's campaigns as member for the University. In return for his support Wilberforce was not shy in asking favors, most often assistance with regard to ecclesiastical appointments. Just how close the two men were is hard to say. They wrote each other a good deal, but almost always on public matters. Gladstone served as a member of the committee to organize a memorial to Wilberforce's son Herbert, and Wilberforce undoubtedly appreciated what Gladstone had tried to do at the time of Robert's conversion. He never opened himself up to Gladstone, however, as he did to old friends like Charles Anderson and Louisa Noel. Gladstone had not known Emily as they had. He had begun to play a part in Wilberforce's life after they both had become public men. Their friendship was likewise public; they met at country houses and over breakfasts in London; they relied upon each other for information and opinions gathered from the lives they led; but their friendly and respectful acquaintanceship never matured into intimate friendship.

After Wilberforce's death Gladstone wrote Reginald Wilberforce that he had been "far from satisfied" with his father's politics.[10] Undoubtedly as Gladstone moved toward Liberalism, Wilberforce found it difficult to move with him. He preferred to think of Gladstone as a sort of thwarted

9. Gladstone took much the same view as Wilberforce. "As far as the *controversy* between the North and South," he wrote the Duchess of Sutherland on May 29, 1861, "is a controversy on the principle announced by the vice-president of the South, viz. that which asserts the superiority of the white man, and therewith founds on it his right to hold the black in slavery, I think that principle detestable, and I am wholly with the opponents of it. . . No distinction can in my eyes be broader than the distinction between the question whether the Southern ideas of slavery are right, and the question whether they can justifiably be put down by war from the North" (John Morley, *Life of William Ewart Gladstone,* 2 vols. [London, 1905], I, 705).

10. July 6, 1882, BD, I. C200.

follower of Peel, the one politician the Church could trust, and as such the man best qualified to be Prime Minister. Following Gladstone's defeat at Oxford in 1865, when Wilberforce wrote to console him upon his loss, Gladstone replied with his famous and cryptic remarks as to his future:

There have been two great deaths, or transmigrations of spirit, in my political existence—one, very slow, the breaking of ties with my original party; the other, very short and sharp, the breaking of the tie with Oxford. There will probably be a third, and no more.[11]

Whatever Gladstone meant by this—in a subsequent letter he declared that "the oracular sentence has little bearing on present affairs or prospects, and may stand in its proper darkness" [12]—Wilberforce took it to mean that he was contemplating a move toward the premiership and wrote to encourage him to make it. "Your charge is what Pitt's was, it is to make England wealthy, to diffuse that wealth specially among the working classes, to enlarge and to purify our institutions." He worried, however, lest Gladstone allow himself to be led astray among a Radical party, "until its fully developed aims assault all that you most value in our country, and it [the Radical party] turns upon you and rends you." [13]

Wilberforce shared Gladstone's inability to find himself a political home during the fifties and sixties. He considered himself a Peelite, and for that reason welcomed the accession of Peel's heir, Aberdeen, in 1852. In spite of his less than enthusiastic response to the revival of Convocation, Aberdeen proved a friend to the Church, and Wilberforce mourned his fall in 1855. "For Church matters how dark a prospect! The only Government which could or was minded to be fair to the Church overthrown, because six miles of road not made from Balaclava to Sebastopol." [14] His friend Arthur Gordon, Aberdeen's son, wrote asking Wilberforce's opinion as to whether his father and his band should join with Palmerston to form a new government. Wilberforce advised against it. He speculated that perhaps without the support of the Peelites, Palmerston would find himself unable to proceed, and that the initiative might once more rest with Aberdeen. In that case, and if he refused the premiership, "is it impossible to put Gladstone into that place (though I think your father would be best for all, and that his noble simplicity and truth of conduct would be above price)." [15] As a piece of political prognostication the letter was no more accurate than most. Gladstone, Sidney Herbert, and Sir James Graham joined the cabinet and gave it strength. Even without them, Palmerston had the support to carry on, as he proved

11. July 21, 1865, BD, II. K.   12. July 25, 1865, Add Mss. 44345.
13. Ibid., July 24, 1865.
14. Diary, January 29, 1855, in Ashwell and Wilberforce, Life, II, 270–271.
15. Ibid., II, 277–278, February 5, 1855.

when the three almost immediately resigned in opposition to an inquiry into the conduct of the Crimean War. The letter was less an educated guess than a pious hope. Wilberforce did not want to believe that Palmerston could be Prime Minister, since he knew very well that of all the likely candidates he would probably be least inclined to deal with the Church as Wilberforce thought it should be dealt with.

What worried him most was the matter of episcopal preferment. Russell's appointments had displeased him. He thought they were made for no other purpose than to promote a party, by sacrificing Churchmen on the grounds that they preached a subversive Tractarianism.[16] Palmerston, who was believed to be without any religious convictions whatsoever, would in all probability intensify this same process, aided and abetted by his ultra Low Church stepson-in-law, Lord Shaftesbury. At first, when Gladstone accepted office with Palmerston in 1855 there was hope that he might act as a counterweight,[17] but once he had departed the prospect appeared bleak. Palmerston had a simple-minded understanding of Church divisions which he once spelled out in a matter-of-fact statement to Sir Charles Wood, his First Lord of the Admiralty. He estimated that of the population of England and Wales, two-thirds were Churchmen, and one third Dissenters. "The Dissenters pretend equality. I do not believe it." The Churchmen were, in turn, split into two factions, High and Low.

The High Church are few in numbers and are found chiefly in the higher classes; the different degrees of Low Church or at least of those who are against the High Church are numerous, among the higher classes, and one may say universal among the middle and lower classes of Churchmen.

The dignitaries of the Church who are of the High Church Party are verging towards Papacy, and are in constant antagonism with their Low Church brethren and with all the Dissenters. The dignitaries who are of the Low Church School are more forebearing towards their High Church brethren and are at peace with the Dissenters.

Under these curcumstances, far wiser to lean to the Low Church. "A few more Bishops like Oxford and Exeter [Phillpotts] would raise a flame throughout the country and even Blomfield was the cause of great discontent." [18]

Whether this was Palmerston's own analysis or Shaftesbury's, secondhand, is difficult to say. Shaftesbury was inclined to take credit for the religious attitudes Palmerston professed. He tendered advice freely, and

16. To Robert I. Wilberforce, February 23, 1853, Wrangham papers.
17. Wilberforce recorded a conversation with Aberdeen: "'Suppose Montagu Villiers [the Low Church rector of Bloomsbury] *must* be a Bishop. But Palmerston will beware of Shaftesbury, for fear of Gladstone, etc.'" (Diary, February 7, 1855, in Ashwell and Wilberforce, *Life*, II, 279).
18. November 20, 1856, Add Mss. 48580.311–313.

Palmerston appears to have taken it when it suited him, although he occasionally relied upon others to assist him—and not just Low Churchmen. Shaftesbury once gave vent to anger in his diary at Palmerston's unwillingness to take the task of ecclesiastical appointments seriously and at his readiness to listen to the opinions of dangerous Tractarians.[19] Though Palmerston may have refused to see the matter as Shaftesbury did, his appointments followed the general pro-Evangelical line he had sketched to Wood. According to Shaftesbury's own count, Palmerston had by November 1862 appointed five Low, three "moderately" High, two "Broad," and no "ultra" High bishops. "A fairer distribution could not have been made," he reported.[20]

Wilberforce, had he read the memorandum, would have seethed. To him the appointments had been a collective misfortune and in some cases individual disasters for the Church. None of the recently elevated bishops understood churchmanship as he believed it had to be understood if the Church was to survive. He had taken hope when Gladstone had rejoined the Cabinet in 1859. But Gladstone insisted he could not do much to alter Palmerston's already firm convictions and exercised little control over appointments.

The dismay Wilberforce felt at Palmerston's treatment of the Church was intensified by his fear that he would himself experience no further advancement as long as Shaftesbury remained the Prime Minister's confidante in matters ecclesiastical. He heard from Arthur Gordon that Aberdeen, had he remained in office, hoped to make him bishop of Durham and eventually archbishop of York.[21] He believed that had he been willing to attach himself to the Evangelical party he might have succeeded to Canterbury. "You do not suppose," he wrote Golightly during the attack upon Cuddesdon, "that I am so blind as not to see perfectly that I might have headed the Evangelical body and been seated by them at Lambeth." [22] To assume that throne a bishop had to impress the Queen and her Consort, as well as the Prime Minister, with his ecclesiastical probity. And this Wilberforce had found increasingly difficult. When Aberdeen resigned, he asked him, through Gordon, to inquire as to the reason for the royal couple's coolness toward him. He believed that others had attempted to injure his character with the Queen,

19. Diary, March 11, 1860, Broadlands Mss.
20. The Low Churchmen: Villiers of Durham; Waldegrave of Carlisle; Baring of Durham (following Villiers); Pelham of Norwich; and Bickersteth of Ripon. The "moderately" High Churchmen: Longley of York and Canterbury; Philpott of Worcester (not to be confused with Phillpotts of Exeter); Wigram of Rochester. The Broad Churchmen: Tait of London and Thomson of Gloucester and Bristol, and York (to Palmerston, November 18, 1862, Broadland Mss.). His characterizations of Wigram and Thomson would certainly have been challenged by Wilberforce, who believed neither was a real "Church" man.
21. Diary, April 14, 1855, in Ashwell and Wilberforce, *Life*, II, 283.
22. *Ibid.*, II, 360.

and especially to make her *distrust* me. . . Now what I should like would be, if it were possible, for your father to have said anything to show what I believe would be his estimate of me, in any conversation with the Queen. Whilst he was the dispenser of honour and place I should never have breathed this wish, even to you. But now, when what he might do would only be, in her secret mind, to redress an injustice, I, with much hesitation, name it to you. But I leave it absolutely to your judgment whether you should even name the subject to your father; and I can readily understand why, even if you do, he may not think it fit, or wise, or possible to do anything in the matter.[23]

Aberdeen did as Wilberforce asked, and received the answer that the bishop could not act disinterestedly. As two particular instances, the Prince cited his seeking out the position as preceptor of the Prince of Wales, and his tailoring a sermon on the Gadarene swine to suit the Prince's theological tastes. When Gordon relayed the news, Wilberforce expressed surprise. He had not sought the preceptorship—"the thought of it was my special horror"—though he believed the Queen had wanted it for him. Had it been offered he could not have refused. "It was therefore the *bête noire* of my expectations." As for the sermon, he had argued it at some length with the Prince,

and the only thing like the 'convenient' averment I said was that it was far best for us to believe in a Devil who suggested evil to us; for that otherwise we were driven to make every man his own Devil; and I thought that this view rather touched him. I cannot say how grateful I feel to Lord Aberdeen, not so much (though a good deal, too, for that) for his doing battle for me, as for his *belief* in me.[24]

Wilberforce could hardly deny that he had courted royal favor. He had pressed his suit upon Victoria and Albert in the early forties and been amply repaid for his pains. Although unmentioned, apparently, in the conversation with Aberdeen, the Hampden controversy had subsequently served to discredit him, as he recognized himself at the time. Thereafter, the Queen, tutored in matters theological by her "Germanic," Broad Church-minded Consort, looked upon Wilberforce as High, and would remember him as one of those who had opposed the will of her minister. As such she would not have inclined to offer him further preferment. Her letter to Gladstone at the time of Wilberforce's death reflected her opinion of him accurately enough.

23. *Ibid.,* II, 273–274, February 2, 1855.
24. *Ibid.,* II, 275, October 30, 1855. In a letter to Louisa Noel, July 22, 1846, he recounted a conversation with Victoria and Albert on the subject of the preceptorship. "They did exceedingly wish to get me for it, and, therefore, did not like my being made a Bishop. But they thought it unfair to me to let their wish for a future and contingent appointment stand in the way of my present position, and so they gave me up as *Tutor,* thinking that as 'friend and adviser' I might be perhaps in many ways as useful. It is a very great relief to me; for I always felt so much afraid that I should really find the two offices clash and interfere with one another when I came indeed to exercise both" (BD, II. F).

The Queen had known him ever since 1842, and admired and liked him *most before* he became a Bishop, and before he leant so much to those High Church views which did harm, and which are so great a misfortune to the Church.

But apart from all that he was a most able, agreeable man, and very kind-hearted, and had shown great attachment to the beloved Prince and great sympathy for the Queen in her great sorrow.[25]

Realizing that neither Palmerston nor the Queen favored him or his work, Wilberforce could not suppress the hope that somehow advancement might still come to him. When Archbishop Sumner died on September 6, 1862, he believed his chance had arrived. He undertook to confer with Gladstone. Longley of York should be translated to Canterbury or, if Longley did not suit, then Bishop Sumner of Winchester, the late Archbishop's brother. On the ninth he wrote again, confiding that should Longley vacate York he would stand ready to assume the duties there. He reminded Gladstone that the Wilberforces were a Yorkshire family.

If a Yorkshireman: with a Yorkshire *tradition:* a power of moving the masses: a power of getting at the Methodists, were placed there, there might be a true revival of the Church and the faith. To you in solemn secrecy I may say that it was Lord Aberdeen who placed this vision before me. Then for *you—the* one thing your warm friends want at Oxford is one definite, tangible proof that at least you *can* fix your mark somewhere for the Church's good on a great appointment.

After despairing at the thought that a man such as the Low Church Baring of Durham might be elevated, he concluded that "it seems humanly speaking as if all the next great strength of our Church life now trembled in the balance. May the Lord direct the hearts of rulers aright." [26]

Gladstone replied that if he were to try to intervene in the appointment it would have to be without consideration of his political strength at Oxford, "because in order to *do* any good I must as I well know forego altogether then the idea of appearing before my constituents to do good." He had hesitated to mention the matter to Palmerston at all, but had eventually indirectly suggested Longley for Canterbury, without much hope that the suggestion would be taken. If it were, and York was vacated, "you are the person who ought to succeed to it." But Gladstone worried that to mention Wilberforce to Palmerston "would not succeed and would even in all likelihood cause a positive recoil and tend to dam-

25. July 22, 1873, in *Letters of Queen Victoria,* 2d ser., 3 vols., ed. G. E. Buckle (London, 1926), II, 264. Wilberforce lavished praise upon the Prince in his review of *The Early Years* in the *Quarterly,* 123:279ff. (1867). For further discussion of the Queen's attitude toward ecclesiastical appointments, see Dudley W. R. Bahlman, "The Queen, Mr. Gladstone, and Church Patronage," *Victorian Studies,* 3:349 (1960).

26. September 9, 1862, Add Mss. 44344. After a meeting in Leeds in 1857, Wilberforce had been moved to comment to Charles Anderson on the superiority of the North country man. "Yorkshire heart. Yorkshire sense. Yorkshire humour, fully comprehending. . . Oh how unlike they are to our South country boors" (October 17, 1857, BD, I. C191).

Bishop Samuel Wilberforce ca. 1865.

age." [27] Wilberforce, whose hopes had been fed by word from Dean Gerald Wellesley of Windsor that the Queen might favor "the *double* appointment I told you he sought," [28] convinced himself that Gladstone should nevertheless plead his case. He had undertaken a preaching tour of Yorkshire at the time, on behalf of Hawaiian missions, and lost no opportunity to think himself into a Yorkshire frame of mind. He found Gladstone's reticence difficult to understand. Others, he wrote him, were "busy at work for the most destructive purposes." Such was his confidence in Gladstone's judgment, "that if I saw *all,* as you do, I should *approve* of your comparative inactivity at such a crisis. I can only trustingly acquiesce," he added rather sourly, "though to *others* I defend your course altogether." [29]

Gladstone replied that Wilberforce had an altogether inflated idea as to his influence with Lord Palmerston. "It is not the usage nor the duty of the First Minister to consult his colleagues on such a subject. The utmost I can do is, considering that I sit for Oxford, to make a representation and recommendation, and there is absolutely nothing more which consistently with usage and with propriety is in my power." He reminded Wilberforce that he had not declined absolutely to undertake a mission on his behalf. He believed his own unstable relationship with Palmerston argued against such a plan. "But I do not hesitate to say that if you on the whole, after considering what I have said, shall wish that I should to it, not only shall I not misconstrue the wish but I will at once do it, and if I do it will certainly do it as well as I can." [30]

On September 25 Wilberforce learned that Longley had received appointment to the See of Canterbury. It seemed to him that Gladstone, with only one case left to make, was now in a position to make it with success. Accordingly he wrote the next day:

> . . . after weighing as carefully as I can all that you say, I cannot but believe that your recommendations could now do no harm and might under God's blessing save the Church an appointment which would indefinitely prolong all the evils she groans under here [in Yorkshire]. There is everything to appeal to. I have been preaching in that great Doncaster Church today crowded from one end to the other with a congregation so attentive that it was delightful to preach to it, and if our Church's system were faithfully upheld in the highest parts the results might be incalculable for both Provinces.[31]

Gladstone did as he was asked, first pointing out to Wilberforce that he might have difficulty in persuading Palmerston that Wilberforce had always acted as wisely as he might have in the matter of Church-State relations. Meanwhile, Palmerston had offered Tait the position, which Tait declined to remain in London. William Thomson, the recently ap-

---

27. September 10, 1862, Add Mss. 44344.   28. *Ibid.,* September 21, 1862.
29. *Ibid.*   30. *Ibid.,* September 23, 1862.   31. *Ibid.,* September 26, 1862.

pointed bishop of Gloucester and Bristol, saw no reason to reject the promotion when approached in turn, and Wilberforce had to endure the galling appointment of his none-too-capable former curate at Cuddesdon to a position which he had craved for himself.

He believed he had been sorely misused. "There must be some history," he wrote Charles Anderson,

if we could get it. Because only last week at Stickleton Sir C. Wood told Admiral Meynell that I was to be appointed. Well it is best as it is for those who will make it best: but there is no denying that I should have liked if it had been God's will to work amongst my father's people.[32]

He could take comfort in the knowledge that others in Yorkshire felt as he did about the rebuff. Longley wrote that he had indulged until the last the hope that Wilberforce might succeed him, "tho' I knew what the force of prejudice was and how possible it was that my hope might be disappointed." [33] Upon the first public occasion following the enthronement of the new archbishop, Wilberforce, and not Thomson, was invited to preach in York minster by the dean.[34] "I think that I am not wrong in telling you," he reported to Gladstone while on another preaching tour in the north,

that cool, calm men whom I have in this past week been with in Yorkshire . . . expressed in the very strongest language both their disappointment at my not having been appointed, and (to use W. Beckett's words) their sense of 'the affront' of the actual appointment.[35]

He had not been building castles in the air. He was the choice of the *Guardian,* by no means his consistent supporter. And, as Disraeli commented in a memorandum the following year, the time seemed ripe for the appointment of a bishop of Wilberforce's theological temper. "It was the height of his ambition. I think he would have preferred it to Canterbury. He was a Yorkshireman, and the son of a great Yorkshireman, who had represented the undivided county of York, and had fairly won it." The "Low Church vein" had been overworked and the death of the Prince had checked the ambitions of Broad Church partisans. Wilberforce had relied upon Gladstone to put his case, and had Gladstone threatened to resign, "he must have gained his point." He did not, and Thomson won the place. "An excellent appointment, in my opinion," Disraeli commented, "but that does not alter the circumstances." [36]

What had kept Wilberforce from York? He did not believe the Queen had put him down. Dean Wellesley had told him she favored "the double

32. November 11, 1862, BD, I. C192.   33. November 11, 1862, BD, I. C194.
34. Kirk-Smith, *William Thomson,* p. 84.
35. November 13, 1862, Add Mss. 44344.
36. Hughenden papers. A/X/A/56. 1863.

appointment"; and later Wellesley reported that "if London [Tait] had taken York I was to be offered London." [37] The scraps of evidence are inconclusive, and one can only conjecture. Palmerston had declared it a senseless policy to promote the interests of the High Church. He and Shaftesbury considered Wilberforce to be of that stripe. Furthermore the two men had disliked each other since that day twenty-five years before, when the clergyman had challenged the cabinet minister at the meeting of the Winchester Diocesan Education Society. Palmerston could mask his personal distaste with the argument Gladstone had brought home to Wilberforce—that he was a prelate getting everything he could for his Church, "asking more, giving nothing." If that remained his opinion of Wilberforce, he could be certain that Wilberforce bore no better one of him. In a letter to Gordon the following year, Wilberforce poured out his disgust with the man whom he had never trusted or respected, and who had now confirmed him in his long-lived enmity.

... That wretched Pam seems to me to get worse and worse. There is not a particle of veracity or noble feeling that I have ever been able to trace in him. He manages the House of Commons by debauching it, making all parties laugh at one another—the Tories at the Liberals by his defeating all Liberal measures, the Liberals at the Tories by their consciousness of getting everything that is to be got in Church and State, and all at one another by substituting low ribaldry for argument, bad jokes for principle and an openly avowed vainglorious imbecile vanity as a panoply to guard himself from the attack of all thoughtful men. I think if his life lasts long it must cost us the slight remains of constitutional government which exist among us.[38]

Six years after his disappointment over York, Wilberforce had occasion once more to hope for promotion. In October 1868 Archbishop Longley died. Disraeli, in the final days of his administration, translated Tait from London to Canterbury, and many people speculated that he might move Wilberforce to London in Tait's place. They speculated without much real knowledge of the complicated relationship between Disraeli and his bishop, which, as Wilberforce himself recognized in the end, made the appointment less than likely. His attachment to Gladstone had, over the years, done nothing to endear him to Gladstone's chief political rival. Disraeli had wanted Wilberforce to help lure Gladstone back into the Tory party before he had returned to service with Palmerston in 1859. "I wish you could have induced Gladstone to have joined Lord Derby's government, when Lord Ellenboro' resigned in 1858," Disraeli wrote later. "It was not my fault he did not. I almost went on my knees to him. Had he done so, the Church, and everything else, would have been in a very different position." [39] Instead, Disraeli complained to

37. Diary, December 16, 1862, in Ashwell and Wilberforce, *Life,* III, 64.
38. *Ibid.,* III, 91, June, 1863.   39. October 28, 1862, BD, II. E.

Wilberforce in a conversation the latter recorded in his diary, "I and others kept the Church as [Gladstone's] nest-egg when he became a Whig, till it was almost too addled." [40]

Wilberforce was not unprepared to cooperate with Disraeli or his party, persuaded that doing so might serve the interests of the Church. He would occasionally drop hints designed to convince Disraeli of his interest in his political future. After inviting him to dine and sleep at Cuddesdon when he entertained the mayor and corporation of Oxford, he added: "It *might* do good. The Duke of Marlborough etc. commonly are my guests on the occasion but this year cannot be." [41] His readiness to cultivate Disraeli's friendship stemmed from his disappointment in Gladstone's effectiveness as a spokesman for the Church within Palmerston's cabinet, and from his dismay at Gladstone's growing willingness to disestablish the Irish Church. Much as he admired Gladstone, and despite the fact that he had encouraged him to step forward as leader of the Whigs, Wilberforce could not help believing that Tories, traditional allies and defenders of Church interests, were more to be trusted than their opponents. When the Whigs fell at last in 1866, Wilberforce wrote his son Reginald that for a time there was hope. "I wish the moribund bishops would arrange their affairs before the Whigs are in again," he remarked with macabre wistfulness. "It would be a grand thing if we could get a few really good men in whilst there is this chance. For no one knows when it will come again." [42]

Along with his hope that Tories might promote Churchmanship as Whigs had not, went Wilberforce's fascination with Disraeli as a person. To Charles Anderson he wrote from Blenheim in the winter of 1867 of an encounter with him there. "He is a marvellous man, not a bit a Briton, but all over an Eastern Jew, but very interesting to talk to." And then, believing perhaps that he had allowed his enthusiasm to carry him too far, he added: "He *always* speaks as if he did believe in the Church." [43] As he admitted in a letter to Gordon the following summer, it was impossible to remain unimpressed. "It is not the mere assertion of talent, as you hear so many say. It seems to me quite beside that. He has been able to teach the House of Commons almost to ignore Gladstone; and at present lords it over him, and, I am told, says that he will hold him down for twenty years." [44] At Blenheim again, the following fall, Wilberforce allowed Disraeli to reconcile him to the Reform Bill. "No man living,

40. October 30, 1862, Ashwell and Wilberforce, *Life,* III, 70.
41. January 24, 1863, Hughenden papers, B. XXI. W362.
42. July 2, 1866, Chichester, 30.
43. February 14, 1867, BD, I. C192. Anderson had a low opinion of Disraeli. He had written Wilberforce in 1857 that he "wouldn't sit on the same bench with Dizzy. Everything he touches he defiles like a Yahoo" (n.d., BD, I. C190).
44. August 18, 1867, Ashwell and Wilberforce, *Life,* III, 227.

in my judgment, can form any idea of the result of the Reform Bill," he told Gordon.

I incline to believe that its earlier effects will be favourable to the Church, and therefore to the monarchy. But in its ultimate consequences I cannot see how it can be otherwise than democratic. It is an appeal to the people against the Whigs. Disraeli speaks exactly as he wrote in 'Sybil.' I had a good talk with him lately at Blenheim. He is full of hope, and speaks, when most confidentially, *à la* 'Sybil.' [45]

Disraeli could count on more than talk by this time to make a political ally of his bishop. Gladstone had made a national issue of his conviction that Ireland's woes demanded the disestablishment of her Church. Wilberforce, though aware that the Irish Church needed a thorough reforming,[46] refused to believe it could be severed from the State without endangering the union of English Church and State as well. "For if England and Ireland be one united kingdom," he declared in the *Quarterly*, "the destruction of the Church's nationality in one island must logically imply its destruction as national Church in both, although it may still survive as an anomaly in one." [47]

When Gladstone introduced his resolutions in favor of disestablishment in the spring of 1868, Wilberforce lamented to Anderson that it was "altogether a bad business." Gladstone, he averred, had been "drawn into it from the unconscious influence of his restlessness at being out of office." And had the Irish Church not been characterized by such a "low tone" Gladstone would never have been moved to destroy it.[48] Wilberforce took to the public platform to defend the status quo. At a large meeting in St. James's Hall in May, he played on popish fears by declaring that a disestablished Church of Ireland would mean the automatic establishment of Roman Catholicism. To those who argued that the dearth of Churchmen left the Church without influence, Wilberforce retorted that the Church's influence was out of all proportion to its numbers. "From every one of those parsonage-houses in which a man of God and a holy family are living are daily diffused a thousand influences which are modifying the superstition around, correcting evil influences, and tending to raise men to the true liberty of the Son of God." [49] In the Lords he attempted to prove St. Patrick a crypto-Anglican and the Roman Catholics unwanted latter-day intruders.[50]

All of which inevitably drew Wilberforce to Disraeli. In order to

45. *Ibid.*, III, 236, November 24, 1867.
46. Wilberforce recorded impressions of the Church of Ireland while on tour there in 1861 (see Ashwell and Wilberforce, *Life*, III, 23–27).
47. "Archbishops of the Reformation," *Quarterly Review*, 125:125. (1868).
48. April 25, 1868, BD, I. C192.   49. *Times*, May 7, 1869, p. 7.
50. *Hansard*, 3rd ser., CXCIII (June 29, 1868), 201ff.

"strengthen our friends at Oxford," he wrote to recommend Francis Leighton, Warden of All Souls to the vacant See of Hereford and, later in the summer, to that of Peterborough. But when Disraeli passed the suggestion to Bishop Ellicott, he received the reply that although Leighton's Church views were "perfectly right," the "ill natured would specify him as more 'high' than he really is; and his being a Rural Dean in the Diocese of *Oxford* would *not* be left unnoticed." [51] Disraeli needed nothing more to convince him that he must look elsewhere for a candidate. For at the same time that Wilberforce found himself drawn by political circumstances into Disraeli's camp, political circumstances had convinced Disraeli that his bishop was a distinct liability. Faced with an election in the fall on the issue of the Irish Church, Disraeli believed that he must, to win, identify himself with the extreme Protestant elements within the country, those ready to rally to a "no popery" cry in defense of the Establishment. He needed to repudiate Churchmen like Wilberforce who were believed dangerously High. As he wrote the Queen: "The great feature of national opinion is an utter repudiation by all classes of the High Church party. It is not only general but universal." [52] The pressures Disraeli felt were real enough. The Low Church *Record* had cautioned him only four days before he wrote the Queen against the machinations of "The Bishop of Oxford, a Prelate who probably knows less of the real state of the Church of England than almost any other Prelate on the Bench, the Archbishop of Canterbury [Longley] only excepted." [53] The Prime Minister could only conclude, as he wrote the Queen, that Wilberforce was at the moment "a prelate who, tho' Mr. Disraeli's Diocesan, he is bound to say is absolutely more odious in this country than Archbishop Laud." [54]

The country got its first taste of Disraeli's determination to court Low Churchmen when he appointed Hugh McNeile, a ferociously Evangelical Liverpool canon, to the Deanery of Ripon in August. When the bishopric of Peterborough came vacant soon after, Wilberforce, not knowing that Disraeli had determined to reject High Churchmen out of hand, wrote to warn him that unless he balanced McNeile's elevation, he would lose two seats at Peterborough in the coming election.[55] Disraeli did not take

51. April 24, 1868; August 11, 1868; September 16, 1868, Hughenden papers, C. III. a 47a; C. III. a 49; C. III. a 49g.

52. August 21, 1868, Royal Archives, A.37.49. Quoted in Robert Blake, *Disraeli* (New York, 1967), p. 508. Disraeli had remarked to Stanley that no one was for High Churchmen "except some University dons, some youthful priests, and some women; a great many of the latter" *(ibid.,* p. 506).

53. *Record,* August 17, 1868, p. 2.

54. September 10, 1868, Royal Archives, D.1.87.

55. September 11, 1868, Hughenden papers, C.III.a 49n. Disraeli appointed William Connor Magee, dean of Cork, a moderate Evangelical.

the opportunity to make his own position clear to Wilberforce until the end of the month. He wrote then to complain of a public letter by W. F. Hook declaring that further appointments of men like McNeile would drive the Church to disestablishment.

> ... Notwithstanding the fine sentiments in which it is very easy to indulge for those who are not responsible, it is all over with the Church of England if she be disconnected with the State.
> Even the Roman Catholic Church without Rome would be weakened...
> I think the chief Minister of this country, if he be ignorant of the bent of the national feeling at a crisis, must be an idiot. His means of arriving at the truth are so multifarious. Now certainly I hold that the long pent-up feeling of this nation against ultra-Ritualism will pronounce itself at the impending election...
> The questions of labour and liberty are settled, the rise of religious questions may be anticipated in an eminently religious people, undisturbed in their industry and secure in their freedom.[56]

"No popery" was in the saddle, and Disraeli intended to ride with it. Wilberforce responded with what in the end proved a more accurate picture of the state of religious sentiment in the country. He argued that Hook's impulsiveness had lent his letter a Laudian tone that did not correspond to reality. He was a man "of large sympathies, not of Laud's pinched up mind and sensibilities." Wilberforce was ready to agree that "the Protestant side" must be secured for the Tories. It was not the Evangelicals, however, but "the strong middle party of orthodox English Churchmen" who would do the job. "I want to keep them yours." [57]

Convinced that he knew better, Disraeli would have none of this argument. One further opportunity presented itself to follow the line Wilberforce had sketched for him. On October 28 Archbishop Longley died, following a month's illness. With the election at hand, Disraeli, in desperation, placed a number of names before the Queen for consideration. She had already determined upon Tait. As Robert Blake has made clear, her broad acquaintance with matters ecclesiastical allowed her to outmaneuver her Prime Minister, who, in the end, found himself pleading for the colorless busybody Ellicott.[58]

Who, then, for London? Many thought it might be Wilberforce, but the public announcement at that moment of a circumstance known to Wilberforce himself for over two months dashed whatever hopes he still har-

56. September 23, 1868, BD, II. E.
57. September 28, 1868, Hughenden papers, B. XXI. W376.
58. Four days after Tait's nomination, Ellicott wrote him: "My modest name had only this advantage, that Disraeli knows me to be a firm conservative and thorough old-fashioned High Churchman: if then I was warmly for you it must be inferred that the Central High Church party would (to say the least) not be unfavourable. The Low Church party at first were a little unmanageable and looked northward [to Thomson of York] (Tait Correspondence, LPL.85.223).

bored: his daughter Ella and her husband, Henry Pye, had been taken into the Roman Catholic Church. Wilberforce had had to reassure himself again and again that this blow would not fall; he could never quite believe that Pye's faith was in the Church of England. When Robert had gone over, he wrote Anderson that his son-in-law remained unshaken, but he could not forebear adding that "his own position is not what *I* like. I mean he does not feel as I do about Rome and England, though he is heartily loyal to our own Church." [59]

Henry Wilberforce's wife, Mary, believed from the start that Pye's faith might be won. She wrote to inform her Roman Catholic brother-in-law George Ryder that the Pyes would be living ten miles from the Ryders, "so we may see something of her, and who knows what turn Pye may take. He has only just been ordained and he may be a Catholic in a few years." [60] So Wilberforce continued to fear. In 1856 he heard from Bishop Denison of Salisbury who had heard from Gladstone that Pye stood at the brink. He hurried to contradict the rumor and confided to Anderson that "it is a great weight off my mind to find that Pye is stable, for I have often doubted it, and felt that sort of shrinking, which I cannot help, with anyone when I once mistrust them." [61] By the time Pye was made a prebend of Lichfield in 1865, Wilberforce had almost stopped worrying. The appointment would keep him safely within the Church, he wrote Reginald, "to which he has been ever since the condemnation of Essays and Reviews by Convocation very loyal." [62] But three years later while at Lavington he received a letter telling him what he then realized he should never have ceased to fear.

He is going over, after all, to Rome, and, of course, my poor Ella. For years I have prayed incessantly against this last act of his, and now it seems denied me. It seems as if my heart would break at this insult out of my own bosom to God's truth in England's Church, and preference for the vile harlotry of the Papacy. God forgive them. I have struggled on my knees against feelings of wrath against him in a long, long weeping cry to God. May He judge between this wrong doer and me! [63]

The pain he had felt at the time of Robert's conversion returned to smite him, made all the more bitter because Ella was "out of my bosom," and because he was an older and a more vulnerable man. It also stung him that though the decision had been reached in August, it was not announced until the end of October, coincident with the death of Archbishop Longley. Wilberforce and his friends believed it a plot on Manning's part to keep him from the promotion that was his due. "I feel sure that Manning kept Pye as a bagged fox," Anderson wrote later to Reginald,

59. November 30, 1854, BD, I. C191.   60. Undated. Clutton papers.
61. March 21, 1856, BD, I. C190.   62. August 3, 1865, Chichester, 30.
63. Diary, August 29, 1868, in Ashwell and Wilberforce, *Life,* III, 255.

"and turned him out at this particular time to prevent S. O. from going to Lambeth. At all events the fact of Archbishop Longley's death and the defection of the Pyes appearing side by side in the newspaper is remarkable and more than suspicious when one knows the creeping slyness and unscrupulous crafts of Romish tactics." [64]

That he had been privy to the Pyes' decision for two months did not make it easier to bear when publicly proclaimed at the end of October. To his son Ernest he wrote bitterly from Hawarden, where he was visiting the Gladstones.

I do not feel to care about anything; everything has lost its interest. I know by experience that if I am brave, and go on, by degrees life, if I live, will resume its powers. I was up early, and walked with dear Prevost to church. Gladstone comes back today. It feels almost a pain meeting him. The Irish Church difference was of itself bad enough, and now this uncommunicated load adds to the heaviness. The wet day, the sighing wind, the falling rotting leaves, the heavy drifting clouds, all seem in unison. It is, too, so difficult to guard my spirit from anger and impatience. The whole thing lies so clearly before me that I am for ever needing to discipline my spirit not to feel unkindly to one who has been my plague ever since I knew him and has robbed me of my only daughter in blood and brought reproach on the Church I have, however imperfectly, ever endeavoured to serve. As to the Papistry itself, I only more than ever see it to be the great Cloaca into which all vile corruptions of Christianity run naturally, and loathe it.[65]

Wilberforce was not a man to abandon himself to despair. When Emily died, when Robert left the Church, when Herbert died, he had on each occasion buried the pain by burying himself in work. He tried once more, but he found the cure came less readily. Never had tragedy pushed him to the edge as it did now. To both Reginald and his brother-in-law, John James, he declared that he would have rather "followed her to her grave" than have Ella cast this reproach upon her Church and upon her own soul.[66]

As to the bishopric of London, the Pyes' conversion scotched the slight chance that Wilberforce might have succeeded to the place. Disraeli was reported to have remarked: "How could I? His daughter by some strange malignity turned Papist just at that moment. The father's appointment would probably have cost me several seats at the General

64. Note on the back of a letter, dated October 30, 1868, from W. F. Hook to Anderson asking what they can do to promote the appointment of Wilberforce as Archbishop (BD, I. C192). Few thought as Anderson and Hook apparently did that Wilberforce would be named Archbishop. It was London upon which their hopes were focused.

65. October 24, 1868, BD, I. C205.

66. October 23, 1868, Chichester, 30; November 9, 1868, BD, I. C205. In a letter to Wilberforce at the time of Robert's conversion, Gladstone had said much the same thing: "For could I, with reference to my own precious children, think that one of them might possibly live to strike, through sincerity of thinking he did God service, such a stroke, how far rather would I that he had never been born" (October 17, 1854, Add Mss. 44467. 193).

Election." [67] Instead, he appointed the nondescript John Jackson of Lincoln. Wilberforce's friends attempted to console him. Tait, by no means an ecclesiastical ally, told him he had wanted him for London. Wellesley, at Windsor, poured him an earful of angry venom when next he visited there.

The Church does not know what it owes the Queen [Wellesley reported]. Disraeli has been utterly ignorant, utterly unprincipled: he rode the Protestant horse one day; then got frightened that it had gone too far, and was injuring the county elections, so he went right around and proposed names never heard of. Nothing he would not have done; but throughout he was most hostile to you; he alone prevented London being offered to you; the Queen looked for Tait [for Canterbury], but would have agreed to you.

Disraeli recommended [Ellicott] for Canterbury!!!—the Queen would not have him; then Disraeli agreed most reluctantly and with passion to Tait. Disraeli then proposed [Christopher] Wordsworth for London. The Queen objected strongly; no experience; passing over bishops, etc; then she suggested Jackson, and two others, not you, because of Disraeli's expressed hostility, and Disraeli chose Jackson. . .

How can [Ellicott] have got that secret understanding with Disraeli? You are surrounded by false, double-dealing men.[68]

Chastened by the blow the Pyes had dealt him, Wilberforce took the rebuff without much rancor. "Disraeli has done exactly as I expected with his Church appointments," he wrote Anderson. "For myself I really thank God it very little disturbs me. I, in my reason, apprehend that by the common rule in such matters I had no right to be so treated; but I am really thankful for feeling so coolly about it." [69] Wilberforce had the satisfaction of seeing Disraeli's elaborate electoral contrivance splintered. He had overestimated Protestant sentiment and underrated the resentment that "the strong middle party of orthodox Churchmen" would register at the polls against his politically motivated ecclesiastical appointments. Wilberforce never again found Disraeli a very fascinating person. From 1868 he turned wholeheartedly to Gladstone. In a crude parable he wrote on foreign affairs in 1871, his caricature of Disraeli probably seemed to him no more than an accurate description:

He was always playing his own game, and he liked to talk big words like an African mystery man. . . Still nobody really trusted Ben, for they saw that he always threw everyone over—no matter what promises he had made him—if he thought he could get anything by doing so.[70]

67. Recorded in Sir Edward Hamilton's Diary, January 11, 1894, Add Mss. 48662.56.
68. Diary, November 28, 1868, in Ashwell and Wilberforce, *Life,* III, 268–269. "Ellicott" appears as a blank in the printed version of the diary. From other references there can be no doubt that his is the correct name. Wordsworth was appointed to the See of Lincoln, vacated by Jackson's translation to London.
69. November 16, 1868, BD, I. C192.
70. *The Break-up of Dame Europa's School* (London, n.d. [1871]), n.p. The pamphlet was written in praise of Gladstone's restraint in keeping England out of a war with Germany.

Wilberforce was ready to acknowledge that despite disagreement over the Irish Church his views on religious matters had far more in common with Gladstone's than with "those of the snuffling clique which believes only in the lion and the unicorn and anoints them with sour stuff." [71] More important, the election convinced Wilberforce that further disagreement over disestablishment would prove futile. On November 20 he wrote the first of many letters preaching accommodation to his old friend Archbishop Trench of Dublin, who continued to believe that much might be gained from die-hard opposition to Gladstone. Wilberforce's arguments suggested his willingness to apply in this case the lesson Gladstone had tried to teach him in 1862: that to survive, the Church would have to moderate its demands and show itself more than merely obstructive. To Trench's contention that the Church should hold out so as to strike a better bargain, he answered:

... This would be wise if you were dealing with a minority, guided by a Master of selfish cunning and unprincipled trickery. Doubtless it would be the wise way to meet a mere mystery-man like Disraeli, who was trading upon the principles and ultimate existence of an honorable minority and had no real principle.

This case was altogether different. Gladstone was "a man of the highest and noblest principle, who has shown unmistakably that he is ready to sacrifice every personal aim for what he has set before himself as a high object." More important, Gladstone could claim the support of a large majority, not just in the House but throughout the country. This, to Wilberforce, had become the determining factor.

The decision of the constituencies seems to me incapable of misapprehension or reversal. Has there ever yet been any measure, however opposed, which the English people have been unable for its difficulty to carry through, when they have determined to do so? ... You may frighten away a fox by an outcry; but you only wake up the strength and the fury of the lion.

He retained his conviction that disestablishment would not relieve Irish distress. "If I thought it possible to resist it successfully I would resist

---

Disraeli, in turn, modeled his bishop in *Lothair* upon his reading of Wilberforce's character. "The Bishop was high-church, and would not himself have made a bad cardinal, being polished and plausible, well-lettered, quite a man of the world. He was fond of society, and justified his taste in this respect by the flattering belief that by his presence he was extending the power of the Church; certainly favouring an ambition which could not be described as being moderate" (*Lothair* [London, 1927], Bradenham Edition, p. 205). Trollope also caricatured Wilberforce, along with Phillpotts and Blomfield, in chap. VIII of *The Warden*.

71. To Charles Anderson, November 25, 1868, BD, I. C192. Anderson found it less easy to accommodate Gladstone: "I think it perfectly scandalous that the country should be made a shuttlecock between two unscrupulous Battledores like Gladstone and Dizzy for I will *never* believe that this Church question was brought forward on any but party grounds to gather together the heterodox mass which had become scattered, just as this precious Reform Bill was brought in by Dizzy to outbid the Radicals" (December 4, 1868, BD, I. C190).

it still. But I think it impossible, and I never have met in the last two months any man of thought and capacity who appeared to me honestly to believe it to be possible." Disraeli was no decent alternative to Gladstone; he would starve the Church if necessary to gain popularity. Better surrender the Church into the compassionate hands of Gladstone, than into the hands of Disraeli, who would slowly torture it to death.[72]

Gladstone was prepared to act on principle and carry disestablishment. Evidence in the Wilberforce correspondence shows the length to which he was prepared to go to accomplish the end that had become his obsession. He wanted help from the bishops—a public statement of some sort declaring a change of heart and a willingness to compromise. In late December 1868 he asked Sir Robert Phillimore, chancellor of the diocese of Oxford, to ascertain his bishop's willingness to write a "public or private" letter to Trench, not aware that Wilberforce had already been at work to alter the Archbishop's mind for a month. Phillimore put the proposal to Wilberforce in a letter on December 24.[73] Wilberforce replied on the 31st, informing Phillimore that he had already written Trench, enclosing a copy of the long letter he had mailed the day before. "You can let Gladstone see it if you think fit. But I doubt whether I ought to publish anything until the Irish prelates or the best of them are ready to take my council." Phillimore had warned him of the obloquy that might attach to his name if he made public his sudden change of heart. Wilberforce again stated that the election had settled the matter for him. Gladstone was, in politics, his "natural leader"; obloquy or not he would do what he could for him. "But I should lose all power of doing good in the matter if it were to seem that I deserted [the Irish bishops] in their difficulty; and this hindrance is aggravated by the way in which Disraeli has avenged the sin of my known affection to Gladstone in those recent ecclesiastical appointments which are likely to outlast my life, and which will give so easy a handle for attributing my action to personal pique." [74] Best to wait until he had privately won the Irish bishops to his side before trying to convince others by a public declaration.

While Wilberforce was writing Phillimore, Lord Lyttelton, Gladstone's brother-in-law, and at the moment his host as well, wrote a letter to the bishop. In effect, it was a genteel bribe. He decried the recent ecclesiastical appointments of Palmerston and Disraeli—"a scandal to the Church and a reproach to the Ministers who made them." He then proceeded to an outline of "the actual state of things" as they stood on the eve of the new Parliament. Parliament was determined on disestablishment, and patronage "according to universal and ancient usage" would be employed to see it carried.

72. December 30, 1868, BD, I. C200.   73. *Ibid.*, December 24, 1868.
74. *Ibid.*, December 31, 1868.

Now of course what I am saying and about to say cannot but have the look of suggesting a temptation to you to let personal motives have weight with you in a grave public question. I cannot help that, as it is irrelevant in the case. If you are liable to be moved even in the least degree, in such a way, so, I apprehend, must any one be: and it would be very unseemly in me to think of offering any advice or caution on such a point to such an one as you.

Everyone recognized that the expected demise of Sumner of Winchester "may furnish the *only* opportunity, *for years,* of a recognition—and though not an adequate, not a *very inadequate,* recognition of your great claims." Loss of this opportunity to advance Wilberforce "would be to thousands of us a matter of unspeakable regret and annoyance."

Yet I do not know that I should have thought there was sufficient hope of gaining my object to warrant me in writing, had I had to do so just after your speech of last Session [against disestablishment]. But now I am writing not only in a materially altered state of things, but not without having heard of indications —I do not mean positive or conclusive ones—that your own political view has been modified.

Lyttelton next provided Wilberforce with grounds for changing his mind—the same grounds Wilberforce had been pressing upon Trench: that the recent election made no other course possible. He concluded with a specific request.

If you should be disposed to adopt some such view as the above, I venture confidently to assert that in your position, you are called on to make it known and to act upon it, and that not at some future period but *now.*

How to do so in the most effective and at the same time discreet manner, I shall not presume to suggest—beyond one step at least; I think you might make some such communication, in a formal or at least in a grave and deliberate way, to the Irish Bishops and above all to Archbishop Trench.

If you should have already determined on adhering to you former course, or on any line essentially different from what I have indicated, what I have written will of course have been thrown away: but not even so, I hope, shall I fail to receive your kind indulgence for having ventured to write.[75]

Wilberforce sent no answer to this letter until January 18. In the interim he pursued the same course with Trench that he had followed since November, asking him, in addition, if he would favor a public letter of the sort suggested by Phillimore and Lyttelton. Trench continued to oppose negotiations on the simple ground that parley with Gladstone would win him no advantage, while alienating the entire body of Irish Churchmen. A letter from Wilberforce, far from helping, would only tell those Churchmen that they had lost an ally and convince them that they must accordingly fight all the harder. Because of his power within the Church, he, of all people, must not seem to desert them.[76] Wilberforce nevertheless proceeded to draft a statement which he enclosed

75. *Ibid.,* December 31, 1868.   76. *Ibid.,* January 5 and 11, 1869.

with his January 18 reply to Lyttelton. He confessed to Lyttelton that for the first time he had been forced to look at the Irish question from the point of view of personal interest. If Gladstone were to appoint him, he hoped it would be for the sake of the Church, and for the support he had lent him while the member for Oxford. He informed Lyttelton of his correspondence with Trench, and his willingness to publicize his views.

> But your letter suggests to me a new fear, which, to anyone who knows the deceitfulness of his own heart, must, I suppose, be a terrible fear, of listening in such grave matters to the dictates of self-interest. With this I must grapple as best I may; and I have so far overcome it as to have put down in the shape of a letter to you my present views on the question, and I now ask whether, if I do publish, you have any objection to this form of publication. I cannot in the face of their earnest entreaty address it to my Irish brethren.

Wilberforce asked Lyttelton to weigh the question of publication in the light of two further considerations. Would he subject his office and therefore the Church to odium if he came forward publicly to announce a change that many would believe "tuned and timed to the interest of personal advancement"? And would a public declaration really work to Gladstone's advantage, assuming Gladstone anxious to reach a compromise solution acceptable to all but die-hards on both sides. "It is one thing for *him* to know that he will have such support: another that the world should know it. When it might be presumably useful to him to be able to point to a possible adverse House of Lords majority, to render with his own followers an unpalatable moderation possible." [77]

The public letter to Lyttelton, entitled "The Answer to the Constituencies," was set in type when Wilberforce sent it off. It contained a general statement of his belief that further opposition would only endanger the Church's chance of obtaining an equitable endowment once disestablishment had been forced upon it. "We may," Wilberforce warned at its conclusion,

> alienate from ourselves regards which yet cling warmly to us if we show a readiness to change the just courage of our past action into the adoption of a system which can be nothing else than the interposing, when it is too late for success, the hesitating delays of a hopeless resistance. Above all, do not let us, through any refusal of ours to adjust the only questions which, in fact, remain open, suffer our Church to continue one unnecessary day the battlefield of faction—the watchword and the prey of opposing parties in the State. In such a course we risk too great a stake. When for the chance of a doubtful victory the men of Israel took the Ark of God into the battle, they did but leave it after their overthrow as a trophy in the hands of the Philistines. [78]

77. *Ibid.*, January 18, 1869.
78. "The Answer to the Constituencies," BD, I. C200.

Gladstone pressed hard for publication. Wilberforce, who continued to hear from Trench, eventually concluded that such a course would only encourage intransigence. "The Archbishop, after counselling with his brethren says 'our worst enemy could not do us a greater harm,'" he reported to Gladstone. He promised to write Trench once more and to seek the advice of Bishop Magee of Peterborough, until recently the dean of Cork. Gladstone fired back what he described to Lord Granville as a stout reply, insisting that Wilberforce make public his change of heart. "Those of whom the world knows nothing except that to the utmost of their power they opposed us last year, count with the world as opponents still, and the private change in their opinion *cannot* weigh with us in the foundation of the Bill." [79] Once more Wilberforce wrote off to Dublin, but Trench could not see the reason in his argument. Nor could Magee of Peterborough, who congratulated Wilberforce on having printed but not published his letter. Printed, it might circulate among those willing to moderate their position. Published, it would be "a gun seized by the enemy and turned against the [Irish?] with such deadly effect that they must surrender on any terms." [80] At this point Gladstone gave up. "I return the Bishop of Peterborough's letter," he wrote Wilberforce at the end of January. "I do not agree in all he says of the publication: but I think it is too much to put upon you individually thus to step out in the front of the ranks and decide the matter by single combat." He hoped now that an Irish convocation might be assembled to deal with the matter as a joint endeavor.[81]

Thereafter Wilberforce played little part in Gladstone's campaign. He served occasionally as go-between for Gladstone in Convocation. When debate on the Bill commenced in the Lords, Gladstone gave his friend a prod: "When I was a youth sitting behind Sir Robert Peel there was a famous old Whig landlady . . . on the road to Edinburgh who had known me from a child and who though on the other side, used to say to me 'Now, mind I always see your name in the Divisions.' That is what I constantly say to you, by no means thinking only of the mere unit in reckoning the members." [82] Wilberforce neither spoke nor voted until the Bill had gone into Committee after the second reading. On amendments he voted more often against than for the Government. He explained in Committee that he had planned to make his position clear during the second reading, that the accidents of debate had kept him from doing so, and that he held himself "incapacitated, as a Bishop of the Church of England, from giving the vote I should otherwise have given, no opportunity of stating the grounds on which I did so having presented itself." [83] He stated his grounds for the benefit of those still

79. January 21, 1869, Add Mss. 44345.   80. January 28, 1869, BD, I. C200.
81. *Ibid.,* January 30, 1869.   82. *Ibid.,* June 12, 1869.
83. *Hansard,* 3rd ser., CXCVII (June 29, 1869), 715.

unfamiliar with them, and added a plea for understanding in the matter of the distribution of endowments.

Two months later Charles Sumner, still ailing but still alive, took advantage of the recent Bishop's Resignation Act to announce his retirement from the See of Winchester.[84] Gladstone had Wilberforce in his mind from the start. The announcement, he wrote Granville wryly, "and the prominence of the figure of S. O. on the canvas will lead to his being much more microscopically than goodnaturedly examined and criticised." Granville replied that he feared the appointment would not be well received in Surrey.[85] The Prime Minister pressed ahead and recommended Wilberforce to the Queen in the same letter that he recommended Frederick Temple to Exeter, as replacement for the ancient and all but extinct Phillpotts. Wilberforce accepted Gladstone's offer "with many feelings of thankfulness that it comes from your hands... It costs me almost more than I can express to leave the Diocese. But I do trust that if my life and health are spared me I may by God's Grace do in my remaining years those there that I could do here. As proof of your esteem and in your estimate of the Queen's consent as a proof of her feeling it is a great gratification to me." [86]

After the long years of waiting the appointment came to Wilberforce, as to most—as the *Guardian* remarked—"almost as a matter of course." [87] Winchester, though a venerable See, was not at the top of any pole. As Wilberforce later admitted candidly to Gladstone: "It is not *the* post for which after so many years of labour and gathered experience I should have chosen to leave Oxford." [88] The thought that he might still move higher flickered for a moment in late November when Tait lay dangerously ill. "Everyone takes for granted without any foundation, that if he is removed, I shall go there," he wrote his son Ernest. "I pray God to keep me from all bad thoughts, and I do feel very quiet indeed about it." [89] Tait recovered; Wilberforce moved willingly enough to Winchester, though, one senses, without the feeling of challenge and without the energy that he might have brought with him had he been called to London or Lambeth.

As he had prophecied, the unkind saw the appointment as payment of a political debt. Wilberforce replied to the charge when a clergyman in the diocese wrote to ask if the rumor had any foundation. After cataloging for what he must have hoped would be the last time his reasons for supporting disestablishment, he added indignantly:

84. The others who retired at the same time: Auckland of Bath and Wells (who could no longer sign his own name); Phillpotts of Exeter; Gilbert of Chichester; and Waldegrave of Carlisle.
85. August 24 and 27, 1869, in *The Political Correspondence of Mr. Gladstone and Lord Granville*, ed. Agatha Ramm (London, 1952), pp. 47, 50.
86. September 15, 1869, Add Mss. 44345.   87. October 6, 1869, p. 1089.
88. November 30, 1869, Add Mss. 44345.   89. November 24, 1869, BD, I. C205.

The class of minds who indulge in these base suspicions may perhaps be affected by considering that, in making the change, I undertake (1) harder work; (2) during the life of the present Bishop a smaller income; (3) far greater expenses; (4) the sacrifice of the love and affection of 24 year's growth. I end with saying I am ashamed for those who ask it at giving such explanations.[90]

In spite of his protestations, Winchester meant advancement. Wilberforce had acknowledged the fact in his response to Lyttelton. But to admit that much is not to say that Wilberforce took the line he did to win himself a better place. Gladstone had dangled place in front of him. Lyttelton informed Canon Ashwell in 1874 that he had written "almost in Mr. Gladstone's name." Gladstone, a week after Lyttelton wrote the bishop, informed Granville that he thought he had "got the Bishop of Oxford right on the Irish Church:—which will be rather material. I got two friends [Lyttelton and Phillimore] to write him: of course not in my name." [91] Gladstone never got Wilberforce quite right on the matter. Wilberforce continued to pursue a policy already determined by the election results. He refused Gladstone's request that he make public his printed letter until satisfied himself that it would help persuade Irish Churchmen to moderate their position; and he never received that satisfaction.

When Reginald Wilberforce began writing the third volume of his father's *Life* he came across the Lyttelton letter and wrote in some concern to Gladstone, asking if it was what it seemed to be. The reply he received, if it says little of Wilberforce, says something of Gladstone.

I do not feel that you need be under any difficulty or pressure with respect to the letters you have sent me. My memory does not record any single instance in which your father's advancement to Winchester was associated even by the most censorious of men with political subserviency. It was a very small acknowledgment of his vast services to the Church of England, given when greater ones had been, as I think, unhappily withheld. Undoubtedly he gave me a warm personal support, and probably he suffered for it, but with his politics generally I was far from satisfied... To shew you how small a space relative to other matters connected with his name and action, politics occupy my mind, I remain under the impression, perhaps erroneous, that he offered some opposition to the Bill for the disestablishment of the Irish Church. This did not I think much surprise me. A Bishop is apt to get a twist in these matters... I have no recollection of Lord Lyttelton's having written 'in my name' but it is perfectly possible that I may have said to him what I had said to the Bishop and if he asked my opinion about his also conveying it [I] may have encouraged the idea.[92]

Reginald published evidence enough to convince readers—as he apparently felt he must convince them—that his father had not swallowed the bribe. He chose to leave unpublished the letter over which Gladstone had sprinkled his politician's dust.

90. To the Reverend H. Majendie, October 13, 1869, BD, I. C200.
91. January 6, 1869, in *Political Correspondence,* ed. Ramm, p. 7.
92. July 6, 1882, BD, I. C200.

CHAPTER X

The Final Years

The See of Winchester had throughout Sumner's long episcopate continued to remunerate its bishop with the princely salary of £10,500. Once Sumner declared his intention to retire, the Ecclesiastical Commissioners moved to redistribute the revenues which they had been unable to touch until then. They reduced the income to £7000, £2000 of which Wilberforce was to pass to Sumner until his death. With £5000 per year—the same sum he had received as bishop of Oxford [1]—Wilberforce would be expected to maintain the ancient dignity of a See far larger than that from which he had been called. Bishop Sumner continued to live in the palace at Farnham while Wilberforce moved between large establishments in Winchester and London. Clergy and laymen would naturally expect him to contribute—his time, certainly, but his money, as well—to the projects which they confidently expected him to initiate and to continue. Financially, the translation was for Wilberforce anything but a boon.[2]

In addition to the money he received as bishop, he depended at this time upon his income from the Lavington estate, the rents of which totaled about £2400.[3] His writings brought him another £150 to £200 per year—he had received 100 guineas for his article on *Essays and Reviews.*[4] But if his income was large, so were his expenses. His style of life drained him of his money. The constant entertaining at Cuddesdon— ordination retreats, lay and clerical synods, ecclesiastical dinner parties and house parties—this meant never-ending expense. Until his daughter married, Wilberforce maintained a residence in London as well as fully staffed households in Oxfordshire and Sussex. His willingness to travel about at everyone's beck and call did nothing to reduce his spending.

1. After 1845 he received £3500 a year from the Ecclesiastical Commission; the remaining income—sometimes more than £2000, sometimes less, derived from such sources as fines on renewals of leases. Parliamentary Papers, XLII (1851), 497.

2. See Archbishop Tait's letter to Gladstone, written in 1871, detailing the financial burden he had assumed when he succeeded to the throne of Canterbury (June 19, 1871, in LPL, Tait Correspondence, 89. 220).

3. From the report of a surveyor and valuer, Robert Carr, February 8, 1865 (Chichester, 43). Wilberforce rented the "rectory house" on the estate for £150 a year. Carr estimated that if the estate were offered for sale "it would realize upwards of £60,000."

4. Diary, January 25, 1861, in Ashwell and Wilberforce, *Life,* III, 14. *Agathos,* his book of parables, brought him from £50 to £75 per edition, of which the 27th was published in 1868. See letter from Seeley, Jackson, and Halliday of December 21, 1868 (BD, I. C202).

And, after 1860, he found himself called upon to make provisions for his sons. Their coming of age did not reduce their dependence on their father, any more than Samuel's had reduced his reliance upon his father William. Reginald, after serving with the army in India, embarked upon a career as a tea planter. Wilberforce backed him enthusiastically, willingly mortgaging Lavington for £10,000 to help him, and peddling Reginald's product among his friends. "I want to know exactly what printed labels I may give to people to tell them what tea to ask for. . . I am sure that if a dozen great folk write to [the importer] for it he will buy your tea at a higher price. So many people now like it. I like it far better than the China." [5] Reginald remained in India until 1866, when he returned home to find a bride. He found a second cousin of Charles Anderson, Anna Marie Denman, and with her settled down at Lavington. Wilberforce received them gladly but fretted as to how Reginald would support himself, and worked hard to help him sell his interest in the plantation so that he could live in comfort at home.

Ernest and Basil, after carefree and not particularly productive lives at Oxford, decided to follow their father into the clergy. Ernest pleased the family by binding them ever more closely to the Andersons. He fell in love with Sir Charles's daughter, Frances Mary, a nurse. They were married in June 1863 after a long courtship and before Ernest had taken orders. The negotiations between the two fathers, Samuel and Charles, recall those between William Wilberforce and John Sargent thirty-five years before. Ernest, like his father, had fallen in love young—when he was eighteen. Samuel worried that he had formed the attachment too early. "But," he acknowledged to Anderson, "we have to deal with facts." [6] Samuel allowed Ernest £300 a year, and wondered if Anderson "could conveniently have made Fan's allowance £150." In a letter several years later, he asked Anderson to help pay for the children's furniture.[7] Basil, who married a Caroline Langford in 1867, did not apparently tax his father's resources as Reginald and Ernest did, his wife possessing a comfortable fortune of her own.

Money problems, which had haunted the Wilberforces when Samuel was a young man, never left him as he lived out his own broad, expansive life and raised his family. He borrowed, he mortgaged, and he assumed that somehow he would always find enough money to satisfy his extravagant demands. Against this background his biographer must weigh evidence brought against him in an extraordinary document written by his brother-in-law, George Dudley Ryder, sometime after Mrs. Sargent's death in 1861. In it, Ryder accused Wilberforce of exercising undue in-

5. January 2, 1866, Chichester, 30.   6. April 26, 1858, BD, I. C191.
7. May 6, 1863 and May 10, 1866, BD, I. C192.

fluence upon his mother-in-law and thereby making off with money rightfully due to him and to Mary Sargent Wilberforce, Henry's wife.[8] The
facts suggest that while Samuel did not act illegally, he did take what his
mother-in-law willingly gave him, as he had taken from his own mother
and father, convinced that his sisters-in-law, by forfeiting their faith, had
forfeited their legacy as well.

Charles Sumner bequeathed Wilberforce a sprawling, thriving diocese,
bearing the impress of his more than forty years as its bishop. He had
instituted there many of the reforms Wilberforce introduced to Oxford.
With visitations, ordinations, training colleges, and church building, he
had attempted to keep pace with the growing populations of Hampshire
and of Surrey which, in 1861, numbered 1,267,794. Between 1830 and
1854 he raised and spent £883,077 on new churches. In 1865 he established a South London Church Extension Fund, which collected over
£20,000 for new churches, schools, and clergymen in Southwark.[9] Various schemes had been proposed for dividing the diocese, which included
the Channel Islands, as well as Surrey and Hampshire. Wilberforce,
who relished a challenge, wrote to ask Gladstone not to take Southwark
from him, although he expressed himself willing to part with the Islands.[10]

He ended by keeping it all. His years as bishop of Winchester were
like a coda to his years at Oxford, echoing the major themes of his work
there on a grander scale. Only by stretching himself to the limit of his
endurance could he achieve in his new diocese the goals he had set himself in the old. He had over a thousand clergymen to get to know. He
kept a map and marked with a red line the parishes he had visited. Instead of holding ordinations at his palace, as he had done at Cuddesdon,
he conducted them in major parishes throughout the diocese—Lambeth,
Guildford, Southampton, Reigate, Surbiton, Dorking, and, in the summer
of 1870, on the island of Guernsey. Church building proceeded steadily.
The diocesan Act Book [11] records the licensing of a multitude of school
rooms for temporary services as inspection and reconstruction proceeded
under the provisions of the Church Dilapidations Act of 1871. Wilberforce's major innovation was the creation of two county-wide associations amalgamating various clerical societies under one administration—
something he had tried to accomplish when he was archdeacon of Surrey.

His correspondence shows him mired even more deeply than at Oxford
in ritual controversy. When he came into the diocese he feared that he
would find its clergymen of almost wholly Evangelical persuasion. "You
can conceive some of the many difficulties bred for me by my dear friend

8. Details of the accusation will be found in the Appendix on p. 319 of this volume.
9. G. H. Sumner, *The Life of Charles Sumner* (London, 1876), pp. 365, 427.
10. October 7, 1869 and November 24, 1869, Add Mss. 44345.
11. Deposited in the library of the Hampshire Records Office, Winchester.

Bishop Sumner's long rule," he wrote Bishop Gray. "Personally he is as kind as possible but the Diocese is most one-sided." [12] But he soon found his troubles coming from all directions. The Low Churchmen lived up to Wilberforce's expectations. Shaftesbury warned him that he could expect only trouble if he permitted ritualism to seep into his clergy's services. "Do not be led to accept a statement that will be made to you that the people like these things. They loathe them. Whenever crowds have been gathered at St. Alban's and other places of Popish revival, it has been to indulge their curiosity and not to satisfy their devotions." Shaftesbury took less than six months to sniff out the masquerading presence of infidel Rome. In May he refused an invitation to attend a meeting of the Surrey Church Extension Fund after reading reports of "highly artistic" ritual practices in that part of the diocese.[13] So upset was a group of Low Churchmen in New Malden that it broke with the parish to form a "Free Church" in opposition to the vicar, who, by lifting up and worshipping the elments and by other similar excesses, had allowed his Tractarianism "slowly and craftily to develop into the idolatry of Rome." [14]

The Purchas judgment [15] merely compounded Wilberforce's difficulties. Ritualists refused to countenance its proscriptions. "I *cannot* make myself believe that the judgment of any court on earth can possibly override the faith of the universal Church," [16] wrote one High Churchman. It was Gorham all over again. Wilberforce had to write to his clergy forbidding them to ring bells during consecration of the elements and cautioning them against the use of white vestments, candles, and wafers. Protestants seized the chance to importune against anything that seemed in any way tainted by Rome. The parishioners of Ryde objected to the epitaph on a newly erected parish tombstone: "Eternal rest give unto him and let perpetual light shine upon him." Was this not a prayer for the dead? Wilberforce replied that the Church nowhere disallowed the words, "and their disallowance would therefore have been a breach of charity." [17]

Wilberforce tried to mediate as he had at Oxford, but without the success he enjoyed there. Because during Sumner's last years the clergy had had their own way, because Wilberforce was not known personally to many of them, and was in their eyes therefore a dignitary but nothing more, because in a diocese the size of Winchester the bishop could never hope to attend to the minutiae of parochial business as Wilberforce had

12. December 7, 1869, BD, I. C199.
13. December 14, 1869, BD, II.E; May 7, 1870, BD, II.S.
14. *The Free Church of England,* 2d ed. (Kingston-on-Thames, 1872), pp. 4ff.
15. See p. 260 above.
16. From the Reverend Richard Wilkans, December 10, 1872, BD, I. C198.
17. To ?, *ibid.,* July 13, 1871.

done at Oxford—for these reasons the clergy remained less attentive to his pleas for moderation and understanding. When Wilberforce informed the rector of Wandsworth Church that he could not confirm there because of the rector's excessive attachment to ritual, he received the tart rejoinder that "nothing can be more distressing to a parish priest in his relations with his Bishop than to feel he can never again rely on that Bishop's fulfillment of a promise once given. 'Blessed is the man who sweareth to his own hurt; and changeth not.'" [18] When, at the other extreme, the rector of St. Saviour's, Southwark, invited an extremist from the Protestant Educational Institute to lecture, and Wilberforce, upon petition from the church wardens, wrote to request the preacher to stay away, he found himself entangled in a thicket of invective that reached to the House of Lords.

Ritual bitterness meant that Wilberforce set himself an even fiercer pace than he had at Oxford. As he began his episcopate he wrote Arthur Gordon of the task that lay ahead for him. Things had "got a good deal out of gear" because of Sumner's age and infirmity. South London was "a tremendous charge." He determined to know as many of the clergy and important laity as he could.

This is in a great measure my present work: and till it is mastered I do not much mind not having Farnham. This house [Lavington] commands a large part of the south of the Diocese—Reigate, Guildford, Petersfield, Portsmouth, Isle of Wight. And I am more at liberty to go and stay with my squires, all of whom press me to come and see them at home. I have been with Lord Carnarvon, Lord Eversley, Sir H. Mildmay, etc., and am setting off on Friday for Sir W. Heathcote's, Lord Malmesbury's, and the Duke of Wellington's. This will bring me to the meeting of Parliament by which time I hope to establish myself at Winchester House.[19]

These long and constant "diocesan wanderings," as he once called them in a letter to Marianne Thornton, were by no means merely social in nature. Even when meeting his squires, he was at work for the Church. A visit to Ringwood, in 1871, saw him coming "to be the life and soul of parochial missions held simultaneously in the four towns and score of villages of the deanery and to make acquaintance with our leading laymen by staying at as many of their houses as time would permit." The work, now that he was in his sixties, exhausted him as it had not done when he was younger. "He had stipulated that we should spare him after-dinner work," an acquaintance later wrote Reginald.

But this was not always practicable and he was frequently in harness morning, noon and night. The last day he came to Ringwood vicarage late in the afternoon, thoroughly done up, as he confessed to the curate who was acting as his secre-

18. From the Reverend Bradley Abbott, *ibid.*, May 24, 1870.
19. January 16, 1870, Ashwell and Wilberforce, *Life*, III, 339.

tary. . . At 8 o'clock he took his place at the table, somewhat more silent at first than was his want. Soon, however, his spirits regained their elasticity and for two hours he poured forth such a flood of brilliant conversation and amusing anecdote we all felt we never passed such an amiable evening or had known such an inexhaustible man.[20]

Wilberforce kept a promise to himself to undertake little work outside the diocese. He continued a member of the Ritual Commission, whose attention was drawn in 1870 to the advisability of altering in some way the Athanasian Creed. Its condemnatory clauses, consigning nonbelievers forever to hell, seemed to many unnecessarily severe. The Commission found itself unable to agree upon the propriety of either alteration or substitution and passed the controversy to Convocation. The possibility that the Creed might be in some way purged from the Prayer Book aroused the High Church. Petitions poured in upon the bishops: High Churchmen opposed to change of any sort; Broad Churchmen in favor of some sort of alternative. Wilberforce was implored by Liddon to threaten resignation. "If your lordship would but say that so long as you are Bishop of the English Church the position as well as the substance of the creed *must* be left untouched,—we should be safe." [21] With little understanding of the depth of this opposition, Tait pressed on for reform. Wilberforce believed he had talked him out of it in the fall of 1871, but the following spring, making use of a Letter of Business which for the first time granted Convocation the power to legislate fully on its own behalf, the Archbishop proposed a discussion of the Creed. Negotiations between the Upper and Lower House dragged on for over a year. Wilberforce had always favored retention of the Creed, along with an explanatory note of some sort softening the literal meaning of its words. He opposed attempts to have it removed to the back of the Prayer Book, or turned into one of the Articles. He wanted it used "more as one would a hymn or chant, than as a dogmatic assertion, appealing to the intellect." [22] In the end, Convocation agreed to a statement satisfactory to the Broad Churchmen and not distasteful enough to drive High Churchmen any further in their despair over the latitudinarianism they feared.

Their fear was one Wilberforce continued to share. He had not welcomed Temple's appointment to the bishopric of Exeter—announced along with his elevation to Winchester. He wrote at first to congratulate the bishop-elect: "I cannot forbear saying that I do firmly believe we shall not only sympathise with one another but work often together." Soon his second thoughts began to echo with the battles of the early sixties. He begged Tait to try to obtain a recantation of the *Essays*. "Your position

20. From William H. Lucas, July 21, 1881, BD, I. C206.
21. October 19, 1871. BD, I. C199.
22. *Chronicles of Convocation,* May 3, 1872, p. 542.

as Archbishop as well as the line you took in Convocation alike seem to qualify you to obtain this great deliverance for our Church. Pray do it. Blessed are the peacemakers." [23] To Temple's complaint that he had welcomed the appointment with one hand only to smite it with the other, Wilberforce replied:

> The letter of mine to which you refer was written on my first hearing of your nomination. It was the natural outcome of my own feeling to F. Temple. When I wrote it I did not even recall to mind that your Essay was included in any Censure of Convocation.
> My feeling to *you* is now what it was when I wrote that letter.
> My earnest desire that you should, for the Church's sake and that of others, and, I might almost say especially, for the sake of Gladstone, separate yourself from what Convocation has condemned, seems to me not only difficult of reconciliation with this feeling towards you, but to be its necessary consequence.[24]

The explanation, whatever Temple made of it, was consistent with the habit that had led Wilberforce into his difficulties with Hampden: an impetuous first gesture, followed by sober reconsiderations. In January, after Temple's consecration, Wilberforce declared to Arthur Gordon that Gladstone had "produced a very threatening and unwholesome excitement" and deplored the fact that Temple had remained unwilling to give satisfaction to his critics.[25] Temple did withdraw his essay from publication the following month, on the ground that as bishop he must tread a more cautious line. But he declared himself satisfied with the effect his essay and the book had had in stirring debate and encouraging and resolving doubt.[26] He remained unwilling to apologize for what he had written because he felt no need to. Orthodoxy, not latitudinarianism, wanted the weapons of defensive warfare now. Though the orthodox remained strong in number, the tone of their retorts to sallies launched by Broad Church opponents suggested that their confidence, if not their strength, was waning.

Insecurity bred rigidity. And rigidity could not help but reduce the Church's general effectiveness. The so-called "Westminster scandal" of 1870 found the Church standing anxious guard against a comprehensiveness many believed it ought rather to encourage. A committee of Convocation, of which Wilberforce was permanent chairman, had undertaken the task of biblical revision. Wilberforce had favored the project from the start, arguing that "undoubted error and additions" might be expunged without in any way altering the "ring of familiarity" that so many cherished.[27] "I would not give up on translation for any-

23. October 26, 1869, LPL, Tait Correspondence, 87.29.
24. December 20, 1869, BD, I. C201.
25. January 16, 1870, in Ashwell and Wilberforce, *Life*, III, 339.
26. *Memoirs of Archbishop Temple*, ed. Sandford, I, 302–304.
27. *Chronicles of Convocation*, February 10, 1870, pp. 75–76.

thing," he wrote Gladstone. "Nor have I the faintest idea of the Bishop of St. David's vision of a fresh, once for all, version." [28]

Fresh version or not, Convocation argued that its committee must avail itself of the advice of scholarly experts. Accordingly, an invitation was issued to Dr. Vance Smith, among others, a Unitarian of considerable repute. His appointment did not remain unchallenged; there was some fear that his Socinianism might poison the deliberations. Dean Stanley nevertheless managed in the absence of a good many of his committee colleagues—Wilberforce among them—to secure him a place. Before the committee set to work Stanley invited all "who may be willing to come" to a service of Holy Communion in the Henry VII Chapel. Smith came and partook of the elements, and his doing so gave great offense to the orthodox—and especially the High Church orthodox. "This insult to our divine Lord eats to the very quick," Liddon lamented to Wilberforce. Stanley had replaced the divine mystery of the Eucharist with a service that amounted to nothing more than "a mere complement—to be offered to those with whom we differ on fundamental questions, when we wish to be on good terms with them." [29]

Wilberforce shared Liddon's distress. He hastened to explain that he had not been in the chair to disapprove of Smith's appointment. He called upon Convocation to condemn what he believed had been a serious affront to the Church. "I deeply lament that any one professing not only to hold but to be the teacher of a doctrine so dishonouring to our Lord and Saviour as the denial of His Godhead joined in that act of Holy Communion of our Church with the Bishops of that Church." [30] In August Smith declared to Tait that he did not deny the Godhead of Christ, but this did little to assuage the offended Churchmen. Tait tried to mediate, but, as he himself admitted to Carter of Clewer, he could not understand how Smith, who had—Socinian or not—confessed himself unable to recite the Nicene Creed, could "join in a solemn service of which that Creed and its doctrines form from the beginning to the end so prominent a part." [31] The controversy simmered on through the fall and winter. When Convocation assembled in February 1871, Wilberforce put forward a resolution that he hoped would remove it from the fire, by removing Smith from the committee. The motion passed the Upper House by a vote of 10 to 4, not before Connop Thirlwall, chairman of the subcommittee to revise the Old Testament, had spoken in defense of Smith and of scholarly latitudinarianism. No one had disputed Smith's

28. February 22, 1870, BD, II. K.
29. July 11, 1870, and July 6, 1870, BD, I. C201.
30. *Chronicles of Convocation*, July 5, 1870, p. 437. The bishops of Ely and Salisbury had partaken of the Communion with Smith.
31. August 11, 1870, Davidson and Benham, *Tait*, II, 70.

reputation as a scholar, Thirlwall declared. Why, then, deny him a place on this committee, whose task was one of scholarship.

"My answer," Wilberforce replied, "is, that it is not on that ground that my resolution rests. It rests on this . . . that this man's presence in the company now is the presence of one who has been permitted to join in that service in Westminster Abbey, and that, therefore, for the honour of the truth itself, his removal from the company is necessary." [32] Thirlwall considered this explanation unsatisfactory enough to warrant his resignation from the committee. Nor did the clergymen in the Lower House feel obliged to assume the bishops' staunch, defensive stand. Their response, while proclaiming "deep regret at the offence" caused by Smith's participation in the service, ended with the declaration, bland as it was confident, that "after this expression of the feeling of the House, the House is persuaded there will be no repetition of such cause of offence." [33]

Though chairman of the revision committee, Wilberforce devoted little time to its work. He was no scholar, and shared little of the scholars' enthusiasm for their task. Bishop Ellicott, chairman of the New Testament subcommittee, reported to his "chief," the Archbishop: "My only care now is to keep [Winchester] as much out of the chair as can cleverly be done. He has not criticism enough for it, and he gave mortal offence to some during his short tenure of the chair. I received private notice that resignations would be sent in if I did not continue some adjustment." [34] Wilberforce may have sensed this displeasure, which Ellicott may have exaggerated. He left the work to others in order to devote his energy to Winchester.

He could no longer spend that energy as recklessly as in times past. Winchester taxed him as Oxford never had. It pleased him that he could have two of his sons nearby to help him—Ernest as his domestic chaplain and Basil as rector of St. Mary's, Southampton. They worried that enemies would call their father to task for handing them preferment; he refused to deny himself the pleasure they could bring to him.[35] Their

32. *Chronicles of Convocation,* February 14–15, 1871, pp. 4, 89.

33. *Ibid,* February 17, 1871, p. 276.

34. August 14, 1870, LPL, Tait Correspondence, 88.146. When the committee was being formed, Ellicott wrote Wilberforce: "I think I must ask you to give me a position of authority, so as better to negotiate, direct, etc., in all details. If you don't mind then, I will ask you to be general chairman, *i.e.* of the whole concern and its parts, and I will ask you to constitute me company chairman" (May 31, 1870, BD, I. C201).

35. When Wilberforce moved from Oxford to Winchester he proposed to bring Ernest along as his domestic chaplain, and put Basil in Ernest's place as rector of Middleton Stoney, near Bicester. Basil wrote Liddon for advice. "I have positively refused Middleton or any other for which it might be exchanged as it seems to me like a job only short of simoniacal. I should be in a false position every way, and I believe it would be injurious to my father" (October 23, 1869, Liddon House papers). He eventually took the post at Southampton from his father in 1871.

readiness to serve the Church had bound him to them. "Our dear Basil still goes on getting far more sensibly minded to do his life's work for God," Wilberforce reported to the more sober-sided Reginald in 1865. "I Cannot tell you the joy it is to me: and it brings him so much closer to me." [36] Tragedy brought him closer still to Ernest, whose young wife died of consumption in 1870. "Your dear love when you told me that you love me quite overset me," Wilberforce wrote on the second anniversary of her death. "I prize your affection, dear one, so very highly, and I fear sometimes I am too demonstrative for your taste: but it is very hard when you love as I love you not to show it." [37] Though he needed no reminding, the pain he had suffered when Emily died flooded back upon him.

For the first time in many years Wilberforce began to be plagued by serious illness. In 1870 he suffered two heart attacks, the second, in November, severe enough to make him believe he was dying. He had spent the summer attending to episcopal business in the Channel Islands, had followed that visit with a strenuous journey through France, and had returned in the fall to keep another round of diocesan appointments. By November he had exhausted himself; only Reginald's timely administration of a liberal dose of sal volatile saved his life when he was seized by violent spasms in the night at Uppark, near Lavington. Yet within the month he was up and off again:

December 1.—(*Peper Harrow*) Voice so gone that I got Mr. Wilson at last moment to preach. Could scarcely speak in chair at the school. Back, and drove around Park. Wrote. Very pleasant evening.

December 2.—Off early for Southsea. Bishop of Guiana came to help me most kindly; but I struggled through, letting him confirm the boys. Then to Elson, and with difficulty preached. Then to Sir A. Clifford's.

December 4.—At Confirmation address. With Archdeacon Utterton to St. Anne's, Wandsworth. The Archdeacon preached most kindly for me—my voice still gone. On to Surbiton. Confirmed—a very nice Confirmation all round.

December 5.—Seeing people, writing, etc., till six. Then to Fulham, where [the Bishops of] Rochester, Lichfield, and Oxford. Mrs. Jackson did not appear, but the young ladies numerous, and very kindly and pleasant. Cheerful evening.[38]

The following April came a third attack. This time Ernest nursed him through the night. The next day he persuaded Ellicott to take a confirmation for him at Southwark while he consulted a physician, who told him that his brain was overworked. And so, the next day, off to Prince's Risborough, and after that to Dorking to another confirmation.[39] He kept to the pace for two more years. By April 1873 he admitted to Ernest:

36. July 16, 1865, Chichester, 30.   37. October 8, 1872, BD, I. C205.
38. Ashwell and Wilberforce, *Life,* III, 369–370.   39. *Ibid.,* III, 378–379.

"I am well, but I am very much tired, and should like to go to sleep for a week or a fortnight." [40] In July, Ernest, whose own health had failed since his wife's death, departed on a vacation to Lapland. Sir Robert Phillimore, who lunched with Wilberforce afterward, found his spirits low. "He was by himself in the House [Winchester House, in London], and had lost for the time the society which he valued so much of his children and grandchildren." [41] He arranged to travel with Lord Granville to Holmbury the following day for a visit and then on to Lavington and a short stay with Reginald and his family. The two men took the railway to Leatherhead, where they mounted horses to ride the rest of the way. Granville, ahead of the bishop, heard a thump, "and turning round I saw him lying motionless." The groom who accompanied them reported that Wilberforce's horse had stumbled. Whether, as the bishop fell, he suffered some sort of heart seizure, the coroner's jury did not bother to determine. He lay straight out, his arms at his side. "The position," Granville wrote Reginald, "was absolutely monumental.

I took off the Bishop's boots, and his neckhandkerchief. I remember my sense of despair at not knowing whether there was anything I could do which could be of use. For a long time I could feel no pulse; at last I could feel the beating distinctly. I mentioned this to an intelligent bailiff who came with labourers. He said he could see no sign of life. I was afterwards told by the doctor that it was my own pulsations, and not that of what, alas! was a corpse, which I had felt.[42]

The body traveled by slow stages from Abinger to Lavington. The funeral, attended by dignitaries of Church and State transported from London by special train, took place on St. James's Day, July 25. His family, true to his own wish, refused the offer of Westminster Abbey and Winchester Cathedral. He was buried alongside Emily, Herbert, Caroline Manning, and Mrs. Sargent in the Lavington churchyard.

"Alas, what can we say," Tait asked himself. "The particulars are known to all: in a moment that light presence gone. The papers have been full of little or nothing else for the whole week, and the extracts shew what the public feeling is." [43] The papers called him an ecclesiastical statesman; the men and women who had known him mourned a humane and sympathetic friend. He had for many years filled a space in the Victorian world. After his death men looked into that space, and tried

40. Easter Day, 1873, BD, I. C205.
41. To Reginald Wilberforce, n.d., in Ashwell and Wilberforce, *Life,* III, 423.
42. *Ibid.,* III, 424, September 25, 1882. Wilberforce had escaped serious injury when pitched from a horse in June 1864 in London.
43. July 27, 1873, LPL, Tait Correspondence, 50.71ff.

to recall the size and shape of the personality that had stood there. All agreed that he had been a complicated and many-sided man. Canon Ashwell, as he began his biography, confessed to the difficulty of setting down a portrait of someone whose very nature was variety, and "answered to every touch as instantaneously as the Aeolian harp answers to each breath of air." [44] Some called the changing tunes a sign of moral fickleness belying lack of any real conviction. They would have seen in a sketch Wilberforce once drew of Vernon Harcourt a likeness to the artist himself. "There was a charming kindness and love about him," he had written Louisa Noel,

and simplicity and absence of selfishness. The *want* was depth—in every way; in intellect, in moral purpose, in sense of responsibility, in concentration of affection. His face quite expressed it; broad, large, yet fine features, nothing gross or low or Rubens-like, but broad and unconcentrated, a man of unbroken prosperity, whom nothing deeply wounded, from whom no crushing would bring out perfume . . . a man to live with, not to die with, for sunshine, not for clouds and storm and dark, dark night; yet quite very loveable.[45]

Such, perhaps, was the Wilberforce of the 1830's, not yet crushed by the deaths of Emily and Herbert, still lovingly close to his brother Robert, untouched by Henry Pye's treachery that was to carry his daughter Ella away to harlot Rome. But those events had scarred Wilberforce, whose own face, unformed and immature as a young man, in later photographs bore the marks of the tragedies he had suffered, and appeared the opposite of "broad and unconcentrated." Even in those earlier years he expressed in his interests and pursuits a sensitivity that carried him contrary to the way the world expected him to move. He wrote poetry, revealing a readiness to hymn—in romantic fashion—the mystery of the universe:

> What is the end to which we all draw near?
> What does the Soul? to live or *be*
> Which were the best? And why has He,
> The Lord of all, who only can
> Read in His closed book his secret will,
> In fatal union wedded still
> The Chant of Nature and the cry of Man.[46]

---

44. Ashwell and Wilberforce, *Life*, I, xiv.   45. *Ibid.*, I, 418, November 13, 1847.
46. Poetry notebook, BD, I. C203. Another poem, written in October 1840, borders on the Gothic. Entitled "Count Rudolph's Bridal," it recounts the tale of that nobleman's marriage to "fair Alice," and of their perilous return to Rudolph's castle, pursued by a pack of werewolves.

> . . . But not at Rudolph's side in vain
> An idle carbine hung.
> One crack, and lifeless on the plain
> His length the monster flung. . .
> But all night long, that castle round

Wilberforce enjoyed nature as God's uncorrupted handiwork. The sea remained always for him a symbol of God's vastness and his mysterious ways; the land—"The fruitful valleys which laugh and sing"—manifested his jubilation.[47] He was never happier than when at Lavington. He ranged the Sussex hills, hunting specimens for his bird collection. With his guests he would climb to the top of the down that overhung his house and all the neighboring countryside, then climb again to the top of a forty-foot wooden tower, from which they might see as far as Beachy Head, Spithead, and the Isle of Wight. Upon their descent, they walked farther on to a mound of stones. Wilberforce would read the appropriate selection from *The Christian Year*, then produce a piece of paper, upon which all the guests inscribed their names and the date. From underneath the stones he drew out a bottle, put in the paper and placed it again where it had lodged since the previous expedition. Wilberforce delighted in the ritual life that Lavington allowed him to lead. There he was squire, not bishop, and he played the role with gusto. At a county fair in 1862, the dinner over and the toasts drunk, Wilberforce went out to enjoy himself among his tenants. "The bishop was the life and soul of the proceedings," The Sussex *Standard*, a bit breathless, reported after the event.

It was most interesting to observe how he entered into all the fun, throwing sacks before blind-folded boys to throw them down, scoring himself at the women's cricket, looking in at the merry dance, and having a word for each poor person and child on the ground. He was well described as 'our own bishop, living among his own people,' and the only regret was that his many duties enabled him to spend so little time on his Sussex property.[48]

Lavington, if it meant happiness, meant also Emily's churchyard grave. Though it did not blight his times there, it brought the fact of her death back upon him. "I wonder whether coming *home* is ever to you the overwhelming thing it has all my life been to me," he wrote to Butler after Herbert's death. "The meeting the many little splashes of spray gathered by accumulation into one great dash of cold water."[49] The sting of loneliness scourged Wilberforce until he died. At one time he took to studying Mesmerism in the hope that it might let him speak again to Emily. But he was soon disillusioned, and came to believe that it was

---

Until the break of day,
The watchman heard the fearful sound
Of the were-wolf's angry bay.

47. From an introduction written to an anonymously published volume, *Voices of the Sea in Words of Holy Scripture and of Standard English Literature* (by the widow of a naval officer), London, 1866, pp. iv, v.

48. September 25, 1862. Clipping in BD, I. C208.

49. September 13, 1856, BD, I. C205.

only "the work of the Evil Spirit . . . so far forth as all frauds are, and this was a rather clumsy one."[50] He was left lonely and with a longing for affection that no one but Emily could have given him—"a longing for satisfied affection, which is not satisfied. O Lord, let it bind me to Thee in whom is all my spirit longs for." June 11, 1871—the forty-third anniversary of his wedding day: "My great Fast Feast. No one to sympathise with me—till I shivered. None of these care; only I whispered it the last thing to A [Reginald's wife] and she seemed to sympathise."[51]

The loneliness drove Wilberforce out into society, where he could enjoy himself talking to friends and meeting famous acquaintances. There was about him, as Tait remarked to Reginald, "a social and irresistibly fascinating side"[52] which made a place for him whenever he wanted to go about in town or country. In London there was almost always someone new to meet and to appraise. "Emerson is very little Yankee, tall, thin, with no atrabilious look, rather silent." "Then to Stafford House with Lord Harrowby, where all the world assembled in 'Aunt Harriet's Cabin' to see Mrs. Beecher Stowe. She spoke to me with interest. 'There was a time when your father's work seemed as hard as ours does now. Yet he succeeded.' "[53] With those he knew better, he might occasionally try to mix more serious talk with social chatter, much as his father and his friends at Clapham had done.

Up early and to Church, then letters. Breakfast at Mahon's—G. Grey, Macaulay, Duke of Argyle, Lady Craven, Van de Weyer. Macaulay in high spirits and great force. Got on rather new topics. Dutch words, writings, and annals. Courier and his merits, etc. Van de Weyer told about the poor Frenchman after the Revolution. 'Where do you dwell?' 'Rue St.____.' 'Il n'y a pas de Saint.' 'Rue de____.' 'Il n'y a pas de De.' 'Rue No. 6.' Walked home with Macaulay, trying to get him more on religion—'God' and causality.[54]

Wilberforce could put anyone at his ease. John Bright, when first he met the bishop, found him "very clever, and pleasant, and disposed to be civil to me. What a distance separates his position and perhaps his views from mine." [55] The distance did not prove so great as to prevent his being asked to Lavington.

Wilberforce had a sense of humor that could disarm the severest critic. J. B. Mozley, who went to Cuddesdon prepared to scoff reported to his sister Ann: "There was less artificialness about him than I expected. A

50. To the Reverend C. Hewett, August 22, 1853, Letter Book, BD, d.210. 174.
51. Diary, May 21, 1867; June 11, 1871, in Ashwell and Wilberforce, *Life,* III, 223, 379.
52. June 20, 1881, Davidson and Benham, *Tait,* II, 499.
53. To Louisa Noel, March, 1848, BD, II.F; Diary, May 7, 1853, in Ashwell and Wilberforce, *Life,* II, 187.
54. Diary, May 20, 1854, in Ashwell and Wilberforce, *Life,* II, 244.
55. February 8, 1854, *The Diaries of John Bright,* ed. R. A. J. Walling (London, 1930), p. 159.

love of the humourous is a great leveller, and he can no more resist telling a good story, even though it a little compromises his dignity, than a
dog can pass a tit-bone." [56] We shall have to take Mozley and the rest at
their word. Most of the existing fragments of the Wilberforce wit only
illustrate the gulf that divides that portion of the Victorian frame of mind
from our own. Much of the humor was ecclesiastical, although not always the sort that one would expect to emanate from rectory drawing
rooms.

What is the difference between Westminster Abbey and Spurgeon's tabernacle?
In the former the pulpit is in the nave, in the latter the knave is in the pulpit.

> The Pope is infallible so they say
> When he speaks or teaches ex Cathedra.
> Now Cathedra means as we all are aware
> The Papal seat or stool or chair,
> Which all goes to show that the force of the rule
> Comes not from the man but flows from his stool.

From Lord Lyttelton, passed by Wilberforce to Charles Anderson:

Two old ladies enquire about a house in Wales and ask if there is a good W.C. The
much perplexed lodging letting lady asks her husband what is W.C. Much ponder-
ing, after which he suggests a weather cock. This is disallowed. She asks an agent
who says, a wine cellar, to be sure. No, for the old ladies mention that they drink
beer. She then asks a local oracle, a Wesleyan minister, who says—'clearly a
a Wesleyan Chapel.' She writes to the old ladies 'a very good one only a mile off
with seats for 400 people.' [57]

Wilberforce was better, as are a great many people, when he poked fun
at himself. He recorded the experience of a channel crossing in doggerel
in 1851.

> No word he spoke, no foot he moved,
> And when his sides the waitress shoved,
> With 'l'autre coté, Monsieur, quick,
> I see you are going to be sick,'
> He sent the officious friend away
> With 'allez vous en, straight, I say.'
> What others did I hardly know.
> You'd better ask the fish below.[58]

Not infrequently the wit would be at someone else's expense. Wilberforce never completely outgrew the undergraduate debater's delight in a
"sharp" thrust or a "bright" sally. The habit had brought him to grief
in his encounter with Huxley, as it did on more than one occasion in the
House of Lords. Albert's secretary, Anson, warned the new bishop in

56. December 3, 1847, J. B. Mozley, *Letters*, p. 188.
57. Notebook, BD, I. C204; to Charles Anderson. November 15, 1872, BD, I. C192.
58. Notebook, BD, I. C186.

1846: "I think the House will be very much afraid of you and that Peers clerical and lay will think twice before they venture to attack you. If I had your talent and your facility for sending home a *personal* shaft, I could not resist taking advantage of it, but I think it is a little dangerous." [59] Impulse led him on to run the danger more than once, though he was usually repaid in kind. Brougham forced an apology from him after he had accused Russell of introducing a Jewish Disabilities Bill because of a debt to the Rothschilds.[60] In the debate on the Canadian Reserves in 1853 he referred to Burke's declaration that it was wrong to deprive Americans of their rights by force or chicanery, and added that Burke "seemed almost to have foreseen" what was occurring at that moment in the House. Derby objected, and Wilberforce retreated with a disclaimer that his remarks had been uttered with a smile that meant they were not to be taken personally. Derby retorted with the line "A man may smile and smile and be a villain." [61] In his most celebrated exchange in the Lords, Wilberforce chose to abandon "personal shafts" for a high line, less characteristic but echoing the tone generally expected of the Bench. In 1864 Lord Westbury took exception to Convocation's judgment upon *Essays and Reviews*. Aware that Wilberforce had been its author, he remarked that the judgment "is simply a series of well-lubricated terms— a sentence so oily and saponaceous that no one could grasp it—like an eel it slips through your fingers and is simply nothing." "I have good ground," Wilberforce replied,

to complain of the tone of the noble and learned lord on the woolsack. If a man has no respect for himself, he ought at all events to respect the tribunal before which he speaks, and when the highest representative of the law of England in your Lordships' Court, upon a matter involving the liberties of the subject and the religion of the realm and all those high truths concerning which this discussion is, can think it fitting to descend to a ribaldry in which he knows that he can safely indulge, because those to whom he addresses it will have too much respect for their character to answer him in like sort, I say that this House has ground to complain of having its high character unnecessarily injured in the sight of the people of this land by one occupying so high a position within it.[62]

Though he was often called a devious man, there was a kind of impetuous directness in many of Wilberforce's remarks about people that

59. June 15, 1846, BD, I. C193.
60. *Hansard,* 3rd ser., XCVIII (May 25, 1848), 1376, 1405.
61. *Ibid.,* CXXVI (April 25, 1853), pp. 448–449. J. B. Mozley's comment on the episode: "[Derby] has no right to talk of smiling and being a villain, for his face wrinkles into countless smiles at a moment's notice out of the most sour basis. I saw his reception of the Bishop of Oxford [following Derby's installation as Chancellor of the University]. At the levee a general smile went the round of the crowd, and only one quotation was in all memories" (Mozley, *Letters,* p. 221).
62. *Hansard,* 3rd ser., CLXXVI (July 15, 1864), 1563.

must have surprised and disarmed his companions. When Thomson of York told Wilberforce that whenever his wife was "in an interesting condition" preferment came his way, and that she was pregnant once again, Wilberforce retorted: "Well, your Grace, there are only two pieces of preferment before you: Canterbury and heaven, but I must say I don't think you are fit for either." [63] Just before Tait's enthronement as Archbishop, Dean Stanley complained to a clutch of attendant dignitaries that he could not see the proceedings where he stood. Wilberforce suggested that he go sit on the throne first and then let the Archbishop sit upon him. "It's what you want, and what he will have to do, before long. You may depend upon it." James Mackarness, Wilberforce's successor at Oxford, who recounted the story in the *Spectator,* added that "the sally was not taken quite so genially as it was given." [64] Gladstone soon afterward reminded Wilberforce that people did not take kindly to this sort of personal banter. In his letter offering the appointment to Winchester he apologized for mentioning "that you must at one or more times have made observations on persons, perhaps playfully, which have been taken as if they indicated a habit of too full censures or remarks. You will know whether this suggestion can be turned to any account." [65] Wilberforce knew that it could and should be. "How I hate stirring up strife," he lamented once after an angry exchange at the Ecclesiastical Commission. "I could lay me down and let all walk over me rather: so gladly." [66]

Gladstone was not the first to point out what Wilberforce already knew well enough. But critics often seemed to want him to be the sort of pompous man he could never be, to live up to some sort of dry-as-dust beau ideal, denying others the undoubted pleasure of his not inconsiderable good humor. To one such, the clergyman Thomas Fosbery, he replied, perplexed:

I do not at present see what change I could well make. You have seen me at my breakfasts, that I am in London Society. My theory has been to show as much *innocent* hilarity as came naturally to me, to watch against personalities—unkind judgments, etc., but saving these and of course any admission of a wrong principle or word, to endeavour to shew that religion made a man happy and not unhappy. . . It *has* often caused me uneasiness as to the path of duty. But I see no indeterminate line between the ascetic renunciation of society and my own.[67]

Even Charles Anderson worried about his friend, and feared that he might be leading him astray: "I know you feel very much with me or rather are constituted in some degree like me who feel that if one had not a keen

63. ? to Reginald Wilberforce, July 15, 1881, BD, I. C206.
64. *Spectator,* August 27, 1881, pp. 1104–1105.
65. September 12, 1869, BD, II. K.
66. Diary, January 26, 1854, in Ashwell and Wilberforce, *Life,* II, 229.
67. September 4, 1854, BD, I. C193.

perception of the ludicrous one must have died long before this, and I know I often make you joke when I had better have let it alone." [68]

That keen perception of the ludicrous was part of Wilberforce's most precious possession—his keen perception of humanity itself. Though he could laugh at human frailty, he could sympathize at the same moment, as, for example, in a report to Louisa Noel, of Sir Robert Peel.

He was reading the 'Quarterly' [in the train from Oxford to London], and soon settled into Croker's bitter attack upon him, peeping into its uncut leaves with intense interest, and yet not liking to show that interest by cutting; and so, when Madame Bunsen, who saw nothing of what was going on, offered a paper-cutter, courteously declining it and lapsing into an article on Pantagruelism, to fall again into the old article and peep into the uncut leaves as soon as all was quiet.[69]

"The force of conscious sympathy," one eulogist called it at the time of his death.[70] It was a force that drew a sympathy from others, and allowed him, as so many remarked, to become "all things to all men." Liddon, in a sermon on his life and works, noted the ease with which

he could pass from scene to scene, from man to man, the most dissimilar, as though, so far from experiencing any strain upon his sympathies, he found positive relief in the sharpest ethical contrasts; and he made each one feel that his sympathy was perfect, so perfect as to seem for the time to preclude the possibility of sympathy in any opposite direction.

This had made men call him "soapy." "Was he not," his enemies asked, "though he sat in the chair of the Apostles, only after all a consummate actor, who could, in matters of practice, assume any character at will?" The question, Liddon insisted, overlooked "the strong, simple motive which in such a man underlies the varieties of the outward life"—the determination "to bring, at whatever cost, some souls for pardon and peace to the feet of the Crucified."

Dean Wellesley once wrote the Queen that Wilberforce's virtue as an ecclesiastical politician was a lack of moral strength "which prevents him from being really dangerous in the Church." [71] Evidence had led him to the wrong conclusion. What Wilberforce lacked was what he once had criticized Blomfield of London for lacking, the foresight that breeds calmness. "It is this deliberate prescience which enables great men in any unlooked-for extremity to see in the startling suddenness of action what it is really to apply their principles, and so not only to cleave to them with the tenacity of an honest intention, but to give them practical effect in action." [72] Wilberforce could cleave to principle; he had less success

68. March 31, 1856, BD, I. C190.
69. July 5, 1847, Ashwell and Wilberforce, *Life,* I, 398–399.
70. H. P. Liddon, *Samuel Wilberforce* (London, 1873), pp. 19, 22, 24.
71. Royal Archives, D. 1. 89, September, 1868. Quoted in Blake, *Disraeli,* p. 510.
72. "Bishops of the Church of England." *Quarterly Review,* 114: 565–566 (1863).

when trying to put principle into action. His mind, as in the case of the Hampden controversy, had been unwilling to penetrate to the base of the difficult question he had set himself to solve. Then, as at many other times, he substituted activity for thought. He could understand what it was to be up and doing, and he could see what doing had wrought within his diocese. Yet doing—plunging ahead with plans and projects—made it even harder for him to think a problem through. Work dimmed his foresight and in this way encouraged the self-deception that was always a habit with him. He had a knowledge but not an understanding of his own shortcomings. The man's virtues and his faults stand forth in a letter Stanley wrote his sister shortly after Wilberforce had come as a bishop to Oxford.

I was then shown into the Bishop's study, where he was standing at a high desk writing, from whence he immediately descended and after expressing his pleasure at seeing me, began with incredible activity at once to mend pens, and to leap from one subject to another without dwelling for two minutes on any...

Stanley had come hoping to speak about the Tractarians at Oxford, but felt he was being rushed.

Again I was struck by the contrast between his want of power in handling theoretical and his very great power in handling practical subjects; as for the mending of the pens, it was one of the most marvellous feats of manual agility I ever witnessed. If every interview is similarly employed, hundreds upon hundreds must be the result; and one part of the dexterity of it was that it either was, or seemed, intended to relieve the interview from a too great appearance of tedium or stuffiness.[73]

When Robert Wilberforce left the Church of England for Rome, Gladstone wrote Samuel that it might well be his task "to show in the service of the Church ecclesiastically how bricks can be made without straw, how the utmost possible results, whether sufficient or not, may be realized in the most embarrassed position and out of the most hopeless materials." [74] Mark Pattison, in an essay on "Learning and the Church of England," censured Wilberforce for trying to accomplish the very task that Gladstone had set him. He admired the awakening of "zeal and professional energy" that the "Bishop of Oxford's party" had roused. But that zeal would be effective only if "accompanied by a corresponding awakening of the conscience," and he could see little evidence that the awakening had occurred. Public opinion had encouraged activity not thought, while the theological disputes of the 1840's had driven intelligent clergymen either to Romanism or Germanism, leaving "only a residuum of practical men—the working clergy."

73. February 9, 1846, Stanley, *Letters and Verses*, pp. 99–100.
74. September 4, 1854, BD, II. K.

The English Cathedral as it now stands, reformed in the spirit of the age, re-formed by the Church herself as she now understands her mission, has been transferred from the learned class to the working clergy. A modern bishop is a mere vicar-general, having a peculiar department of official business to transact. Up to the moment of his consecration he was a working-clergyman. If any crisis of opinion arises, he is sure to reflect the prejudices of the majority.[75]

Wilberforce defended a "working clergy" as the one instrument capable of effecting genuine religious change in England. "If the clergy of other times and lands may sometimes reproach us with being a body little addicted to deep and abstract thought," he wrote in his Charge of 1848, "we have this great advantage for men of action, that ours is a practical training. With such advantages we ought to have a practical insight into the social evils of our day and be the leaders in their redress." [76] As if with his eye on that same passage, Pattison wrote that a church must above all "grapple intellectually with the actual facts of our social life," and that the Church of England was not attempting to do so. The clergyman wished "to conquer, but not to reform or renew the social life of the regions" he invaded. "Trained not to employ his reason in theology, [he] never thinks of employing it in any other direction." [77] The history of the Church of England in the nineteenth century suggests that Pattison may have been right. Wilberforce and, by extension, the whole Church of England, found it difficult to grapple with the facts of Victorian society. They knew the industrial city and the problems that festered there; they knew of the fear and torment doubt engendered. They worked hard at these new problems. But their work followed the parochial patterns and "practical training" of times past, and their vision was in that sense a narrow one. The present saw their hard work helping the Church hold its own. But the present called as well for an understanding of what the future promised, and that understanding, which admittedly comes to very few, came neither to the Church nor to Samuel Wilberforce.

75. Mark Pattison, *Essays,* 2 vols. (London, 1908), II, 274, 295, 299–300.
76. *Charge,* 1848, p. 49.   77. Pattison, *Essays,* II, 292.

Appendix   Index

Samuel Wilberforce and the Will of Mary Sargent

(Unless otherwise noted, the following evidence is drawn from George Dudley Ryder's statement—forty-three pages long—and from a shorter memorandum which accompanies it, now both in the possession of Sir George Clutton.)

Ryder's account begins with a statement of affairs as they stood at the death in 1836 of Henry Sargent, Mrs. Sargent's sole surviving son. The Lavington estate reverted then to her four daughters: Emily Wilberforce, Mary Wilberforce, Caroline Manning, and Sophia Ryder. Samuel objected to a scheme that would mean the breaking up of the estate.[1] Instead, he proposed that it be made over to his wife Emily, the eldest daughter. According to Ryder, to compensate the other daughters, the remainder of Mrs. Sargent's own fortune was to be divided between them upon her death, once marriage settlements of £5000 had been paid to all four. The Lavington estate was already mortgaged for £15,000, £5200 of which had come from Mrs. Sargent. As part of the new agreement—again according to Ryder—Mrs. Sargent willed Samuel and Emily a further £5200 for use in paying off this encumbrance. This provision was made revocable, however, on the ground that should the Lavington debt have been paid by the time of Mrs. Sargent's death, the £5200 might then go, along with the rest of her own estate, to the three younger daughters. The settlement, to which Ryder claimed all parties agreed, was to Samuel and Emily's obvious advantage. The others acquiesced because they did not want to see Lavington pass from the family and because they believed Mrs. Sargent had a sizeable fortune to leave them.

Following the death of two of the four daughters, Caroline Manning and Emily Wilberforce, Mrs. Sargent, in 1842, made a new will. Samuel was now master of Lavington. Mrs. Sargent left him an additional £2000 of her own money, a gift to her from her cousin, Mrs. Mary Carey. The remainder of her estate she divided between her two surviving daughters, Mary Wilberforce and Sophia Ryder. A memorandum added two

---

1. "Heard, from Mrs. Sargent, Forster's [the lawyer?] first proposal of making it [the estate] over to four daughters. I objected" (Diary, June 27, 1836, BD, I. C186). June 30: "Heard from Mrs. Sargent that she disliked Forster too." July 9: "Heard from Mrs. Sargent. Difficult. Property less than expected. I rather vexed about it."

months later stated specifically that the £2000 for Samuel was to come only from Mrs. Carey's money, invested in Greek bonds and a ship, *Minerva*. "Should these two sources fail in producing £2000 it cannot be made up from any other source." [2]

Somehow, during the 1840's, Wilberforce and Mrs. Sargent, who was now living with him, together paid off the £15,000 debt on the estate. Ryder says that Wilberforce paid £10,000 "of his own"—though where he found it is difficult to say—and that Mrs. Sargent paid the remaining £5000, using Samuel's marriage portion to do so. The only available evidence suggests that Mrs. Sargent paid more than that: Wilberforce sought Anderson's help in 1841 in selling some of her Nottinghamshire property—"from £5000 to £15,000 worth." [3] Affairs remained unchanged until 1853, when Mrs. Carey died. According to Ryder's description of the terms of 1836, her money, had it not already been willed to Samuel, should have formed part of that fund to be divided between Mary and Sophia. By 1853, however, the Henry Wilberforces and the Ryders had converted to Roman Catholicism. Mrs. Carey, before her death, specified that her money must not pass to Roman Catholics; she apparently did not realize that Mrs. Sargent had already made it over to Samuel. [4] During the 1850's, Mrs. Sargent lent money to Henry Wilberforce and to Ryder, despite their conversions and despite the fact that since Sophia's death in 1850, Ryder could be said to have no direct claim upon her assistance. For Henry she sold off enough property of her own to allow him to buy an estate in Ireland. He took the money as a share of his inheritance and paid her interest on the share during her lifetime.

Mrs. Sargent died in 1861, and to the surprise of Henry and of Ryder, died insolvent. Henry inherited some spoons, and Ryder a mirror—for which he was asked to pay. Their suspicions were aroused when they learned that Wilberforce had failed to have the will probated. Ryder wrote to ask the reason and received from Samuel the explanation that Mrs. Sargent's insolvency meant that probation would be a needless expense. He added that the "real difficulty" involved that memorandum concerning the Greek bonds and the ship *Minerva*. "On the second page of her will she originally wrote the source of the fund from which she wished the legacy to be paid to me." That legacy she had revoked by a codicil in 1858, giving the £2000 to Samuel's children, leaving him instead her house in Wilton Place. When the legacy was revoked, Wilberforce wrote, she had desired to have the memorandum destroyed, since

2. The will and memorandum are in Chichester, 167.
3. April 14, 1841, BD, I. C191.
4. Ryder maintained that Henry had asked Samuel about the money and that his answer "was that he had 'considered the matter over on his knees before God and decided on keeping it'!"

she did not want the children to depend solely on the Greek bonds and the ship for their money. "We not knowing it was of any moment," Wilberforce continued, "either by her hand or mine it was torn off. Now we have the best authority for saying that this would in all probability lead to an expense in proving the will which cannot be calculated—and as no one is injured, the Government not defrauded, and no power created by the deed practically needed, I am strongly advised to keep it quietly in the dresser. I earnestly trust that this explanation will fully satisfy you."

It did not have that effect. Ryder demanded a copy of the will and the memorandum. Armed with them, he built a case against his brother-in-law that, he believed, did not come to court only because he was a Roman Catholic and Wilberforce an English bishop.[5] His document makes no direct charge. The implication is that Wilberforce bilked Mrs. Sargent of her money and that, specifically, he tore off the memorandum, thereby insuring for his children the £2000, a sum rightfully belonging to Mary and to Ryder under the terms of the 1836 agreement. "The Bishop would of course . . . desire that it should be as difficult as possible for us to say, that out of £3000 which he had imported into the family compact [i.e. which was a part of Mrs. Sargent's legacy to her daughters under the terms of the 1836 compact] as part compensation to us for the gift of that Lavington mortgage to his wife which had originally been ours [the £5200], he got two-thirds bequeathed to him by a secret will [the will of 1842], made when Mrs. Sargent lived in his house."

What is to be made of all this? Certainly that Ryder bitterly resented Wilberforce's intimacy with Mrs. Sargent; and that he resented as well the way in which he—and his wife, while she lived—had been treated by Samuel since their conversion. Ryder constructed his case from more than personal pique. He believed Wilberforce had acted illegally in diverting money to himself that was not rightfully his. Mrs. Sargent's 1842 will, leaving a further £2000 to Samuel, did not accord with Ryder's version of the 1836 compact. But Mrs. Sargent was by now living with Samuel. She knew the scale of his expenses and what it cost to maintain Lavington. Her memorandum made it clear that the legacy must come from Mrs. Carey's gift, not from her own capital; in this way, perhaps, she excused her infidelity to the former agreement. The codicil of 1858 passed the £2000 legacy directly to Samuel's children. Again, it is not hard to imagine Mrs. Sargent, who had lived with the children for over fifteen years, wanting to leave them something, and ready to remove her 1842 conditions from the bequest. Either she or Samuel may have

5. The lawyers—John Davenport for Wilberforce, and a Mr. Woodrooffe for Henry and Ryder—exchanged letters. Arbitration was proposed, but there is no evidence of its having been undertaken.

torn off the memorandum, a careless and foolish thing to do. Wilberforce, who upon occasion could be both careless and foolish, was nevertheless not accustomed to act with the furtiveness Ryder's insinuation suggests. If the codicil once more operated contrary to the 1836 agreement, Mrs. Sargent could argue that the intervening deaths and conversions had turned not only the agreement but her whole private world upside down. Nor had she ignored her other sons-in-law. Her loans to them were generous, and she expected that they would inherit a part of her estate at her death.

A more puzzling question remains: how did she come to die insolvent? There is evidence that she sold off a great deal of her property to help Samuel. In 1860 he wrote Anderson of a farm, belonging to Mrs. Sargent, that he wished to sell. "It must certainly be sold at her death because it goes to Henry [really Mary] and George Ryder and they would not like to hold it in common. And if much more income could be got through the sale, it is a great pity that Mrs. Sargent should not get it." [6] What happened to this property? If sold, the money never came to Mary Wilberforce or George Ryder. Presumably it went to Samuel, who took it knowing it would not pass to the others. Was Wilberforce constantly "at" Mrs. Sargent about the expenses of Lavington, as Ryder charged? He had never been a saver, and his way of living devoured his income. Mrs Sargent may well have been prevailed upon to turn her property into money for him.

Ryder's dismay at finding himself without a legacy naturally led him to wonder what had happened. When he found out, he resented that the 1836 compact had been disregarded and that his mother-in-law's entire estate had vanished.[7] No one could argue that he was without a case. His understandable outrage at the way he had been treated led him to assume the worst. In fairness to Wilberforce, it also led him to ignore what a more dispassionate observer cannot help but recognize. Ryder could not understand that Mrs. Sargent had committed herself to share her life with Samuel and Samuel's children. She was Samuel's as she would never any more be George Ryder's, or Sophia's, Henry's or Mary's. Their conversions had seen to that. Devoted to Samuel and tied to his life, she would willingly help him in a way she would never help them. And Samuel, needing money as he had always needed it, took what he believed was rightly his, now that his relations had deserted to Rome.

6. July 23, 1860, BD, I. C192.
7. Wilberforce denied the existence of a formal written compact, and Ryder himself could not produce one.

INDEX